LITERACY

Routledge Applied Linguistics is a series of comprehensive resource books, providing students and researchers with the support they need for advanced study in the core areas of English language and Applied Linguistics.

Each book in the series guides readers through three main sections, enabling them to explore and develop major themes within the discipline.

- Section A, **Introduction**, establishes the key terms and concepts and extends readers' techniques of analysis through practical application.
- Section B, **Extension**, brings together influential articles, sets them in context, and discusses their contribution to the field.
- Section C, **Exploration**, builds on knowledge gained in the first two sections, setting thoughtful tasks around further illustrative material. This enables readers to engage more actively with the subject matter and encourages them to develop their own research responses.

Throughout the book, topics are revisited, extended, interwoven and deconstructed, with the reader's understanding strengthened by tasks and follow-up questions.

Literacy:

- integrates psychological, educational and anthropological approaches to literacy and its consequences for individuals and society
- gathers together influential readings from key names in this interdisciplinary field, including Catherine Snow, David Olson, and Mike Cole
- presents teachers, students and researchers with diverse opportunities to explore for themselves a broad range of perspectives and methods of study.

Written by experienced teachers and researchers in the field, *Literacy* is an essential resource for students and researchers of Applied Linguistics.

Brian V. Street is Chair of Language in Education in the Department of Education and Professional Studies at King's College London.

Adam Lefstein is Senior Lecturer in Education at the University of London Institute of Education.

D0431367

ROUTLEDGE APPLIED LINGUISTICS

SERIES EDITORS

Christopher N. Candlin is Senior Research Professor in the Department of Linguistics at Macquarie University, Australia and Professor of Applied Linguistics at the Open University, UK. At Macquarie, he has been Chair of the Department of Linguistics; established and was Executive Director of the National Centre for English Language Teaching & Research (NCELTR) and first Director of the Centre for Language in Social Life (CLSL). He has written or edited over 150 publications and co-edits the new *Journal of Applied Linguistics*. From 1996–2002 he was President of the International Association of Applied Linguistics (AILA). He has acted as a consultant in more than 35 countries and as external faculty assessor in 36 universities worldwide.

Ronald Carter is Professor of Modern English Language in the School of English Studies at the University of Nottingham. He has published extensively in the fields of applied linguistics, literary studies and language in education. He has given consultancies in the field of English language education, mainly in conjunction with The British Council, in over 30 countries worldwide. He was recently elected a fellow of the British Academy of Social Sciences and is currently chair of the British Association of Applied Linguistics (BAAL).

TITLES IN THE SERIES

Intercultural Communication: An advanced resource book
Adrian Holliday, Martin Hyde and John Kullman

Translation: An advanced resource book
Basil Hatim and Jeremy Munday

Grammar and Context: An advanced resource book
Ann Hewings and Martin Hewings

Second Language Acquisition: An advanced resource book
Kees de Bot, Wander Lowie and Marjolijn Verspoor

Corpus-based Language Studies: An advanced resource book
Anthony McEnery, Richard Xiao and Yukio Tono

Language and Gender: An advanced resource book
Jane Sunderland

English for Academic Purposes: An advanced resource book
Ken Hyland

Language Testing and Assessment: An advanced resource book
Glenn Fulcher and Fred Davidson

Bilingualism: An advanced resource book
Ng Bee Chin and Gillian Wigglesworth

Literacy: An advanced resource book
Brian V. Street and Adam Lefstein

Literacy

An advanced resource book

Brian V. Street and Adam Lefstein

Routledge
Taylor & Francis Group

LONDON AND NEW YORK

First published 2007 by Routledge
2 Park Square, Milton Park, Abingdon, Oxon OX14 4RN

Simultaneously published in the USA and Canada
by Routledge
270 Madison Ave, New York, NY 10016

Routledge is an imprint of the Taylor & Francis Group, an informa business

© 2007 Brian V. Street and Adam Lefstein

Typeset in Akzidenz Grotesk, Minion and Novarese by
Keystroke, 28 High Street, Tettenhall, Wolverhampton
Printed and bound in Great Britain by
MPG Books Ltd, Bodmin, Cornwall

British Library Cataloguing in Publication Data
A catalogue record for this book is available from the British Library

Library of Congress Cataloging in Publication Data
Street, Brian V.
  Literacy: an advanced resource book / Brian V. Street and Adam Lefstein.
      p. cm.
  1. Literacy. 2. Literacy programs. 3. Reading. I. Lefstein, Adam. II. Title.
  LC149.S76 2007
  302.2'244–dc22

                              2007025928

ISBN10: 0–415–29181–X (pbk)
ISBN10: 0–415–29180–1 (hbk)
ISBN10: 0–203–46399–4 (ebk)

ISBN13: 978–0–415–29181–1 (pbk)
ISBN13: 978–0–415–29180–4 (hbk)
ISBN13: 978–0–203–46399–4 (ebk)

Contents

Contents

Tables and figures

TABLES

FIGURES

Series editors' preface

The Routledge Applied Linguistics Series provides a comprehensive guide to a number of key areas in the field of applied linguistics. Applied Linguistics is a rich, vibrant, diverse and essentially interdisciplinary field. It is now more important than ever that books in the field provide up-to-date maps of what is an ever-changing territory.

The books in this series are designed to give key insights into core areas of Applied Linguistics. The design of the books ensures, through key readings, that the history and development of a subject is recognised while, through key questions and tasks, integrating understandings of the topics, concepts and practices that make up its essentially interdisciplinary fabric. The pedagogic structure of each book ensures that readers are given opportunities to think, discuss, engage in tasks, draw on their own experience, reflect, research and to read and critically re-read key documents.

Each book has three main sections:

A: An **Introduction** section: in which the key terms and concepts which map the field of the subject are introduced, including introductory activities and reflective tasks, designed to establish key understandings, terminology, techniques of analysis and the skills appropriate to the theme and the discipline.

B: An **Extension** section: in which selected core readings are introduced (usually edited from the original) from existing key books and articles, together with annotations and commentary, where appropriate. Each reading is introduced, annotated and commented on in the context of the whole book, and research or follow-up questions and tasks are added to enable fuller understanding of both theory and practice. In some cases, readings are short and synoptic and incorporated within a more general exposition.

C: An **Exploration** section: in which further samples and illustrative materials are provided with an emphasis, where appropriate, on more open-ended, student-centred activities and tasks, designed to support readers and users in undertaking their own locally relevant research projects. Tasks are designed for work in groups or for individuals working on their own. They can be readily included in award courses in Applied Linguistics, or as topics for personal study and research.

The books also contain a detailed, thematically organised further reading section, which lays the ground for further work in the discipline. There are also extensive bibliographies.

The target audience for the series is upper undergraduates and postgraduates on language, applied linguistics and communication studies programmes as well as teachers and researchers in professional development and distance learning programmes. High-quality applied research resources are also much needed for teachers of EFL/ESL and foreign language students at higher education colleges and universities worldwide. The books in the Routledge Applied Linguistics series are aimed at the individual reader, the student in a group and at teachers building courses and seminar programmes.

We hope that the books in this series meet these needs and continue to provide support over many years.

THE EDITORS

Professor Christopher N. Candlin and Professor Ronald Carter are the series editors. Both have extensive experience of publishing titles in the fields relevant to this series. Between them they have written and edited over one hundred books and two hundred academic papers in the broad field of applied linguistics. Chris Candlin was president of AILA (International Association for Applied Linguistics) 1996–2002 and Ron Carter was Chair of BAAL (British Association for Applied Linguistics) 2003–2006.

Professor Christopher N. Candlin
Senior Research Professor
Department of Linguistics
Division of Linguistics and Psychology
Macquarie University
Sydney NSW 2109
Australia

and

Professor of Applied Linguistics
Faculty of Education & Language Studies
The Open University
Walton Hall
Milton Keynes MK7 6AA
UK

Professor Ronald Carter
School of English Studies
University of Nottingham
Nottingham NG7 2RD
UK

Acknowledgements

Besnier, N. (1999) 'Literacy' in *Key terms in language and culture*, ed. A. Duranti. Oxford and Malden: Blackwell, pp. 136–138. Reproduced by permission of Blackwell Publishing.

Stierer, B. and Bloome, D. (1994) *Reading words: a commentary on key terms in the teaching of reading*. Sheffield: NATE. 'Theoretical influences', pp. 3–10. Reproduced by permission of National Asssociation for the Teaching of English www.nate.org.uk

Snow, C., Burns, M. and Griffin, P. (1998) *Preventing reading difficulties in young children*, pp. 15–31, © 1998 by the National Academy Press, Washington, DC. Reprinted with permission.

Adams, M. (1993) 'Beginning to read: an overview' in Beard, R. (ed.), *Teaching literacy, balancing perspectives* London: Hodder and Stoughton, pp. 204–215. Copyright © 1993 Roger Beard. Reprinted with permission of the publisher.

Goodman, Ken, from *On reading*. Copyright © 1996 by Ken Goodman. Published by Heinemann, a division of Reed Elsevier, Inc., Portsmouth, NH. All rights reserved. Reprinted with permission.

Street, B. and J. 'The schooling of literacy', in *Literacy in the community*, ed. D. Barton and R. Ivanic, London: Sage, pp. 143–166. Copyright © 1991 by Sage Publications. Reprinted by permission of Sage Publications.

Goody, J. (1997) 'Evolution and communication', in *The domestication of the savage mind*. Copyright © 1977 by Cambridge University Press. Reprinted with permission.

Street, B. (1984) 'The autonomous model', *Literacy in theory and practice*. Copyright © 1984 by Cambridge University Press. Reprinted with permission.

Scribner, S. and Cole, M. (1978) 'Unpackaging Literacy', *Social Science Information* 17 (1), 19–39. Copyright © Sage Publications and Foundation of the Maison des Science de L'Homme, 1978, by permission of Sage Publications Ltd. Reproduced with permission.

Olson, D. (1994) 'Demytholgising literacy', *The world on paper*. Copyright © 1994 by Cambridge University Press. Reprinted with permission.

From Barton, D., Hamilton, M. ch. 1 'Literacy practices', pp. 7–15, in *Situated literacies: reading and writing in context* London: Routledge, edited by D. Barton, M. Hamilton, and R. Ivanic. Copyright © 1999. Reproduced by permission of Taylor and Francis UK.

Bartlett, L. and Holland, D. (2002) 'Theorizing the Space of Literacy Practices', in

Ways of Knowing (University of Brighton), 10–22. Reproduced by kind permission of the authors.

Martin-Jones, M. and Jones, K. (eds) (2000) 'Introduction: multilingual literacies', in *Multilingual literacies: reading and writing different worlds* (Amsterdam and Philadelphia: John Benjamins Publishing Company), pp. 1–15, reprinted with permission.

Reder, Stephen and Davila, Erica (2005) 'Context and literacy practices', *Annual Review of Applied Linguistics*, 25, 170–187. Copyright © 2005 by Cambridge University Press. Reprinted with permission of the authors and publishers.

Burningham, John, *The cupboard* (London: Jonathan Cape, 1975). Reprinted by permission of The Random House Group Ltd.

Aiken, Joan, *The bread bin*, Illustrated by Quentin Blake, p. 75 (BBC Knight Books, Jackanory 1974). Reproduced by kind permission of the author.

Milk carton, courtesy of Farmland Dairies www.farmlanddairies.com.

Brunhoff, Jean de, *Histoire de Babar*, © Librairie Hachette 1939.

Gourdie, Tom, *The Puffin book of handwriting* (London: Puffin, 1980). Copyright © Tom Gourdie, 1980.

'Fhamida's register', from Nigel Hall and Anne Robinson, *Exploring writing and play in the early years.* Manchester Metropolitan University Education Series. London: David Fulton Publishers, 1995, reprinted with permission.

From P. Cowan, 'Putting it out there: revealing Latino visual discourse in the Hispanic academic program for middle school students', in B. V. Street (ed.), *Literacies across educational contexts: mediating learning and teaching*, pp. 145–169 (Philadelphia, PA: Caslon Publishing, 2005), reprinted with permission.

How to use this book

Literacy: An Advanced Resource Book aims to introduce readers to key concepts and debates surrounding theory, research and practice in the multi-disciplinary field of literacy and literacies. The book integrates excerpts from classic research studies, editorial commentary, reflective tasks, illustrative analyses, and research topics. It brings psychological, linguistic, anthropological and educational approaches to literacy into dialogue with one another and with the reader.

The book is divided into three sections: (**A**) **Introduction** presents and elaborates upon the central questions, themes and concepts in the literacy field; (**B**) **Extension** engages the reader with classic texts, which demonstrate how scholars from various disciplines have addressed and researched the key questions and themes; and (**C**) **Exploration** offers readers opportunities and tools to explore these themes and issues in their own research. Cutting across each section are four overlapping themes: (1) **Meanings of 'literacy'**, (2) **Literacy acquisition**, (3) **Consequences of literacy** and (4) **Literacy as social practice**. The texts in each of these different areas respond to and build upon the preceding sections, so we recommend reading the book in the order presented. However, for readers interested in tracing the themes throughout the book, we provide a map as a kind of guide – along with greater detail about the book's organisation – in Section A2.

Throughout the book we offer numerous reflective tasks to facilitate readers' engagement with the various texts and the issues they raise. If this advanced resource book is being used in a seminar or workshop context, then tasks can be assigned as individual or group learning activities.

In keeping, then, with other books in this series, we see this volume as a resource on which readers can draw in order to think, discuss, engage in tasks, draw upon their own experience, reflect, research and read – and critically re-read – key documents in the field of applied linguistics in general and – in this case – of literacy in particular. We hope readers will use the volume in this way, and that it will serve both as an introduction to the field and as a valuable resource to which they will return over many years.

SECTION A
Introduction

Unit A1
Why study literacy?

Why study literacy? What makes this topic a 'problem' worthy of attention? In what ways is it important or interesting? And to whom?

Before we address these questions we would like to invite you to reflect on your own responses to them. In other words, before we discuss why we've chosen to write this book, it would be useful for you to think about why you've chosen to read it. This may seem strange: we've barely started and already we're posing questions to the reader.

We see these questions as part of a 'conversation' we would like to conduct with you, the reader, throughout the entire book. This conversational style is partially a function of the book's topic. Since the book explores how literacy functions in society and culture – and how it is constructed in both academic research and in the popular imagination – readers' thoughts and experience are a valuable complement to the scholarly and popular materials which we have assembled. Thus, we will often pose questions for you to consider before offering our own interpretations. Comparing your reflections with ours will hopefully facilitate your critical engagement with and learning from the book. Moreover, we believe that all books should be read in such a conversational manner, whether the authors have explicitly invited such a reading or not – but we'll revisit this point later, when we explore what it means to be literate.

So, returning to our questions: Why study literacy? What makes this topic a 'problem' worthy of attention? In what ways is the issue important or interesting? And to whom?

An initial response to these questions might be incredulity: Haven't we heard the news? Don't we know that we are in the midst of a scandalous 'literacy crisis'? After all, newspaper headlines regularly warn of an 'epidemic of illiteracy' that threatens to destroy our economy, society and culture. We start our exploration of interest in literacy with excerpts from three articles discussing this issue. The first two, from the UK press, amplify the scope and dangers of illiteracy; the third, from the USA, seeks to mitigate the problem and criticises proposed solutions to it.[1]

---

1 Our examples recently appeared in the US and UK press. For further studies of the representation of this 'crisis' see Berliner and Biddle (1995) on the United States and Welch and Freebody (1993) on Australia.

The first article, an opinion-editorial piece by Melanie Phillips entitled, 'One million illiterate children – but how many more will it take before this pernicious ideology is destroyed?', appeared in the *Daily Mail* of 3 March 2005 (p. 14). The article appeared in the wake of a report published on the preceding day by the Centre for Policy Studies (a summary appears on its website: http://www.cps.org.uk/). Contrary to 'one of Tony Blair's proudest boasts', writes Phillips, the government's educational reforms are a failure, leading to '1.2 million children having failed to achieve expected levels of literacy since [the National Literacy Strategy] launch in 1998'. Phillips blames theses alleged failures on 'the teaching establishment', which 'stopped training teachers in the tried-and-tested methods of teaching children to read' on account of 'excessive concern' for struggling children and ideological biases. Instead, teachers used 'a variety of other methods, such as memorising or guessing at words'. Phillips argues that, although children were often able to give 'a convincing impression of being able to read', they were unable to decode unfamiliar texts – because they had not been taught phonics. She claims that the results of this approach have been 'catastrophic', yet 'virtually the entire education establishment defended it with near-religious fanaticism'. She lists the consequences of this policy:

> Because of the grip still maintained by this pernicious ideology upon our teacher-training institutions, British children are less literate than many in the Third World, let alone our major economic competitors.

> Their resulting failure to cope at school is undoubtedly a major cause of the dismaying levels of ill-discipline and truancy at school, not to mention crime and other antisocial behaviour.

> At a deeper level still, if children are not able to read, they are not able to think.

In concluding her article, Phillips asks, 'How many more children will need to be sacrificed before it [the government] finally wakes up?'

The second article also appeared in the *Daily Mail*, following a report on literacy rates – six years before Phillips's editorial. Tony Halpin's 'Illiterate millions shame our schools' (26 March 1999, p. 13) begins with an impressive list of statistics:

> One in five adults, seven million people, cannot use a Yellow Pages directory to find a plumber.

> And a quarter cannot work out the change they should get from £2 if they buy groceries costing £1.58.

> Two million people have 'virtually no ability to read and write functionally'.

Halpin also notes that illiterate people are 'five times more likely than literate people to be unemployed', and 'twice as likely to be in low-paid jobs'. Moreover, he notes that '60 percent of people in prison have reading problems'. Halpin quotes Sir Claus Moser, chairman of the Basic Skills Agency: 'The scale of the problem is staggering and a shameful reflection on past years and decades of schooling.' Moser calls for a 'national crusade' to remedy the problem.

These articles provide powerful material for reflecting on the questions we posed at the outset, and also raise new questions. What is the literacy problem? According to the authors, millions of people, both adults and children, cannot read and write adequately. Why is this important? The authors suggest that the 'crisis' has dire consequences for both the individual and society. For the individual, illiteracy implies 'misery', by impairing the ability to function in everyday life (e.g. to find a plumber), to earn a living, to be part of society and even to think. For society, the authors suggest that the low literacy rates are linked to poor discipline in schools, antisocial behaviour, crime and a lack of economic competitiveness (placing Britain behind Germany, the Netherlands and Sweden and even 'many in the Third World').

Clearly, with so much at stake, literacy is a serious matter, and the authors employ dramatic and harsh language to assert its gravity: 'shameful', 'debacle', 'national disaster', 'cruel deception', 'catastrophic results', 'devastating' and 'scandal'. Such language is usually reserved for matters of a moral or spiritual character and, indeed, both authors evoke religious images. The opponents of phonics are described as defending their methods with 'near-religious fanaticism' as they 'sacrifice' children for the sake of their 'pernicious ideology'. And the proposed solution to the problem is described as a 'crusade'.

Beyond appealing to passions and moral sentiments, what about the arguments and evidence presented? Is there indeed a literacy crisis, and is it as severe as the articles would lead us to believe?

Both articles present numerous statistics: seven million adults cannot use the Yellow Pages, two million are functionally illiterate, and 1.2 million children have failed to achieve the expected standard in literacy. But wait a minute, the numbers don't seem to add up: are there five million adults who are 'functionally literate' but cannot find a plumber (seven million minus two million)? And what about the 44 per cent of 11-year-old boys who did not achieve the expected standard for writing: Are they functionally literate? Can they find a plumber? Or are they being judged according to a different measure of literacy? Even a cursory look at the articles raises the question of what being il/literate means, and how it is measured.

Other writers address the same data from a different political or ideological per-spective and we need to take account of their perspectives too. The third article we summarise here, Mary Lee Griffin's 'Hooked on phonics? We should lose this addiction', was also published in the popular press (*Los Angeles Times*, 22 October 2002, p. B13), but offers a contrasting view to that of the first two excerpts. It challenges the claims advanced by Phillips, Halpin and others about a 'literacy crisis' and cites alternative data to suggest there has not really been much change in literacy levels. Whom are we to believe and how do we decide? Both cite authoritative data, both use heightened rhetorical devices to make their point. Putting them side by side here at the outset can provide us with a term of reference as we proceed through the similar debates in the academic and research literature in this resource book. The same question will arise for us with respect to this more measured body of writing: How do we decide for ourselves? What are credible arguments and data? What frames of reference can help us make sense of these contrasts? Does it matter, and if so why? It is worth taking these questions with us as we now read and then reflect on these excerpts.

Griffin opens her editorial comment with a question: 'How bad is this national reading crisis we keep hearing and reading about?' She musters data from the US government National Assessment of Educational Progress to argue that 'reading achievement has not changed much in 30 years' and that 'our fourth-grade readers rank second in the world'. Given this rosy diagnosis, Griffin asks why politicians constantly talk about a 'reading crisis' and call for more phonics and testing in primary schools. In answering that question, she asks, 'Who profits?' She dismisses the idea that phonics programmes are in the interests of either children or teachers, instead laying the blame at the feet of the publishing industry:

> [C]ommercial publishers, supported by federal policy makers . . . profit most. Phonics materials, programs and assessments represent a lucrative business for textbook publishers. Phonics acquisition is easy to 'quantify' by testing before and after instruction, spawning scores of quasi-experi- mental studies that prove the treatment of phonics works. Publishers and scientists get rich, politicians get elected and students and teachers are bored to tears.

Griffin claims, moreover, that phonics is being and has been taught in schools as part of whole language and balanced literacy programmes. She concludes the article by arguing that the most important ingredient in successful literacy learning is skilful teachers, but that such teachers are a threat to textbook publishers.

These articles raise another dimension of the 'literacy crisis' question: is reading about decoding, recognising words or understanding meaning? The first author, Phillips, suggests that all three are important, but that decoding should come first. The third author, Griffin, argues that the claims for phonics are 'fraught with questionable truths', and that reading is bound up with imagination, thinking, identity and power. Where, if at all, do those concerns fit into the debate about literacy 'standards'? Both Phillips's and Griffin's positions are developed by other authors we meet later in the book.

In this book, then, we will explore those questions – about how literacy should be defined, taught and learned – along with the arguments about its alleged conse- quences. We will also look at the role played by 'literacy' – not the entity but talk about the entity – in society. In other words, we will investigate why the news media regularly carry stories about literacy crises, and how these 'crises' are mobilised in support of various interests and ideologies.

The book is intended to facilitate the reader's own exploration of these and other questions, problems and debates central to the field of literacy studies. Generally, the issues can be divided into four overlapping clusters of questions:

- *Definition and demarcation.* What is literacy? What kind of thing is it (e.g. a skill, capacity, credential, acquired taste)? What is the scope of literacy (e.g. reading, writing, speaking, listening or language, other semiotic modes and media or everyday versus academic genres)?
- *Acquisition.* How is literacy acquired? What are the sources of difficulties in its acquisition? What does research tell us about the relative merits of different approaches – phonics, whole language, 'authentic reading' etc.?
- *Consequences.* What are the benefits of literacy (e.g. cognitive consequences, communication, economic or developmental, instrumental or functional, identity, consciousness, affective dimensions)?
- *In society.* What role does 'literacy' play in contemporary discourse? How is literacy assessed or researched? How is it represented? In whose interests?

So why study literacy? First, literacy is seen as critical for the well-being of individuals and society. Although we have distanced ourselves from that position – note our use of the disclaimer, 'literacy is seen' in the previous sentence – we do consider it to be worthy of serious consideration, and present and discuss texts that make the case much more convincingly than the two articles used to introduce the topic in this section. Second, literacy is currently high on the agenda in public debates. We try to help the reader find their way in these debates through an introduction to and critical discussion of seminal texts and current disputes. Third, study of literacy leads to inquiry into a broad range of social, political and ideological issues. We hope to persuade you that for this reason literacy is an intrinsically interesting topic, worthy of study for the insights it can give us about who we are, what we would like to become and how we conduct our communal affairs.

One final comment about who we are and our positions on the topics discussed in the book. Brian Street is Professor of Language in Education at King's College London. He undertook anthropological fieldwork on literacy in Iran during the 1970s, and taught social and cultural anthropology for over twenty years at the University of Sussex before taking up his current post. He has written and lectured extensively on the topics in this book, and you will encounter excerpts from some of those publications in Section B – Extensions. Adam Lefstein is Academic Fellow in Pedagogy and Classroom Interaction at Oxford University Department of Education. He has worked in schools and informal educational settings in Israel, and is currently researching literacy policy and practice in England. Though we don't agree on all of the issues discussed in the book, we do approach literacy from a common 'social practice' perspective.

We have introduced our own positions at this point in the book for a perverse reason. Our purpose in this book is to assist you in critically engaging with a broad range of ideas, in order to form your own opinion, which may not necessarily coincide with our own. To that end, we've attempted to be balanced in our presentation of ideas, including giving a fair hearing to ideas contrary to our own, and questioning ideas with which we are sympathetic. Nevertheless, our biases undoubtedly influence our presentation, so we thought it would be wise to inform you about them from the outset.

Unit A2
Organisation of the book

The book is organised into three sections, which are intended to (A) introduce and elaborate upon the central questions, themes and concepts in the field, (B) present a number of classic texts, demonstrating how scholars from various disciplines have addressed and developed these questions and themes, and (C) offer readers opportunities and tools to explore the issues on their own.

In the rest of this Section A – Introduction – readers are invited to reflect on their own meanings and experiences of literacy in light of encounters with a series of everyday texts, including, for example, children's literature, household labels and instructions in the workplace. These encounters are designed to stretch the boundaries of commonly held ideas about what 'literacy' involves, inviting you to consider various dimensions of experience implicated in literate activity. Following these everyday encounters, we delve into the scholarly literature (A5 Academic study of literacy: mapping the field), providing you an overview or 'map' of the burgeoning field of literacy studies, which includes contributions from a number of different academic disciplines and fields, especially psychology, linguistics, history, anthropology and education. This overview is organised into five parts, the first four of which correspond to the key issues highlighted at the end of the preceding 'Why study literacy?' discussion: (A5.1) Meanings of 'Literacy', (A5.2) Literacy acquisition, (A5.3) Consequences of literacy, and (A5.4) Literacy as social practice. In the fifth part (A5.5) we address 'New literacies'.

Section B – Extension – is mainly focused on scholarly texts, again divided into these four categories. In each section you will find classic scholarly treatments of these topics, supplemented by questions, tasks and commentaries that are intended to facilitate critical engagement with these specialist approaches without having to become a specialist in these fields. Where appropriate, you will be pointed towards further references but this will not be necessary for an initial encounter with the material. The core readings provided in each section, then, are intended to allow you to review key features of the literature on literacy and to enter the debates amongst researchers and practitioners. References are provided for you to pursue further the ideas encountered.

A central debate, which runs as a fault line throughout these texts, is about the alleged positive effects of literacy for individuals, societies and cultures that acquire or develop it. On the one hand, a number of authors advocate a 'literacy thesis', according to which literacy is a key factor in the development of rational, scientific thought (the article by Goody in Section B3.1 is a key text in this tradition). On the other hand, others argue that the effects of literacy cannot be disentangled from the social, cultural and historical contexts of its use (the article by Street in Section B3.3 is a key text in this tradition). Proponents of the first approach tend to talk about literacy and its consequences as being *autonomous* of the historical or social contexts of its development or use, while their critics insist upon the *ideological* nature of literacy practices and debates (the idea of 'autonomous' and 'ideological' models of literacy is elaborated in Section B3.3). Figure A2.1 charts the texts in Section B according to this distinction.

Most of the texts do not explicitly discuss their model of literacy; this figure is our assessment of the often unstated assumptions guiding their work. As such, it should be read as suggestive, not definitive. We're not at all sure that all the authors would agree with our assessment of their positions on this chart, and we recommend that you return to this figure after reading the relevant texts and judge for yourself.

Section C – Exploration – provides you with questions, tools and materials to build upon and apply the knowledge and ideas gleaned throughout the book in conducting your own literacy investigations. Questions are raised for further study and research, particularly with a view to helping you work with the materials in relation to your own contexts. The materials provide scope for you to research and reflect on aspects of literacy of particular interest to you. Tasks are designed for either groups or individuals. Whilst the examples provided in Section C build on topics addressed in Sections A and B, and you are encouraged to relate these general debates to your own experience in educational settings, there is scope here for you to also develop similar topics of your own, taking advantage of the methods outlined in the activities provided.

TRACING KEY THEMES

One way of reading the book is to trace a theme or domain of literacy across Sections A, B and C. Table A2.1 outlines the progression of such key ideas, from the everyday encounters in Section A3, through the overview of scholarly literature in Section A4, the classic texts in Section B and the explorations in Section C.

TASKS

Throughout the book we offer numerous activities to facilitate readers' engagement with the various texts and issues raised by them. You should feel free to use (or ignore) these tasks as you see fit. Some readers may prefer to read the entire book and then return to consider questions of particular interest. Others may attempt to address each and every task. And, if this resource book is being used in a seminar or workshop, facilitators may assign tasks as individual or group learning activities.

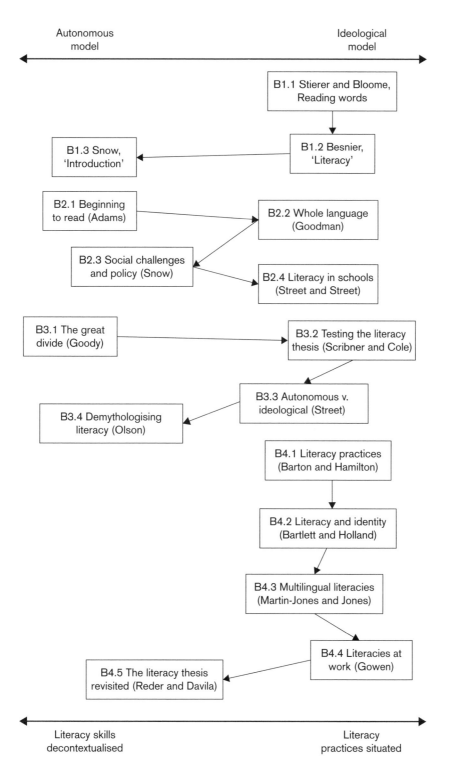

A2.1 Section B texts in the literacy debate

Table A2.1 Map of key themes

Theme or domain	A4 Encounters with literacy	A5 Academic study of literacy	B Extension	C Exploration
Definitions	A3 Keywords	A5.1 Meanings of 'Literacy' in different traditions	B1 Keywords	C1.2 Literacy log
Early reading	■ Burningham, *The cupboard* ■ Aiken, *The bread bin*	A5.2 Literacy acquisition	B2 Literacy acquisition	C3.4 'Literacy problems' and the mass media C2.2 Children's literature – code, content and practice
Schooling	■ Gourdie, *The Puffin book of handwriting: how to write well with everyday materials* ■ Hall and Robinson, 'Fhamida's register' ■ Cowan, 'Putting it out there . . .'	A5.2 Literacy acquisition	B2.4 Literacy in schools	C2.3 Academic literacies
Literacy and identity	■ Brockes, 'The phoney graffiti war and the killing that shocked an estate' ■ Cowan, 'Putting it out there . . .'	A5.4 Literacy as social practice	B4.2 Literacy and identity	C3.2 Everyday writing in modern society
Everyday literacies	■ Brockes, 'The phoney graffiti war and the killing that shocked an estate' ■ Farmland Dairies milk carton ■ Boiler instructions	A5.4 Literacy as social practice	B4.1 Literacy practices	C1.2 Literacy log C3.2 Everyday writing in modern society
Workplace literacies	■ Boiler instructions	A5.4 Literacy as social practice	B4.4 Literacies at work	C3.1 Workplace literacies
New literacies	■ Farmland Dairies milk carton ■ Powers, 'Losing our souls, bit by bit'	A5.5 New literacies		Conclusion: Coming to terms with new literacies
Literacy politics	A1 Why study literacy?	A5.3 Consequences of literacy	B3 Consequences of literacy	C3.4 'Literacy problems' and the mass media C3.3 International policy and practice in the literacy field

Some extracts are accompanied by a variety of tasks and task types, while for others only one or two are provided. Following some of the tasks we have provided commentary, which is intended to exemplify possible responses to the questions, and to open up further questions.

Unit A3
Keywords

What is literacy? As we noted in the introduction (Section A1), the term 'literacy' is highly contested, as are related terms people use to speak about it. Before we survey the scholarly literature on this field, and introduce you to some of the key texts, we thought it might be useful for you to examine your own literacy lexicon: What are the keywords for you in thinking and speaking about literacy?

The idea of a 'keyword' may require some explanation. Cultural critic Raymond Williams (1976) introduced this term in his *Keywords: a vocabulary of culture and society*. In the introduction to that book Williams writes about how disoriented he felt upon his return to Cambridge after serving overseas in the Second World War. Suddenly, people seemed to be speaking 'a different language'. It appears that, in the tumultuous years of the war, the meanings of, attitudes towards and uses of certain words, such as 'culture' or 'class', shifted rapidly. Williams set out to explore those shifts, documenting the historical development of a number of such 'keywords', which together form a core vocabulary for speaking and thinking about culture and society.

'Literacy' was not included among Williams's keywords, though the word is included in his discussion of 'literature'. At least two further books have applied Williams's methodology to the field of literacy and reading: Carter's (1995) *Keywords in language and literacy* and Stierer and Bloome's (1994) *Reading words: a commentary on key terms in the teaching of reading*. We highly recommend both these books, and indeed have included a passage from the latter text in Section B1.2. Before reading those or related texts, we suggest that you engage in this exercise of clarifying your own keywords, and then comparing your literacy vocabulary with those developed by others.

⭐ Task A3.1: Developing a list of keywords

In order to develop your list of keywords, we suggest that you follow Stierer and Bloome's lead. They organised their analysis under twenty-four 'headwords'. To decide on their headwords, they began by writing down every term they could think of which was used in a technical or professional capacity in the field of literacy. This produced a list of over a hundred words. They then grouped the words into clusters of words with linked meanings or uses. Some words were assigned to more than one cluster. This produced about thirty clusters. At this stage they attempted to identify which word in each cluster represented what they called the 'superordinate' term. They did this by discussing the way the words in each cluster were used in the field, and the kinds of relationships they seemed to have with each other. These twenty-five or so headwords then served as their agenda for writing entries, some of which were then were combined, producing the final list. (Stierer and Bloome's list appears in Task B1.1 but we suggest that you develop your own list before you consult theirs.)

Task A3.2: Contrasting literacy vocabularies

Compare your list of keywords with those developed by friends and colleagues:

➤ What are the commonalities and differences?

➤ Discuss how, when and by whom the different words are typically used, and note any variations in use.

➤ Can you account for where the differences came from?

➤ Do they reflect arbitrary idiosyncrasies, or are they indicative of different assumptions regarding and/or different experiences with the field of literacy? For example, someone who has worked as a teacher of reading may have a very different way of talking about literacy from, for example, someone with a background in linguistics or psychology.

➤ What sort of events, sites or practices did you have in mind when you came up with your respective lists of keywords? Different issues are probably raised, for example, when thinking about school versus everyday reading and writing.

We recommend that you maintain your list of keywords, using it as a tool for reflecting on the different texts you encounter in this resource book. We hope that your list will evolve as you engage with the various ways of talking and thinking about literacy, and as you develop an appreciation for the reasons different authors choose their terms. It might also be interesting to note whether the colleagues you set out with have likewise changed their positions over time and what the influence of reading this book might have been for both you and them.

Unit A4
Encounters with literacy

Before delving into the academic debates in the field, we would like to first turn back to our own experience and ask, 'Where and how do we encounter literacy in our daily lives?' As children, most of us first met with literacy through books addressed to early learners, combining pictures with easy text and vocabulary. Schools in particular use such texts as ways of introducing children to what some view as the key building blocks of literacy: the 'alphabetic principle', the phonetic code, elementary vocabulary, etc. Once we have mastered these levels of literacy learning, we are likely to focus more on what is sometimes called 'real reading', i.e. the taken-for-granted ways in which we draw meaning from texts (this position is laid out in Section B2.1 and B2.3). Some commentators, as we shall see, advocate a different sequence, in which the encounter with meaning and 'unfamiliar texts' comes sooner (e.g. Section B2.2).

As adolescents and later as adults, we encounter a range of text types, many of which may be very different from those of school, and as we do so we are learning new things and deriving new meanings that are more complex and varied than those associated with our early learning. We are also engaged, at different stages of this reading process, in learning to write – some literacy campaigns, notably those taken to the 'natives' by early missionaries, tended to focus mainly on reading and to marginalise writing – which can provide a source of relative autonomy and independence for the writer compared with the reader's dependence on what others have already written. Attending to writing, then, is likewise a key component in our understanding of what counts as literacy, whether as a technical skill or an ideological challenge.

Taking these developmental processes as a starting point, then, we will explore below a number of texts that can be characterised as representing different 'stages' in literacy learning and use. In particular, we ask how the key terms you began to list in Section A3.1 can help you to understand your encounter with these texts – and do you now need further terms to make sense of the whole literacy process? It will soon become apparent that even the most innocent of statements – and terms – to describe this process are heavily contested. As you read through the later sections of this book and acquire a wider range of terms and concepts, you may want to revisit this section to put your immediate responses now into that broader perspective. Writing them down now and filing them under explicit headings may facilitate this process of later review. There is, of course, no final resting place from which we can 'view' such data – only a continuing, fluid and recursive series of unfolding encounters. At least, that is the premise on which this resource book is based. You might want to challenge this and propose a more certain direction and point of arrival. Again, that position will give you a way of reading both the texts cited below and the academic material selected in Section B.

We begin with a classic example of an early childhood reading text. We have chosen one from the mid-1970s first, as many readers may have encountered such material as children and then been surprised by how different the texts used by their own children seem to be. Such contrasts can tell us a great deal about what counts as literacy and as 'reading' at different times and places. The first text involves a classic mix of picture and short text.

TEXT

Burningham, John, *The cupboard* (London: Cape, 1975).

There is a cupboard
in our kitchen

Reflections

There are a number of different approaches to this text. We might, for example, call upon the approach indicated by authors such as Snow (Section B1.3; see also B2.1 Adams on 'Beginning to read') in which the reader looks at how units of sound, or 'phonemes' are combined to form syllables, words and a sentence. Or, alternatively, we might take the approach indicated by Goodman and others (Section B2.2) and look at the movement across the page that perhaps prioritises words over the picture. But before we become too deeply embroiled in these (and other) approaches, it will be interesting for you to write down your own response to it. Does it remind you of your own learning of literacy in childhood? If so, what memories are evoked – positive, negative, warm, fearful? Do you use similar texts with children you encounter today – your own or others' – and how would you characterise their responses? With an educational perspective in mind, what do you think such texts contribute to the learning of literacy? Can you find other similar texts and compare them with Burningham's? Are the underlying assumptions similar or different, for example with respect to the layout, use of text/image relations, kinds of words or syllables or phonemes chosen? Is your interest in this kind of literacy mainly to do with its potential for learning or are you more interested in the story and the pleasure it can give?

A book for older children, also from the same period, likewise combines text and image but there are more words and they are different and the picture is also different from those in the early childhood book, in ways you might like to try to describe. As we explore these different examples, our expectations and assumptions will become more apparent.

TEXT

Aiken, Joan, *The bread bin*. Illustrated by Quentin Blake (London: BBC, 1974).

Then he hopped down on to Arabel's pillow.

He hopped close behind her head, and listened at her left ear. He listened for a long time. Then he went round to her other side and listened at her right ear.

Then he croaked a little, gently, to himself, and made a tiny scratching noise with his claws on the pillow. Then he waited.

There was a pause. Then, very slowly, Arabel rolled over on to her stomach. She turned her face a little and opened one eye, so that she could just see Mortimer with it.

"Hello, Mortimer," she whispered.

75

Reflections

You might compare the writing with that in the previous text by Burningham. First, it is longer. What does this tell you about the age of the child being targeted? And what assumptions does this difference reveal about the 'stages' of learning literacy? Do you share these assumptions or have you had different experiences – in your own literacy learning or as you watched other children use such texts? And, what about the picture? How is it different from that in 'The cupboard' and again what assumptions does this reveal about how children are thought to relate to images? Then, you might explore how the image and the text are related to each other. For instance, in 'The cupboard', the image is on a separate page from the text. One might argue that the written text has priority and the image is intended to illustrate or support what is already there in the text (an idea developed by Kress and colleagues, whose work we discuss later in Section A5.5). You might explore this claim and whether you think it is justified here. And then apply it, or other assumptions you bring to this material, to the Quentin Blake picture. The image is at the top of the page of written text and the bird is incorporated into the picture. Does this suggest a different stance on the part of the reader, different expectations as to how they are 'reading' the text? And again what do you see as the relationship between the image and the text? As someone interested in literacy, our first response was that the positioning of the bird near to Arabel's ear signified a close connection between words and image – the bird is croaking into her ears and making a scratching noise on her pillow; it is communicating with her, its 'voice' is part of the text and this verbal participation is signalled by the pictorial representation. But you may have picked up an entirely different point and you may think our interpretation stems from over-interest in literacy. How might others respond to such a text? For example, someone interested in reading – perhaps more than in literacy – might see its function as being to facilitate the learning of 'real reading' mentioned above.

These are only two small examples and you will no doubt have encountered a multitude of such texts, revealing a variety of different points about literacy and the assumptions we make, beyond our own few suggestions. But the point is that by becoming attuned to recognising and unpacking such assumptions we will be better placed to make explicit our own underlying theories and concepts regarding literacy. Again it is worth noting this at this stage and returning to it later, as you read the academic texts and reflect on how well they capture this experience and this encounter.

We now move from reading to writing, considering first children's initial exposure to writing before looking at later experiences. Again you might think about your own early and later experiences, with respect both to your own learning of writing and to that of children you have seen doing this.

TEXT

Gourdie, Tom, *The Puffin book of handwriting: how to write well with everyday materials* (London: Puffin Books, 1980).

Wrong pen-holds such as these can prevent you from writing well.
Do not let the thumb cross over on to the fore-finger (1).
Do not encourage the middle finger to rest on the pencil as in (2).
Do not let the disengaged fingers curl right into the palm – this cramps the muscles.
Here is the proper pen-hold (4)

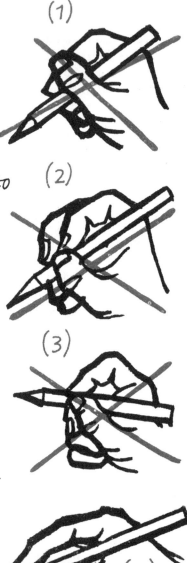

Reflections

Had you expected the text on writing to be so prescriptive? It uses instructions such as 'do not' and evaluative terms such as 'proper'. So this is a different kind of text from the two we have just seen. It belongs, we might say, to a different 'genre' (a term we explore further later, in Sections B3.1 and C2.3). Would you find it helpful, in your list of 'key terms', to make a distinction between 'fiction' and 'non-fiction'? Or is there some other way that you would characterise how the texts differ? The book it is taken from is concerned with 'handwriting', a term that focuses on the material practice rather than the usual more abstract meaning we intend when we talk about 'writing'. 'Writing' usually refers to the production of meanings in verbal form and, in everyday usage, we may not distinguish between various ways of doing this – handwriting, using a computer keyboard etc. – but instead focus on the more general distinction between writing and reading.

Now that we have raised this level of meaning, you might consider the contexts in which you use different material forms – sitting on a bus, in a classroom, at home. Do different forms get associated with different content? That is, do you envisage writing different things – lengthy texts, short notes, highlighted signs etc. – in different forms – hand, keyboard, using pens or chalk? Are these differences simply functional or are some of them symbolic, that is associated with important meanings and ideas irrespective of whether they function efficiently or not in that context? A graffiti writer might spend considerable time – and risk getting caught – because they associate the 'style' of writing with significant cultural or emotional states. The following example is taken from a newspaper article about such use of graffiti in an English housing estate. Ione, a 15-year-old-boy, had put an inscription on the wall and Devon, an 18-year-old, had defaced it. Ione attacked Devon with a knife and he died later that day. Our first response to this event is likely to be shock and horror, but we would justify using it here to make the point that forms of literacy that we sometimes dismiss as trivial or morally offensive may, for the participants, be deeply significant, indeed matters of life and death. Literacy outside of school signifies more than just a skill.

TEXT

Brockes, Emma, 'The phoney graffiti war and the killing that shocked an estate', *Guardian*, 5 September 2001 (excerpts).

> After his arrest, Ione put in a claim of self-defence and said he had been maliciously provoked. It was the manner of this provocation that startled the police. In mitigation, the teenager told them: 'I saw my work had been lined through. I took it as an insult because it dented my pride.' The 'work' he referred to was graffiti.
>
> The first, and possibly biggest, problem this conferred on the authorities was a conceptual one. If Devon had died over graffiti, then graffiti signified

a far deeper estrangement in its young practitioners than had previously been thought.

'Two young lives have been ruined over the most trivial of causes,' said Detective Inspector Martin Ford, the investigating officer. He struggled with Ione's line of defence. 'It was a dispute that would usually end with no more than a black eye.'

What had happened, the police wondered, to promote the status of graffiti on the estate from an idle recreation into something more fundamental? To persuade Ione that the boy who obliterated his graffiti – or tag – obliterated more or less everything of value about him?

. . .

In the late 1990s, a half-hearted gang culture grew up around the Casterbridge estate, the Hilgrove and a third local estate, the Rowley Way. 'Gang rather overstates it,' says Lee Dempster, an officer on the investigating team. 'There were only three people in one and four in another'. . .

Their main recreation was graffiti and in 1999, a phoney war broke out, fought via the medium of competitive tagging. Ione and Devon's graffiti pseudonyms were, respectively, Blast and Mr Reach and they surfaced as far afield as Camden, two miles away.

A4.4 London graffiti (photo Adam Lefstein)

One in particular stands out: in round-handed script, 'Mr Reach', sprayed on a wall on the Rowley Way estate. A line of red paint has been drawn through it and the paint has run, collecting in stalks and baubles down the brickwork. In graffiti parlance, Mr Reach has been lined out and its author insulted.

Reflections

What do we need to know to make sense of this incredible event? And of the role of literacy in it? And does the story challenge our assumptions about graffiti as an aspect of literacy? The report states that the young boy saw his graffiti markings or 'tags' as 'a matter of pride'. When another boy defaced it, there was clearly more being challenged than some obscure or trivial markings. The residents thought that such graffiti were simply 'mindless hieroglyphics'. Is that your view of graffiti? Do you feel morally offended when you see graffiti in public places? And do you tend to think that the content and form are 'mindless'? How, then, do you respond to this example? That the boy was indeed 'mindless' and that his response was out of all proportion? From an ethnographic perspective, explanations can be offered of such a response that still, of course, do not justify such violence but that can help us understand why such things happen and perhaps thereby broaden our expectations of what is associated with this form of literacy.

It is clear that people invest huge amounts of emotional and cultural energy and meaning into different kinds of inscription. Words in holy places, often carved or embedded in tile work, can carry similar weight and it would be considered 'sacrilegious' to deface them. Whilst such meanings are supported by strong institutions and cultural heritage, it may also be true that less recognised forms of inscription also carry such weight for their participants. There is a considerable literature on graffiti and inscription on different surfaces that draws our attention to the cultural meanings of literacy well beyond questions of 'skill' and decoding (see, for example, Baeder, 1996). One of us was struck during a recent visit to India how rural women in a literacy class were quite comfortable using their chalk to write on the floor and on the walls of the building, in ways that would be considered offensive in the classrooms we occupy in London. Whatever our personal opinions of these practices, we are pushed by the analyses to perhaps review our assumptions about what counts as 'literacy', where the boundaries are defined both in terms of what surfaces are appropriate to 'write' on and more broadly what meanings are attached to the concept. Again your checklist of key terms may come in for some revision here. Would you want to include 'graffiti' in such a list? And if so what are the implications for the account of literacy being developed here?

A more conventional example of children's writing is provided overleaf, taken from a helpful book on the subject, *Exploring writing and play in the early years* by Nigel Hall and Anne Robinson. Whilst much school writing is seen as a form of composition according to specific genre constraints, children do also write spontaneously as part of their play activity. This example illustrates such a mix of play and schooling, as Fhamida makes her own version of the teacher's daily register.

TEXT

'Fhamida's register' from Hall, Nigel, and Robinson, Anne, *Exploring writing and play in the early years*. Manchester Metropolitan University Education Series (London: David Fulton Publishers, 1995).

Reflections

Fhamida, who was 5 years old at the time, has copied not only the letter and word forms used by the teacher when taking the class register but also the layout, and has added her own small signs beside each name. Moreover, she linked this with the oral practice she saw her teacher perform, insisting on calling her register each morning. Such engagement with the holistic contextual features of literacy are already present at the age of 5 and suggest we cannot just isolate the word and phoneme levels even for beginning learners – literacy, it seems, comes as a package and part of the learning is knowing how to fit parts of the package together in meaningful ways.

By the time we were teenagers, many of us were doing all kinds of 'real reading' outside of school, including magazines targeted at our age group, specialist journals for enthusiasts etc. We include here one such example because of its richness in evoking issues not only of 'reading' but also of deeply cherished identity, in this case concerning heritage and ethnicity. The data are drawn from an Hispanic Academic Summer Program, reported by Peter Cowan (2005) in his insightful article on the use made of *Lowrider* magazines by a young Hispanic boy in the programme. A lowrider is a genre of customised car associated with the Mexican-American community: lowrider cars are lowered to the ground, ride on small, custom wheels and skinny tyres, and often feature elaborate paint schemes (frequently including icons found in the Mexican-American community). The young students were bringing in to the class magazines associated with this genre which teachers at first dismissed as inappropriate for school and learning, but then began to realise were significant both for the pupils' ethnic identities and for their engagement with writing (cf. http://www.lowridermagazine.com/). A broader theme also emerged as Cowan, drawing upon the work of Kress and van Leeuwen on multimodality (1996), came to recognise the location of such writing in more general semiotic practices, including drawing and photography. He realised, then, that the pupils were using the drawings and their association with the magazines to construct identities in a context where their Latino backgrounds were often marginalised. From the evidence of interviews, the artwork and his own observations, Cowan concludes that such practices can be described as 'visual literacy', a term you might want to scrutinise more closely before considering whether it would be appropriate to add to your list of key terms. (You may find the language he uses to describe these processes unfamiliar but the point is to address the 'visual literacy' issue rather than get caught up in the particular jargon – a principle you will find repeated throughout this volume as you inevitably encounter unfamiliar language by specialist authors.)

TEXT

Cowan, Peter M., 'Putting it out there: revealing Latino visual discourse in the Hispanic academic program' in B. Street, ed. *Literacies across educational contexts: mediating learning and teaching* (Philadelphia: Caslon Publishing, 2005), pp. 145–169.

> My findings reveal that Latino visual discourse is a form of visual literacy and an epistemology that draws on Latin American/Amerindian ways of perceiving, thinking and knowing that is subaltern, because it exists outside of mainstream, Eurocentric cultural practices and institutions that conserve knowledge. The colonization of Mesoamerica resulted in the trans-culturation of practices of literacy and this process of cultural hybridization is at least as old as the Conquest. Transculturation and NLS [New Literacy Studies] theorize the journey of the social practices and icons of Latino visual discourse from south to north, and their neoculturation in Mexican American/Latino communities in the U.S. where practitioners re-imagine, re-envision, and re-invest icons with meanings that Latino youth use to construct affirming cultural identities. Latino visual discourse is a culturally distinct form of visual literacy that some students bring to school where it gets overlooked, underestimated and often denigrated by school officials who fail to see how these visual literacy practices are related to literacy.

A4.6 Artwork from the June/July 2004 issue of *Lowrider Arte* magazine

Reflections

Whilst the discourse here may be unfamiliar, with its technical terms from the field of Latin American studies, such as 'transculturation', 'subaltern' etc., the point may look more familiar as we consider the ways in which minority groups in our own societies, like the Hispanic youths in Cowan's account, use a blend of literacy and art work to express themselves. Cowan analyses the use of Aztec icons, such as the Plumed Serpent and religious icons such as the Virgin of Guadalupe, in such youths' art work and as they appear in lowrider art and magazines. You might consider what work the icon in this particular picture from the June/July 2004 issue of *Lowrider Arte* magazine is doing and then use that approach to look for similar examples in your own context. A good starting point might be the shelves of newsagents where teen and specialist magazines abound, to consider the ways in which such material is indicative of the 'literacy' engagement of readers who in other contexts may be considered poor readers or even, on the basis of formal schooled tests of their 'reading', as 'illiterate'.

Likewise you might begin to follow up the work in multimodality (see references in the bibliography, e.g. Kress and van Leeuwen 1996, 2001) that locates written production in the context of other modes – visual, oral, kinaesthetic etc. Again does your list of key terms in literacy have to adjust to take account of this phenomenon? Does 'reading' shift its meaning to include the mix of art work and written words, including the use of elaborate fonts that are part of both genres, as in the earlier example? Are you happy with the term 'visual literacy' or are there limits, do you feel, to the use of literacy as a metaphor for other skills and competences? Elsewhere one of us has argued for using literacy to refer to texts that involve some reading and writing and that terms such as 'political literacy', 'emotional literacy' etc. lose the precision that this narrower usage provides (Street, 2000). But Cowan is using the term for texts that do involve both art work and written material, so perhaps it makes the point well that the two are often combined?

Having looked at just a small – and unrepresentative but we hope indicative – sample of children's and teenage engagement with reading and writing, and considered some responses and tasks, you might now like to find further examples of your own. In doing so you might like to consider, first, texts that speak to your own experience – whether in your own early learning, in encounters with others' learning or not at all associated with learning but rather embedded in everyday life. As you develop the latter approach, you might like to look forward to Section C3.2, where material from the writing of 'ordinary' people for the Mass Observation archive is discussed, or Section C3.1 where we look at 'workplace literacies'. Then you might like to use a more academic criterion, selecting texts according to what they tell you about your ideas on literacy. As we have seen, the different texts might highlight for you whether your dominant assumption is that literacy is equivalent to 'reading'; or that your interest is implicitly about the cognitive implications of writing; or of writing as a social process. Each text is probably capable of revealing aspects of any of these approaches, but particular choices of text may perhaps indicate a particular focus or interest. Connected with this reflective activity, you might then like to review your list of key terms and check whether particular texts – such as the graffiti text above – may push you to revise the list. Do you now need to put the term 'reading' or 'writing' in the list, if they were not there before; and what about 'graffiti'? Or 'handwriting'? In this way you will develop further your own take on the field and have a conceptual and linguistic apparatus on which to draw as you encounter further texts in subsequent sections of the resource book.

We provide some examples of 'everyday' literacy below, and there are fuller accounts for further exploration in Section C (C3.1 and C3.2). You might like first to consider whether you would have included these under 'literacy' and second what exactly are the literacy skills involved in making sense of them. At first sight the two examples below may not appear to be part of what you would have called 'literacy'. And whilst the first one – the label from a milk carton – may seem somewhat trivial and mundane, the second – from a workplace sign with instructions for setting a heater – may appear ordinary if complex. But the very unusual nature of using such material in a resource book on literacy already makes the point – that it is not self-evident what we include under this heading and that in everyday life we encounter a variety of demands on our literacy skills and understandings.

TEXT

Farmland Dairies milk carton

TEXT

Boiler settings

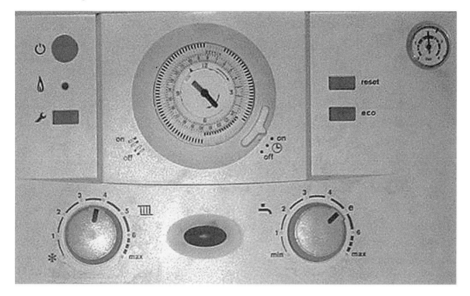

A4.8 (photo Brian Street)

Reflections

In your everyday life you no doubt encounter labels and packaging like the milk carton here all the time and usually don't stop to consider the 'literacy' involved in making sense of them. When someone knowing only the English alphabet travels to another country, especially where the writing system is different with perhaps Greek characters, Cyrillic alphabet or Japanese or Chinese ideographs, then the 'work' of interpreting such packets, road signs, 'information' posters etc. becomes more obvious and important. This reminds us of how much we take for granted in our own literacy environment and what we must know in order to access and decode information in even the most mundane of circumstances. The milk carton is representative of many such moments, from the breakfast table through to bedtime as we engage with the mix of words, fonts, colours, images, layout, numbers, dashes and brackets etc. that make up the meaning of even this simple literacy experience.

What about the numbers there, for instance (an important theme, as numeracy is often treated as secondary to literacy and yet much of our daily life hinges on getting the figures right as well as the letters)? There are three sets of percentages: 100%, 2% and 38%. Did you note these at first reading, and what role did they play in your making sense of the text? At one level, they can be seen as part of advertising discourse, framed around healthy eating and drinking and addressed to those of us who think about the fat intake of a given food. The word 'real' after 100% points up this wholesome framing of the text and the '2% reduced fat milk' is meant to provide scientific information, although we might have trouble following through what it is '2%' of! Meanwhile, the phrase '38% less fat than whole milk' says something similar with another set of figures that do not seem to correspond easily to the previous '2%'. Apart from percentages, there are also ordinary whole numbers, attached to measurements of various kinds; 'Fat reduced from 8g to 5g'. How does this relate to the percentages? We confess we got lost at this point and maybe it doesn't matter – except we might ask, what are all the figures doing there if they are not meant to communicate with the reader in some way? Then we have a mix of numerical notation '(3.78L)' and of numbers written out as words 'One Gallon'. This indexes the mix of weight systems still in use in the UK, switching between imperial and metric, although using different signifiers to do this – words in one case and numbers plus a letter that stands for a word in another (i.e. 'L' for 'Litre'). Is the second presented in reduced form because the writer assumes that the reader is less comfortable with the metric system? Or is the reason for this difference that it is assumed litres are better known so only the initial letter is needed? Our sense is that it is recognised that in the UK we have traditionally measured milk in pints and gallons, so the notation here is appealing to our cultural knowledge and familiarity but that regulations require the use of metric notation so this is added on (in parentheses).

Finally, what is the figure '1914' doing there? Again this can be seen as part of the advertising, signalling a company that has sufficient history in the field to be trusted. But why that year rather than the number of years it has been going? The effect is that the reader has to do a quick calculation to fill in the information implied by the figure – that Farmland Dairies is 91 years old (we are writing this in 2005) – or is the subject of the phrase 'since 1914', 'Farm Fresh' indicating that the production of milk has been 'fresh' over this period? In either case, for this part of the text the exact figure matters less than it does in the percentage claims – '2% reduced fat milk' – which are probably subject to regulatory mandates. We hope that we have done enough here to indicate just how complex even the simple texts of our everyday life are – and we have scarcely got to the words on this particular page, having chosen to focus on numbers. In Exploration C1.2 we invite you to try a similar exercise, keeping a log of your literacy practices from the moment you awake – through eating breakfast, using transportation, reading signs, going to work, shops, leisure sites etc. – all of which involve similar complex mixes of words, numbers and images, and similar mixes of discourse types – information, persuasion, claims, appeals to the reader.

Another 'ordinary' piece of equipment is a heating system, to be found both at home and in the workplace. Like many workplace literacies (see Section B4.4 and C3.1) the sign system associated with the equipment is a complex mix of visuals, words and numbers – and yet it is taken for granted in contemporary society that we can all handle this. Or is it? Do you, in fact, leave it to fellow workers who claim skill and expertise in technology – not necessarily so overtly in literacy – but can you trust them with such potentially dangerous equipment? At home, do you leave such things to the children? Or is that just for computers and videos, whilst heating systems are too potentially dangerous for young ones? The role of literacy and more broadly of sign systems, with visuals, numbers, layout etc. is brought home by such mundane equipment and the instructions associated with it.

Let us try to describe it. There is a clock at the centre with two sets of figures around the edges – on the outside ring a full 24-hour clock with gradations signified by small lines for quarters of an hour; and an inner circle in which only four numbers appear: 3, 6, 9 and 12. The outer set allows the user to select periods of time at which the heater will be operating – the inner set, with bold clock hands, indicates the current time. To the bottom right, there is a switch with three options, the position being indicated by a bullet point and by a mixture of words – 'on', 'off' – and an image – a picture of a clock face with hands. Further down is another dial with both numbers from 1 to 6 and words 'min', 'max'. In addition there is a letter 'e' between the numbers 4 and 5 and the line around the outside gets gradually thicker from min to 6 and then shreds into a dotted line. On the upper right side are two oblong light indicators with words beside them – 'reset' and 'eco'.

There are two literacy issues here – the first is reading, how we make sense of such diagrams; the second is writing, how we might write out our understanding of the meaning of such diagrams for others. We found it difficult to present this image in words and you might like to have your own go at it – or better, check out some similar piece of equipment in your workplace or at home and try to describe it to someone else – and then write out your description for someone not present. As we shall see, in the passages and activities we include on workplace literacies (Section B4.4, C3.1), ordinary workers are confronted with such complex semiotic systems all the time and yet, according to such researchers as Gowen whose text we reproduce in Section B4.4, often employers do not give them credit for the skills they show in 'reading' such material. Or else the employer's educational programmes fail to address the on-site knowledge workers already have of such complexities and address them as simple and in deficit, with levels of literacy that are anyway irrelevant to their everyday workplace practice. Gowen's account and our reading of it in relation to the materials presented here have implications both for workplace relations and for the kinds of educational programmes deemed appropriate in the workplace, issues we will raise in more detail later in the resource book (Section C3.1). For the moment you might just like to consider, have you ever had any training in this kind of literacy and if not how did you come to command such texts? Would you even call your 'reading' of such instructions 'literacy' – a question also raised with respect to the dairy carton? Both texts raise the opening questions of this resource book, what counts as literacy – and who decides?

TEXT

Richard Powers, 'Losing our souls, bit by bit', *New York Times*, 15 July 1998 (excerpts).

The cold war may be ancient history, but the Code War is only now beginning to heat up.

As more Americans do business on line, Internet commerce has created new worries about the security of personal information. Many consider encryption – the technology used to encode information and keep it private – to be the solution. As the networked world wires together our newly digital dens, we are drawn into a struggle with as great a consequence as the geopolitical one that shaped the last half century.

Reflections

These first two paragraphs of Powers's essay introduce us to another aspect of what it means for many people (at least in the West) to be literate today: the ability to 'find one's way around' cyberspace and to participate in the emerging forms of literate activity that take place there. While many observers have celebrated the many opportunities that such digital literacy poses, Powers sounds a note of alarm. So much of our lives have now been registered in some archive system, which he terms 'universal bookkeeping', that he claims we have already lost the battle for privacy and can only try to hold on to some zones of secrecy, that is 'the registered data that only authorized personnel can call up'. Powers notes: 'We have conceded the right to be recorded and we quibble only over the question of access.' He links this to our everyday lives, where phone calls, purchases, subscriptions etc. leave an audit trail that is easily followed by those with the authority to do so. Such systematic record-keeping has been made possible by the 'technologies of writing, print, telegraphy, telephony and tape' but more recent technologies such as encryption have made it ubiquitous and have changed the focus from privacy to secrecy. It was these early phases of print literacy that brought into being the idea of privacy in the first place – before the development of mass record-keeping the issue did not arise in the same way. But now, with the new technologies, the issue is not how to preserve privacy in a context where most of our activity is recorded anyway but rather how to get access to that recorded information: 'so now we fight the battle of encryption, a war over who gets access to what data about whom'.

Accompanying Powers's article is a clever illustration: the profile of a human head – eye and mouth wide open as if to suggest a scream of terror – made entirely out of telephone numbers, addresses, account numbers, passwords, licence numbers, etc. (We recommend you look up Powers's article and the accompanying illustration as our summary and description cannot do them justice.) The illustrator represents all these numbers as embedded in our heads and bewildering us as we try to perform simple functions in daily life. If the milk carton looked complex, and the heating system elaborately embedded, this is incomprehensible – and yet every day we engage in such transactions, call up such data from our mental memories and other storage devices (computers, notes on the home notice board, familiar objects, diaries etc.), attempt to decode it and, perhaps forlornly, to protect it from the gaze of others. You might take a stimulus from this perhaps overdrawn account to check out the kinds of data you call upon in your daily routines, how it is represented – in numbers, letters, words, objects – and how you store and call upon it (and protect it from undesired gaze).

Where does this all fit in the list of literacy terms you have been compiling? What role does literacy play in 'encryption' – or would you call the whole process 'encryption literacy'? How well prepared are we to engage with these levels of 'reading and writing' and how do they relate to the procedures being inculcated in those early texts we viewed above? How well do researchers' models hold up against these new communicative practices? Does the understanding of learning and literacy suggested earlier and developed further in Section B2 prepare us for this? Do the accounts of cognition argued about in Section B3 cover this level of our experience? And can the 'social practice' approaches developed in Section B4 help us engage with all of this complexity? Or do we need new models and theories?

Moving backwards and forwards across the resource book, from data and experience that evoke such questions, as we have been doing in Section A1–A4; to academic research that attempts to describe and analyse them in Section B; to 'Explorations' where we use these insights to pursue our own deeper understandings and research, will we hope help us deal with this complexity in a reasonably systematic way. By the time you get to the end of the resource book and come back to this section, you may feel you need yet another resource book to carry you forward into the new zones being mapped out.

Unit A5
Academic study of literacy – mapping the field[1]

A5.1 MEANINGS OF 'LITERACY' IN DIFFERENT TRADITIONS

The meaning of 'literacy' as an object of enquiry and of action – whether for research purposes or in practical programmes – is, as we have seen, highly contested and we have argued that we cannot understand the term and its uses unless we penetrate these contested spaces. This resource book has been organised around three major traditions or areas of enquiry that, despite inevitable overlaps, provide a heuristic by which we can begin to understand different approaches and their consequences. These comprise: *literacy acquisition, consequences of literacy*, and *literacy as social practice*. We have already begun to explore these areas with the help of some introductory texts, encounters and reflections. The next section of the resource book, Section B Extension, is organised into subsections with readings drawn from each of the three areas or traditions. In order to prepare for those readings, we will now provide our own 'mapping' of those traditions. You might want to skip this for the moment and go straight from the introductory materials and tasks to the academic readings, in which case it will be interesting to come back to this mapping part afterwards and compare what the sources have said to our representation of them and their place in the different fields. On the other hand, you might find it helpful to enter the terrain of these academic papers with some initial mapping – that, at least, is the aim of the following account.

Whilst, as we have seen, attention to reading has traditionally been seen as the main thrust of literacy work, and attention to cognition has driven many academic and policy claims for the 'consequences' of literacy, recent social and sociocultural approaches and adult learning theories as well as the impact of multimodal studies and discourse analysis have broadened what counts as literacy and challenged claims for its consequences. The authors cited here represent a variety of responses to these changes: some, such as Adams (1993) and Snow et al. (1998) (see Section B2.1; and Sections B1.3 and B2.3), privilege a more decontextualised account of the learning process; others such as Scribner and Cole (1978b) (see Section B3.2) attempt to link cognitive processes with social practices; others are moving to locate the teaching

---

1 Parts of this account are taken from a paper commissioned as preparatory work for the Unesco 2005 Global Monitoring Report; these parts are reproduced here by kind permission of the Unesco GMR Team, Paris.

of literacy within broader social and political contexts and to be more sensitive to the variety of backgrounds and language styles that learners bring with them, rather than imposing a single standard on all (Street and Street, 1991, see Section B2.4; and Rogers, 1992); and others locate literacy within other semiotic means of communication, such as visual and gestural 'modes', thereby focusing on 'multi-modality' or on 'multiliteracies' rather than on just 'literacy' which they see as less central to the communicative needs of a globalising world (Kress and Van Leeuwen, 2001; Cope and Kalantzis, 2000). All of these authors, some more explicitly than others, address contested issues of power and social hierarchy as they affect both definitions and their outcomes for practice.

A5.2 LITERACY ACQUISITION

For many, use of the term 'literacy' evokes the question of how children learn to read and this, then, is what the concept has been taken to mean. A similar metonymy is evident in adult literacy circles, where reference to an interest in 'literacy' is taken to be an interest in how to overcome 'illiteracy' by teaching adults how to *read* (even though for many a major motivation in entering literacy programmes is to learn how to write).

The issue of how children learn to read has been highly contested in recent years and those debates have implications for how adult literacy is conceived. The distinction between a focus on 'phonic' principles on the one hand (Adams, 1993, see Section B2.1) and on 'reading for meaning' on the other (Goodman, 1996, Section B2.2) has led to what are sometimes termed the 'reading wars'. More recently, researchers have argued for a 'balanced' approach that is less divisive and that recognises the strengths of each perspective (Snow, 1988, Section B2.3). In many circles, still, the term 'literacy' is interpreted to refer to 'reading' and more particularly to the learning of reading by young children. Adams (1993), for instance, herself a key figure in the US National Commissions on Literacy, begins an overview of the literature on 'Literacy' with the claim:

> The most fundamental and important issues in the field of reading education are those of how children learn to read and write and how best to help them.

The piece from which this comes was included in a book entitled *Teaching literacy, balancing perspectives* (ed. Beard (1993), p. 204, see Section B2.1) and offers a further introduction to some of the key terms in the field of reading that we have already encountered, such as 'phonics', 'whole language', phonemic awareness' etc. It also makes claims about what 'scientific' research now tells us about learning to read. There is now a requirement in some countries for 'scientific-based' approaches that can provide sound evidence of which methods and approaches are superior and that can claim to 'soundly refute' some hypotheses in favour of others. Adams's work, which can be situated within this aspiration, was based on a year reviewing the literature on the 'reading wars' and looking for alternatives. She concludes that the different disciplinary strands have begun to converge, and that the different perspectives are beginning to agree on what counts. The whole language view of learners engaging in a 'guessing game' (Goodman (1967) or the notion that spellings of words are minimally relevant to reading (Smith, 1971) have been rejected, she claims, in favour of attention to 'phonics'. The key to improvement in literacy, especially amongst the 'economically disadvantaged', includes phonemic awareness, phonic knowledge, word recognition, spelling and vocabulary.

If one were only to read such accounts, then the picture would seem clear enough and the task of increasing literacy – not only within the USA, as in this case, but across the world, for adults as well as children – would be simply a matter of putting these principles into practice. However, once you read other authors, then other views of what counts as literacy begin to emerge – and these authors speak with as much authority, for instance about 'what research tells us', as does Adams. Ken Goodman, for instance, who is largely seen as the leading international figure in 'whole language' approaches, refers like Adams, to 'what we have learned' and to 'scientific knowledge' – but in this case that requires a different 'knowledge', namely 'of language development, of learning theories, and of teaching and curriculum' (Goodman, 1996, see Section B2.2), not just of 'spelling-sound relations'. For him learning literacy is a more 'natural' process than described in the phonics approach and he likens it to the way in which humans learn language: 'Written language is learned a little later in the life of individuals and societies, but it is no less natural than oral language in the personal and social development of human beings' (Goodman, 1996).

Whether language, and by analogy literacy, are 'taught' or 'learned naturally' represent extreme poles of what, for most educators is a 'continuum': as Goodman states, 'while I separate *learning* reading and writing from *teaching* reading and writing, I can't do so absolutely'. What is evident from these accounts, then, is that underpinning approaches to literacy are theories of learning. These too need to be taken into account both in defining literacy and in developing policies for the spread of literacy, whether with respect to children or to adults.

A.5.2.1 Learning

Like theories of literacy, theories of learning have themselves been opened up more broadly in recent academic debate. Social psychologists and anthropologists such as Rogoff, Lave and Wenger (Lave, 1988; Lave and Wenger 1991; Rogoff, 2003; Rogoff and Lave, 1984) have invoked terms such as 'collaborative learning', 'distributed learning' and 'communities of practice' to shift the focus away from the individual mind and towards more social practices. To cite just one example, Barbara Rogoff and her colleagues, in their discussions of informal learning, have distinguished between 'the structure of *intent participation* in shared endeavors' and '*assembly-line preparation* based on transmission of information from experts, outside the context of productive activity':

Intent participation involves keen observation of ongoing community events with the anticipation of growing participation in the activity at hand.

(Rogoff et al., 2003)

Intent participation involves a collaborative, horizontal structure varying in roles, with fluid responsibilities, whereas assembly-line preparation employs a hierarchical structure with fixed roles. In intent participation, experienced people facilitate learners' roles and often participate alongside them; in assembly-line preparation, experienced people are managers, dividing the task often without participating. The learners' roles correspond to taking initiative to learn and contribute versus receiving information. Along with these interrelated facets of the two processes are differences in motivation and purposes, in sources of learning (e.g. observant participation or lessons out of the context of productive, purposeful participation), in forms of communication and in forms of assessment (to aid or test learning).

This account links closely to Rogers's (2003) work in adult education. Drawing upon Krashen's (1982) classic distinction with respect to language learning between 'acquisition' and 'learning', Rogers refers to 'task-conscious' learning and 'learning-conscious learning'. For Rogers, these forms of learning are to be distinguished by their methods of evaluation (task fulfilment versus measurements of learning). Whilst this may at times appear to differentiate adults strongly from children, Rogers and others argue that both children and adults do both – that in fact they form a continuum rather than two categories. Whilst adults are less often engaged in formal learning than children, the difference, he suggests, really lies in the *teaching* of adults (i.e. the formal learning) and in the power relationships, the identities built up through experience and the experiences adults bring to their formal learning. Much of what originally counted as learning theory in the discipline of psychology has been criticised for its failure to address these features. One consequence has been that aspects of the more traditional literacy learning of children (including 'assembly-line preparation' and 'test learning') have been used for adults, as evident in many adult literacy programmes; adults, for instance, as Rogers and others have shown, have been encouraged to join younger age groups, to take tests, to decon-textualise learning, ignore their own previous knowledge etc. (Freire, 1985; Freire and Macedo, 1987; Robinson, 2003; Rogers, 1994; Rogers et al., 1999; UNESCO, 2005).

A5.3 CONSEQUENCES OF LITERACY – THE LITERACY THESIS

Many of these theories of literacy and of learning have rested on deeper assumptions about cognition and in particular regarding the 'cognitive consequences' of learning or acquiring literacy. A dominant position, until recently, was to apply the idea of a 'great divide' – originally used to distinguish 'primitive/modern' or 'under-developed/developed' to 'literates' and 'non-literates', a distinction that implicitly or explicitly still underpins much work in and justifications for literacy programmes.

Anthropologists, such as Goody (1977; see Section B3.1), and psychologists such as Olson (1977, 1994; see Section B3.4), have linked the more precise cognitive argument to broader historical and cultural patterns regarding the significance of the acquisition of literacy for a society's functioning, economic development and scientific potential. These claims often remain part of popular assumptions about literacy and have fed policy debates and media representations of the significance of the 'technology' of literacy.

Whilst rejecting an extreme technological determinist position, Goody for instance does appear to associate the development of writing with key cognitive advances in human society: the distinction of myth from history; the development of logic and syllogistic forms of reasoning; the ability of writing to help overcome a tendency of oral cultures towards cultural homeostasis; the development of certain mathematical procedures, such as multiplication and division (for further discussion of the debates in mathematics see Street, Baker and Tomlin, 2005); and – perhaps the key claim for educational purposes – that literacy and the accompanying process of classroom education bring a shift towards greater abstractedness. Whilst he is careful to avoid claiming an absolute dichotomy between orality and literacy, it is partly on the grounds that his ideas do lend credence to technological determinism that he has been challenged, through the experimental data provided by Scribner and Cole (1978b, see Section B3.2; 1981) and the ethnographic data and arguments by Street (1984, see Section B3.3) and others (see Finnegan, 1999; Maddox, 2005). Goody himself has criticised many of these counter arguments as 'relativist', a term that might be applied to much contemporary thinking about literacy (and social differences in general) and has considerable implications for our approach to literacy whether within education or in everyday life.

During the 1970s the social psychologists Sylvia Scribner and Michael Cole conducted a major research project amongst the Vai peoples of Liberia in order to test the claims of Goody and others about the cognitive consequences of literacy in a 'real life' setting. Their accounts of the outcomes of this research (Scribner and Cole, 1978b; see Section B3.2; 1981) represented a major landmark in our understanding of the issues regarding literacy and cognition that we have been considering here. As we shall see in the excerpted material in Section B3.2, they quote Farrell, as a classic example of such claims (1977, p.451) – 'the cognitive restructuring caused by reading and writing develop the higher reasoning processes involved in extended abstract thinking' – and they argue, 'Our research speaks to several serious limitations in developing this proposition as a ground for educational and social policy decisions'. They address the limitations of these claims in both empirical and theoretical terms. For instance, many of the claims derive from abstract hypotheses not based in evidence, or the evidence used is of a very specific form of written text, such as use of western scientific 'essay text' literacy as a model for accounts of literacy in general (cf. Olson, 1977; Street, 1984). Many of the assumptions about literacy in general, then, are 'tied up with school-based writing'. This, they believe, leads to serious limitations in the accounts of literacy: 'The assumption that logicality is in the text and the text is in school can lead to a serious underestimation of the cognitive skills involved in non-school, non-essay writing.' The writing crisis, to which many of the reports and commissions cited above under 'Literacy and Learning' refer, 'presents itself as purely a pedagogical problem' and arises in the first place from these limited assumptions and data.

Scribner and Cole, instead, test out these claims through intensive psychological and anthropological research of actual practice, taking as a case study the Vai peoples of Liberia, who have three scripts – Vai (an invented phonetic script), Arabic and English – each used for different purposes.

> We examined activities engaged in by those knowing each of the indigenous scripts to determine some of the component skills involved. On the basis of these analyses, we designed tasks with different content but with hypothetically similar skills to determine if prior practice in learning and use of the script enhanced performance.
>
> (1978b, p. 13)

The tests were divided into three areas: Communication skills; Memory; and Language analysis. On the basis of the results, they argue that all we can claim is that 'specific practices promote specific skills': the grand claims of the literacy thesis are untenable:

> there is no evidence that writing promotes 'general mental abilities'. We did not find 'superior memory in general' among Qur'anic students nor better language integration skills 'in general' among Vai literates . . . There is nothing in our findings that would lead us to speak of cognitive consequences of literacy with the notion in mind that such consequences affect intellectual performance in all tasks to which the human mind is put.
>
> (1978b, p. 16)

This outcome suggests that the metaphor of a 'great divide' may not be appropriate 'for specifying differences among literates and nonliterates under contemporary conditions. The monolithic model of what writing is and what it leads to . . . appears in the light of comparative data to fail to give full justice to the multiplicity of values, uses and consequences which characterize writing as social practice' (p. 17). Scribner and Cole, then, were amongst the first to attempt to retheorise what counts as literacy and to look outside of school for empirical data on which to base sound generalisations (cf. Hull and Schultz, 2002, on literacy in and out of school).

One of the main proponents of the 'strong' thesis regarding the consequences of literacy has been David Olson (1977; see Section B3.4), who has been and is one of the sources for claims about the 'autonomous' model of literacy (cf. Street, 1984; see Section B3.3) and was indeed cited by Scribner and Cole in their account. But in a later book (1994) he, like them, tries to modify the inferences that can be drawn from his own earlier pronouncements and to disentangle myth and reality in our understanding of literacy. He draws an analogy with Christian theologians trying to put their faith on a firmer basis by getting rid of unsustainable myths that only weakened the case. As he describes the unsustainable myths of literacy he seems to be challenging those put forward by Goody, Farrell and others. In arriving at 'the new understanding of literacy' he describes six 'beliefs' and the 'doubts' that have been expressed about them as a helpful framework for reviewing the literature on literacy.

1 Writing as the transcription of speech
2 The superiority of writing to speech
3 The technological superiority of the alphabetic writing system
4 Literacy as the organ of social progress
5 Literacy as an instrument of cultural and scientific development
6 Literacy as an instrument of cognitive development

He then outlines the 'doubts' that modern scholarship has thrown on all of these assumptions. For instance, with respect to (4) Literacy and social development, he cites counter-arguments from anthropologists such as Lévi-Strauss (1961), who argued that not only is literacy not the royal route to liberation, it is as often a means of enslavement.

> It seems to favour rather the exploitation than the enlightenment of mankind . . .

> The use of writing for disinterested ends, and with a view to satisfactions of the mind in the fields either of science or the arts, is a secondary result of its invention – and may even be no more than a way of reinforcing, justifying, or dissimulating its primary function.
>   (Lévi-Strauss, 1961, pp. 291–292, cited in Olson, 1977)

With respect to (5) Cultural development, Olson cites the work of cultural historians and anthropologists (cf. Finnegan, 1999) who 'have made us aware of the sophistication of "oral" cultures . . .' and from whose work it appears that 'No direct causal links have been established between literacy and cultural development'.

Like Scribner and Cole's, Olson's conclusion challenges the dominant claims for literacy for adults as well as for children:

> the use of literacy skills as a metric against which personal and social competence can be assessed is vastly oversimplified. Functional literacy, the form of competence required for one's daily life, far from being a universalizable commodity turns out on analysis to depend critically on the particular activities of the individual for whom literacy is to be functional. What is functional for an automated-factory worker may not be for a parent who wants to read to a child. The focus on literacy skills seriously underestimates the significance of both the implicit understandings that children bring to school and the importance of oral discourse in bringing

those understandings into consciousness in turning them into objects of knowledge. The vast amounts of time some children spend on remedial reading exercises may be more appropriately spent acquiring scientific and philosophical information.

(Olson, 1977, p. 12)

He concludes: 'For the first time, many scholars are thinking the unthinkable: is it possible that literacy is over-rated?'

We might ask, in the light of this academic challenge, what are literacy policy makers and practitioners to do? Does the academic challenge undermine their current work in literacy and development or are there things they can get on with whilst the scholars argue? Whatever response we make, it is apparent that we cannot ignore such findings. As we shall see below, for many researchers the rejection of the 'literacy thesis' does not necessarily mean that we should abandon or reduce work in literacy programmes in or out of school: but it does force us to be clearer as to what justifications we use for such work and how we should conduct it. The next section shows how new theoretical perspectives, themselves growing from the debates outlined previously, have proposed a way of continuing to pursue productive work in the literacy field without the 'myths', overstatements and doubtful bases for action of some of the earlier positions.

A5.4 LITERACY AS SOCIAL PRACTICE

Whilst the concern with cognition and with 'problems' of acquisition continue, a recent shift in perspective has emphasised understanding of literacy practices in their social and cultural contexts. This approach has been particularly influenced by those who have advocated an 'ethnographic' perspective, in contrast with the experimental and often individualistic character of cognitive studies, and the textual, etic perspective of linguistic-based studies of text. These social developments have sometimes been referred to as 'New Literacy Studies' (Barton and Hamilton, 1998; see Section B4.1; Collins, 1995; Gee, 1999a; Heath, 1983; Street, 1993). Rogers argues that much of the work in this tradition focuses on the everyday meanings and uses of literacy in specific cultural contexts. This, like the work of Street and others, links directly to the application of ethnographic enquiry to literacy programmes (Rogers, 2005a; Street, Baker and Rogers, 2006).

In trying to characterise these new approaches to understanding and defining literacy, one of us has referred to a distinction between an 'autonomous' model and an 'ideological' model of literacy (Street, 1984; see Section B3.3). The 'autonomous' model of literacy works from the assumption that literacy in itself – autonomously – will have effects on other social and cognitive practices, much as in the 'cognitive consequences' literature cited above. The model, I argue, disguises the cultural and ideological assumptions that underpin it and that can then be presented as though they are neutral and universal. Research in the social practice approach challenges this view and suggests that in practice dominant approaches based on the autonomous model are simply imposing western (or urban etc.) conceptions of literacy on to other cultures (Street, 2001). The alternative, ideological model of literacy offers, I argue, a more culturally sensitive view of literacy practices as they vary from one context to another. This model starts from different premises than the autonomous model – it posits instead that if we were to view literacy as a social practice, not simply a technical and neutral skill, then it would become apparent that it is always embedded in socially constructed epistemological principles. The ways in which people address reading and writing would themselves be seen as rooted in conceptions of knowledge, identity and being. Literacy, in this sense, is always contested, both its meanings and its practices, hence particular versions of it are always 'ideological', they are always rooted in a particular world-view and a desire for that view of literacy to dominate and to marginalise others (Gee, 1990). The argument about social literacies (Street, 1995) suggests that engaging with literacy is always a social act even from the outset. The ways in which teachers or facilitators and their students interact is a social practice that affects the nature of the literacy being learned and the ideas about literacy held by the participants, especially the new learners and their positions in relations of power. From this perspective, it is not valid to suggest that 'literacy' can be 'given' neutrally and then its 'social' effects only experienced or 'added on' afterwards.

The question this approach raises for policy makers, programme designers, teachers and practitioners is, then, not simply that of the 'impact' of literacy – to be measured in terms of a neutral developmental index – but rather of how local people 'take hold' of the new communicative practices being introduced to them, as Kulick and Stroud's (1993) ethnographic description of missionaries bringing literacy to New Guinea villagers suggested. Literacy, in this sense, is, then, already part of a power relationship and how people 'take hold' of it is contingent on social and cultural practices and not just on pedagogic and cognitive factors. This raises questions that need to be addressed in any literacy activity: What are the power relations between the participants? What are the resources? Where are people going if they take on one literacy rather than another literacy? How do learners challenge the dominant conceptions of literacy?

This approach has implications for both research and practice. Researchers, instead of privileging the particular literacy practices familiar in their own culture, now suspend judgement as to what constitutes literacy among the people they are working with until they are able to understand what it means to the people themselves, and which social contexts reading and writing derive their meaning from. Many people labelled 'illiterate' within the autonomous model of literacy may, from a more culturally sensitive viewpoint, be seen to make significant use of literacy practices for specific purposes and in specific contexts. For instance, studies suggest that even non-literate persons find themselves engaged in literacy activities so the boundary between literate and non-literate is less obvious than individual 'measures' of literacy suggest (Canieso-Doronila, 1996). Academics have, however, often failed to make explicit the implications of such theory for practical work. This resource book attempts to enable readers to make explicit the variety of such positions as a basis for their own engagement with practice, whether as everyday participants in literacy practice or as teachers, policy makers or programme designers.

One way of facilitating such explicitness has been to suggest we make out lists of 'key terms' in the field and explore what they tell us about our own and others' assumptions. We looked earlier at our own vocabulary, and will encounter in Section B1 terms offered by Stierer and Bloome on the one hand and by Snow on the other. The field of New Literacy Studies has offered further concepts that claim to help us to answer some of the questions raised above. These include the concepts of *literacy events* and of *literacy practices*. Shirley Brice Heath characterised a 'literacy event' as 'any occasion in which a piece of writing is integral to the nature of the participants' interactions and their interpretative processes' (Heath, 1983, p. 50). One of us employed the phrase 'literacy practices' (Street, 1984, p. 1) as a means of focusing upon 'the social practices and conceptions of reading and writing', although he later elaborated the term both to take account of 'events' in Heath's sense and to give greater emphasis to the social models of literacy that participants bring to bear upon those events and that give meaning to them (Street, 1988). David Barton, Mary Hamilton and colleagues at Lancaster University have taken up these concepts and applied them to their own research in ways that have been hugely influential both in the UK and internationally (cf. Barton and Hamilton 1998; see Section B4.1). The issue of dominant literacies and non-dominant, informal or vernacular literacies is central to their combination of 'situated' and 'ideological' approaches to literacy. You might like to see if there is room in your growing list for these terms and if so what work they would do in helping you make explicit the meanings and assumptions you bring to the field. Some further examples of this 'new literacy studies' approach, which you will encounter in Section B, are Bartlett and Holland's examination of the relationships between literacy and identity (B4.2), Martin-Jones and Jones's study of literacy in multilingual contexts (B4.3) and Gowen's study of literacy and literacy education in the workplace (B4.4).

Again, these ideas are contested and, before you settle too firmly with them, you might also like to consider recent critiques of these 'new' approaches. Brandt and Clinton (2002), for instance, refer to 'the limits of the local' – they and others (cf. Collins and Blot, 2003) question the 'situated' approach to literacy as not giving sufficient recognition to the ways in which literacy usually comes from outside of a particular community's 'local' experience. Street (2003) summarises a number of these texts and the arguments they put forward and offers some counter-arguments from an ethnographic perspective. More recently, Maddox (2005) has attempted to bring together the 'situated' approach with that of 'New Literacy Studies', using his own ethnographic field research in Bangladesh to explore the relationship. For instance, he critiques NLS for its 'reluctance . . . in examining the role of literacy capabilities and practices in progressive forms of social change and the production of agency'. Like Brandt and Clinton, he wants to recognise the force of 'outside' influences associated with literacy, including the potential for helping people move out of 'local' positions and take account of progressive themes in the wider world.

The 'desire to keep records of household income and expenditure' was not just a technical issue but one of authority, gender relations and kinship – literacy (and numeracy) could play a catalytic role in such women's breaking free from traditional constraints. He wants, then, to 'shift away from the binary opposition of ideological and autonomous positions that has dominated . . . debates in recent years' and develop a 'more inclusive theory that can link the local and the global, structure and agency and resolve some of the theoretical and disciplinary tensions over practice and technology'. These issues are nicely summarised by Reder and Davila (B4.5).

Stromquist (2004), in a recent paper for a conference on gender and education, also critiques aspects of the 'social' perspective on literacy from the perspective of someone wishing to build upon literacy interventions for equity and justice agendas. She accepts the arguments put by NLS against the strong version of the cognitive consequences of literacy but does not believe that means entirely abandoning recognition of where literacy and cognition are associated: 'Understanding the contributions of literacy does not mean that one needs to see literacy functions as the only way to develop cognitive ability and reasoning powers, but rather that there be acknowledgement that literacy does enable people to process information that is more detailed, deliberate and coherent than oral communication.' For instance, 'Literacy enables people to participate in modern life processes such as reading newspapers and maps, following instructions, learning the law, and understanding political debates'. Without returning to the now discredited claims of the autonomous model, she and others in the field of adult literacy want to hold on to some of the powers of literacy associated with it.

The positions and arguments outlined here, whether just the privileging of the 'local' evident in some early NLS positions or the recognition of 'outside' and global as well as cognitive influences, as in Brandt, Maddox, Stromquist and others, imply different approaches to what counts as 'literacy' and to how programmes for the extension and enhancement of literacy may be conceptualised and designed. From this point of view, then, any project for developing or enhancing the literacy either of children or of adults needs to indicate which literacies are under consideration. The implications of these scholarly debates for practical interventions are not that we abandon work in this field – despite the occasional tendency in that direction as researchers question many of the supposed gains associated with literacy – but rather that we put it into perspective and recognise the limitations and constraints imposed by the different theoretical positions we adopt.

However, before moving to the detailed academic texts in Section B, we will outline one further position that is turning out to have perhaps even greater implications for our understanding of literacy. That is the approach to literacy as text, and in particular the focus on new communicative practices, sometimes referred to as 'multimodality' or 'multiliteracies'. There is no space to pursue this further here, although we take up the issue again in the book's Conclusion. Moreover, you might like to bear some of the following account in mind and perhaps follow up some of the references, as you work through the three areas or traditions around which the resource book is structured.

A5.5 NEW LITERACIES

Linguists, literary theorists and educationalists have tended to look at literacy in terms of the texts that are produced and consumed by literate individuals. Linguists have developed a variety of complex analytic tools for 'unpacking' the meanings of texts, both those that can be extracted by a skilled reader and those that a writer implicitly or explicitly deploys (Hornberger, 2003). Educationalists have then applied some of this knowledge to the development of skilled readers and writers. For instance, a movement that began in Australia focused on the analysis of writing into different 'genres' (cf. Cope and Kalantzis, 1993) and became significant in educational contexts more generally (underpinning aspects of the National Literacy Strategy in the UK (cf. Beard, 1999). Theorists and practitioners working from this perspective aim to provide learners with the full range of genres necessary to operate in contemporary society and indeed treat this as the crucial dimension of the social justice and 'access' agenda. In doing so, they could be criticised from an ethnography of literacies perspective for attempting to generalise 'contemporary society' rather than to particularise it. Similarly, building on work by linguists, more radical critics have focused on stretches of language larger than the sentence, referred to by sociolinguists as 'discourse'. Influenced by broader social theory and by uses of the term discourse by Foucault and others, they have developed an approach to what Gee (1990) calls Discourse with a big D. This locates literacy within wider communicative and sociopolitical practices – at times the term Discourse looks very like what anthropologists used to mean by 'culture'. The work of Gee (1990) and Fairclough (1991) represents a central plank in this approach.

Kress and others have developed this position further, arguing that language should be seen as just one of several modes through which communication is conducted (Kress and van Leeuwen, 2001): 'We suggest that, like language, visual images, gesture and action have been developed through their social usage into articulated or partly articulated resources for representation' (p. 2). Individuals make choices from the 'representational resources' available amongst these various modes, and a multimodal perspective enables us to identify the traces of these decisions – of the interests of the parties to a text. This approach sees literacy practices as one set amongst many communicative practices at the same time applying the social, ideological and functional interpretations that have been developed with respect to discourse-based studies of communication. It recognises, for instance, that many people, including those defined as 'literate' by standard measures, use other strategies to deal with literacy tasks – in determining bus or train times for instance, or in finding their way to addresses, people do not necessarily 'decode' every word or number but instead 'read off' from a range of signs, including colour, layout, print font etc. (Cope and Kalanztis, 2000; Street, 1998). Approaches to understanding such 'multimodality' can also be applied to the work of classrooms – science classrooms employ diagrams, objects, notation systems etc. in addition to language itself in spoken and written forms, as means whereby pupils learn what counts as 'science' (Kress et al., 2001). Similar analyses can be applied to a range of subject areas both within schooling and in adult programmes and less formal educational contexts.

A new book (Pahl and Rowsell, 2005) attempts to bring together the two fields of study signalled here – New Literacy Studies and multimodality. The volume is helpful in guiding us away from extreme versions of these approaches. For instance, the term literacy is sometimes broadened well beyond the NLS conception of social practice to become a metaphor for any kind of skill or competence: at one extreme we find such concepts as 'palpatory' literacy (skill in body massage) or 'political' literacy, whilst somewhat closer to the social literacies position we find reference to 'visual' literacy or computer literacy, both of which do involve some aspects of literacy practices but may not be wholly defined by them. From the perspective of multi-modality, we likewise find uncertainty about what to include and exclude, what goes with what: Do we classify a single mode, say visual literacy, with its affordances, in an entirely separate category from other modes, say, writing? How do we avoid a kind of technological or mode determinism? Can we find ways of describing the overlap and interaction of such modes according to context and 'practice'? (cf. Street, 2000).

One way of tracing a path through this semantic and conceptual confusion is to engage in research on the practices described: labelling the object of study forces us to clarify what exactly we include or exclude and what are the links between various modes, a principle that is important not only for research but also for policy and practice. Ethnographic-style methods of enquiry may be particularly appropriate to this endeavour, since they involve the reflexivity and the closeness to the ground that enable us to see more precisely what multimodal practices and literacy practices consist of. Future developments, then, both conceptual and applied, may involve some marriage of the last two approaches signalled here – literacy as social practice and literacy as one component of multimodal communicative practices. This is sometimes signalled as a relationship between 'texts and practices', an approach that may come to inform literacy work more in the coming years.

The broader policy question raised by all of this work is whether the literacies being taught in schools and in mainstream adult programmes are relevant to the lives that learners are leading and will have to lead in the globalised world with its 'new work order' demands of flexibility, multimodality and multiliteracies (cf. Gee et. al., 1996). In recent years a number of researchers have addressed the issue of the variety of literacy practices evident in workplaces. From a theoretical perspective, Gee et al. have considered the new literacies required of workers in the 'new work order', exemplified for example in ethnographic studies of a factory in Cape Town (Prinsloo and Breier, 1996), a Boston milk depot (Scribner, 1984) and a hospital and church in the USA (Gowen, 1992). There are often conflicts between such actual uses of literacy in the workplace and the kinds of literacy skills prioritised in official strategies and campaigns. Chris Holland's (1998) annotated bibliography of this area provides a useful way in to this field and signals materials produced by Trade Unions and NGOs, for example, 'Workplace Basic Skills Network' (UK) (cf. also Hull, 2000, 2001; O'Connor, 1994), that you might like to follow up as you explore these areas further. Gowen's account (Section B4.4) of workplace literacies in the US setting provides a useful summary of the issues with a detailed description of the struggles of a particular individual across different sites.

The work on multimodality or on multiliteracies makes especially apparent the general theme of this introductory section – that we cannot avoid the implications of the deeper conceptual frameworks that underpin our approach and our practice, in the field of literacy as in other domains. If we want to have some control over the effects of our engagement in this area, then we need first to make explicit what these underlying assumptions are and to take cognisance of what research tells us of their implications and of their consequences when they have been enacted in other contexts. Understanding and defining literacy lies at the heart of 'doing' literacy, and the new understandings and definitions outlined above are likely to lead to quite different ways of doing in the next era. We now move into a closer engagement with some of the texts summarised above as a way of refining further the developing conceptions of literacy with which this resource book is working.

SECTION B
Extension

In this Section we provide extracts from a range of articles and books on Literacy and we suggest tasks for you to engage with in order to help make sense of the extracted passages, linking them to each other and to the key themes we are pursuing throughout the book. We have divided the material according to the following headings, which correspond of course to the key sections in our review of the field in Section A5:

B1   Keywords
B2   Literacy acquisition
B3   Consequences of literacy
B4   Literacy as social practice.

Following these sections you will be offered opportunities to explore these issues in depth in Section C Exploration.

Unit B1
Keywords

Under this heading we introduce you to some of the terms used by various practitioners and theorists in the field of literacy. We have subdivided these into educational, anthropological and psychological terms. You might note how different (and similar) such terms are in the different disciplines. This section builds upon the earlier Task A3, 'Developing a list of keywords'. In that task you generated a list of key terms you associate with the field of literacy. We suggest that you revisit that list as you read the following extracted discussions, comparing your keywords with those identified by Stierer and Bloome, Besnier and Snow. (And if you haven't generated your own list yet, we recommend you do so now, using the method outlined in Section A3.)

B1.1 EDUCATIONAL TERMS

Barry Stierer and David Bloome, in a paper for the National Association of Teachers of English in the UK, likewise set out some of the key terms associated with literacy. In this case, their focus is on the association between literacy and reading and in particular on the ways in which children are taught how to read (see texts in Section B2). For many people this is where 'literacy' starts – indeed the term literacy is often seen as synonymous with reading. For those interested in the educational dimension of literacy, their account is especially informative. They start with their own theoretical assumptions, recognising like Besnier (see later) that the account of literacy they give will be rooted in their underlying assumptions and ideas, including what Besnier terms 'prescriptive normativity' (which will become clearer once you have read the Besnier article and done some of the tasks we suggest there).

Stierer and Bloome start with the point that many key terms associated with the learning of reading or literacy are contested – a point that recurs throughout the accounts provided in this book. As teachers as well as researchers, they ask the reader to share with them the assumptions they bring to such learning. For instance, in this field, terms such as 'phonics' and 'whole language' have been the sites of much debate and argument: according to which label is used to describe a teacher or a learner, the judgement of them and of the work they needed to do differed.

➤ Can you describe situations where you have used labels such as 'dyslexic' or 'remedial' to describe someone's way of learning how to read – perhaps your own, when you were at school or in an adult literacy class?

➤ Were there other terms used to label you or those you know?

They cite two different kinds of study that have informed their development of a vocabulary for describing reading and literacy – studies in language and ideology; and studies of the social construction of reading and literacy.

- Have you come across these fields of study before, perhaps under different labels?
- Using the description offered of each field by Stierer and Bloome, write down ways in which these relate to or help you articulate your own experience – or are they completely different from your experience and from the keywords that you are used to employing when you talk about literacy and reading?
- If so, what terms are you more familiar with? And what fields do they derive from, for example psychology, government reports, newspapers?
- Can you identify an implicit set of values beneath each position? Would you call these positions 'ideological' in the sense used, according to Stierer and Bloome, by Fairclough?
- Does this add anything to your understanding of literacy?

Text B1.1
B. Stierer and
D. Bloome

Stierer, B. and Bloome, D. (1994) *Reading words: a commentary on key terms in the teaching of reading* (Sheffield: National Association for the Teaching of English), 'Theoretical influences', pp. 3–10.

Theoretical influences

We knew from our experiences working in classrooms that the meanings of key terms in the teaching of reading were often more complicated than what was written in technical dictionaries. We also knew that certain words in the teaching of reading – like 'phonics' and 'whole language' – were the sites of much debate and argument. These debates had real consequences. Teachers and pupils were often labelled by these words: Ms Smith is a 'real books' teacher; Ms Jones is a 'phonics' person; Stephen is a 'remedial' reader; John is 'dyslexic'. The labels had real consequences for the opportunities teachers and pupils had, and for how their behaviour was interpreted.

In addition to our experiences in classrooms, there have been a number of scholarly works that have helped us to articulate a critical examination of the vocabulary of the teaching of reading. Two different but related fields of scholarship have been especially influential on our work here. The first consists of studies in language and ideology; and the second consists of studies of the social construction of reading and literacy. Part of what brings these two fields together is their interest in revealing the ideologies behind everyday language and literacy practices, including those that occur in classrooms.

Language and ideology

The first body of theoretical work which has strongly influenced us in our thinking about this project is scholarship which has examined the relationship between language in use (or discourse) and the exercise of power. The field of critical discourse analysis offered us two related theoretical tools: first, a set of ideas which helped to explain the way in which the vocabulary used in the teaching of reading is linked to wider power relationships; and second, a practical method for unpacking this vocabulary in a way which located it in its contexts of use.

B. Stierer and
D. Bloome

Explanatory ideas

The first tool, the explanatory ideas, appealed to us because they related to our starting point: that the more widely used terms in the teaching of reading – which can often seem so neutral and innocuous – contain, and at the same time transmit, an implicit set of values, assumptions and definitions. These have real consequences for teachers' thinking and practice, and for the educational experience of children in school. Moreover, they are related to powerful interests in education and society. Our starting point was therefore a recognition that the dominant vocabulary in reading pedagogy is *ideological* – that is, it is an example of:

> an implicit philosophy in the practical activities of social life, backgrounded and taken for granted, that connects it to common sense.
>
> (Fairclough, 1989, p. 84)

Practical approach to language study

The other theoretical tool offered by this work on language and ideology is a practical approach for analysing spoken and written language in a range of social contexts – from immediate interactive contexts (like classrooms), to institutional contexts (like schools), to wider societal contexts (like the political and cultural constraints within which schools operate). Since our aim was to scrutinise a particular kind of language which is an integral part of these different levels of social context, and to try to do so systematically, this work offered an approach well-suited to our purpose.

The social construction view of reading and literacy

In reflecting on the vocabulary of the teaching of reading, we have been influenced by studies that have viewed reading and literacy as socially constructed. These studies have influenced us in two related ways. First, they have emphasised that there is not a single predetermined definition of reading; rather, there are many definitions of reading which emerge from how people actually use written language to interact with each other and to act on the world in which they live. From this perspective, reading and literacy are social and cultural practices and not just a set of decontextualised intellectual skills. This understanding of reading helped us to focus attention on how the vocabulary of the teaching of reading often promotes a single and narrow definition of reading, and it helped us ask questions about the social and cultural dynamics involved in dismissing a broader range of definitions of reading.

A second way in which studies of reading and literacy as socially constructed influenced our investigation was by focusing our attention on the ideological work accomplished by reading. How people engage in reading – how they interact with each other during a reading event, how they interpret a text, how they define what is and what is not reading, and how they connect reading to other events in their lives – reflects a cultural ideology and helps to shape it. Studies of reading as socially constructed give us a warrant for considering reading and the teaching of reading as ideological practices.

Reading and literacy have traditionally been viewed as a kind of technology, a technical skill acquired by individuals to be used across situations and texts. Although there might have been some disagreement about which intellectual skills make up reading, there was little disagreement about reading being a set of skills, and that these skills needed to be taught. The view of reading and literacy in general as socially constructed has fundamentally challenged this traditional view of reading. Rather than viewing reading as a decontextualised set of intellectual skills, reading is viewed as a set of social practices and social events involving the use of written language. Researchers studying reading from this perspective ask questions such as: How are people in different situations using written language? What are people using written language for? How do people use written language to interact with each other? What social values are associated with the use of written language? In what ways do people interpret written language? Implicit in these questions is the proposition that the answers will not be generalisable or universal, but specific to a cultural group, a social institution, or perhaps even limited to a particular situation or event. In other words, this view of reading provides a new set of questions to ask about reading and a new definition of knowledge about reading.

Part of the picture that emerges from studies of reading and literacy in specific situations shows that, beyond superficial similarities, there is a great deal of variation in how people use and constitute reading and writing across situations and across cultural groups. For example, in some cultures it is not appropriate to write a letter to express emotion while in others it is the appropriate social practice. In some cultures it is appropriate in particular situations to allow each individual to derive their own interpretation of a written text, while in other cultures in analogous situations the appropriate social practice is to insist on one, single authorised interpretation.

Although there is wide variation in how people engage in reading events, within a social or cultural group people share assumptions about how to engage in reading (including how they should interact with each other) in particular types of situations. For example, members of a church share assumptions about how the prayer book should be read during Sunday services; lawyers share assumptions about how a contract should be read and how it should be disputed; cooks share assumptions about how to use a cookery book; and pupils and teachers share assumptions about how a textbook should be used and read. The wide variation in literacy practices makes it clear that there is not one way of doing reading, but many ways of doing reading, not one literacy but many literacies – and this is true not only across cultural groups but within them as well.

Although it is important to highlight variation, studies of reading as socially constructed have also shown how certain reading practices within an institution and a society may be associated with the exercise of power. Further, particular reading practices may be associated with greater social prestige and may provide greater access to economic rewards and social mobility. This insight leads to questions such as: Who has access to these reading practices and how do they get access? How is the association between reading practices and the exercise of power rationalised (that is, the ideological justification)? What are the social and cultural consequences of the exercise of power through these reading practices? How is the power which is exercised through these reading practices related to other ways of exercising power? How and to what effect is the exercise of power through these reading practices contested?

. . .

One implication of viewing reading as socially constructed is that the attempt to create a single definition of reading is nonsensical. This is the fundamental disagreement between traditional perspectives on reading and views associated with the social construction of reading. Unless the definition is so superficial as to be of no use (as in 'reading involves written language'), the effect of a single definition of reading is to deny the great variation of social practices that would otherwise count as reading, and would in effect be a description of a specific reading practice rather than a definition of reading per se. When a specific reading practice (or a specific set of reading practices) is taken as the definition of reading, other reading practices may be marginalised, or dismissed as not being reading and therefore as not legitimate ways to use written language. *Whoever has the authority to define reading has the power to determine who is a reader and who is not, whose interpretation of a text is acceptable and whose is not, and how and for what written language may be used.* The creation of a single definition of reading (which is itself a literacy practice) creates a standard that legitimates giving power, rewards and resources to those who adhere to authorised reading practices and denies it to others; and, perniciously, it makes the distribution of power based on adherence to a standard model of reading seem common-sensical and unassailable.

Task B1.1: Comparing keywords

Stierer and Bloome's list of keywords is as follows:

> ability, accuracy, assessment, bedtime story reading, code, comprehension, curriculum, development, dyslexia, failure and success, functional reading, instruction, motivation, phonics, reader, reader response, readiness, reading age, reading schemes, real books, remedial reading, skills, standards, word attack.

➤ How does this list compare to your own?

➤ In what places do the two lists converge or diverge?

➤ And what might be the reasons for the similarities and differences?

Commentary

Stierer and Bloome deliberately left the word 'reading' out of their list of 'key terms'. They said:

> The implication of these studies of reading as socially constructed, for our project on the vocabulary of reading pedagogy, is that it is more useful not to define 'Reading' and to leave it vague and indeterminate, than it would be to replace one set of definitions with another. There is, therefore, no entry on 'Reading' in this book.

It is likely that in your own list you did put 'reading' in, especially if you have young children and have seen their growing efforts to get to grips with early books and school learning or if you have been involved in education. For many, the term reading has become almost synonymous with literacy. In keeping with Stierer and Bloome's problematisation of this taken for granted idea, we have chosen to not begin the book with in-depth discussion of reading and its acquisition. In this way, we hope to facilitate the reader's own raising of these questions. Indeed, you may already have asked, 'How can this book on literacy say so little about reading?' There will, of course, be texts in the next section (B2) that do address this issue but we wanted to establish the point that even the most self-evident of terms that go to make up the complex or cluster under the heading of literacy need to be justified rather than taken for granted.

B1.2 ANTHROPOLOGICAL TERMS

The following selection from an article by an anthropologist, Niko Besnier, provides a similar starting point for reflecting upon our own uses of the term 'literacy', drawing upon the author's discipline of anthropology. You are again encouraged to write down some of the key terms for yourself, provide a gloss and then relate them to your own starting assumptions about and experience of literacy. A series of tasks will be provided after the excerpt to enable you to begin the process of reflection and 'taking hold' of the ideas that will continue to weave throughout the book.

Text B1.2
N. Besnier

Besnier, N. (2001) 'Literacy', in A. Duranti (ed.) *Key terms in language and culture* (Oxford and Malden, MA: Blackwell), pp. 136–138.

Literacy can be roughly defined as communication through visually decoded inscriptions, rather than through auditory and gestural channels. Literacy as a human activity has lurked in the background of both anthropological and linguistic research throughout its history, thought about but not investigated systematically; borne in mind but marginalized. Social anthropologists have long speculated on the peculiar thinking processes, social structures, and cultural patterns that characterize literate individuals and groups. Until not long ago, linguists viewed literacy as what linguistics does not study, a reaction, in part, to the association in popular thinking of written language with prescriptive normativity. Only in recent decades have these speculations and negative definitions given way to systematic investigations and a more centralized focus in both disciplines.

Several identifiable currents underlie contemporary research on literacy in linguistic anthropology. First, attempts to deconstruct age-old statements about the funda-mental differences between literate and pre-literate societies have led researchers to explore the vast patterns of diversity covered under the umbrella term 'literacy.' . . . For example, the pedagogical literacy that children practice at school and the literacy activities that their parents engage in at home can differ widely. Similarly, literacy in the workplace, during leisure time, in the courtroom, and at church all have particular characteristics, associations, and implications. Literacy varies widely in form and context across societies as well: contexts of use, levels of prestige, communicative norms, identities of users, and social dynamics all shape literacy in particular ways in each society or community. Each society or community is literate in ways that differ from the ways in which other societies or communities are literate. Research in the diversity and heterogeneity of literacy experiences is thus explicitly particularistic and ethnography-driven.

The drawback of this particularistic approach is that it is potentially too generalization-shy; at worst, it becomes an amalgamation of anecdotes collected by researchers marveling at the diversity of humankind. The second current in recent works on literacy saves it from these dangers: linguistic anthropologists strive to apprehend the meaning of reading and writing as social, cultural, and cognitive activities. This meaning may consist of symbolic relationships, associations and connections between reading and writing, on the one hand, and other aspects of human existence, on the other. For example, ethnographers of literacy have demonstrated that for participants in literate communication, the activities that take place 'around' literate communication (i.e., simultaneously, in the same social space, with the same people) provide a specific flavor to the literacy activity, a flavor that becomes part of its inherent meaning. Thus, for instance, literacy produced or consumed during religious ceremonies highlights the same aspects of the self, the same emotions, the same power and authority relations that are foregrounded in the religious ritual. These aspects of self, emotions, and relations are evident in the way that participants handle written texts (reading them, memorizing them, talking about them, touching them, etc.) and, often, in the form of the texts themselves. They become an integral part of the social and cultural meaning of the literacy activity.

Arriving at an understanding of this meaning therefore consists in searching for relationships and connections which leads one to the third current identifiable in the linguistic anthropological investigation of literacy. Like all other communicative activities most reading and writing activities are often 'microscopic,' i.e., they consist in messages exchanged over short periods of time between restricted numbers of persons, whose scope and consequences are minimal. (Of course, widely disseminated published writing is potentially more 'macroscopic,' but it is only one of many manifestations of literacy.) Despite their microscopic form, literate exchanges articulate the larger structures in which they are embedded. For example, when literate communities are embedded in a colonial context, or when they constitute different social classes or gender groups in a complex society, the differences in their literacy activities are no longer simply instances of the heterogeneity of literacy as a mode of communication. Rather, they become part of dynamics of domination and resistance, structure and agency, and reproduction and change. In such contexts, certain literacy activities are valued, exalted, and employed as gate-keepers restricting access to institutions and other organs of power. Others are devalued or simply not defined as literacy or communication at all. In other words, each act of reading and writing potentially re-enacts in a moment-by-moment ('microscopic') fashion the macroscopic structures in which it takes place. Literacy, like many other social activities (even beyond the realm of communication), thus mediates between microscopic, person-centered, and agentive behavior and macroscopic, structural, overarching, and reproduction-centered institutions, ideologies, and similar categories.

Task B1.2: Assumptions about literacy

Besnier here draws attention to the popular assumption that literacy is associated with *prescription*, that is with rules about what is 'correct' and 'proper' usage.

➤ Are your own assumptions of this kind and if so do they stem in some way from your experience of schooling?

➤ What might literacy look like if not viewed from this perspective? That is, can you think of contexts where it is less important that the writing is correct and proper rather than, for instance, that it evokes feeling, communicates a message etc.?

➤ Similarly, Besnier signals the ongoing debates about differences between literate and pre-literate societies. Do you hold assumptions about such a difference – which may be not so much about 'pre-literate' society as about 'illiterate' people in your own society?

➤ Are there situations where you use literacy as a 'cornerstone' to help 'distinguish between kinds of people, groups, cultures, and thinking activities'?

Again you might write down examples from your own experience where these distinctions have been significant, for example at school, in overseas work, in community projects. Besnier talks of the different 'flavour' of literacy activities, a term not usually associated with literacy: he gives the example of those associated with ritual evoking particular kinds of identity.

➤ Can you list some uses of literacy which you associate with particular emotions, identities, aspects of your life?

➤ What do you feel about the different 'flavours' evoked by such different literacy practices?

Finally, Besnier says that

> Literacy, like many other social activities (even beyond the realm of communication), thus mediates between microscopic, person-centered, and agentive behavior and macroscopic, structural, overarching, and reproduction-centered institutions, ideologies, and similar categories.

➤ Can you list situations where you have used literacy in a more local, person-centred way – for example writing a Christmas card to friends – and then work out how this is associated with larger institutions and ideologies – for example in this case the rituals and commercial practices associated with Christmas?

Some readers may not feel particularly positive about such associations, some may worry about the hegemony of particular religious institutions and others may worry about commercialisation. All of these 'ideological' and value positions may be significant in our approaches to the uses and meanings of literacy in our daily lives.

➤ What do all of these personal experiences and assumptions tell you about your own definitions of literacy – and how do these relate to those put forward by Besnier?

Besnier signals a wider literature that we will come back to in Section B3, regarding the use of literacy as a sign of the difference between kinds of society and ways of thinking:

> In the works of Lucien Levy-Bruhl, Claude Levi-Strauss, Walter Ong, Jack Goody, and many others, literacy was foregrounded as a cornerstone that distinguished the 'primitive' from the 'civilized' [see texts in Section B3]. Along with the rest of anthropology, students of literacy have re-examined the Orientalist and 'othering' assumptions and consequences of such statements [see texts in Section B4]. Like all other products of human thinking, literacy is a complex and heterogeneous phenomenon, and certainly not one which we can privilege as a 'cornerstone' that would help us distinguish between kinds of people, groups, cultures, and thinking activities. Like all other aspects of human existence, literacy is part of the complex web of activities through which humans organize themselves socially and culturally.

Besnier, then, disagrees with the earlier claims signalled here and claims that literacy cannot be used as a 'cornerstone' to 'distinguish between kinds of people, groups, cultures, and thinking activities'.

➤ Do you agree or disagree with this conclusion and what do you think are the implications of each position for how we view literacy in our own social contexts?

➤ How would you present your own view of this debate?

Your response to these questions is likely to affect your reading of the texts and arguments presented throughout the book, so it may be helpful to spend some time thinking about the issues at this stage and perhaps to write down your current views, as you have done with the 'key terms', so that you can check them as you work through this resource book.

B1.3 PSYCHOLOGICAL TERMS

We now look at one of the most influential accounts of reading, produced by Catherine E. Snow and her colleagues on the Committee on the Prevention of Reading Difficulties in Young Children in the USA, as a way in to the debates about reading and where it might fit in the larger classification of literacy. You might read the following passages from the Report with these questions in mind and then try to bring together the various texts and approaches we have addressed in this section as well as developing your list of key terms (there is a longer passage from this Report in Section B2 which will enable you to develop these ideas further and link them to other influential texts in the field).

Text B1.3 C. E.
Snow et al.

Committee on the Prevention of Reading Difficulties in Young Children, C. E. Snow, et al. (1998) *Preventing reading difficulties in young children* **(Washington, DC: National Academy Press), 'Introduction', pp. 15–31.**

Introduction to Reading

Reading is a complex developmental challenge that we know to be intertwined with many other developmental accomplishments: attention, memory, language, and motivation, for example. Reading is not only a cognitive psycholinguistic activity but also a social activity.

Being a good reader in English means that a child has gained a functional knowledge of the principles of the English alphabetic writing system. Young children gain functional knowledge of the parts, products, and uses of the writing system from their ability to attend to and analyze the external sound structure of spoken words. Understanding the basic alphabetic principle requires an awareness that spoken language can be analyzed into strings of separable words, and words, in turn, into sequences of syllables and phonemes within syllables.

Beyond knowledge about how the English writing system works, though, there is a point in a child's growth when we expect 'real reading' to start. Children are expected, without help, to read some unfamiliar texts, relying on the print and drawing meaning from it. There are many reasons why children have difficulty learning to read. These issues and problems led to the initiation of this study.

Even though quite accurate estimates can be made on the basis of known risk factors, it is still difficult to predict precisely which young children will have difficulty learning to read. We therefore propose that prevention efforts must reach all children. To wait to initiate treatment until the child has been diagnosed with a specific disability is too late. However, we can begin treatment of conditions associated with reading problems, for example, hearing impairments.

Ensuring success in reading requires different levels of effort for different segments of the population. The prevention and intervention efforts described in this report can be thought of in terms of three levels (Caplan and Grunebaum, 1967, cited in Simeonsson, 1994; Pianta, 1990; and Needlman, 1997). *Primary prevention* is concerned with reducing the number of new cases (incidence) of an identified condition or problem in the population, such as ensuring that all children attend schools in which instruction is coherent and competent.

Secondary prevention is concerned with reducing the number of existing cases (prevalence) of an identified condition or problem in the population. Secondary prevention likewise involves the promotion of compensatory skills and behaviors. Children who are growing up in poverty, for example, may need excellent, enriched-preschool environments or schools that address their particular learning needs with highly effective and focused instruction. The extra effort is focused on children at higher risk of developing reading difficulties but before any serious, long-term deficit has emerged.

Tertiary prevention is concerned with reducing the complications associated with identified problem, or conditions. Programs, strategies, and interventions at this level have an explicit remedial or rehabilitative focus. If children demonstrate inadequate progress under secondary prevention conditions, they may need instruction that is specially designed and supplemental – special education, tutoring from a reading specialist – to their current instruction.

Task B1.3: Comparing keywords continued

In the spirit of critiquing keywords, try to write down which terms here are significant and consider what you take them to mean. For example, 'phoneme', 'alphabet', 'writing system', 'prevention', 'deficit' are all technical terms within the field of 'reading' that did not appear at all in the discussions of 'literacy' cited earlier. If you consider, like Snow, that they are key components of any discussion of literacy, then consider where they might be placed in your clusters, 'family trees', lists of literacy terms. You might also begin to address the question of why different groups of authors have shown preference for different clusters of terms:

➤ What are Bloome and Stierer signalling by excluding reading and what are Snow and her colleagues signalling by foregrounding it?

➤ What is implied by their use of medical sounding terms such as 'diagnosis', 'disability', 'treatment' in contrast with the terms favoured by Besnier – 'pedagogical literacy', 'literacy activities', 'literate communication', 'flavour'?

In a book on literacy (and language) we cannot treat such choices as innocent or purely technical – there are associations being drawn upon and messages being conveyed beyond the referential meanings of the words themselves. It is our contention, as the 'authors' of this volume, that if from the early section of this book you become attuned to such 'readings' of the language used by different writers, then as you go through the longer passages selected in Section B and the tasks set out in Section C you will be in a stronger position to 'take hold' of the meanings that matter to you, to interpret critically the different perspectives on literacy being presented and to develop your own language for talking about the subject.

Unit B2
Literacy acquisition

Until recently the term 'literacy' was often interpreted, as we have pointed out above, to refer to reading and more particularly to the learning of reading by young children. Adams, for instance, in the section selected opposite, begins her account with the claim:

> The most fundamental and important issues in the field of reading education are those of how children learn to read and write and how best to help them.

Whilst Adams's work has been highly influential in the field of reading studies, later sections will show how the assumption from which she begins has been challenged and a wider perspective has taken hold (see Sections B3 and B4). Nevertheless, we begin with that aspect of literacy which is familiar to anyone engaged in schooled literacy – debates over how children learn to read. Adams's article is an apt place to set out from, both because it is written by a key actor in the field (as she says, she was called upon by the US Congress to help evaluate the alternatives) and because it helpfully sets out the various poles of the debate. The distinction between a focus on 'phonic' principles on the one hand and on 'reading for meaning' on the other (represented for example by selections from Goodman in Section B2.2) has led to what is sometimes termed the 'reading wars'. More recently, researchers have argued for a 'balanced' approach (Adams's article included here was itself published in a book on 'balancing perspectives') that is less divisive and that recognises the strengths of each perspective.

The theories discussed in this volume, both those concerning acquisition and cognition and, more recently, those concerning texts and practices, all impact upon how teachers in schools attempt to facilitate their pupils' literacy. Whilst the approaches indicated in Sections B2 and B3 derive mostly from narrower views of literacy as reading – and sometimes writing as Adams indicates – some have recently begun to take account of social and sociocultural approaches (see Section B3.3, B3.4) in trying to understanding children's learning. One feature of these recent changes, and perhaps what is represented by the 'balanced' approach, has been that researchers and teachers not only explore the cognitive and individual aspects of learning to read but they have also attempted to locate classroom practice within broader social and political contexts and to be more sensitive to the variety of backgrounds and language styles that pupils bring with them, rather than imposing a single standard on all.

As the authors in this section indicate, any approach is highly contested, and issues of power as well as 'skill' loom large. Moreover, the very research methods and theoretical paradigms used to make claims in this field have themselves been subject to critical and political scrutiny. There is now a requirement in some countries for 'scientific-based' approaches that can provide sound evidence of which methods and approach are superior and that can claim to 'soundly refute' some hypotheses in favour of others.

We have selected passages that, we hope, will provide you with a feel for the key arguments and the ways they are encapsulated in the styles of major authors in the field. You might like to note that many of the authors address the reader directly as 'you' in an attempt to engage directly in the issues rather than simply to preach their point of view and that is the form of 'addressivity' that we have adopted too in attempting to make this resource book a genuine dialogue and a source of exploration.

B2.1 BEGINNING TO READ

The following passage is taken from a longer piece by Marilyn Jager Adams that was included in a book entitled *Teaching literacy balancing perspectives* (edited by Roger Beard). You might like to use it, first, to become more familiar with the terms of the debates in the field of reading, for example 'phonics', 'whole language', phonemic awareness' etc. Second, you might like to consider the claims about what scientific research now tells us about learning to read. Third, since the paper appeared in a book attempting to 'balance' the perspectives previously seen as 'at war', it will be interesting to consider how far the approach is 'balanced' and how far it might be seen to privilege a particular viewpoint. In order to pursue this question, you may next want to read another of the papers selected here, by one of Adams's protagonists Ken Goodman. These contrasts raise the deeper question with which you might approach this whole volume: 'How far can any of us be neutral in considering literacy?'

Adams, M. J. (1993) 'Beginning to read: an overview' in R. Beard (ed.) *Teaching literacy balancing perspectives* **(London, Hodder and Stoughton), pp. 204–215.**

Text B2.1
M. J. Adams

The most fundamental and important issues in the field of reading education are those of how children learn to read and write and how best to help them. Moreover, these issues are nowhere more important than in the initial stages of literacy instruction. Every child enters school expecting to learn to read. Those who make reasonable progress are well on their way to a successful school career. Those who do not, experience disappointment in school and in themselves as students, even in their very introduction to the system. Understandably, children who have struggled in vain with reading soon decide that they neither like nor want to read (Juel, 1988). But without reading, what is their future – academic or otherwise?

Today, more than ever before, we need to understand the knowledge and processes involved in learning to read and the methods, manner, and progression through which

Extension

M. J. Adams

their development may best be fostered. Levels of literacy that were held, even recently, to be satisfactory will be marginal by the year 2000 (National Academy of Education, 1985). But even as the social and economic values of literacy are multiplying, so too is the evidence that many children are not adequately learning to read beyond a basic level (Chall, 1983). Moreover, the dropout and illiteracy statistics are especially marked among those very children who depend most of all on schooling for their formal literacy education.

Yet, the effectiveness of literacy instruction cannot be expected to improve measurably until our understanding of what it must entail improves significantly: what do our students and pupils need to learn in service of reading and writing? With what knowledge and expectations do different children approach the challenge of learning? How can we modify our classrooms so as to reach *all* of them most effectively and engagingly? How can we enable teachers to understand and build on their students' and pupils' knowledge and expectations so as to lead them to become reflective and self-improving readers and writers?

In recent years, progress in the domain of beginning reading and writing instruction has been stymied by the heat of the debate in the United States of America over phonics versus whole language. Indeed, so paralysing and divisive had this debate become that, in 1986, the United States Congress passed a law requiring an evaluation of the alternatives. That task fell to me. To produce the report (Adams, 1990), I spent a year reviewing not just the literature on the merits and demerits of phonics instruction per se but also theory and empirical research related to the nature of reading and its acquisition and mastery. I reviewed the history of the debate, the literature on the relative effectiveness of different instructional approaches, the theory and research on the knowledge and processes involved in skilful reading, and the various literatures relevant to reading acquisition.

Making this task still trickier was the fact that the relevant information and arguments are scattered across so many fields. The relevant research literature divides itself not only across the fields of education, psychology, and linguistics, but also the fields of computer science and anthropology. Within each of these fields, moreover, it is divided again and across scores of subdisciplines. Inasmuch as each of these subdisciplines is supported by its own separate sets of journals and books, each has accrued its own perspective on the issues – along with its own relatively distinct terminology and knowledge base.

Within education, for example, there exist essentially separate literatures on classroom research and practice, on preschool literacy development, on special education and disabilities, on educational psychology, on policy research, and on large-scale statistical modelling and meta-analyses. Within psychology, the relevant literatures include not just those focused rather directly on reading and its acquisition, but also those on cognitive development, on language and text comprehension, on visual perception and pattern recognition, on eye movements, on the dynamics and limitations of attention and memory, and on the nature of thinking and learning. Within computer science, the work on machine learning, artificial intelligence, and computer modelling has provided important means of expanding and testing our theories about learning and the structure of knowledge. At the same time, the linguistics literature provides key insights into the orthography, phonology, syntax, and semantics of English while the anthropological literature offers ethnographic studies of home literacy support and practice as they vary across different cultures and neighbourhoods.

Although this cross-disciplinary dispersion of the literature made my task more difficult, I think it also made it far more worthwhile. Clearly it was past time to bring the pieces together. More than that, however, the overlap was there: key issues had been recognised again and again, both within and across the different fields. Within fields, as researchers scrutinised, challenged, and reassessed each others' hypotheses and findings, they gradually peeled away mistaken notions even while gradually defining, affirming, and refining their successors. Across fields, meanwhile, research has not only given us independent validations of this work, but more: approaching the issues from different perspectives and through different methods of inquiry, the various literatures tended, not merely to replicate, but also to complement and extend each other in invaluable ways.

In all, the work synthesised in my report stands as awesome testimony to the progress these fields have made towards understanding the knowledge and processes involved in reading and learning to read – so much more complex and powerful than any armchair vision. Bit by bit, by testing theories and observations through the sometimes slow and assiduously self-critical cycles of science, we have collectively learned a great deal. I stress this point because there is now developing in the United States a wholesale rejection of the value of using or attending to the results of the scientific method. Do not let this movement overtake you. Qualitative and quantitative research are productive only in complement. Where the former gives us values and direction, the latter protects us from letting the strengths of our beliefs blind us to their limitations.

In many ways, the debate over phonics versus whole language can be seen as a dramatic reflection of these very tensions. Grown from qualitative observations of learners and learning, the whole language movement is an impassioned assertion that there is far more to literacy than phonics. Through such activities as read-alouds, big-book sharing, language experience, and creative writing, an effort has been made to invite active exploration and appreciation of its many dimensions. It is a reaction to routines evolved to mindlessness, and a movement to replace them with activities that will usefully develop and enrich. It is a reaction to overly controlled stories in children's reading books, and a movement to provide text that is worth reading and learning to read. It is a reaction to compartmentalisation of instruction, and a movement towards integration across the curriculum. Most of all, perhaps, the whole language movement is an unflagging effort to remind us that effective instruction depends on meeting and responding to children's individual needs by building on their strengths, interests, and confidences.

In fact, the value of most of the whole language initiatives are increasingly endorsed through research. But there are exceptions. Most troublesome among these are the notions that the spellings of words are minimally relevant to reading and to the challenge of learning to read. As initially put forth by Frank Smith in his seminal book, *Understanding Reading* (1971), these hypotheses were received with enormous excitement, and not just by teachers. Indeed, researchers eagerly flocked to the laboratory to affirm and extend Smith's ideas. But that is not how it worked out. Over the twenty years since publication of Smith's book, science has over and over, firmly and indisputably, refuted both of these hypotheses. In the course, however, it has also significantly advanced our understanding of the knowledge and processes involved in language and reading. (See Adams, 1991, for an overview of this saga.).

Most of all, learning to read is not natural (see especially Liberman and Liberman, 1990). Rather, it depends critically on certain insights and observations that, among many if not most children, are not forthcoming without some special guidance. In particular, to read with fluency and comprehension children must develop a functional understanding of the alphabetic basis of English print along with working knowledge of its spellings.

Skilful reading, moreover, is scarcely a 'psycholinguistic guessing game', as Goodman (1967) termed it. Instead, for skilful adult readers, meaningful text – regardless of its ease or difficulty – is read through what is essentially a left to right, line by line, word by word process. Furthermore, skilful readers visually process virtually every individual letter of every word they read, tending strongly to translate print to speech as they go. True, skilful readers neither look nor feel like that's what they do when reading. Yet, that is only because they recognise the words so quickly and easily that their conscious, reflective attention is all the while focused on monitoring and extending the meaning of the text (see Adams, 1990, Section 3).

More specifically, research indicates that the skilful reader's remarkable ability to recognise printed words derives from a deep and ready knowledge of their composite sequences of letters along with the connections of those spellings to speech and to meaning. Even as the print on the page activates this knowledge, by its very structure, it serves reciprocally to organise, recognise, and give base meaning to the print. Indeed, provided that this knowledge is reasonably well developed, word recognition proceeds all but automatically – and that is very important because active, thoughtful attention is limited. Where readers must instead struggle with the words, they necessarily lose track of meaning.

Because, in the end, the words on the page are authors' principal means of conveying their message, it will not do for readers to ignore them. Nor will guessing suffice: even skilful adults are unable to guess correctly more than 25 per cent of the time (Gough *et al.*, 1981); besides that, the process of guessing itself requires time and effort that can only be found at the expense of the normal processes of comprehension. In fact, contextual cues contribute significantly to the speed and accuracy of word recognition only for those whose word identification skills are poor; meanwhile, poor word identification skills are strongly coupled with poor reading comprehension (for a more recent view of these issues, see Vellutino, 1991).

Because visual knowledge of words consists, at core, of knowledge of the ordered identities of their component letters, its growth depends on solid visual familiarity with the letters of the alphabet. To the extent that a child's attention is focused on the identity of any single letter, it cannot be usefully distributed across the sequence as a whole. Worse still, to the extent that any letter cannot be recognised, it obstructs learning of the sequence as a whole. For children who, on entering the classroom, do not yet have a comfortable familiarity with the letters of the alphabet, finding ways to help them is of first order importance.

Even so, knowledge of letters is of little value unless the child knows and is interested in their use: correctly perceived and interpreted, print conveys information. In keeping with this, children's concepts about print are also strong predictors of the ease with which they will learn to read. Before formal instruction is begun, children should possess a broad, general appreciation of the nature of print. They should be aware of how text is formatted; that its basic meaningful units are specific speakable words; and that its words are comprised of letters. Of equal importance, they should have a solid sense of its various functions – to entertain, inform, communicate, record – and the potential value of each such function to their own selves.

All such awarenesses are powerfully fostered by reading aloud to children, by engaging them regularly and interactively in the enjoyment and exploration of print. As it happens, in homes where book-sharing with preschool children occurs with any appreciable frequency, it tends to occur with great regularity – and significant impact. An hour a day cumulates to more than 2000 total hours of lap-time reading across the preschool years. Moreover, this is 2000 hours of very special print exploration – one to one, face in the book, and with all the love, attention, and discussion that comes alongside. Yet, ethnographic studies show that many children have barely even seen a book before entering school. To learn to read, a child must learn first what it means to read and that he or she would like to be able to do so. Our classrooms, from preschool on up, must be designed with this in mind.

Although the ultimate goal of instruction on word recognition is to develop immediate pathways from print to meaning, the growth of young readers' visual vocabularies depends vitally on knowledge of spelling-sound relations. In keeping with this, research demonstrates that, when developed as part of a larger programme of reading and writing, phonics instruction leads to higher group achievement at least in word recognition, spelling, and vocabulary, at least in the primary grades, and especially for economically disadvantaged and slower students or pupils (see Adams, 1990, Chapter 3).

[In the original text there then follows a closer account of the nature of phonemic awareness and of ways in which teachers can help children with reading, including a list of recommendations. You might like to compare Adams's headings with Goodman's which follows once you have read both – hers include: 'Predictors of reading acquisition'; 'Before formal instruction begins'; 'Beginning to read'; 'Phonics instruction'; 'Beyond the basics'.]

Commentary

We would like to pause and reflect upon this text and how we read it. We will engage in similar tasks after most of the texts in Sections B2 to B4. These activities are intended to help you make sense of and critically engage with the texts. Most of the questions we offer you are ones we posed to ourselves in trying to come to terms with these texts; occasionally, we also share some of our 'answers' in the form of commentary or dialogue. We hope that by modelling for you our own processes of reading we will encourage and facilitate your own readings. In many of the discussions we will highlight an interpretative perspective which you can apply to other texts (including the other texts in this book, among them our own commentaries). These discussions are not just about the Extension readings: taken together, they also serve as an investigation of different ways of engaging with texts. So, let us begin with some tasks connected with Adams's 'Overview'.

Task B2.1.1: Balance?

Adams's article appears in a book entitled *Teaching literacy balancing perspectives*.

➤ To what extent do you think she has succeeded in balancing between phonics and whole language?

➤ Which side in this 'great debate' (Chall, 1983) or 'reading war' (Pearson, 2004) do you think can most easily identify with her position?

➤ Do you think that this question is fair and/or helpful?

➤ Or is there another set of positions that you think better characterise what Adams is trying to say?

★ Task B2.1.2: A rhetorical reading

What is Adams doing in this passage? That may seem like a strange question: she's providing an overview of what is known about learning how to read. But that is only a partial answer. Why is she presenting the overview? What is she trying to achieve? And how is she doing that? In posing these questions, we're assuming that most communication – including academic articles – involves not only the transmission of information but also the attempt to persuade the reader to accept a certain position. This interpretative perspective is nicely developed by Lloyd Bitzer (1968), and the following discussion is partially based upon his framework. According to Bitzer, discourse (i.e. a speech or article) is shaped by the 'rhetorical situation' that gives rise to it, including

1 a problem or 'exigence': 'an imperfection marked by urgency; it is a defect, an obstacle, something waiting to be done, a thing which is other than it should be';
2 an audience or audiences who can act to change the exigence; and
3 constraints: elements of the situation – for example 'beliefs, attitudes, documents, facts, traditions, images, interests, motives and the like' – which constitute both resources for and limitations on the author's attempts at mobilising the audience to change the exigence.

As an initial task, we suggest you try out this framework – that is, exigence(s), audience and constraints – to analyse the rhetorical situation of Adams's article and to develop an interpretation of what she is doing. Whilst starting with the general questions – What are her purposes? And how does she attempt to accomplish them? – you might use Bitzer's framework to go into these questions in more detail:

1 What is the 'problem' or 'exigence' she is raising?
2 Whom is she addressing who she thinks might help change the situation?
3 What are the constraints in this situation? For example teacher attitudes? Government policy? Research traditions and conflicts?

Commentary

The following are notes from our rhetorical reading of Adams's article. Our interpretation is of course, not necessarily the best one. We challenge you to advance a better one, using evidence from Adams's text to support your argument.

What are the exigences that Adams is trying to solve?

In the beginning of the article she introduces a chain of four 'problems': (1) literacy is important for individuals' futures – 'academic or otherwise'; (2) literacy levels are unacceptably low (and indeed this 'problem' is growing as 'levels of literacy that were held, even recently, to be satisfactory will be marginal' in ten years' time); (3) improvement of literacy instruction depends upon improvement of our understanding of reading and how it is acquired; and (4) our understanding of reading and its acquisition has been impaired by the 'heat of the debate . . . over phonics versus whole language'. Thus, Adams suggests, in order to solve 'the literacy problem', we need to overcome this 'paralysing and divisive' debate. Note that the final problem – the polarisation of positions in debates about how to teach reading – is also a constraint: readers undoubtedly hold positions in and on this debate, and will likely judge the article in light of the debate and the article's position on it.

Who are the audiences of Adams's article?

The article appeared as a chapter in a UK book on teaching literacy, so it seems a safe bet that the article is intended for people in the UK – policymakers, educators, parents and members of the public – who can influence the way reading is taught. Adams also signals this audience by referring to events that have happened 'in the USA' (as opposed to 'here'), and even by warning the audience not to let the movement for the 'wholesale rejection of . . . scientific method' in the USA 'overtake you'. Which 'camps' is Adams addressing here? At first glance, it would appear that she is trying to address everyone, since she is very inclusive and complimentary in her mentions of the many approaches that have contributed to our understanding of reading. Moreover, the article appears in a book with the phrase 'balancing perspectives' in its title. However, as we will try to show in what follows, she may have a more specific audience in mind.

What are the situation's constraints?

As noted in the discussion of exigences above, the first constraint is the heated debate over teaching reading – or, 'reading wars'. In the context of this divisive and polarised discourse, statements and speakers tend to become associated with one camp or the other, thereby alienating the other side. Likewise with regard to disciplinary identifications and loyalties. Adams was trained as a cognitive and developmental psychologist, which gives her authority to speak on the matter, but might also deter researchers and practitioners from other backgrounds. (Perhaps, for that reason, she does not mention her own disciplinary background when reviewing the different disciplines that have contributed to our understanding of reading.)

So what is Adams doing?

Purposes are closely related to exigences. The final exigence noted above – the heated debate between whole language and phonics – gives rise to purpose number 1: to defuse the reading wars by synthesising the conflicting ideas. The other three exigences – the need to improve literacy through a better understanding of how to teach reading – give rise to purpose number 2: to promote phonics instruction as the first step in formal reading instruction.

Purpose number 1: We need to synthesise contradictory approaches

Synthesis of opposing methods and perspectives is a central theme throughout the article. This includes of course integrating whole language and phonics, but also synthesis of the many disciplinary perspectives that have contributed to study of reading acquisition, and synthesis of qualitative and quantitative methodologies. The structure of the article captures this dialectical movement between whole language and phonics. Adams begins her review by complimenting the whole language movement for its many contributions to research on reading acquisition: advancing the assertion that 'there is far more to literacy than phonics', replacing mindless routines with rich language experience and real books, and 'remind[ing] us that effective instruction depends on meeting and responding to children's individual needs'. But then she criticises whole language for the 'troublesome' hypotheses that 'the spellings of words are minimally relevant to reading and to the challenge of learning to read'. Adams contests these hypotheses and advances the (phonics) position – that skilful readers use knowledge of letters in order to decode words. But she then appears to modify this position, stating 'Even so' as she returns to whole language concerns about children's appreciation of and interest in the meaning of print, which can be fostered 'by engaging them regularly and inter-actively in the enjoyment and exploration of print' (a classic whole language position). Finally, Adams returns back to phonics concerns with a section (not included in the extracted passage) on phonemic awareness and how teachers can and should develop it.

Purpose number 2: Phonics and phonemic awareness should be the first topics taught in formal reading instruction

This issue is not highlighted as explicitly as the need for synthesis in the excerpted passage. Nevertheless, this proposition is the 'bottom line' of Adams's recommendation about how to teach reading in schools. Having established her authority (as surveyor of the entire field and author of a prestigious, government-mandated report) and impartiality (as appreciative of the contributions of whole language and as committed to synthesis), Adams essentially advances the central argument of the phonics camp: since phonics knowledge is a prerequisite for fluent word recognition (which is a prerequisite for comprehension), 'finding ways to help [children who do not yet have a comfortable familiarity with the letters of the alphabet] is of first order importance'. Synthesising phonics and whole language, for Adams, means striking a conciliatory tone towards the latter while advancing the central tenets of the former. We might ask how 'balanced' is this perspective and how far the conciliatory tone is a rhetorical strategy for pursuing her own position.

With this interpretation of Adams's purposes, we now revisit the question of the article's primary audience. Above we conjectured that the article was addressed equally to members of both the phonics and the whole language camps. However, on closer consideration, it seems that she is addressing mainly the whole language group as her ideas about teaching reading are objectionable primarily to them, and it is to this audience that most of her rhetorical energies are devoted. Thus, although Adams is careful to congratulate whole language for its many contributions, and to note that 'most of [its] initiatives are increasingly endorsed through research', she in fact goes on to criticise fundamental aspects of the approach. Similarly, she avoids mention of 'phonics' throughout her critical discussion of whole language, instead talking about the 'connections of spellings to speech' and the 'letters of the alphabet'.

Task B2.1.3: Rhetorical reading critiqued

➤ How has this rhetorical reading of Adams's article affected your interpretation of it?

➤ In what ways has it improved and constrained your understanding?

➤ For what kinds of text is such an interpretive perspective more or less appropriate?

➤ How 'balanced' do you feel *our* reading (i.e. the authors of this volume) has been?

Task B2.1.4: Problems with phonics?

In her overview, Adams discusses the shortcomings of approaching reading as a 'psycholinguistic guessing game' (using contextual and other cues to predict and check a word's meaning, an approach associated especially with Goodman whose article follows). Instead, she proposes developing children's phonemic awareness and knowledge of spelling-sound relations.

> What are the possible shortcomings of this approach? (The exercise in Section C2.1 should help stimulate your thinking about this topic.)

 Task B2.1.5: The main issues in the phonics versus whole language debate

Adams gives us an initial overview of the great debate about teaching reading. You may find it helpful, as you progress through the articles in this section, to map out the main issues in this debate.

Table B2.1.5 Main issues in the phonics / whole language debate

Source	Issue	Phonics	Whole language
Adams	Children's needs	Phoneme-grapheme decoding	
	?	?	
Goodman	?	?	

We would recommend that you consider which aspects of the controversy each author has emphasised and/or downplayed in their respective accounts. This will allow you to compare the way the debate is represented by each of the participants. Take note of how the table changes as you progress through the other articles:

> What are the significant differences between the different authors?

> How useful is the division of the positions into these two categories?

> How could you change the table to give a better account of the issues and positions in this debate?

Further reading on the World Wide Web

Adams was interviewed as part of the US Public Broadcasting Service programme, 'The children of the code': http://www.childrenofthecode.org/interviews/adams. htm. She is currently Chief Scientist for Soliloquy Reading Assistant: http://soliloquy learning.com/index.html (click on the 'Take the tutorial' to see how the Company's interactive reading software works). See the DfES Phonics seminar: March 2003 (collection of papers on the phonics element in the British National Literacy Strategy): http://www.standards.dfes.gov.uk/primary/publications/literacy/686807/.

B.2.2 WHOLE LANGUAGE

Ken Goodman represents the kind of approach that Adams was challenging. Indeed, in Adams's article, she refers to Goodman directly, writing that 'Skilful reading . . . is scarcely a "psycholinguistic guessing game", as Goodman (1967) termed it'. In the following text you will have a chance to begin to judge for yourself the merits of Goodman's approach, which is commonly called 'whole language', because it emphasises the importance of teaching language in context and texts in their entirety, and resists the isolation of phonetic decoding from larger units of meaning.[1] (Some commentators would disagree with this characterisation of 'whole language'; we recommend you revisit and reassess it after you have read Goodman and others.)

Ken Goodman and Frank Smith are often cited as the 'founding fathers' of the whole language movement.[2] Goodman's seminal article on the topic, 'Reading: a psycholinguistic guessing game', was published in 1967 (also reprinted in Singer and Ruddell, 1976). In the 1970s and 1980s whole language came to be seen as the 'conventional wisdom' of language education in the US and UK educational establishments. In the 1990s it lost its primacy, in part because of a series of pro-phonics research reports (Snow et al., 1998; NRP, 2000), and in part because of political and policy developments – culminating in the 1998 National Literacy Strategy in England and the 2001 No Child Left Behind Act in the USA (see Pearson, 2004, for a review of the reasons for the movement's demise).

We have chosen the passage reproduced here, which was published at about the same time as the Adams piece, in order to facilitate comparisons. The succession of articles enables you to begin, in a preliminary way, to accumulate sufficient knowledge of their different positions to be able to make up your own mind – and, of course, to be inspired to read further in each author. Goodman, like Adams, refers to 'what we have learned' – in this case 'about written language': again you might like to consider what we know and how we know it – what are the bases for the various claims with which you are being regaled and how can you assess them? You might also reflect on the rhetorical strategies the authors use to make their claims, subjecting this text to analysis similar to that received by Adams's article. We propose some ways you might address this at the end of the article. In particular, you might want to consider their different sources of authority, and how that relates to their views of what counts as literacy and how we acquire it. Another question to take forward might be when different authors assume literacy learning starts and the relationship between learning and teaching – the role and importance of schooling as opposed to that of home and community for instance, is addressed by both

1 The term 'whole language' is popular in the United States; in the UK this approach was called 'real books', on account of its proponents' preference for authentic literature instead of using reading textbooks with highly controlled vocabulary and syntax (you might check out Meek, 1991).
2 But see Goodman (1992). For accounts of the history of the whole language movement see K. Goodman (1989) and Y. Goodman (1989).

Adams and Goodman. Both authors address teachers and parents and offer strategies and guidance for how to help children learn literacy. Consider:

■ Do their recommendations simply complement each other, or do they point us in different directions and suggest different kinds of teaching and learning?

■ Where they disagree explicitly, for example on 'guessing', what evidence would you need to make up your own mind and what theoretical assumptions do their respective claims and advice rest upon?

**Text B.2.2
K. S. Goodman**

Goodman, K. S. (1996) *On reading* (Portsmouth, NH: Heinemann), Chapter 8: 'Learning and teaching reading and writing', pp. 117–125.

'Teaching can support and extend learning, but it can never make it happen.'

I plan to focus on teaching and learning in another book, but it seems to me that I owe you, here, some sense of what I believe. What we've learned about written language processes has major implications for understanding how written language is learned, and for building a pedagogy: a principled stance for the teaching of reading and writing. Fortunately, a rich professional literature already exists on that topic. Many teachers have already put into practice what we know about literacy processes, and some have had their teaching stories published. You'll find a representative bibliography at the end of this book.

Let me make two things perfectly clear at the start:

There is simply no *direct* connection between knowing about language competence and understanding how that knowledge is developed, or how to teach it.

The relationship between theory and practice is a two-way street.

First, it seems obvious that teaching reading and writing requires knowing what competent reading and writing is. A sound approach to teaching must be consistent with and build on a scientific knowledge of literacy and how it is learned, but it must also build on knowledge of language development, sound learning theories, and an understanding of teaching and curriculum.

Second, educators don't just apply knowledge, they produce it. Classroom teachers have taught me a lot about learning and teaching literacy; they've also taught me a lot about the reading process in the real world of classrooms – knowledge that researchers and theoreticians need to add to what they learn under research conditions. Whole language teachers have taken control of the body of knowledge about how reading and writing work and have built their own pedagogy on that knowledge – their teaching theory and practice. What we know is important for teaching, but who knows it and what they do with the knowledge is even more important.

Later in this chapter that point is demonstrated in four classroom vignettes that show teachers playing a much wider range of roles than 'direct instruction' entails. But first I'll describe how literacy begins and develops in literate societies.

Growing into literacy in a literate environment

A baby is born. Anxious parents are reassured by doctors and nurses that the baby is 'healthy and normal.' In comparison with most animal babies, human babies are born quite helpless and immature; it takes them a long time to be able to do the things adults do. But their proud parents are patient and confident that in due course they will smile, turn themselves over, sit up, crawl, stand, walk, and so on. Given a nurturing home and normal human associations, the baby will grow, develop, change and learn. (Of course I know that not all babies are born normal in every respect, but we need to understand normal development before we can understand the abnormal development of a few children.)

In due course, human infants also begin to understand the spoken language around them, and to speak it themselves. Because it happens as naturally as standing and walking, it seems like just another result of their physical maturation. But that's only partly true; other animals have the same control over the sound-producing organs, but only human beings develop language. Human language is qualitatively different from the rudimentary, limited communication of other animal species.

What makes language both necessary and possible is that our brains have the ability to think symbolically: we let things represent other things. Because we can create complex abstract systems for representing the most subtle experiences, concepts and ideas, we are able to reflect on our experiences and communicate our needs, experiences and ideas to others. All human societies, at all times in recorded history and before, have created and used oral language.

That doesn't mean that no learning is involved, of course. But learning language is different in important ways from learning to walk, and from the learning of other animals. Human language learning is *both personal and social*. It is the medium for thought and learning, but also, since we are born dependent, our survival and development depend on our ability to join a social dialog as we join a social community. So, language is essential not only for our physical and social survival, but also for our sharing in the collective knowledge of our families, communities and societies.

Written language is learned a little later in the life of individuals and societies, but it is no less natural than oral language in the personal and social development of human beings. And the process by which written language develops is the same as that for oral language development. Both develop out of the need of humans to think symbolically and to communicate in a growing range of contexts and functions, as individuals and as societies. Written language is an extension of human language development that occurs when it's needed: when face-to-face and here-and-now language is no longer sufficient.

We've learned a lot over the last few decades about how children develop as readers and writers. What it took was a liberation from the mistaken view that written language learning is fundamentally different from oral language learning, a view that led to the equally mistaken notion that literacy learning begins when children enter school. As a result, most of us, including parents, simply didn't see the literacy learning going on all around us. As Yetta Goodman says, generations of parents have washed off their walls the evidence of their children's writing development. The truth is that children come to school already rich in literacy experiences, and having already learned to make sense of print.

As we take a look at schools in this chapter, you need to keep in mind that, while I separate *learning* reading and writing from *teaching* reading and writing, I can't do so absolutely. Children continue to learn to read and write while they're receiving instruction, and it's hard to separate the results of learning from the results of instruction. Also, some of what parents and others do outside of school can be seen as instructional, even when instruction isn't explicitly intended – for example, when a child shows a parent a box of cereal, points to the print and says, 'What does this say?' In his study of his son's language development, Halliday (1975) identified a phenomena he called 'tracking': the child takes the lead in language development and the parent follows and supports that development. Children and parents do it all the time.

Extension

In any case, instructional programs in school must build on the beginnings children have already made. Instead of regarding the reading-writing curriculum as a set of new skills children have to learn, teachers have to recognize and build on the development already taking place. Classrooms ought to be richly literate environments, providing lots of support for extending and strengthening the literacy development that began before the children ever entered school.

Language acquisition and development

I need to digress briefly to put my view of learning, particularly literacy learning, in context. Two views of human language learning are commonly contrasted: 'nature' vs. 'nurture.' These, and my own view, can be described as follows:

In the 'nature' view, language is considered innate. It's not learned at all, but acquired by bringing the innate, universal language into harmony with the particular language community the child is born into. For many who hold this view, only oral language is innate, written language an abstract representation of it. Written language is acquired through instruction.

The 'nurture' view is mainly a behaviorist approach. In it, language, like everything else, is learned through some kind of operant conditioning. Environmental stimuli require responses, and somehow in the process language is shaped.

'Invention and convention' is what I label my own view, which draws on the work of the Russian psychologist Lev Vygotsky, the Swiss psychologist Jean Piaget and the Anglo-Australian linguist Michael Halliday.

I see human learning, including language learning, as a *process of invention*. Human beings invent (socially construct) language to communicate with each other and to learn and think with. Language is therefore a social invention. But since society is made up of people, it is also a personal invention. In fact, we each individually invent language and keep inventing it throughout our lives.

But we invent our own language within a family and community which already have a language loaded with the *conventional* ways of doing the things we are inventing. Piaget calls this kind of tension 'disequilibrium.' Our personal inventions and the social conventions of the language of the people around us pull and push us in opposite directions. As Vygotsky puts it (1978), our personal language moves toward the social language until, eventually, we appear to have 'internalized' the latter. At that point, the social language becomes the basis for our inner speech, the language we use for learning and for reflecting on experience.

As we move toward conventional language, we also come to share the values and life views of our family and society. Halliday called the book in which he presented his research on language development *Learning How to Mean*. We learn how our culture organizes and expresses meaning through language. Language is learned in the process of its use, through participation in speech acts and literacy events. Lots of participation in talk is what makes it possible for children to learn oral language. And lots of writing and reading make it possible for children to build written language.

Building on what children know

Surrounded by print in a literate society, children become aware that written language is a way of making sense. They begin very early to respond to print as meaningful, recognizing logos and signs as a way of identifying places and products: a stop sign or the Golden Arches, for example. Gradually they learn, in succession: that print makes sense, what sense print makes, how print makes sense – that is, they come to control the system of written language. Children play at the activities of the adults around them, and much of their early literacy is developed in playing at reading and writing. Yetta Goodman and others, in many places and languages, have documented how children first invent written language and then move toward the conventions.

In literate societies, some children move easily into literacy. They write notes and cards (which adults often can't read), compose shopping lists, create signs (KEP AWT) to put on their bedroom door, read 'McDonald's', 'CREST' and 'Sesame Street'. By the time they enter school, they read and write more or less conventionally. Most other children, through their transactions with print in the environment, have at least begun their journey into literacy, and many are well into it.

Learning to transact with text

As we've discovered, reading and writing is making sense by transacting with text, using the three systems of language simultaneously. So what is it that children must learn to do? Essentially, they must develop strategies and learn to use textual cues to make sense of text – that is, construct meaning. They can do that only by transacting with real texts in which the three systems of language relate authentically to each other. They can't learn to control written language by focusing separately on each system. They can't learn phonics, vocabulary and grammar in isolation because, in the real world, those systems don't occur in isolation from language or from each other. Just as children learn to talk and listen in authentic oral language settings, they learn to read and write in authentic literacy settings.

Only in the context of real language do the graphophonic, lexico-grammatic and semantic language systems occur in the proper relationships so that young learners can develop and use strategies for making sense. They need to learn to sample the print selectively, predict and infer, and self-correct as needed, all within a focus on making sense of print. And as they develop these strategies, they need to become confident in playing the psycholinguistic guessing game getting to meaning with minimal effort and input. On the other hand, they need to be cautious enough that they can monitor their good guesses and make sure they fit the developing text. Finding a balance between confidence and tentativeness is essential to reading development.

[Like Adams, Goodman goes on to offer some strategies for helping learners' reading development. These include: 'Building a sense of text'; 'Inventing the spelling system'; 'How vocabulary is built'; 'Learning by doing'; 'Learning in and out of school' and 'Lifelong learning'. You might like to compare these headings with those offered by Adams and relate this to the arguments they put forward.]

Task B2.2.1: Fitting it all together

How do the different parts of Goodman's article add up? Goodman makes a series of claims about the relationship between theory and practice, children's oral and written language development, and how reading should be taught in school.

➤ How do the discussions of these various issues fit together into a coherent whole?

Task B2.2.2: Approaches to language learning

In the section entitled 'Language acquisition and development' Goodman offers three views of human language learning: nature, nurture and invention-and-convention.

➤ Which of these views is closest to your own?

➤ Are there any other views excluded by this categorisation?

➤ How, if at all, might one view be proven to be correct?

Task B2.2.3: Whole language versus phonics?

Both Adams and Goodman address teachers and parents and offer strategies and guidance for how to help children learn literacy.

➤ Do their recommendations simply complement each other, or do they point us in different directions and suggest different kinds of teaching and learning?

➤ Where they disagree explicitly, for example on 'guessing', what evidence would you need to make up your own mind and what theoretical assumptions do their respective claims and advice rest upon?

Task B2.2.4: The main issues in the phonics versus whole language debate (continued)

Revisiting your table from earlier (Section B2.1.5):

➤ Are there any additional issues that Goodman raises?

➤ Do his characterisations of the phonics and whole language positions differ from Adams's?

➤ How might you be able to account for these discrepancies?

Task B2.2.5: Goodman's rhetoric

You might want to subject Goodman's article to the same sort of rhetorical reading with which you read Adams's 'Beginning to read: an overview'.

➤ What is Goodman doing?

➤ What are the exigencies that he is trying to solve?

➤ Who are the audiences of his article?

➤ What are the situation's constraints?

➤ What are his purposes?

After you're finished, we suggest that you compare your interpretation with that developed by Moorman et al. (1994), and of course make sure to read also the responses by Goodman and others in the same issue of that journal.

B2.3 SOCIAL CHALLENGES AND POLICY

Like Adams, Catherine Snow is not only a commentator on the field of early reading and literacy but also a major participant in the public debate in the USA, where she was chair of a committee convened to address the problems that children were perceived to have in reading. The selection here is taken from the introduction to the frequently cited report of that committee, part of which we have already considered in Section A. Despite the fact that the report attempts 'balance', seeing reading as 'not only a cognitive psycholinguistic activity but also a social activity', and offering a detailed summary of studies by anthropologists such as Heath on home literacy practices, Jim Gee and Gerald Coles both argue, in a book provocatively entitled *Literacy as snake oil* (edited by J. Larson, 2001), that this work has been misrepresented for policy purposes by those advocating a strong phonics and regulatory position. A question to keep in mind, therefore, in addition to those already raised concerning the nature of reading and of literacy, is how supposedly technical accounts of the reading process (phonemic awareness etc.) and 'balanced' accounts of cognitive and social factors are harnessed to political agendas. You might also consider, again, the use of specialist discourse in describing these issues: at points, for instance, the report employs medical-style discourse, referring to 'condition and risks' associated with early literacy problems, such as 'innate predispositions' and advocating 'prevention with a remedial or rehabilitative focus': again the language in which the analysis is couched can tell us a lot about the author's conceptual framing of the issues. Despite this apparent focus on the individual child as in need of attention, the report does again acknowledge a more social point, in this case regarding the changing definitions of literacy, citing Stedman and Kaestle (1987): 'Current difficulties in reading largely originate from rising demands for literacy, not from declining absolute levels of literacy.'

You might like to consider how definitions of literacy and of what counts as adequate levels of literacy have changed over time, or vary from one country or locality to another. In the end, the report attempts to link the theory and research to practical proposals for intervention: 'We attempt to identify the characteristics of the preschool and school environments that will be effective for such children.' You might like to align these proposals with those by Adams and Goodman and to see how they stand up to your own experience. The report provides another detailed and scholarly account of the nature of the English writing system and its respective problems and advantages.

■ How does this account relate to those offered by other authors, such as the Adams and Goodman selections above?

■ Are there differences in the supposedly 'scientific' and neutral accounts that mean what we know is still contested – or do you feel relatively secure that there is a basis of agreement at this level?

Text B2.3 C. E. Snow et al.

Committee on the Prevention of Reading Difficulties in Young Children, C. E. Snow et al. (1998) *Preventing reading difficulties in young children* (Washington, DC: National Academy Press).

(Editor's note: this passage is the immediate continuation of Text B1.3.)

Introduction

Reading is essential to success in our society. The ability to read is highly valued and important for social and economic advancement. Of course, most children learn to read fairly well. In fact, a small number learn it on their own, with no formal instruction, before school entry (Anbar, 1986; Backman, 1983; Bissex, 1980; Jackson, 1991; Jackson et al., 1988). A larger percentage learn it easily, quickly, and efficiently once exposed to formal instruction.

Societal challenges

Parents, educators, community leaders, and researchers identify clear and specific worries concerning how well children are learning to read in this country. The issues they raise are the focus of this report:

1. Large numbers of school-age children, including children from all social classes, have significant difficulties in learning to read.
2. Failure to learn to read adequately for continued school success is much more likely among poor children, among nonwhite children, and among nonnative speakers of English. Achieving educational equality requires an understanding of why these disparities exist and efforts to redress them.
3. An increasing proportion of children in American schools, particularly in certain school systems, are learning disabled, with most of the children identified as such because of difficulties in learning to read.
4. Even as federal and state governments and local communities invest at higher levels in early childhood education for children with special needs and for those from families living in poverty, these investments are often made without specific planning to address early literacy needs and sustain the investment.
5. A significant federal investment in providing bilingual education programs for nonnative speakers of English has not been matched by attention to the best methods for teaching reading in English to nonnative speakers or to native speakers of nonstandard dialects.
6. The passage of the Americans with Disabilities Act (ADA) provides accommodations to children and to workers who have reading disabilities. In order to provide full

access for the individuals involved, these accommodations should reflect scientific knowledge about the acquisition of reading and the effects of having a reading difficulty.

7. The debate about reading development and reading instruction has been persistent and heated, often obscuring the very real gains in knowledge of the reading process that have occurred.

In this report, we are most concerned with the children in this country whose educational careers are imperiled because they do not read well enough to ensure understanding and to meet the demands of an increasingly competitive economy. Current difficulties in reading largely originate from rising demands for literacy, not from declining absolute levels of literacy (Stedman and Kaestle, 1987). In a technological society, the demands for higher literacy are constantly increasing, creating ever more grievous consequences for those who fall short and contributing to the widening economic disparities in our society (Bronfenbrenner et al., 1996). These economic disparities often translate into disparities in educational resources, which then have the self-reinforcing effect of further exacerbating economic disparities. Although the gap in reading performance between educational haves and have-nots has shrunk over the last 50 years, it is still unacceptably large, and in recent years it has not shrunk further (National Academy of Education, 1996). These rich-get-richer and poor-get-poorer economic effects compound the difficulties facing educational policy makers, and they must be addressed if we are to confront the full scope of inadequate literacy attainment (see Bronfenbrenner et al., 1996).

Despite the many ways in which American schools have progressed and improved over the last half century (see, for example, Berliner and Biddle, 1995), there is little reason for complacency. Clear and worrisome problems have to do specifically with children's success in learning to read and our ability to teach reading to them. There are many reasons for these educational problems – none of which is simple. These issues and problems led to the initiation of this study and are the focus of this report.

The many children who succeed in reading are in classrooms that display a wide range of possible approaches to instruction. In making recommendations about instruction, one of the challenges facing the committee is the difficult-to-deal-with fact that many children will learn to read in almost any classroom, with almost any instructional emphasis. Nonetheless, some children, in particular children from poor, minority, or non-English-speaking families and children who have innate predispositions for reading difficulties, need the support of high-quality preschool and school environments and of excellent primary instruction to be sure of reading success. We attempt to identify the characteristics of the preschool and school environments that will be effective for such children.

The Challenge of a Technological Society

Although children have been taught to read for many centuries, only in this century – and until recently only in some countries – has there been widespread expectation that literacy skills should be universal. Under current conditions, in many 'literate' societies, 40 to 60 percent of the population have achieved literacy; today in the United States, we expect 100 percent of the population to be literate. Furthermore, the definition of full-fledged literacy has shifted over the last century with increased distribution of technology, with the development of communication across distances, and with the proliferation of large-scale economic enterprises (Kaestle, 1991; Miller,

1988; Weber, 1993). To be employable in the modern economy, high school graduates need to be more than merely literate. They must be able to read challenging material, to perform sophisticated calculations, and to solve problems independently (Murnane and Levy, 1993). The demands are far greater than those placed on the vast majority of schooled literate individuals a quarter-century ago . . .

Academic success, as defined by high school graduation, can be predicted with reasonable accuracy by knowing someone's reading skill at the end of grade 3 (for reviews, see Slavin et al., 1994). A person who is not at least a modestly skilled reader by the end of third grade is quite unlikely to graduate from high school. Only a generation ago, this did not matter so much, because the long-term economic effects of not becoming a good reader and not graduating from high school were less severe. Perhaps not surprisingly, when teachers are asked about the most important goal for education, over half of elementary school teachers chose 'building basic literacy skills' (National Center for Education Statistics Schools and Staffing Survey, 1990–1991, quoted in National Center for Education Statistics, 1995: 31).

The special challenge of learning to read English

Learning to read poses real challenges, even to children who will eventually become good readers. Furthermore, although every writing system has its own complexities, English presents a relatively large challenge, even among alphabetic languages. Learning the principles of a syllabic system, like the Japanese *katakana*, is quite straightforward, since the units represented – syllables – are pronounceable and psychologically real, even to young children. Such systems are, however, feasible only in languages with few possible syllable types; the *hiragana* syllabary represents spoken Japanese with 46 characters, supplemented with a set of diacritics (Daniels and Bright, 1996). Spoken English has approximately 5,000 different possible syllables; instead of representing each one with a symbol in the writing system, written English relies on an alphabetic system that represents the parts that make up a spoken syllable, rather than representing the syllable as a unit.

An alphabetic system poses a challenge to the beginning reader, because the units represented graphically by letters of the alphabet are referentially meaningless and phonologically abstract. For example, there are three sounds represented by three letters in the word 'but,' but each sound alone does not refer to anything, and only the middle sound can really be pronounced in isolation; when we try to say the first or last consonant of the word all by itself, we have to add a vowel to make it a pronounceable entity.

Once the learner of written English gets the basic idea that letters represent the small sound units within spoken and heard words, called phonemes, the system has many advantages: a much more limited set of graphemic symbols is needed than in either syllabic (like Japanese) or morphosyllabic (like Chinese) systems; strategies for sounding out unfamiliar strings and spelling novel words are available; and subsequences, such as prefixes and suffixes, are encountered with enough frequency for the reader to recognize them automatically.

Alphabetic systems of writing vary in the degree to which they are designed to represent the surface sounds of words. Some languages, such as Spanish, spell all words as they sound, even though this can cause two closely related words to be spelled very differently. Writing systems that compromise phonological representations in order to reflect morphological information are referred to as deep orthographies. In English, rather than preserving one-letter-to-one-sound correspondences, we preserve the spelling, even if that means a particular letter spells several different sounds. For example, the last letter pronounced 'k' in the written word 'electric' represents quite different sounds in the words 'electricity' and 'electrician,' indicating the morphological relation among the words but making the sound-symbol relationships more difficult to fathom.

The deep orthography of English is further complicated by the retention of many historical spellings, despite changes in pronunciation that render the spellings opaque. The 'gh' in 'night' and 'neighborhood' represents a consonant that has long since disappeared from spoken English. The 'ph,' in 'morphology' and 'philosophy' is useful in signaling the Greek etymology of those words but represents a complication of the pattern of sound-symbol correspondences that has been abandoned in Spanish, German, and many other languages that also retain Greek-origin vocabulary items. English can present a challenge for a learner who expects to find each letter always linked to just one sound.

Sources of reading difficulties

Reading problems are found among every group and in every primary classroom, although some children with certain demographic characteristics are at greater risk of reading difficulties than others. Precisely how and why this happens has not been fully understood. In some cases, the sources of these reading difficulties are relatively clear, such as biological deficits that make the processing of sound-symbol relationships difficult; in other cases, the source is experiential such as poor reading instruction.

[The report goes on to detail these difficulties under the headings: 'Biological deficits', 'Instructional influences'.]

Demographics of reading difficulties

A major source of urgency in addressing reading difficulties derives from their distribution in our society. Children from poor families, children of African American and Hispanic descent, and children attending urban schools are at much greater risk of poor reading outcomes than are middle-class, European-American, and suburban children. Studying these demographic disparities can help us identify groups that should be targeted for special prevention efforts. Furthermore, examining the literacy development of children in these higher-risk groups can help us understand something about the course of literacy development and the array of conditions that must be in place to ensure that it proceeds well.

One characteristic of minority populations that has been offered as an explanation for their higher risk of reading difficulties is the use of nonstandard varieties of English or limited proficiency in English. Speaking a nonstandard variety of English can impede the easy acquisition of English literacy by introducing greater deviations in the representation of sounds, making it hard to develop sound-symbol links. Learning English spelling is challenging enough for speakers of standard mainstream English; these challenges are heightened for some children by a number of phonological and grammatical features of social dialects that make the relation of sound to spelling even more indirect.

. . .

Non-English-speaking students, like nonstandard dialect speakers, tend to come from low socioeconomic backgrounds and to attend schools with disproportionately high numbers of children in poverty, both of which are known risk factors. Hispanic students in the United States, who constitute the largest group of limited-English-proficient students by far, are particularly at risk for reading difficulties. Despite the group's progress in achievement over the past 15 to 20 years, they are about twice as likely as non-Hispanic whites to be reading below average for their age. Achievement gaps in all academic areas between whites and Hispanics, whether they are U.S. or foreign born, appear early and persist throughout their school careers (Kao and Tienda, 1995).

One obvious reason for these achievement differences is the language difference itself. Being taught and tested in English would, of course, put students with limited English proficiency at a disadvantage. These children might not have any reading difficulty at all if they were taught and tested in the language in which they are proficient. Indeed, there is evidence from research in bilingual education that learning to read in one's native language – thus offsetting the obstacle presented by limited proficiency in English – can lead to superior achievement (Legarreta, 1979; Ramirez et al., 1991). This field is highly contentious and politicized, however, and there is a lack of clear consensus about the advantages and disadvantages of academic instruction in the primary language in contrast to early and intensive exposure to English (August and Hakuta, 1997; Rossell and Baker, 1996).

In any event, limited proficiency in English does not, in and of itself, appear to be entirely responsible for the low reading achievement of these students. Even when taught and tested in Spanish, as the theory and practice of bilingual education dictates, many Spanish-speaking Hispanic students in the United States still demonstrate low levels of reading attainment (Escamilla, 1994; Gersten and Woodward, 1995; Goldenberg and Gallimore, 1991; Slavin and Madden, 1995). This suggests that factors other than lack of English proficiency may also contribute to these children's reading difficulties.

One such factor is cultural differences, that is, the mismatch between the schools and the families in definitions of literacy, in teaching practices, and in defined roles for parents versus teachers (e.g., Jacob and Jordan, 1987; Tharp, 1989); these differences can create obstacles to children's learning to read in school. Others contend that primary cultural differences matter far less than do 'secondary cultural discontinuities,' such as low motivation and low educational aspirations that are the result of discrimination and limited social and economic opportunities for certain minority groups (Ogbu, 1974, 1982). Still others claim that high motivation and educational aspirations can and do coexist with low achievement (e.g., Labov et al., 1968, working in the African American community; Goldenberg and Gallimore, 1995, in the Hispanic communities) and that other factors must therefore explain the differential achievement of culturally diverse groups.

Literacy is positively valued by adults in minority communities, and the positive views are often brought to school by young children (Nettles, 1997). Nonetheless, the ways that reading is used by adults and children varies across families from different cultural groups in ways that may influence children's participation in literacy activities in school, as Heath (1983) found. And adults in some communities may see very few functional roles for literacy, so that they will be unlikely to provide conditions in the home that are conducive to children's acquisition of reading and writing skills (Purcell-Gates, 1991, 1996).

It is difficult to distinguish the risk associated with minority status and not speaking English from the risk associated with lower socioeconomic status (SES). Studying the differential experiences of children in middle- and lower-class families can illuminate the factors that affect the development of literacy and thus contribute to the design of prevention and intervention efforts.

The most extensive studies of SES differences have been conducted in Britain. Stubbs (1980) found a much lower percentage of poor readers with higher (7.5 percent) than with lower SES (26.9 percent). Some have suggested that SES differences in reading achievement are actually a result of differences in the quality of schooling; that is, lower-SES children tend to go to inferior schools, and therefore their achievement is lower because of inferior educational opportunities (Cook, 1991). However, a recent study by Alexander and Entwisle (1996) appears to demonstrate that 'it is during nonschool time – before they start and during the summer months – that low-SES children fall academically behind their higher SES peers and get progressively further behind. During the school months (at least through elementary school) the rate of progress is virtually identical for high- and low-SES children.

Regardless of the specific explanation, differences in literacy achievement among children as a result of socioeconomic status are pronounced. Thirty years ago Coleman et al. (1966) and Moynihan (1965) reported that the educational deficit of children from low income families was present at school entry and increased with each year they stayed in school. Evidence of SES differences in reading achievement has continued to accumulate (National Assessment of Educational Progress, 1981, 1995). Reading achievement of children in affluent suburban schools is significantly and consistently higher than that of children in 'disadvantaged' urban schools (e.g., NAEP, 1994, 1995; White, 1982; Hart and Risley, 1995). An important conceptual distinction was made by White (1982) in a groundbreaking meta-analysis. White discovered that, at the *individual level*, SES is related to achievement only very modestly. However, at the *aggregate level*, that is, when measured as a school or community characteristic, the effects of SES are much more pronounced. A low-SES child in a generally moderate or higher-SES school or community is far less at risk than an entire school or community of low-SES children.

The existence of SES differences in reading outcomes offers by itself little information about the specific experiences or activities that influence literacy development at home. Indeed, a look at socioeconomic factors alone can do no more than nominate the elements that differ between middle-class and lower-class homes. Researchers have tried to identify the specific familial interactions that can account for social class differences, as well as describe those interactions around literacy that do occur in low-income homes. For example, Baker et al. (1995) compared opportunities for informal literacy learning among preschoolers in the homes of middle-income and low-income urban families. They found that children from middle-income homes had greater opportunities for informal literacy learning than children of low-income homes. Low-income parents, particularly African-American parents, reported more reading skills practice and homework (e.g., flash cards, letter practice) with their kindergarten-age children than did middle-income parents. Middle-income parents reported only slightly more joint book reading with their children than did low-income families. But these middle-income parents reported more play with print and more independent reading by children. Among the middle-class families in this study, 90 percent reported that their child visited the library at least once a month, whereas only 43 percent of the low-income families reported such visits. The findings of Baker et al. that low-income homes typically do offer opportunities for literacy practice, though perhaps of a different nature from middle-class homes, have been confirmed in ethnographic work by researchers such as Teale (1986), Taylor and Dorsey-Gaines (1988), Taylor and Strickland (1986), Gadsden (1993), Delgado-Gaitan (1990), and Goldenberg et al. (1992).

⭐ **Task B2.3.1: Continuing the debate**

➤ How is Snow's account similar to and/or different from Adams's and Goodman's? In what ways has she contributed to the preceding debates?

➤ How do you think Adams and Goodman might respond to her analysis?

➤ What parts would each of them find more or less problematic?

⭐ **Task B2.3.2: Literacy in a medical frame**

As we noted in our introduction to this excerpt, Snow employs clinical-medical language in discussing the issues of reading difficulties. For example, at one point she writes:

> Even though quite accurate estimates can be made on the basis of known *risk factors*, it is still difficult to predict precisely which young children will have difficulty learning to read. We therefore propose that prevention efforts must reach all children. To wait to initiate *treatment* until the child has been *diagnosed* with a specific *disability* is too late. However, we can begin *treatment of conditions* associated with reading problems, for example, *hearing impairments*. (our emphasis)

➤ How does framing the issue in this way affect the way we think about the scope and nature of problems and possible solutions?

For example, one assumption underlying medical knowledge is the distinction between 'normalcy' or 'health' on the one hand, and 'pathology' or 'illness' on the other.

➤ What are the advantages and disadvantages of casting reading difficulty as a pathological state?

➤ Moreover, how does this emphasis on prevention, diagnosis and treatment fit in with Snow's later discussion of the 'Demographics of Reading Difficulties'?

⭐ **Task B2.3.3: Your own experiences**

So far we have presented you with excerpts from three different accounts of the reading process and the difficulties associated with it: Adams, Goodman and Snow.

➤ How do your own experiences – and those of people close to you, for example a daughter or son, a younger sibling – compare to these expert explanations?

➤ Which parts of the different theories discussed best approximate the way in which you learned to read?

➤ And how would you position yourself relative to the 'at risk' populations surveyed by Snow?

Task B2.3.4: Gee versus Snow ⭐

As noted above, the linguist Jim Gee criticised Snow and colleagues' report as '[framing] the issues and problems too narrowly in terms of 'reading', construed as what the Academy report calls "real reading", that is, decoding, word recognition, and comprehension of "literal meaning", rather than in terms of language, literacy, and learning as they are situated in multiple sociocultural practices in and out of schools' (Gee 1996b, p. 358). In particular, Gee cites the 'fourth grade slump' (Chall et al., 1990) – the phenomenon in US education whereby pupils from lower socioeconomic backgrounds, who attain expected achievement standards in the initial grades, begin to lag behind their more privileged peers in the fourth grade (9-year-olds) – a problem not adequately addressed by the narrow focus on reading as decoding and literal comprehension. He concludes his 'reframing' of the problem thus:

> The Academy report is built around an all too common divide between reading in the early primary grades as 'real reading' (decoding, word recognition, and comprehension of 'literal meaning') and reading in the later grades as reading within specific learning-focused, content-based or disciplinary practices. Such a divide fails to ensure we won't simply reproduce the fourth-grade slump. The New Literacy Studies would argue that 'real reading' decontextualised from social practices is, at any age, useless. It would focus, instead, on how people, from childhood to adulthood, learn to leverage new school-based (and other public sphere) social languages – in speech, writing and action – to participate in, and eventually critique and transform, specific sociocultural practices.

➤ How do you think Snow and colleagues might respond to such a critique?

➤ For example, are there any potential advantages of treating reading as decontextualised?

➤ Why might they have opted to not include the infamous fourth-grade slump in their discussion of reading difficulties?

➤ Gee quotes at length from their report in substantiating his claims; what might account for the different conclusions at which he and Snow arrive?

➤ And are these differences that make a difference for policy and practice? In what way?

If you do not yet fully recognise what Gee is speaking about when he talks about 'the New Literacy Studies', 'school-based social languages' and reading as 'sociocultural practice', do not despair. The next article in this section provides a New Literacy Studies critique of the sociocultural practice of reading in school, and Section B4 also provides a number of articles that expand on this approach.

The debate between Snow and Gee continued beyond this one essay, and you might find it interesting to trace its trajectory, from Snow and colleagues' Report (of which the preceding passage is only one small excerpt), Gee's critique cited above, and Snow's (2000) and Gee's (2000) rejoinders on the pages of that same journal.

➤ What are the central issues and arguments?

➤ On which points do you agree and/or disagree with each of the two authors?

➤ What further evidence would you need in order to make up your mind?

➤ How might you find that evidence, and/or how might it be created (e.g. what kind of research study could provide it)?

➤ In what ways has the debate shed light on the problem of how to prevent reading difficulties?

Task B2.3.5: The main issues in the phonics versus whole language debate (continued)

Revisiting your table from earlier:

➤ Are there any additional issues that Snow raises?

➤ How do her views fit into the categories you have already constructed?

➤ In what ways does her discussion approximate Adams's and/or Goodman's views? (It is noteworthy that she does not use the terms 'whole language' or 'phonics' in the excerpt.)

➤ What new issues does her excerpt bring to the discussion?

➤ On the basis of your reading, how do you think Adams and Goodman might respond to her analysis?

B2.4 LITERACY IN SCHOOLS

The 'Snow' Report selection ends with reference to research on cultural and class factors that might explain low literacy performance by children from minority groups in both the USA and the UK. The next selection indicates the kind of research that ethnographers are conducting both in and out of schools (cf. Hull and Schultz, 2002). Street and Street used ethnographic-style methods to study primary classrooms and followed up some of the children into their homes. A key question to ask in this context is whether their work simply fits the pattern of discussion already addressed, perhaps being located under what Snow et al. refer to as 'Demographics', or whether there is a qualitative shift in focus in such an approach, of the kind signalled by Gee in his reference to 'New Literacy Studies'? For instance, the article questions the dominant association between literacy and schooling that is at the heart of the reports and studies previously listed.

■ Are these two sets of researchers simply talking across each other and not listening, can you identify overlaps and is any synthesis possible?

For instance, the Streets contend that literacy is not just a set of technical skills, of the kind described by Snow and others regarding phonemic awareness etc., but is also always part of social practices. They raise the question of how it is that, amongst the many varied cultural uses and meanings of literacy, one particular variety – 'schooled literacy' – has come to be taken as the only literacy, the standard to be taught in the ways described in earlier articles. What this means, and how it affects the account of classrooms where reading and writing are being taught, are questions highlighted by the inclusion of this piece in a section on literacy and learning. You might also bear in mind the reference to New Literacy Studies above and consider whether or how this article might be seen as part of that tradition – one way of addressing this might be through consideration of the relationship between this piece and the excerpts that follow.

Street, B. V. and Street, J. (1991) 'The schooling of literacy', in D. Barton and R. Ivanic (eds) *Writing in the community* (London: Sage Publications), pp. 143–166.

Text B2.4
B. V. Street and
J. Street

The meanings and uses of literacy are deeply embedded in community values and practices, yet they tend to be associated in many accounts simply with schooling and pedagogy. Recent approaches to literacy, however, have come to focus upon the varied social and cultural meanings of the concept and its role in power relations in contemporary society (Besnier, 1989; Bledsoe and Robey, 1986; Cook-Gumperz, 1986; Fingeret, 1983; Finnegan, 1988; Heath, 1983; Tannen, 1985; Varenne and McDermott, 1983). Literacy is not a given, a simple set of technical skills necessary for a range of educational competencies, as much of the earlier literature would suggest. Literacy practices are neither neutral nor simply a matter of educational concern: They are varied and contentious and imbued with ideology. There are different literacies related to different social and cultural contexts rather than a single Literacy that is the same everywhere (Street, 1984, 1993). This raises the question of how it is that one particular

B. V. Street and
J. Street

variety has come to be taken as the only literacy. Among all of the different literacies practiced in the community, the home, and the workplace, how is it that the variety associated with schooling has come to be the defining type, not only to set the standard for other varieties but to marginalize them, to rule them off the agenda of literacy debate? Nonschool literacies have come to be seen as inferior attempts at the real thing, to be compensated for by enhanced schooling.

We are interested in exploring the ways in which, both at home and at school, dominant conceptions of literacy are constructed and reproduced in such a way as to marginalize alternatives and, we would suggest, to control key aspects of language and thought. We hypothesize that the mechanism through which meanings and uses of 'literacy' take on this role is the 'pedogogization' of literacy. By this we mean that literacy has become associated with educational notions of Teaching and Learning and with what teachers and pupils do in schools, at the expense of the many other uses and meanings of literacy evident from the comparative ethnographic literature. We use pedagogy not in the narrow sense of specific skills and tricks of the trade used by teachers but in the broader sense of institutionalized processes of teaching and learning, usually associated with the school but increasingly identified in home practices associated with reading and writing. Whether we are observing parent-child interactions, the development of educational toys and 'software' in the home, or the procedures associated with classroom learning, *pedagogy* in this sense has taken on the character of an ideological force controlling social relations in general and conceptions of reading and writing in particular.

The chapter is organized around a number of key theoretical concepts, informed by some illustrative data from fieldwork undertaken in the United States during 1988. We begin with an analysis of what we mean by the 'pedagogization' of literacy, highlighting the cultural specificity of this form with reference to comparative material from social situations in which literacy is not associated with schooling or pedagogy. We then briefly describe the school and community from which we draw some illustrative data; we consider in this context some of the processes of pedagogization, such as the objectification of language, metalinguistic usages, space labeling, and classroom procedure. After having suggested some of the ways of studying *how* the schooling of literacy is effected, we conclude with some suggestions as to *why* this form of literacy has acquired such importance in contemporary society, focusing on the relationship between literacy, ideology, and nationalism. Finally, we draw some conclusions regarding possible directions for future research. The chapter as a whole is informed by an 'ideological' model of literacy. It eschews the notion of a great divide between literacy and orality; and it develops earlier critiques of the 'autonomous' model of literacy, with specific reference to its role in contemporary schooling (Street, 1984).

Literacy without schooling

We begin by establishing what is meant by the notion of different 'literacies' and of conceptualizing literacy outside schooling and pedagogy. Literacy is so embedded within these institutions in contemporary society that it is sometimes difficult for us to disengage and recognize that, for most of history and in great sections of contemporary society, literacy practices remain embedded in other social institutions. While Ogbu's definition of *literacy* as 'synonymous with academic performance,' 'the ability to read and write and compute in the form taught and expected in formal education' (Ogbu, 1990), would probably receive general agreement in contemporary society, it is put into perspective by [recent work in the ethnography of literacy which shows multiple literacy practices in different cultural contexts associated with varieties of 'performance' and meaning] Reid (1988); Yin-yee ko (1989); Barton and Ivanic (1991); Barton and Padmore (1991); Rockhill (1987); Scribner and Cole (1981); Bledsoe and Robey (1986); Harbsmeier (1988); Kulick and Stroud (1993).

. . .

[What these accounts show is that] literacy need not be associated with schooling or with pedagogy: Ogbu's definition is inappropriate if we are to understand the full and rich meanings of literacy practices in contemporary society. Research needs, instead, to begin from a more comparative, more ethnographically based conception of literacy as the *social* practices of reading and writing and to eschew value judgments about the relative superiority of schooled literacy over other literacies.

Literacy in the community and in the school

While mainly concerned with exploring these issues at a theoretical level, we suggest how they might be developed empirically by reference to a small, pilot research project we conducted on home and school literacy practices in a community in the United States. Just as we wish to eschew culturally biased judgment of different literacies in different communities, so we wish to avoid making judgments on schooled literacy. We are not concerned with evaluating the practices we describe below but with analyzing them ethnographically as social phenomena. The peculiar practices associated with literacy in schools and, increasingly, in the home and community in much of late twentieth-century American society represent a fascinating and important addition to the complex and varied repertoire of literacy practices across both time and space that ethnographers and historians are now beginning to reveal. Why and how this particular version of literacy practices is reproduced and sustained in contemporary society is a theoretical and ethnographic question – crucially bound up with issues of power in the wider society – rather than a matter of educational evaluation. While Cook-Gumperz (1986), Soltow and Stevens (1981), and Howard (1991) have amply documented the historical processes by which 'schooled' literacy has become the dominant mode over the last century, the comparative questions their work poses have less often been applied to the current situation itself and to the reproduction of that dominance. It is within this framework that we developed a small pilot project to attempt to work out how such research might be framed and conducted. The material presented here is not sufficiently full or detailed to merit the term *ethnography*, rather, we see it as contributing toward future research of an ethnographic kind in this area.

The school on which we focused was set in an upper-middle-class suburb of a major American city that suffered from gross poverty, social inequality, and inner-city decline. Many of those who lived in this suburb had fled there to avoid these problems. The school was one of the few state schools that enjoyed a high reputation in middle-class and professional circles, and many families made considerable financial efforts to buy themselves into the area. House prices were high, and, in most families, both partners were obliged to work to meet mortgage costs. They would frequently leave for work in the city early in the morning, leaving their children at the day-care center at the school, and returning in the evening to pick the children up from the center, which remained open well after school closing time. The school had classes from first grade through

B. V. Street and
J. Street

fifth with about 20 pupils per class and two or three classes in each year. We observed and taped classroom practices, in the first and fifth grades, each of us spending three mornings or afternoons in each class. We also taped discussion sessions with each of the teachers in which we asked about their conceptions of literacy. Outside of the school, we conducted interviews with half a dozen parents of children who attended the school and the classes we were observing, asked them to keep a 'Literacy Diary' by recording literacy events in their homes, and asked some families to tape-record the speech around these events . . .

We began the project by assuming a distinction between literacy practices in the community and in the school. We wanted to explore the ways in which the particular variety of literacy that we labeled 'school literacy' comes to dominate other forms of literacy in contemporary society. Our experience forced us to refine these ideas, particularly those regarding home and school literacies, and to recognize that the extent of similarity between practices of literacy in the community, in the home, and in the school make our earlier dichotomy unhelpful. Underlying literacy in all of these contexts is a common thread, derived from wider cultural and ideological processes. We focus here on one particular aspect of this common thread, the processes of pedagogization.

Processes of pedagogization

We found that one way of answering our questions about the pedagogization of literacy was to break it down into a number of specific processes and then to examine these processes in both home and school. In this chapter, we are particularly concerned with the processes that help construct an 'autonomous' model of literacy – in which many individuals, often against their own experience, come to conceptualize literacy as a separate, reified set of 'neutral' competencies, autonomous of social context – and with the procedures and social roles through which this model of literacy is disseminated and internalized.

The construction and internalization of the autonomous model of literacy is achieved by a number of means, some of which we will briefly attempt to illustrate from our data: the distancing of language from subjects – the ways in which language is treated as though it were a thing, distanced from both teacher and learner and imposing on them external rules and requirements as though they were but passive recipients; 'metalinguistic' usages – the ways in which the social processes of reading and writing are referred to and lexicalized within a pedagogic voice as though they were independent and neutral competencies rather than laden with significance for power relations and ideology; 'privileging' – the ways in which reading and writing are given status vis-à-vis oral discourse as though the medium were intrinsically superior and, therefore, those who acquired it would also become superior; and 'philosophy of language' – the setting of units and boundaries for elements of language use as though they were neutral, thereby disguising the ideological source of what are in fact social constructions, frequently associated with ideas about logic, order, scientific mentality, and so on.

Among the institutional processes that contribute to the construction and internalization of the pedagogic voice in school, we focus on 'space labeling' and 'procedures.' The institutionalization of a particular model of literacy operates not only through particular forms of speech and texts but in the physical and institutional space that is separated from 'everyday' space for purposes of teaching and learning and that derives from wider social and ideological constructions of the social and built world. 'Procedures' represent the way in which rules for the engagement of participants as teachers and learners are continuously asserted and reinforced within practices supposedly to do simply with using and talking about literacy: While apparently simply giving instructions about handling a text, for instance, teachers and parents are also embedding relations of hierarchy, authority, and control.

A 'mix' of oral and literate media, sometimes referred to as an 'oral-literate' continuum, is to be observed in all of these processes: Participants employ both oral and literate discursive strategies as they interact, in both home and school. But this interactive aspect of literacy and orality tends, within actual practice, to be disguised behind prescriptions and linguistic conventions that represent the linguistic modes as entirely separate, as though there were a 'great divide' between orality and literacy. This conception of literacy appears to be one of the major means whereby an autonomous model of literacy is internalized and disseminated in contemporary society. It is a conception endemic to pedagogized literacy.

[The sections on 'objectifying language' and space labelling have been omitted.]

Procedures

Procedures for organizing classroom time, work practices, and literacy materials dominate the classroom and form a major part of the pedagogic voice. One teacher told her students explicitly that they had to speak differently in class: 'Now you are in school, use your inside school voice.' Thereby school is separated from other times and places, and familiar everyday processes of speaking, reading, and writing are given a distinct character and a special authority. A session is divided into phases by means of linguistic markers that have illocutionary force in actually constructing the separate times and spaces (but compare with Collins, 1996). The teacher continually interrupts students' work with statements about where the class are in her time frame and what to do next: 'Journals now: write how the group work went'; 'close your scripts up, all the pages inside. You're going to be putting them inside'; 'the first thing you're going to do when everyone gets back is go over the homework so this would be a marvellous time to get it finished'; 'get out last night's reading assignment'; 'break now, have a snack now.' 'Now we're running overtime. Quick, reading groups. Get your maths papers out.' 'We'll finish now. A new book on Monday.' These interjections are not simply practical features of classroom activity, although they do have specific surface functions in organizing the day where only one teacher takes a class right through. They also, however, help to define what literacy is: They define the organization of texts, papers, and reading and writing materials as the organization of cultural time and space. While they appear to be teaching strategies, they in fact set the boundaries of literacy itself and assert its place within a culturally defined authority structure. The teacher has the authority to bound time and space for the students, and this authority reinforces her control over the definition and bounding of linguistic practices: Literacy is placed in relation both to oral discourse and to specific material practices with which it becomes entwined and defined.

In the same voice as she marks phases of time during the day, the teacher sets out procedures for this material practice of literacy: 'When you've finished, put all the papers in the folder I gave you. You're going to be responsible for finding all the things when we're going through it. That's why you have the folder'; 'If you want to write the sentences on lined paper, then take some from your book.' 'Turn over on the back of the paper.' The ending of a session is defined by a combination of linguistic markers and literacy practices: 'Put your scripts in a folder. You may fold it in half once to get it in.'

Oral procedures for finding their way around a written text also combine teacher authority over texts with a 'mix' of oral and written conventions that is not explicitly addressed. It is as though the words were not being spoken but assimilated to the written form:

> TEACHER: 'Top of page 62. What does C's mother do about that? . . . Let's look at page 66 now. I'm sorry, page 64. Read to me the third sentence. That's the third sentence not the third line. How can you find a paragraph? It starts in.'
>
> STUDENT: 'It starts with a capital letter.'
>
> TEACHER: 'Yes, but it also starts in. . . . Can you tell me the last word of the sentence? What was that word? Page 59 now. So D. was going home . . . what was the friend's name? . . . the last two lines tell you. Page 60 now. Read what Steve says . . . Bob says that.'

Much of this discourse depends upon shared assumptions about the visual perception of a text, its layout and organization – a paragraph 'starts in,' page numbers mark the physical boundaries of written material, 'sentences' are visual presences whose opening and closing words can be easily identified (unlike in much oral discourse). The oral representation of the materiality of the written medium becomes a means of organizing actual social relations in the classroom.

Another teacher, getting students to read the parts in a television script, similarly combines oral and written strategies in asserting her authority to determine who has the right to speak at different defined points and where they are in the text:

> TEACHER: 'Page 5, first column, down near the bottom . . . we'll switch reader when we get to that spot. Narrator for 1, 2 and 3. For 4, 5 and 6 Sarah. M for all those sections David. That should take care of everything up to the end of 6. If you get stuck on a word don't worry about it, everyone can see it and knows it. Try to pronounce it . . . Wait, remember to read that dark print stuff first, where is it happening now, the dark print tells you that. We'll finish at the end of 7. I'm going to do 7. I know I said we'd finish at 6, but we're going to do to the end of 7.'

The visual and linguistic markers for moving around a text dominate the discourse and establish the teacher's authority over the direction readers will take. The text becomes a concrete set of signs on a pathway and students are busy looking for cues to their own involvement and for ending. It is interesting that there is much scope here for the teacher to address metalinguistic features of oral/literate interaction (Fairclough, 1989) and to decode the significance of different print faces and so on but these are not the kinds of metalinguistic issues with which the pedagogic voice is concerned. Rather, it develops procedural skills in moving around texts, asserts who has authority over the text, and reinforces the pressure on students to see written language as something separate and detached.

Homogenization or variation?

B. V. Street and
J. Street

There is not space here to extend the analysis in this degree of detail of literacy practices in the home, although our experience was that there were many similarities, particularly in the link between literacy and linguistic practices, on the one hand, and the organization of time and space, on the other. A key question for future research in both contexts is how the assertion of authority and the allocation of participants to specific roles and relationships are inscribed within particular literacy events and practices. At first, this may lead us to conclude that the conception of literacy associated with schooling and pedagogy, in particular the emphasis on Teaching and Learning, is transforming the rich variety of literacy practices evident in community literacies into a single, homogenized practice. Mothers and children in the home adopt the roles of teachers and learners; a toy is treated not as a source of 'play,' to be used according to the cultural conventions associated with leisure, relaxation, childhood, and so on, but instead is located within a framework of teaching and learning, scaffolding the child to future academic achievement; reading a story aloud is transformed by the pedagogic voice from a context of narrative, character, and morality to a prescribed role for the listening child in the achievement of school 'readiness.'

However, as ethnographies of literacy in the community proliferate, a more complex picture may emerge, and we expect to find forms of resistance and alternative literacies alongside 'schooled' literacy. Moreover, it is already apparent that the process of pedagogization of literacy does not derive solely from schools, although its institutional and historical roots are clearly found there, as Cook-Gumperz (1986) and Soltow and Stevens (1981) have demonstrated. It is not simply a matter of how school imposes its version of literacy on the outside world – as we originally imagined and as a rich educational literature has presumed. Rather, the question to be explored is how and why this version of literacy is constructed, assimilated, and internalized in many different contexts, including the school itself. We have tried to suggest ways in which the question of *how* this process is effected may be answered.

. . .

Task B2.4.1: How universal is the pedagogisation of literacy?

Street and Street emphasise that their analysis is preliminary: the results of a pilot study of literacy in two classrooms intended to contribute 'toward future research in this area'.

➤ How do their descriptions compare to your own experiences as a pupil and/or teacher?

➤ Which, if any, of the processes of pedagogisation they outline have you encountered?

➤ How would you respond to their interpretation of those phenomena?

For further reading: Bloome, Puro, and Theodorou (1989), Bloome (1993), and Collins (1996).

⭐ Task B2.4.2: Literacy or literacies?

The Streets' analysis is predicated upon the idea that the different ways that people 'take hold of' literacy constitute different 'literacies'. Thus, commercial literacy is different from religious literacy which differs from schooled literacy. We suggest that you discuss with a colleague the potential advantages and problems with such an approach. For example, the Streets could have referred to different uses or genres of literacy, with their corresponding social practices, rather than calling each genre a different 'literacy'.

➤ Why do you think they might have chosen to use the more radical set of terms? (You might find some answers from their perspective in other writings by Street, see e.g. B3.3.)

➤ Does their analysis of schooled literacy justify this move?

➤ What is gained and/or lost in the process?

⭐ Task B2.4.3: Methods for studying reading

You've undoubtedly noticed a major shift in research methods between this and the preceding three articles, with regard to (1) the objects of inquiry, (2) methods of data collection and (3) analysis, (4) scope of relevant information, and (5) type of claims being advanced. You might outline the different methods used by Adams, Goodman, Snow and the Streets, and then discuss:

➤ What are the advantages and problems of each approach?

➤ To what extent are differences between the authors' conclusions the result of differences between their respective methodologies?

➤ And to what extent are differences between their methodologies a reflection of different epistemological assumptions?

These questions might help bridge the articles in Sections B1 and B2 and those you will encounter later in B3 and B4 – such methodologies and assumptions help explain the differences you will observe as you move between the extracts in these different sections.

Unit B3
Consequences of literacy

As we saw in Section A and earlier in this Section (e.g. B2.3, Snow), a number of writers have discussed the 'cognitive consequences' of acquiring literacy, suggesting the idea of a 'great divide' between 'literates' and 'non-literates'. Anthropologists such as Goody and psychologists such as Olson have linked the more precise cognitive argument to broader historical and cultural patterns, regarding the significance of the acquisition of literacy for a society's functioning, such as levels of metalinguistic awareness, sense of history, ability to be reflexive and explicit etc. These claims often remain part of popular assumptions about literacy and have fed policy debates and media representations of the significance of literacy (see e.g. Section C3). These were classically challenged by Street, who described the approach in terms of an 'autonomous' model of literacy – that is a view of literacy that assumes its characteristics to have 'effects' for the mind and for society independent of (or autonomous of) context. We reproduce later (Section B3.3) an early summary of the autonomous model in Street's (1984) *Literacy in theory and practice*. There he posed an alternative perspective, which he termed an 'ideological' model, that takes account not only of context but also of power relations in interpreting the meanings of literacy and the claims that can be made for its acquisition. This distinction, and the 'practices' approach with which it is associated, drew on the classic study by Scribner and Cole of Vai literacy, which used standard psychological instruments to test such hypotheses regarding the significance of literacy for cognition (Section B3.2). Their research helped to modify the claims of the earlier 'Literacy Hypothesis' whilst wishing to maintain the focus on the relationship between literacy and cognition. Scribner and Cole's work contributed to approaches to cognition as situated, drawing on Vygotsky, which, to some extent, lie between traditional 'great divide' approaches on the one hand and new 'ideological' approaches on the other. Olson has been associated with earlier 'autonomous' approaches but in his more recent work he has proposed a more nuanced understanding of the 'effects' of literacy which he sees as arising not so much from literacy per se as from the associated models of language and thought which the distancing provided by writing facilitates. We conclude this section with Olson's paper (Section B3.4) to give you an opportunity to reflect on whether and how this approach resolves some of the issues raised earlier regarding the cognitive consequences of literacy – in the tasks we invite you to consider whether Olson is still appropriately placed within the 'autonomous' model or whether he has helped move the field on beyond Street's distinction. We also take up this question in a dialogue between Adam and Brian that appears at the end of Section B3.

B3.1 THE GREAT DIVIDE

Jack Goody's classic early account of literacy as heralding *the* significant move forward in human society remains one of the most influential accounts of the 'consequences' of a society acquiring the 'technology' of reading and writing. It forms the basis for many of the more recent challenges, from within his own discipline of anthropology (see Finnegan, 1988; Street, 1984) and also from cultural psychologists (Scribner and Cole, 1981), as the extracts in this section demonstrate. His views are probably still close in broad terms to those of popular and policy perceptions of the importance of literacy, so it is important to read what he has to say in his own words, before moving on to the numerous critical accounts. Goody claims that he is not trying to put forward a single 'technologically determined, sequence of cause and effect' and yet his critics, as we shall see later, seem often to accuse him of exactly this. After you have read this selection, we will ask you to consider whose claims seem to you most valid in the light of the theory and evidence being presented by the various authors in this section (and in the other references). Similarly, we suggest that you might want to use the other readings here and your own experience to test out some of Goody's larger claims, for example that 'logic' (admittedly, in a narrow sense) is more likely to be associated with writing, that is that it is 'easier to perceive contradictions in writing than it is in speech'; his claims about the significance of literacy for certain mathematical procedures, such as multiplication and division (for further discussion of the debates in mathematics see Street, Baker and Tomlin, 2005); his carefully phrased assertions that 'literacy and the accompanying process of classroom education brings a shift towards greater "abstractedness"' and about 'the tendency of oral cultures towards cultural homeo-stasis'. Whilst he is careful to avoid claiming an 'absolute dichotomy', you might like to check how well even these modified claims stand up to the data provided by Scribner and Cole, the arguments by Street and others, and the refined position offered more recently by Olson. Finally you might like to follow through Goody's critique of counter-arguments as 'relativist': is this a valid and useful counter to much contemporary thinking about literacy (and social differences in general) and what are its implications for the role of literacy in your own experience? After each text we will raise questions and tasks such as these to help you structure your response and come to your own conclusions about these complex – and still very relevant – issues.

Text B3.1

J. Goody

Goody, J. (1977) *The domestication of the savage mind* (Cambridge: Cambridge University Press), 'Evolution and communication', pp. 1–18.

. . . an examination of the means of communication, a study of the technology of the intellect, can throw further light on developments in the sphere of human thinking. For those studying social interaction, developments in the technology of the intellect must always be crucial. After language the next most important advance in this field lay in the reduction of speech to graphic forms, in the development of writing. Here we can see not one single leap but a series of changes, many of them spread through a process of diffusion that can be reconstructed in its broad terms and which culminated in the relatively simple form of alphabetic writing in widespread use today, and whose proposed adoption in China Lenin once described as the revolution of the East. Of course changes in the means of communication are not the only significant factor; the system or mode of communication also includes the control of this technology, whether it is in the hands of a religious or political hierarchy, whether indeed it is a scribal or 'demotic' system. Nevertheless differences in the means of communication are of sufficient importance to warrant an exploration of their implications for developments in human thought; and, in particular, to see whether they can give us a better account of observed differences than the dichotomies we have earlier rejected ['traditional/modern'; 'primitive/advanced' etc.]. The challenge then is not merely to criticise the existing framework (that is never very difficult) but to offer an alternative account that explains more.

If we think of changes in communication as being critical, and if we see them as multiple rather than single in character, then the old dichotomy between primitive (or 'prior') and advanced disappears, not only for 'thought' but for social organisation as well. For the introduction of writing has had a great influence on politics, religion and economics; kinship institutions seem influenced only in a secondary way, for reasons that will be mentioned shortly. In saying this I am not attempting to put forward a simple, technologically determined, sequence of cause and effect; there are too many eddies and currents in the affairs of men to justify a monocausal explanation of a unilinear kind. On the other hand, there is a halfway house between the choice of a single cause and the complete rejection of causal implications, between the diffuseness of structural causality and of functional fit and the selection of a single material factor as the dominant or even determinant cause; there is the whole area of causal arcs, of feedback mechanisms, of the attempt to weigh a plurality of causes. Regarding the nature of these causal factors, a major line of thinking in sociology and anthropology, especially in that which follows the Durkheimian tradition, has tended to neglect the technological changes that other disciplines, such as prehistory, have found so significant. There were two reasons for this trend. One was the attempt to establish sociology as a distinct subject dealing with a special category of facts deemed 'social'; in social anthropology there was a parallel attempt (deriving from the same Durkheimian source) to steer clear of the study of material culture and concentrate exclusively upon the 'social'. The second reason lay in Weber rather than in Durkheim; his qualifications to Marx's thesis involved a partial shift in emphasis from production to ideology, from 'infrastructure' to 'superstructure', a trend that has become increasingly dominant in some later social theory.

The significance of technological factors has to be judged independently of such ideological considerations. In the cognitive sphere they are important for two special reasons. We are dealing with developments in the technology of communicative acts, a study of which enables us to make a bridge between various branches of knowledge interested in the science of society, in its cultural products and in the instruments of cultural production that it has at its command. Secondly a stress upon the implications of changes in the technology of communications can be seen as an attempt to discuss in more manageable terms a topic that has become increasingly obscure and scholastic.

In an earlier paper (1963) Watt and I tried to lay out some of the features we saw as being closely linked to the advent of writing and in particular to the invention of the alphabetic system that made widespread literacy possible. We suggested that logic, 'our logic', in the restricted sense of an instrument of analytic procedures (and we did not give the same overwhelming value to this discovery as Lévy-Bruhl and other

Extension

philosophers) seemed to be a function of writing, since it was the setting down of speech that enabled man clearly to separate words, to manipulate their order and to develop syllogistic forms of reasoning; these latter were seen as specifically literate rather than oral, even making use of another purely graphic isolate, the letter, as a means of indicating the relationship between the constituent elements. It is a suggestion consistent with Luria's research in Central Asia where he found schooling associated with an acceptance of the highly artificial assumptions on which logical syllogisms were based (Scribner and Cole 1973: 554). A similar argument applies to the law of contradiction, which Lévy-Bruhl deemed absent in primitive societies. From one standpoint his claim was nonsense. Yet it is certainly easier to perceive contradictions in writing than it is in speech, partly because one can formalise the statements in a syllogistic manner and partly because writing arrests the flow of oral converse so that one can compare side by side utterances that have been made at different times and at different places. Hence there is some element of justification behind Lévy-Bruhl's distinction between logical and pre-logical mentality, as well as behind his discussion of the law of contradiction. But the analysis is totally wrong. Because he fails to consider the mechanics of communication, he is led to make wrong deductions concerning mental differences and cognitive styles.

The same kinds of consideration apply to numbers as apply to other words. The development of Babylonian mathematics also depended upon the prior development of a graphic system, though not an alphabetic one. The relationship between writing and mathematics holds true even at an elementary level. In 1970 I spent a short time revisiting the LoDagaa of Northern Ghana, whose main contact with literacy began with the opening of a primary school in Birifu in 1949. In investigating their mathematical operations I found that while non-school boys were expert in counting a large number of cownes (shell money), a task they often performed more quickly and more accurately than I, they had little skill at multiplication. The idea of multiplication was not entirely lacking; they did think of four piles of five cownes as equalling twenty. But they had no ready-made table in their minds by which they could calculate more complex sums. The reason was simple, for the 'table' is essentially a written aid to 'oral' arithmetic. The contrast was even more true of subtraction and division; the former can be worked by oral means (though literates would certainly take to pencil and paper for the more complex sums), the latter is basically a literate technique. The difference is not so much one of thought or mind as of the mechanics of communicative acts, not only those between human beings but those in which an individual is involved when he is 'talking to himself', computing with numbers, thinking with words.

There are two other general points I want to make about the mental processes involved. I remarked that most LoDagaa were quicker in counting large sums of cownes. Indeed my method caused some amusement since I was seen as moving the shells in an uneconomic manner, one by one. I later observed that only schoolboys, accustomed to the more individualising ways of 'abstract' counting, used the same technique. When a normal bridewealth payment adds up to 20,000 cownes, counting can be a time-taking procedure. The LoDagaa themselves recognised a special mode of 'cowne counting' (*libie pla soro*), where they moved first a group of three, then two, to form a pile of five. Apart from being a fraction of twenty, which was the base for higher calculations, five represented a number which a person could check by a glance as he moved his hand forward again to collect the next group of cownes. The possibility of such a double check clearly increased the accuracy of the computation. Four piles of five were then aggregated into a pile of twenty; five twenties into a hundred, and so on till the bridewealth was counted. But the point I want to make has nothing to do with the speed or accuracy of counting, but with the relative concreteness of the procedure. When I first asked someone to count for me, the answer was 'count what?'. For different procedures are used for counting different objects. Counting cows is different from counting cownes. We have here an instance of the greater concreteness of procedures in non-literate societies. It is not the absence of abstract thought, as Lévy-Bruhl believed; nor is it yet the opposition between the 'science of the concrete' and the 'science of the abstract', of which Lévi-Strauss speaks. The LoDagaa have an 'abstract' numerical system that applies as well to cownes as to cows. But the ways in which they use these concepts are embedded in daily living. Literacy and the accompanying process of classroom education brings a shift towards greater 'abstractedness', towards the decontextualisation of knowledge (Bruner *et al.* 1966: 62), but to crystallise such a developmental process into an absolute dichotomy does not do justice to the facts either of 'traditional' society, or of the changing world in which the LoDagaa now find themselves.

The other general point is this. There are some specialist groups of traders, such as the overseas Yoruba, whose ability to calculate relatively complex sums is linked to their role as distributors of European goods, breaking down bulk items into small packages. Such transactions require a careful consideration of the profit and the loss, and this attention the Yoruba certainly give. How far their ability in this direction is a feed-back of literate achievement is difficult to know; the 'table' is essentially a graphic device, yet it is used as an instrument of oral calculation. Among the Yoruba this ability to calculate is normally transmitted in 'family' lines; it is subject to the limitations of oral transmission, which tends rapidly to incorporate or reject outright a new element in the body of knowledge. I have already mentioned that the absence of writing means that it is difficult to isolate a segment of human discourse (e.g. mathematical discourse) and subject it to the same highly individual, highly intense, highly abstract, highly critical analysis that we can give to a written statement. But there is also a further point, for which I provide a simple illustration to show the difference made by writing. If an individual Yoruba were to develop a new mode of calculation, the chance that this creative achievement would survive him depends primarily upon its 'utility'. I do not give this term the narrow meaning assigned by Lévi-Strauss (1962) in his dismissal of Malinowski but simply intend to infer that it is a now or never matter; there is no chance that his discovery will be acclaimed at a later date; there is no store for subsequent recall.

This is no trivial consideration; what happens here is part and parcel of the tendency of oral cultures towards cultural homeostasis; those innumerable mutations of culture that emerge in the ordinary course of verbal interaction are either adopted by the interacting group or they get eliminated in the process of transmission from one generation to the next. If a mutation is adopted, the individual signature (it is difficult to avoid the literate image) tends to get rubbed out, whereas in written cultures the very knowledge that a work will endure in time, in spite of commercial or political pressures, often helps to stimulate the creative process and encourage the recognition of individuality.

The growth of individualism is another of the vague generalities applied to the cognitive development of mankind. Once again, there is something to be explained. Durkheim tried to do so by means of another dichotomy, the shift from mechanical to organic solidarity; the growth of the division of labour meant the increasing differentiation of roles; advanced society was characterised by heterogeneity as against homogeneity and this state of affairs was reflected in the *conscience collective* of uncomplicated societies, and in the kinds of solidary bond that existed between persons and groups.

Again there is something to the Durkheimian argument. But the process he describes is more likely to produce a series of partially differentiated sub-groups rather than the kind of activity usually associated with the growth of individualism in the West. There was certainly more than one factor involved in this vaguely defined process; but the changes in human communication that followed the extension of alphabetic literacy in Greece and the introduction of the printed word in Renaissance Europe were surely important factors. Yet they are given no consideration at all in his argument.

Another common theme in differentiating between societies, one that is discussed by Lévi-Strauss as well as by Cassirer before him, has to do with the contrast between myth and history (Goody and Watt 1963: 321–6). There is, of course, a simple-minded sense in which history is tied to the use of documentary material and hence is inseparable from literate cultures; before that, all is prehistory, the prehistory of societies dominated by myth. Without going into the many ambiguities involved in the definition of myth, there is a sense in which this concept often involves a backward look at that which is either untrue or unverifiable. And in the most literal sense the distinction between *mythos* and *historia* comes into being at the time when alphabetic writing encouraged mankind to set one account of the universe or the pantheon beside another and hence perceive the contradictions that lie between them. There are thus two senses in which the characterisation of the 'savage mind' as 'pre-historical' or atemporal relates to the distinction between literate and pre-literate societies.

While the focus of this book is specifically upon cognitive factors, it is worth indicating two other sociological discussions that would gain from a consideration of the consequences of the changes that have taken place in systems of communicative acts, even though these relate to social institutions. The written word does not replace speech, any more than speech replaces gesture. But it adds an important dimension to much social action. This is especially true of the politico-legal domain, for the growth of bureaucracy clearly depends to a considerable degree upon the ability to control secondary group relationships by means of written communications. Indeed it is interesting to note that the terms in which Cooley originally defined the primary group are very close to those used for pre-literate societies. 'By primary group, I mean those characterised by intimate face-to-face association and co-operation. The result of intimate association, psychologically, is a certain fusion of individualities in a common whole, so that one's very self, for many purposes at least, is the common life and purpose of the group' (1909: 23). A face-to-face group has no great need of writing. Take the example of the domestic group, the prototypical primary group, which brings us back to the reasons why writing has had little direct influence on kinship, since intercourse between kin is largely oral and often non-verbal.

[Goody goes on to link literacy with the development of bureaucracy and political systems, themes he develops further in later publications (Goody 1986, 1987). He concludes with a major broad claim about the significance of literacy in explaining the differences between different types of society, a claim that may still underlie many of the policy approaches to literacy education and that you might like to keep an eye out for in the other texts included here.]

I have tried to take certain of the characteristics that Lévi-Strauss and others have regarded as marking the distinction between primitive and advanced, between wild and domesticated thinking, and to suggest that many of the valid aspects of these somewhat vague dichotomies can be related to changes in the mode of communication, especially the introduction of various forms of writing. The advantage of this approach lies in the fact that it does not simply describe the differences but relates them to a third set of facts, and thus provides some kind of explanation, some kind of mechanism, for the changes that are assumed to occur.

A recognition of this factor also modifies our view of the nature of those differences. The traditional characterisation is essentially a static one in that it gives no reason for change, no idea of how or why domestication occurred; it assumes the primitive mind has this particular character, the advanced has that, and it is due to the genius of the Greeks or the Western Europeans that modern man emerged. But modern man is emerging every day in contemporary Africa, without, I suggest, the total transformation of processes of 'thought' or attributes of 'mind' that existing theories imply. The content of communication is clearly of prime significance. But it is also essential, for social theory and historical analysis, for present policy and future planning, to recall the limitations and opportunities offered by different technologies of the intellect.

In the chapters that follow, I try to analyse in a more particular way the relation between means of communication and modes of 'thought'. In this endeavour I want to maintain a balance between the refusal to admit of differences in cognitive processes or cultural developments on the one hand and extreme dualism or distinction on the other. The thought ways of human societies resemble each other in many respects; individual intellectual activity is a feature of the social life of the LoDagaa of Northern Ghana as it is of Western cultures. Indeed the next chapter is directed to making this very point, the point that some versions of the dualistic view tend to overlook. On the other hand, the extreme form of relativism implicit in much contemporary writing neglects the fact that the cognitive activities of individuals differ from society to society in many ways. Some of the general differences that marked the binary approaches can be attributed to the new potentialities for human cognition that are created by changes in the means of communication.

Task B3.1.1: The 'technology of the intellect': your experience

⭐

We ended the previous section, B2 on 'Literacy acquisition', with a paper by Street and Street that provided a 'social practices' view of literacy acquisition that the authors claimed challenged the dominant emphasis on decontextualised skills. The papers in that section moved across a spectrum of positions regarding how important 'context' is in understanding learning in general and literacy acquisition in particular. The papers in this Section B3 on cognitive consequences of literacy make explicit some of the broader philosophical underpinnings of these debates and help us focus on what we mean when we refer to literacy and what we assume are the consequences of its acquisition, both by individuals and also for whole societies. Goody's arguments can be seen as spelling out what often remains implicit in such discussions.

Drawing upon his anthropological expertise in cross-cultural comparison, he explores the question of what generalisations can be made about the 'technology of the intellect', as he deems literacy, and he draws upon specific examples from his own field research in West Africa, and also on the Vai studies that are represented in Section B3.2 here, to illustrate his points. As he takes us through the arguments you might like to reflect, likewise from an anthropological perspective, on whether they hold true for your own experience of social life and of the role of the technology of the intellect in it. For instance, Goody argues that, after language, the development of writing is 'the next most important advance' in human intellectual activity. Getting into practice at questioning the assumptions of the authors represented in this volume, you might reflect upon this claim and consider what evidence would support or challenge it. For instance, you might be inclined to be suspicious of claims that appear to attribute 'determinism' to such technology. If so, Goody is ready for you as he cites a significant history of western sociological thought that might agree with you but that, he claims, fails to give due credit then to material conditions, perhaps by overstating the role of 'ideology' or of the 'social'. So, challenging Goody's view on literacy forces you back into your deeper assumptions about cause and effect in social and material life. He concedes that certainly a simple dichotomy between pre- and post-technology is not very helpful (although this has perhaps been the dominant position in many western societies committed to a belief in 'Progress' – with the West, of course, at the apex of that development). But the flaws of these earlier arguments are, he claims, no reason to throw out any understanding of the role of technology; rather 'there is a halfway house between the choice of a single cause and the complete rejection of causal implications' and it is this half-way house that he wants to occupy. The following questions should help you clarify your own position in this respect.

➤ Do you feel comfortable sitting there with him?

➤ Is that what follows from rejecting the 'great divide' theory of literacy or do you work with other metaphors, other base lines from which to view the question?

➤ What are the consequences of adopting his position?

Whilst rejecting crude determinism, Goody does argue that certain mental developments can indeed be associated with the technology of writing: logic, contradictions, decontextualisation, developments in mathematics. He backs this up with evidence from LoDagaa using cownes (shell money), and Yoruba commercial transactions. You might like to use the same procedure to argue for your own position, whether it is the same as Goody's or whether it is more like that signalled by Street in Section B3.3 – or some further position that you would like to argue for.

➤ Can you think of examples that illustrate the role of literacy in such mental processes as 'abstraction' or 'decontextualisation' from your own ethnographic experience of living in society?

If you have travelled you might like to use the anthropological comparative method, bringing together examples from cultures that on the face of it may seem very different but which may address similar underlying issues, such as the problems Goody cites of handling contradictions or of disembedding from one's own cultural context – does literacy play a significant role in such processes as he claims?

Task B3.1.2: Theoretical positions and their empirical bases

Having clarified your own position you might then like to move on to set it against the views of others through discussion. A group of people might go through the questions above and then list your findings and their consequences for the 'Literacy Thesis'. You might then draw up a table (see Table B3.1.2) on which each person signals their own example – of the kind indicated earlier by Goody with his LoDagaa and Yoruba examples – then signal the cognitive features associated with it – in Goody's case this included, as we have seen, logic, contradictions, decontextualisation, developments in mathematics. Finally indicate in the last column what you take the implications of your examples to be for the overall hypothesis Goody is putting forward. This would certainly put you in a strong position for reading the next papers in this section, as you encounter different authors who take Goody to task from different perspectives. As they put forward their positions, you can call upon your data set and your conceptual listing to check how well their arguments hold up.

Table B3.1.2 Theoretical positions and empirical bases

Name	Literacy / oral example	Cognitive features	Implications for Goody hypothesis
Goody	LoDagaa counting	'Abstract' but not 'decontextualised'	Supports claim for difference but not divide between oral and literate mental processes
Street			
Scribner and Cole			
Olson			
Reader 1			

You might now like to consider some questions regarding your responses in this table:

➤ How difficult was that task?

➤ Which terms were easier or harder to categorise?

⮞ What are the differences between your list and Chandler's? (See below.)

⮞ What contexts of reading and/or listening were you thinking about when you created your categories? What are the advantages and disadvantages of such binary categorisations?

⭐ Task B3.1.3: Written versus spoken language – a great divide?

Much of Goody's argument is predicated upon a fundamental difference in the nature of written and spoken language. Many theorists have joined him in postulating such a division. In the following tasks we invite you to test your own instincts regarding what Daniel Chandler calls the 'biases of eye and ear':

⮞ Divide the following terms into two lists under the headings 'spoken word' and 'written word': Eye, Ear, Impermanence, Space, Abstract, Fixed, Permanence, Fluid, Ordered, Subjective, Objective, Quantifying, Inaccurate, Resonant, Time, Timeless, Present, Rhythmic, Participatory, Communal, Individual, Detached

⮞ Compare your response to Chandler's categorisation (in 'Biases of the ear and eye: "great divide" theories, phonocentrism, graphocentrism and logocentrism', http://www.aber.ac.uk/media/Documents/litoral/litoral1.html).

You should now be in a good position to consider what your responses to these questions and tasks have indicated about your position in the larger debates signalled by Goody, Street and others. You can now carry this forward into your reading of Scribner and Cole and then of Street and of Olson.

B3.2 TESTING THE LITERACY THESIS

During the 1970s the cultural psychologists Sylvia Scribner and Michael Cole conducted a major research project amongst the Vai peoples of Liberia in order to test out claims about the cognitive consequences of literacy in a 'real life' setting. Their accounts of the outcomes of this research represented a major landmark in our understanding of the issues regarding literacy and cognition that we have been considering here. The selections reproduced here, taken from their 1978 article, published before their major book (see Scribner and Cole, 1981) on the research, were an attempt to provide a more accessible account for a general audience. The paper was prepared for a conference on writing, sponsored by the National Institute of Education in the USA, in June 1977. In it they address many of the points raised by other authors in this section, such as Goody and Olson, and provide us with an opportunity to test out some of their claims on specific data.

They use anthropological perspectives to inform their work as psychologists in addressing psychological propositions of the kind put forward by Farrell (1977,

p. 451) that we encountered briefly in Section A: 'the cognitive restructuring caused by reading and writing develop the higher reasoning processes involved in extended abstract thinking'. They address the limitations of these claims in both empirical and theoretical terms and they also add to the ethnographic methods some traditional psychological tools such as experimental tasks (for instance, they set participants a version of 'Kim's game' in which they are shown a series of objects that are then removed and the participants are asked to name as many as they can recall – the 'success' rate was correlated with the various factors that interested the researchers – which language the participant used, whether they had been to school and which writing system they knew).

From this more empirical perspective, Scribner and Cole challenged many of the claims that derive simply from abstract hypotheses not based in evidence, or where the evidence used is of a very specific form of written text, such as Olson's use of western scientific 'essay text' literacy as a model for accounts of literacy in general. From this they argue that many of the assumptions about literacy in general are 'tied up with school-based writing'. This, they believe, leads to serious limitations in the accounts of literacy: 'The assumption that logicality is in the text and the text is in school can lead to a serious underestimation of the cognitive skills involved in non-school, non-essay writing.' The writing crisis, to which many of the reports and commissions cited in Section A1 refer, can be seen from this perspective to 'present itself as purely a pedagogical problem' and to arise in the first place from these limited assumptions and data.

Scribner and Cole, then, were amongst the first to attempt to re-theorise what counts as literacy and to look outside of school for empirical data on which to base sound generalisations (cf. Hull and Schultz, 2002, on literacy in and out of school). Their account of Vai literacy involved both ethnographic description of context and psychological testing and measurement of the consequences of different uses and forms of literacy. Whilst it would be difficult for any of us to replicate such in-depth studies of literacy in use, we suggest below that you might want to use their account as a benchmark for asking questions about other accounts of literacy, including those you encounter in everyday life (e.g. in the media, in international development projects, in educational contexts): What evidence are the claims in these accounts based upon and what assumptions about literacy are they making? Are schooled notions of literacy being applied to out of school practices? Are there equivalent empirical studies of the literacies being described? What kinds of generalisations can validly be made on the basis of what is known about, for instance, children's home literacy practices, changes in schooled literacy etc.?

Thinking about the studies reported in Section B2, the Vai studies lead us to ask: What is the relationship between our understanding of such technical skills as phonetic decoding and our understanding of such social skills as the uses of literacy for letter writing or record keeping? If you know of multilingual contexts for the uses of literacy, you might apply the question Scribner and Cole ask about uses of Vai literacies: What are 'the personal and situational factors which may influence the allocation of literacy work to one or another script', a question that underlay much of the work reported in Marilyn Martin-Jones and Katherine Jones's book *Multilingual literacies*, from which the extract in Section B4.3 is drawn? Again, the studies reported here can help us reformulate the questions we ask about literacy in our own contexts, leading to new and interesting observations and understandings.

Text B3.2
S. Scribner and
M. Cole

Scribner, S., and Cole, M. (1978) 'Unpackaging literacy', *Social Science Information*, 17(1), 19–39.

One of the important services anthropology has traditionally provided the other social sciences is to challenge generalizations about human nature and the social order that are derived from studies of a single society. The comparative perspective is especially valuable when the topic of inquiry concerns psychological 'consequences' of particular social practices, such as for example different methods of child-rearing (permissive vs. restrictive) or schooling (formal vs. nonformal) or mass communication (oral vs. literate). It is surely a hazardous enterprise to attempt to establish causal relationships among selected aspects of social and individual functioning without taking into account the totality of social practice of which they are a part. How are we to determine whether effects on psychological functioning are attributable to the particular practices selected for study, or to other practices with which they co-vary, or to the unique patterning of practices in the given society? When we study seemingly 'same' practices in different societal contexts, we can better tease apart the distinctive impact of such practices from other features of social life.

Here we apply one such comparative approach to questions about reading and writing practices and their intellectual impact. Our approach combines anthropological field work with experimental psychological methods in a study of 'literacy without schooling' in a West African traditional society. We hope our findings will suggest a new perspective from which to examine propositions about the intellectual and social significance of literacy whose uncertain status contributes to our educational dilemmas.

These dilemmas have been repeatedly stated. They revolve around implications for educational and social policy of reports that students' writing skills are deficient, and that there is a 'writing crisis'. Is this the case if so, is it really a matter for concern? Does it call for infusion of massive funds in new research studies and methods of instruction? Or is it merely a signal that we should adjust our educational goals to new 'technologies of communication' which reduce the need for high levels of literacy skill? (See for example Macdonald, 1973.)

These questions call for judgments on the social importance of writing and thus raise an even more fundamental issue: on what grounds are such judgments to be made? Some advocate that pragmatic considerations should prevail and that instructional programs should concentrate on teaching only those specific writing skills that are required for the civic and occupational activities student groups may be expected to pursue. Many educators respond that such a position is too narrow and that it overlooks the most important function of writing, the impetus that writing gives to intellectual development. The argument for the general intellectual importance of writing is sometimes expressed as accepted wisdom and sometimes as knowledge revealed through psychological research. At one end of the spectrum there is the simple adage that 'An individual who writes clearly thinks clearly,' and at the other, conclusions purporting to rest on scientific analysis, such as the recent statement that 'the cognitive restructuring caused by reading and writing develop the higher reasoning processes involved in extended abstract thinking' (Farrell, 1977, p. 451).

This is essentially a psychological proposition and one which is increasingly moving to the forefront of discussion on the 'writing problem.' Our research speaks to several serious limitations in developing this proposition as a ground for educational and social policy decisions. One of these is the frailty of the evidence for generalizations about the dependency of certain cognitive skills on writing, and the other is the restricted model of the writing process from which hypotheses about cognitive consequences tend to be generated. Before presenting our findings on Vai literacy, we shall briefly consider each of these in turn.

[The authors next review, under the heading 'Speculations about cognitive consequences of literacy', the literacy thesis advanced by Goody and other scholars. They emphasise, among other points, that there is no empirical evidence to support theoretical speculations about the causal relationship between writing and thinking, and that many authors make an unwarranted leap from discussions of historical and cultural changes to individual psychological effects. Even if we accept, for example, that the invention of the alphabet was critical for the advent of scientific thinking in ancient Greece, that does not necessarily imply that learning or not learning an alphabetic script will make *individuals* more or less scientifically minded. Next they discuss 'some dominant conceptions of writing', showing how 'most of our notions of what writing is about, the skills it entails and generates, are almost wholly tied up with school-based writing'. These issues raise questions about the implications of the acquisition of different forms of literacy – that is, school-based versus informal – for individual psychological development.]

Three literacies among the Vai

The Vai, a Mande-speaking people of northwestern Liberia, like their neighbours, practice slash-and-burn rice farming using simple iron tools, but they have attained a special place in world history as one of the few cultures to have independently invented a phonetic writing system (Dalby, 1969; Gelb, 1952; Koelle, 1854). Remarkably, this script, a syllabary of 200 characters with a common core of 20–40, has remained in active use for a century and a half within the context of traditional rural life and in coexistence with two universalistic and institutionally powerful scripts – the Arabic and Roman alphabets. Widely available to all members of the society (though in practice confined to men), Vai script is transmitted outside of any institutional setting and without the formation of a professional teacher group.

The fact that literacy is acquired in this society without formal schooling and that literates and non-literates share common material and social conditions allows for a more direct test of the relationship between literacy and thinking than is possible in our own society. Among the Vai we could make direct comparisons of the performance on cognitive tasks of reasonably well-matched groups of literate and non-literate adults. To do so, however, required us from the outset to engage in an ethnographic enterprise not often undertaken with respect to literacy – the study of literacy as acquired and practised in the society at large. Our effort to specify exactly what it is about reading and writing that might have intellectual consequences and to characterize these consequences in observable and measurable ways forced us away from reliance on vague generalizations. We found ourselves seeking more detailed and more concrete answers to questions about *how* Vai people acquire literacy skills, *what* these skills are, and *what* they do with them. Increasingly we found ourselves turning to the information we had obtained about actual literacy practices to generate hypotheses about cognitive consequences.

From this work has emerged a complex picture of the wide range of activities glossed by the term 'writing', the varieties of skills these activities entail and the specificity of their cognitive consequences.

What writing 'is' among the Vai

Our information about Vai literacy practices comes from a number of sources: interviews with some 700 adult men and women, in which anyone literate in one of the scripts was questioned extensively on how he had learned the script and what uses he made of it; ethnographic studies of literacy in two rural towns; observations and records of Val script teaching sessions amid Qur'anic schools; analyses of Vai script and Arabic documents as they relate to Vai social institutions (see Goody, Cole and Scribner, 1977).

We estimate that 30 percent of the adult male population is literate in one of the three scripts, the majority of these in the indigenous Vai script, the next largest group in Arabic and the smallest in English. There is a substantial number (20%) of literate men who read and write both Vai and Arabic and a small number of triliterates. Since each script involves a different orthography, completion of a different course of instruction and, in the case of Arabic and English, use of a foreign language, multiliteracy is a significant accomplishment.

As in other multiliterate societies, functions of literacy tend to be distributed in regularly patterned ways across the scripts, bringing more clearly into prominence their distinctive forms of social organization, and transmission and function. In a gross way, we can characterize the major divisions among the scripts in Vai life as follows: English is the official script of political and economic institutions operating on a national scale; Arabic is the script of religious practice and learning; Vai script serves the bulk of personal and public needs in the villages for information preservation and communication between individuals living in different locales.

In daily practice these distinctions are often blurred, raising a host of interesting questions about the personal and situational factors which may influence the allocation of literacy work to one or another script.

English script has least visibility and least impact in the countryside. It is learned exclusively in Western-type government and mission schools, located for the most part outside of Vai country. Students leave home to pursue their education and to win their place in the 'modern sector'. Little is seen of English texts in the villages, but paramount chiefs and some clan chiefs retain clerks to record court matters in English, and to maintain official correspondence with administrative and political functionaries.

Arabic writing, on the other hand, is an organic part of village life. Almost every town of any size has a Qur'anic school conducted by a learned Muslim (often the chief or other leading citizen). These are usually 'schools without walls' – groups of boys ranging in age from approximately 4 years to 24 who meet around the fire twice a day for several hours of recitation and memorization of Qur'anic verses which are written on boards that each child holds. In Islamic tradition, committing the Qur'an to memory (internalizing it in literal form) is a holy act and the student's progress through the

S. Scribner and
M. Cole

text is marked at fixed intervals by religious observances and feasting. Initially, learning can only proceed by rote memorization since the students can neither decode the written passages nor understand the sounds they produce. But students who persevere learn to read (that is sing out) the text and to write out passages still with no understanding of the language. Some few who complete the Qur'an go on to advanced study under tutorship arrangements, learning Arabic as a language and studying Islamic religious, legal and other texts. In Vai country there are a handful of out-standing scholars with extensive Arabic libraries who teach, study and engage in textual commentary exegesis and disputation. Thus Arabic literacy can relate individuals to text on both the 'lowest' (repetition without comprehension) and 'highest' (analysis of textual meaning) levels. Arabic script is used in a variety of 'magico-religious' practices, its secular uses include correspondence, personal journal notes and occasionally trade records. The overwhelming majority of individuals with Qur'anic training however, do not achieve understanding of the language and their literacy activities are restricted to reading or writing out known passages of the Qur'an or frequently used prayers, a service performed for others as well as for oneself.

Approximately 90 percent of Vai are Muslim and, accordingly, Qur'anic knowledge qualifies an individual for varied roles in the community. Becoming literate in the Arabic language means becoming integrated into a close-knit but territorially extended social network, which fuses religious ideals, fraternal self-help, trade and economic relationships with opportunities for continuing education.

Knowledge of Vai script might be characterized as 'literacy without education'. It is typically learned within a two week to two month period with the help of a friend, relative or citizen who agrees to act as teacher. Learning consists of committing the characters to memory and practice in reading, first lists of names, later personal letters written in the Vai script. Demonstration of the ability to write a letter without errors is a common terminating point for instruction. With rare exceptions, there are no teaching materials except such letters or other written material as the teacher may have in his personal possession. 'Completion of lessons' is not the endpoint of learning: there are frequent consultations between ex-student and teacher. For the practised scribe as well as the novice, literacy activities often take a cooperative form (e.g. A goes to B to ask about characters he cannot make out) and sometimes a contentious one (e.g. A and B dispute whether a given character is correct or in error).

Vai script uses are overwhelmingly secular. It serves the two classical functions of writing: memory (preserving information over time) and communication (transmitting it over space) in both personal and public affairs, with a heavy emphasis on the personal.

From an analytic point of view, focusing on component skills, it is useful to classify script functions according to whether or not writing involves the production of text or non-text materials. Non-textual uses range from very simple activities to complex record keeping. Among the simple activities are the uses of individual written characters as labels or marking devices (e.g., marking chairs lent for a public meeting with the names of owners, identifying one's house, clarifying information displayed in technical plans and diagrams). Record-keeping, most typically a list-making activity, fulfills both social cohesion and economic functions. Lists of dowry items and death feast contributions, family albums of births, deaths, marriages all help to regulate the kinship system of reciprocal rights and obligations. Lists enlarge the scope and planful aspects of commercial transactions these include records of yield and income from cash-crop farming proceeds netted in marketing, artisan records of customer order; and payments received.

S. Scribner and
M. Cole

A mere 'listing of lists', however, fails to convey the great variation in levels of systematicity, organization and completeness displayed in records. Some are barely decipherable series of names; others orderly columns and rows of several classes of information. Some genealogies consist of single-item entries scattered throughout copy books, others of sequential statements which shade off into narrative-like texts.

The more expert Vai literates keep public records from time to time when asked to do. These are less likely to be continuing series than single list assignments, house tax payments for the current year, work contributions to an ongoing public project such as road- or bridge-building, a population headcount and the like.

Personal correspondence is the principal textual use of the script. Letter-writing is a ubiquitous activity which has evolved certain distinctive stylistic devices, such as conventional forms of salutation and signature. It is not uncommon to see letters passed from hand to hand in one small town, and many people who are not personally literate participate in this form of exchange through the services of scribes. Since Vai society like other traditional cultures developed and still maintains an effective system of oral contact and communication by message and 'grapevine', reasons for the popularity of letter-writing are not self-evident, especially since all letters must be personally sent and hand-delivered. Protection of secrets and guarantee of delivery are among the advantages most frequently advanced in favour of letters rather than word-of-mouth communication.

For all its popularity, letter-writing is circumscribed in ways which simplify its cognitive demands: a majority of Vai literates correspond only with persons already known to them (78 percent of literates interviewed in our sample study reported they had never written to nor received a letter from a stranger). Many factors undoubtedly contribute to this phenomenon, among which the non-standardized and often idiosyncratic versions of script characters must figure prominently, but it is significant for hypotheses about intellectual skills that written communication among the Vai draws heavily upon shared background information against which the 'figural' news is exchanged.

. . .

It is apparent from this quick review that Vai people have developed highly diversified uses for writing and that personal values, pride of culture, hopes of gain and a host of pragmatic ideological and intellectual factors sustain popular literacy. The level of literacy that obtains among the Vai must, however, on balance be considered severely restricted. Except for the few Arabic scholars or secondary school English students, literacy does not lead to learning of new knowledge nor involve individuals in new methods of inquiry. Basic processes of production, trade and education are little affected by the written word.

Effects of literacy

Should we conclude that these restrictions disqualify indigenous Vai literacy as 'real literacy'? It clearly has social consequences for its practitioners and (we hypothesized) might have identifiable cognitive consequences as well. It seemed unlikely however that it would have the very general intellectual consequences which are presumed to be the result of high levels of school based literacy.

Nonetheless, this possibility was explored as part of our major survey of Vai adults at the outset of the project. In fact, we found no evidence of marked differences in performance on logical and classificatory tasks between non-schooled literates and non-literates. Consequently we adopted a strategy of making a functional analysis of literacy. We examined activities engaged in by those knowing each of the indigenous scripts to determine some of the component skills involved. On the basis of these analyses, we designed tasks with different content but with hypothetically similar skills to determine if prior practice in learning and use of the script enhanced performance.

[The tests were divided into three areas: Communication skills; Memory; and Language analysis. Scribner and Cole conclude by drawing out the implications of their findings for generalisations about literacy. On the basis of the results, they argue that all we can claim is that 'specific practices promote specific skills'.]

Implications

Perhaps the most challenging question of all, is how to balance appreciation for the special skills involved in writing with an appreciation of the fact that there is no evidence that writing promotes 'general mental abilities'. We did not find superior memory 'in general' among Qur'anic students nor better language integration skills 'in general' among Vai literates. Moreover, improvements in performance that appear to be associated with literacy were thus far only observed in contrived experimental settings. Their applicability to other domains is uncertain. We do not know on the basis of any controlled observation whether more effective handling of an experimental communication task, for example, signifies greater communication skills in non-experimental situations. Are Vai literates better at communicating anything to anybody under any circumstances than Arabic literates or non-literates? We doubt that to be the case, just as we doubt that Qur'anic learning leads to superior memory of all kinds in all kinds of situations. There is nothing in our findings that would lead us to speak of cognitive consequences of literacy with the notion in mind that such consequences affect intellectual performance in all tasks to which the human mind is put. Nothing in our data would support the statement quoted earlier that reading and writing entail fundamental 'cognitive restructurings' that control intellectual performance in all domains. Quite the contrary: the very specificity of the effects suggests that they may be closely tied to performance parameters of a limited set of tasks, although as of now we have no theoretical scheme for specifying such parameters. This outcome suggests that the metaphor of a 'great divide' may not be appropriate for specifying differences among literates and non-literates under contemporary conditions.

The monolithic model of what writing is and what it leads to, described at the beginning of this paper, appears in the light of comparative data to fail to give full justice to the multiplicity of values, uses and consequences which characterize writing as social practice.

Task B3.2.1: Divergent disciplinary perspectives

Scribner and Cole start from the general anthropological debate reflected in Section B3.1, but they take some of the claims made as essentially 'a psychological proposition' and they bring to bear psychological tests for checking their validity. In this sense the arguments about 'cognitive consequences' are conducted from within the camp as it were, whereas anthropologists and often educationalists, as we shall see, invoke other paradigms to make their case. So you might start your reflection on this text by considering the differences between these ways of making sense of the world. Before you even move on to trying out some of these techniques for yourself, you might step back and consider where you stand in assessing the disciplines from which the different techniques arise. The anthropologists, as we have seen, cited data from different societies in West Africa such as LoDagaa and Yoruba. Helpfully for our comparison, the psychologists also use data from this part of the world, in this case from Vai peoples. But here the similarity ends. Try to articulate for yourself the different ways in which they cite their data and then consider which you are most comfortable with. Having done that you will then be in a good position to move on to consideration of the merits of these different approaches. You may even find there is not agreement about how to describe the methods used:

➤ Does 'ethnographic' versus 'experimental' capture the differences?

➤ Or do they both have elements of the other?

➤ What are the relative advantages of each discipline for the study of literacy and its consequences?

★ Task B3.2.2: Assessing literacy and cognitive skills

One of the difficult problems faced by Scribner and Cole was how to tease apart literacy and cognition in the tests they administered. After all, most traditional 'Intelligence Quotient' (IQ) tests are pen and paper tests, which assume that the test subject is to a certain extent literate. Consider how you might deal with this challenge:

➤ How might you test someone's cognitive abilities in a way that does not confound cognition and literacy?

➤ Scribner and Cole used tests to assess subjects' sorting ability, categorisation, memory, logical thinking and language objectivity. Try to design a (literacy-independent) task to assess each of those abilities.

You might want to compare your tasks to those developed by Scribner and Cole (described in chapter 8 of *The psychology of literacy*). Here is an example of a logic task (Scribner and Cole, 1981, p. 127):

> All women who live in Monrovia are married.
> Kemu is not married.
> Does Kemu live in Monrovia?

➤ How well does that task test logical thinking?

➤ What problems might arise in making inferences on the basis of such a task (and similar tests)?

➤ How can negative and positive responses to that question be interpreted? (See Scribner and Cole's discussion for some of the problems they encountered, and how they tried to come to terms with them.)

B3.3 AUTONOMOUS VERSUS IDEOLOGICAL MODELS OF LITERACY

Street, who is an anthropologist like Goody, mounted a major critique of the position put forward by his colleague regarding the 'consequences' of literacy. Just as Goody drew upon his own and colleagues' field experience in West Africa, as we saw earlier, so Street used his field work in Iran to provide case study evidence that challenged the tenets of the 'Literacy Thesis', that is the theory that literacy is the key factor in the development of 'advanced' civilisation. There is a great deal of careful positioning here as Street responds to Goody's own concern not to appear 'determinist' and yet argues that 'the language, the texture of the argument, and the treatment of the ethnography tend to override such warnings and justify the claim that Goody does lay himself open to being interpreted in this way'. Street lays out a list of critiques of what he terms the 'autonomous' model of literacy and replaces it with features of what he terms an 'ideological' model – both of which we shall hear more of as we work through this resource book.

By bringing together ideas that may not have been explicitly laid out in this way, the notion of 'models' offers a way of representing conceptions about literacy that, once we look, we may find we all hold in one form or another. This provides a potential framework, then, for considering the various positions put forward as we work through the texts in Section B Extension and we suggest some exercises at the end that draw upon Street's models (cf. Figure A2.1). However, other authors may want to frame the field in a different way. Street himself cites Scribner and Cole as, like him, favouring a more social practice view that critiques the Goody position, but there are also differences between their more psychologically based account and that of what became the 'New Literacy Studies'. The latter is more rooted in social theory and concerned with discourse and power – an approach we will see especially developed in Section B4, 'Literacy as social practice'.

Street, B. V. (1984) *Literacy in theory and practice* (Cambridge: Cambridge University Press), 'The autonomous model', pp. 1–11.

Text B3.3
B. V. Street

I shall use the term 'literacy' as a shorthand for the social practices and conceptions of reading and writing. I shall be attempting to establish some of the theoretical foundations for a description of such practices and conceptions and will challenge assumptions, whether implicit or explicit, that currently dominate the field of literacy studies. I shall contend that what the particular practices and concepts of reading and writing are for a given society depends upon the context; that they are already embedded in an ideology and cannot be isolated or treated as 'neutral' or merely 'technical'. I shall demonstrate that what practices are taught and how they are imparted depends upon the nature of the social formation. The skills and concepts that accompany literacy acquisition, in whatever form, do not stem in some automatic way from the inherent qualities of literacy, as some authors would have us believe, but are aspects of a specific ideology. Faith in the power and qualities of literacy is itself socially learnt and is not an adequate tool with which to embark on a description of its practice.

I shall demonstrate that, nevertheless, many representations of literacy do rest on the assumption that it is a neutral technology that can be detached from specific social contexts. I shall argue that such claims, as well as the literacy practices they purport to describe, in fact derive from specific ideologies which, in much of the literature, are not made explicit. I claim, then, that analysis of the uses and consequences of literacy frequently fails to theorise, in a way that is adequate for cross-cultural comparison, just what is the nature of the practice which has these 'uses and consequences'.

In order to clarify the differences between these different approaches to the analysis of literacy, I shall characterise them as the 'ideological' model and the 'autonomous' model of literacy respectively. I shall deal firstly with the 'autonomous' model. This model is often at least partially explicit in the academic literature, though it is more often implicit in that produced as part of practical literacy programmes. The model tends, I claim, to be based on the 'essay-text' form of literacy and to generalise broadly from what is in fact a narrow, culture-specific literacy practice. The main outlines of the model occur in similar form across a range of different writers and I shall summarise these before investigating variations. The model assumes a single direction in which literacy development can be traced, and associates it with 'progress', 'civilisation', individual liberty and social mobility. It attempts to distinguish literacy from schooling. It isolates literacy as an independent variable and then claims to be able to study its consequences. These consequences are classically represented in terms of economic 'take off' or in terms of cognitive skills.

An influential example of the former representation is the claim by Anderson (1966) that a society requires a 40% literacy rate for economic 'take off', a hypothesis that recurs with apparent authority in many literacy programme outlines. What is not specified is what specific literacy practices and concepts 40% of the population are supposed to acquire. Yet comparative material, some of which Anderson himself provides, demonstrates that such practices and conceptions are very different from one culture to another. The homogenisation of such variety, which is implied by the statistical measures and the economic reductionism of these approaches, fails to do justice to the complexity of the many different kinds of literacy practice prevalent in different cultures. It also tends implicitly to privilege and to generalise the writer's own conceptions and practices, as though these were what 'literacy' is.

The theory behind these particular conceptions and practices becomes apparent when we examine the claims made for the cognitive consequences of literacy by many writers in the field. These claims, I argue, often lie beneath the explicit statistical and economic descriptions of literacy that are currently dominant in much of the development literature. The claims are that literacy affects cognitive processes in some of the following ways: it facilitates 'empathy', 'abstract context-free thought', 'rationality', 'critical thought', 'post-operative' thought (in Piaget's usage), 'detachment' and the kinds of logical processes exemplified by syllogisms, formal language, elaborated code etc.

Against these assumptions I shall pose an 'ideological' model of literacy. Those who subscribe to this model concentrate on the specific social practices of reading and writing. They recognise the ideological and therefore culturally embedded nature of such practices. The model stresses the significance of the socialisation process in the construction of the meaning of literacy for participants and is therefore concerned with the general social institutions through which this process takes place and not just the explicit 'educational' ones. It distinguishes claims for the consequences of literacy from its real significance for specific social groups. It treats sceptically claims by western liberal educators for the 'openness', 'rationality' and critical awareness of what they teach, and investigates the role of such teaching in social control and the hegemony of a ruling class. It concentrates on the overlap and interaction of oral and literate modes rather than stressing a 'great divide'.

The writers I am discussing do not necessarily couch their argument in the terms I am adopting. But, nevertheless, I maintain that the use of the term 'model' to describe their perspectives is helpful since it draws attention to the underlying coherence and relationship of ideas which, on the surface, might appear unconnected and haphazard. No one practitioner necessarily adopts all of the characteristics of any one model, but the use of the concept helps us to see what is entailed by adopting particular positions, to fill in gaps left by untheorised statements about literacy, and to adopt a broader perspective than is apparent in any one writer on literacy. The models serve in a sense as 'ideal types' to help clarify the significant lines of cleavage in the field of literacy studies and to provide a stimulus from which a more explicit theoretical foundation for descriptions of literacy practice and for cross-cultural comparison can be constructed.

In the light of these different perspectives on literacy, and following the critique of the 'autonomous' model, we will, I hope, be in a position to pose some general questions of both a sociological and practical kind. Are there, for instance, any significant general or universal patterns in the practices associated with literacy in different cultures? What concrete practices and ideological formations have been characteristically associated with shifts from memory to written record, and how can the associations be explained? How can the findings of theorists and in particular of those associated with the 'ideological' model be fruitfully put into practice?

Chapter 1 offers an exposition and critique of what I take to be a 'strong' version of the 'autonomous' model of literacy – that put forward by Olson, Hildyard and Greenfield. Hildyard and Olson (1978) argued that written forms enable the user to differentiate the logical from the interpersonal functions of language in a way that is less possible in oral discourse. Patricia Greenfield (1972), whose work they refer to for ethnographic support, applied aspects of Bernstein's concepts of elaborate and restricted codes to schooled and unschooled children amongst the Wolof of Senegal. Her conclusions were that unschooled children lacked the concept of a personal point of view and the cognitive flexibility to shift perspective in relation to concept-formation problems. All three authors then related such differences to the intrinsic qualities of writing. I argue that such conceptions are mistaken on a number of grounds:

1. The work of social psychologists, social anthropologists, philosophers and linguists challenges the representation of certain forms of language use, in different cultures or social groups, as 'embedded' and 'illogical'. This work, notably by Evans-Pritchard (1937), Lévi-Strauss (1962), Labov (1973), Rosen (1972), Stubbs (1980), Crystal (1976) etc., demonstrated the logic beneath unfamiliar conventions. It challenged the general significance attributed to tests that are claimed to demonstrate the

working of logic and suggested that they often test instead such factors as explicitness, the nature of which is more clearly dependent on the cultural context.

2. From this and other literature it can be argued that the 'rationality' debate is itself embedded in particular ideological and political contexts. The introduction of literacy to the classic debate can be seen as an attempt to give the legitimacy of the 'technical' to statements about rationality that would otherwise appear to be culturally loaded.

3. The justification made by Hildyard and Olson of elaborate and expensive education systems on the grounds that they foster improved 'logic' and 'scientific' thought are circular in that the tests for 'success' are those of the education systems themselves.

4. It is, in any case, virtually impossible to set up a measure by which different performances of logic across different social groups can be reliably assessed.

5. Claims for the objectivity and neutrality of 'sentence meaning *per se*' (Olson, 1977) are themselves socially constructed conventions, developed within specific social traditions. They should not be taken at face value since they serve more often to privilege the users' own beliefs than as rigorous standards of 'truth'.

6. The claims that texts embody 'autonomous' meaning which does not change over time and space is not proven. The 'meaning' of texts lost for years and then rediscovered (Popper's World Three) in fact depends upon the learnt conventions of the discoverer's society.

7. The actual examples of literacy in different societies that are available to us suggest that it is more often 'restrictive' and hegemonic, and concerned with instilling discipline and exercising social control.

8. The reality of social uses of varying modes of communication is that oral and literate modes are 'mixed' in each society. There is nothing absolute about a shift to greater use of literate modes, which is better described as a change in the 'mix'. Oral conventions often continue to apply to literate forms and literate conventions may be applied to oral forms.

9. What is taken in the 'autonomous' model to be qualities inherent to literacy are in fact conventions of literate practice in particular societies.

While the descriptions of literacy provided by the writers described in Chapter 1 probably represent the most extreme version of the 'autonomous' model, the most influential presentation of it has probably been that of the social anthropologist Jack Goody. In a number of publications since the 1960s he has attempted to outline what he sees as the importance, 'potentialities' and 'consequences' of literacy. His views have been adopted by, amongst others, fellow anthropologists as the authoritative position on the subject, particularly where they themselves have devoted little explicit attention to the question of literacy. This implicit acceptance leads, I argue, to problems not only in the representations of literacy itself made by these anthropologists but also in their more general accounts of social change, religious thought and ideology in the societies they describe. It is, therefore, important for anthropological work in general that the concepts underlying Goody's representation of literacy should be made explicit and their implications followed through.

Goody's perspective, which I examine in Chapter 2, includes many of the characteristics of what was outlined in Chapter 1 as the 'autonomous' model of literacy, but he extends its scope across grand sweeps of culture and history (Goody, 1968, 1977). He would explicitly replace the theory of a 'great divide' between 'primitive' and 'modem' culture, which had been employed in earlier anthropological theory and which is now discredited, with the distinction between 'literate' and 'non-literate'. He believes that this distinction is similar to, but more useful than, that traditionally made between 'logical' and 'pre-logical' . . . This, he claims, is because of the inherent qualities of the written word: writing makes the relationship between a word and its referent more general and abstract; it is less closely connected with the peculiarities of time and place than is the language of oral communication. Writing is 'closely connected to', 'fosters', or even 'enforces' the development of 'logic', the distinction of myth from history, the elaboration of bureaucracy, the shift from 'little communities' to complex cultures, the emergence of scientific thought and institutions, and even the growth of democratic political processes. Goody does, in fact, enter caveats against taking these views too literally and, in particular, claims that he is not arguing a determinist case. But the language, the texture of the argument, and the treatment of the ethnography tend to override such warnings and justify the claim that Goody does lay himself open to being interpreted in this way.

I argue that Goody overstates the significance that can be attributed to literacy in itself; understates the qualities of oral communication; sets up unhelpful and often untestable polarities between, for instance, the 'potentialities' of literacy and 'restricted' literacy; lends authority to a language for describing literacy practices that often contradicts his own stated disclaimers of the 'strong' or determinist case; and polarises the difference between oral and literate modes of communication in a way that gives insufficient credit to the reality of 'mixed' and interacting modes. Despite the density and complexity of social detail in Goody's descriptions of literacy practice, there is a peculiar lack of sociological imagination in his determination to attribute to literacy *per se* characteristics which are clearly those of the social order in which it is found.

I also argue that the use by social anthropologists in particular of the 'autonomous' model of literacy, notably in the Goody version of it, affects not only their representation of literacy practices in specific societies but also their descriptions of the processes of social change and the nature of religious and political ideology in those societies.

[Street goes on to cite the work of Clammer (1976) on literacy in Fiji as an example of how anthropologists have been led astray by Goody's model.]

B. V. Street

A number of writers from many different disciplines and over a period of time have, therefore, expressed doubts about the grander claims made for literacy. These criticisms have not previously cohered in an explicit alternative model of the kind I describe as the 'ideological' model of literacy. However, work produced in the last few years in this field has made it possible to begin such a process. In Chapter 4, I examine some of this work, link it with the arguments examined above, and attempt thereby to lay the foundations for the construction of such a model.

Ideas being developed in a number of different disciplines can be seen to have significant underlying premises in common which, I argue, provide a coherent challenge to the 'autonomous' model of literacy. This coherence can be usefully pre-sented through the representation of these ideas as forming an 'ideological' model of literacy. Those working through these ideas do sometimes make explicit the challenge to the theories which I have collectively labelled as the 'autonomous' model, although they do not necessarily address it in those terms. I argue that the application of those terms enables us to see more clearly the underlying theoretical assumptions in writing on literacy, to recognise cleavages in the field, to expose hidden contradictions, and to begin the work of cross-cultural comparison and generalisation on the basis of a worked out model of literacy. This model has the following characteristics:

1. it assumes that the meaning of literacy depends upon the social institutions in which it is embedded;
2. literacy can only be known to us in forms which already have political and ideological significance and it cannot, therefore, be helpfully separated from that significance and treated as though it were an 'autonomous' thing;
3. the particular practices of reading and writing that are taught in any context depend upon such aspects of social structure as stratification (such as where certain social groups may be taught only to read), and the role of educational institutions (such as in Graff's (1979) example from nineteenth century Canada where they function as a form of social control);
4. the processes whereby reading and writing are learnt are what construct the meaning of it for particular practitioners;
5. we would probably more appropriately refer to 'literacies' than to any single 'literacy';
6. writers who tend towards this model and away from the 'autonomous' model recognise as problematic the relationship between the analysis of any 'autonomous', isolable qualities of literacy and the analysis of the ideological and political nature of literacy practice.

I examine these conceptions, then, as they are represented in the work of a number of writers. The writers I cite are identified with a range of disciplines and, significantly, many of them have themselves consciously attempted to cross disciplinary boundaries. Within the collection of essays on literacy edited by Goody in 1968 there was already a challenge to his position. Gough, for instance, argued that he had overstated the case for the 'consequences' of literacy (Goody, 1968 p. 69). She emphasised that literacy is perhaps a necessary but not a sufficient cause for specific social developments (ibid. p. 153). She showed, for instance, that within the centralised bureaucratic states which Goody claimed are facilitated by literacy, varieties of political formation are in fact possible and not just the single outcome that his 'literacy determinism' suggests. Classes and the development of individualism, which Goody related to the spread of literacy, were taken by Gough to derive from the 'division of labour and the relationship to the mode of production'. Differences 'in levels of literacy and reading habits tend to spring from these arrangements rather than giving rise to them' (ibid.). History may be re-constructed in literate as well as in oral societies. The scientific exploration of space and the sceptical questioning of authority are widely variable 'as between comparably literate societies'. Literacy 'forms part of both the technological and ideological heritage of complex societies as well as being intrinsically involved with their social structures' (ibid. p. 84). These arguments and others put forward by contributors to the 1968 volume and elsewhere, worked out in close relation to ethnographic data, provided an important early check to the easy acceptance of Goody's ideas and therefore to the 'autonomous' model with which I would link them.

Goody's later work, while repeating many of these formulations, does also present material and ideas that could be construed as lending support to the 'ideological' model of literacy and as a challenge to the 'autonomous' model. In *The Domestication of the Savage Mind* (1977) he emphasises the importance of tables, lists and bureaucratic devices as being part of the corpus of 'literacy', and in doing so moves attention away from the cognitive consequences of literacy and towards the social practice. He does not, however, make this explicit. I maintain that an analysis of his work in terms of the models of literacy that I have outlined exposes and helps to resolve contradictions which Goody himself has not so far confronted.

Within social psychology too there has been some challenge to the 'autonomous' model without entirely confronting its implications. Scribner and Cole (1981) argue that studies of the kind that I describe in Chapter 1 make inferences about 'cognitive' consequences of literacy that are too general and vague to be of any use. Instead they propose testing for specific language skills rather than for 'cognition' and they relate these skills to particular social practices. What is acquired in a particular literacy, they argue, is closely related to the practice of that literacy. They conducted social psychological surveys, linked with anthropological field research by M. Smith, amongst the Vai peoples of Liberia. These people have three forms of script available, Latin, Arabic and Vai, and different individuals make use of different ones in different contexts. Cole and Scribner and their team of researchers tested different Vai literates for the transfer of specific skills that were practised in different literacies. They then formulated their findings in specific terms. If those literate in Vai script, for instance, develop certain skills of contextualisation and word recognition which are transferable to other contexts, it is in very specific ways. If, for instance, particular uses of Vai script promote memorisation, it has to be established which aspects of memory are involved: it cannot be assumed that memory in general is facilitated by literacy in general. Since Vai script is not learnt in schools but through personal tuition, Cole and Scribner hoped that their study would contribute towards an analysis of the significance of literacy separately from the influence of schooling, with which it is generally conflated.

Although this approach provides a useful corrective to the grander claims of Goody and others, it poses an unresolved contradiction between the possibility of isolating ever more precisely the 'technical', 'autonomous' qualities of literacy and the understanding that any literate practice is a social practice and thus cannot be described as 'neutral' or in isolation. Vai literate practices may be usefully isolated from formal schooling, but they are embedded in other socialising practices and in the beliefs and customs which accompany them and give them meaning. The Vai material poses and highlights the basic sociological questions about literacy to which the 'ideological' model of literacy addresses itself.

Michael Clanchy, an historian, describes the shift from memory to written record in medieval England in such a way as to highlight the social and ideological nature of literacy practice (1979). He argues that the shift was facilitated by the continuing 'mix' of oral and literate modes and that written forms were adapted to oral practice rather than radically changing it. He thus provides evidence to challenge the grander claims for the radical shift supposedly entailed by the acquisition of literacy. His carefully documented account of the growth of a 'literate mentality' emphasises the necessity of examining the real social practice involved rather than attempting to infer the nature of literacy itself from introspection or experimentation.

Harvey J. Graff, a social historian, likewise provides a basis for an alternative more socially based view of literacy (1979). He challenges what he calls the 'literacy myth' whereby it is contended that literacy of itself will lead to social improvement, civilisation and social mobility. With reference to nineteenth century Canada he analyses the statistics for occupational and ethnic groupings in relation to evidence of their respective literacy achievements. He discovers that literacy itself made very little difference to occupation and wealth as compared with the significance of ethnic and class origin. He argues that the presentation of literacy as 'autonomous' and 'neutral' is itself part of the attempt by ruling groups to assert social control over the potentially disruptive lower orders. Schooling and the techniques for teaching literacy are often forms of hegemony and it would be misleading in such contexts to represent the process of literacy acquisition as leading to greater 'criticalness' and logical functioning.

Developments in sociolinguistics, of the kind examined in Chapter 4, can also be linked with recent work in literacy criticism which lends support to the 'ideological' model of literacy and helps to move us away from the 'autonomous' model.

Some of the writers I identify as contributing towards the development of an 'ideological' model of literacy may be more aware of the points outlined above than others. Certainly no one of them necessarily represents all of the features outlined, and the model itself is a development from them. But I will attempt to justify the claim that taken together their work represents a significant challenge to the ideas about literacy that have been generally accepted until recently and provides the essential starting point from which to construct an alternative approach.

Task B3.3.1: Street versus Goody

You may have already followed our suggestion with respect to the Goody material and drawn up a list of examples of literacy and orality and their consequences for the Literacy Thesis (Task B3.1.2: Theoretical positions and their empirical bases). If so you are well placed to now use the Street paper to check out your position so far and conversely to enable you to check out the validity of Street's arguments in the light of this position. Even without doing this exercise, the juxtaposition of the Goody and the Street papers can give you ample scope for reflection. For instance, each of the authors denies the kinds of accusations the other might make against them – Goody that he is being a technological determinist, Street that he is being a 'social' determinist or 'relativist' (see also Street's Foreword to Prinsloo and Breier, 1996 for a refutation of the relativist position). You might then ask:

➤ How well do these authors justify their positions and how do they use data to support them?

➤ How might your own position and evidence weigh in these scales?

➤ Would you want to adjust the measures in the first place and 'start from somewhere else'? If so, where?

Task B3.3.2: Extending the debate

Having thought this through on your own, perhaps with the help of notes, diagrams or a table of the kind indicated in Section B3.1.2, you might now like to enter into discussion with others:

> How have they answered the questions posed above, where do they stand and what evidence do they use to support that position?

> How does it look compared to your arguments and your evidence?

> Have you accepted each other's evidence or have you argued about whether some data count more than others, for example classroom experience versus everyday, or experience from one culture versus many.

You might like to stage a debate in which one person or group takes on the Goody position and one takes on the Street position (you may need a Chair to keep order!) and then appeals to an audience who might even have a vote at the end.

Task B3.3.3: Models of literacy and empirical data (alternative suggestion)

It might help to systematically set out the differences between Street's and Goody's positions. To do this, you might take the two lists provided by Street – the nine 'grounds' he cites to show that the conceptions of literacy put forward by Goody, Olson and Greenfield, which he terms the 'autonomous' model, 'are mistaken'; and the six characteristics of the 'ideological' model – and check each against your own data, in order to clarify where you stand on each of the issues.

Table B3.3.3 Models of literacy and empirical data

Autonomous model	Supporting data	Ideological model	Supporting data	Your position
Texts embody 'autonomous' meaning which does not change over time and space		The meaning of literacy depends upon the social institutions in which it is embedded		

B3.4 DEMYTHOLOGISING LITERACY

David Olson has been one of the main proponents of the 'strong' thesis regarding the consequences of literacy and is one of the sources for claims about the 'autonomous' model of literacy (Street 1984). But in this section from a later book he tries to modify the inferences that can be drawn from his own earlier pronouncements and to set out what is myth and what is reality in our understanding of literacy. He draws an analogy with Christian theologians trying to put the faith on a firmer basis by getting rid of unsustainable myths that only weakened the case. As he describes the unsustainable myths of literacy you might like to look back at the accounts in Section A and to that by Goody in this section and also to review the assumptions you encounter in your own social context and check which ones remain dominant despite such debunking.

Where do they – and you – stand on what Olson calls 'the new understanding of literacy'? His list of six 'beliefs' and the 'doubts' that have been expressed about them provide a helpful framework for reviewing any of the literature in this (and other) books on literacy. It can help you, for instance, to answer the difficult question Olson poses: 'Is literacy an instrument of domination or an instrument of liberation?' His own answer – that it depends which literacy you are focusing on – refers forward to the material in the next section (B4), where authors argue that there are multiple literacies rather than a single all-embracing Literacy. If we adopt this position, then not only the answers but the questions we can ask will also change and that might make us re-read some of the earlier material in Sections A and B1 to B3 with a different eye.

<table>
<tr><td>Text B3.4
D. R. Olson</td><td>**Olson, D. R. (1994)** *The world on paper: the conceptual and cognitive implications of writing and reading* **(Cambridge: Cambridge University Press), 'Demythologizing literacy', pp. 1–19, and selections from the Conclusion.**</td></tr>
</table>

Demythologizing

> The noblest acquisition of mankind is SPEECH, and the most useful art is WRITING The first eminently distinguishes MAN from the brute creation; the second, from uncivilized savages.
>
> (Astle, 1784, p. i)

There can be little doubt that a major feature of modern societies is the ubiquity of writing. Almost no event of significance, ranging from declarations of war to simple birthday greetings, passes without appropriate written documentation. Contracts are sealed by means of a written signature. Goods in a market, street names, gravestones – all bear written inscriptions. Complex activities are all scripted whether in knitting pattern books, computer program manuals, or in cooking recipe books. Credit for an invention depends upon filing a written patent while credit for a scientific achievement depends upon publication. And our place in heaven or hell, we are told, depends upon what is written in the Book of Life.

. . .

Where does this enthusiasm for literacy come from? For some three hundred years we in the West rested our beliefs in our cultural superiority over our pre-literate ancestors as well as over our non-Western neighbors, on our access to a simple technological artifact, an alphabetical writing system. Our social sciences tended to help us sustain that view. Theories of evolution, progress, and development all contributed to the comfortable view of our own superiority and the superiority of the means that allowed us to develop it.

In the past two decades this comfortable view has begun to come apart. Cultures with less literacy have come to see the value western cultures set on literacy as self-serving, as a form of arrogance (Pattanayak, 1991) and western scholars have found the rhetoric of literacy far exceeding the validity of the claims. Indeed, the evidence has begun to accumulate that our beliefs about literacy are a blend of fact and supposition, in a word a mythology, a selective way of viewing the facts that not only justifies the advantages of the literate but also assigns the failings of the society, indeed of the world, to the illiterate.

The situation in regard to literacy is not dissimilar to that faced a century ago by Christian theologians who began to cast a critical eve over the tradition that had come down to them and, recognizing certain archaic modes of thought and expression, adopted the task of 'demythologizing' Christianity. The justification for this activity was not to undermine the hopes of the faithful but to put those hopes on a firmer, more truthful ground. Humble faith based on a secure foundation, they urged, was preferable to a robust faith based on surmise. The faithful, of course, were not always willing to cash in the old for the new.

We are faced with a similar choice in regard to our beliefs and assumptions about literacy. The faithful need not be overly alarmed. The assumptions about literacy that we may have to abandon are not worth holding in any case. Indeed, they underwrite poor social policy and poor educational practice. And the new understanding of literacy that may emerge as we critically examine the facts, promises to have implications and uses far greater than those which the old dogma yielded. What we shall lose is the naive belief in the transformative powers of simply learning to read and write and calculate, the magical powers of the three Rs. More importantly for our purposes, we shall be able to move beyond the mere tabulation of pros and cons and set the stage for a new understanding of just what was involved in creating and now living in 'a world on paper.' That is the main purpose of this chapter.

There are six deeply held and widely shared beliefs or assumptions about literacy on which current scholarship has cast considerable doubt.

First the beliefs:

(1) Writing is the transcription of speech. The fact that almost anything we say can be readily transcribed into writing and that anything written can be read aloud makes irresistible the inference that writing is just speech 'put down.' Indeed, this is the traditional assumption dating back to Aristotle but explicitly expressed in the technical writings of Saussure (1916/1983) and Bloomfield (1933). Since readers are already speakers, learning how to read comes to be seen as a matter of learning how one's oral language (the known) is represented by visible marks (the unknown). Old wine, new wineskins.

(2) The superiority of writing to speech. Whereas speech is seen as a 'loose and unruly' possession of the people, as Nebrija, the fifteenth-century grammarian, described oral Castellian to queen Isabella (Illich and Sanders, 1989, p. 65), writing is thought of as an instrument of precision and power. Reading the transcription of one's oral discourse is a humbling experience, filled as it is with hesitations, false starts, ungrammaticalities and infelicities. Speech on important public occasions is scripted written, planned and corrected – to achieve the goals of saying precisely what is meant and yet appearing sincere and spontaneous. One learns to write, in part, as a means of learning to express oneself correctly and precisely in one's oral speech.

(3) The technological superiority of the alphabetic writing system. The invention of the alphabet by the Greeks is taken as one of the high points in cultural evolution, achieved only once in history and its presence serves, to this day, to distinguish alphabetic from non-alphabetic cultures. An early expression of this idea can be found in Rousseau's *Essay on the origin of language*:

> These three ways of writing correspond almost exactly to three different stages according to which one can consider men gathered into a nation. The depicting of objects is appropriate to a savage people; signs of words and of propositions, to a barbaric people, and the alphabet to civilized peoples.
>
> (1754–91/1966, p. 17)

Samuel Johnson, Boswell tells us, considered the Chinese to be barbarians because 'they have not an alphabet' (cited by Havelock, 1982). To this day the French language makes no distinction between knowledge of writing generally and knowledge of the alphabet, both are 'alphabetisme.' Presumably other forms of writing are not 'true' writing systems. The three classical theories of the invention of writing, those of Cohen (1958), Gelb (1963) and Diringer and Regensburger (1968) all treat the evolution of the alphabet as the progressive achievement of more and more precise visible means for representing sound patterns, the phonology of the language. The representation of ideas through pictures, the representation of words through logographic signs, the invention of syllabaries are all seen as failed attempts at or as halting steps towards the invention of the alphabet, it being the most highly evolved in this direction and therefore superior.

. . .

(4) Literacy as the organ of social progress. One of the most conspicuous features of modern western democracies is their uniformly high levels of literacy. It is commonly held that it was the rise of popular literacy that led to rational, democratic social institutions as well as to industrial development and economic growth and that any decline in levels of literacy poses a threat to a progressive, democratic society.

Historians have attempted to specify the relation between literacy and social development in the West. Cipolla (1969, p.8) found that although historical patterns were far from uniform 'it appears that the art of writing is strictly and almost inevitably connected with the condition of urbanization and commercial intercourse.' The correlation invites the inference that literacy is a cause of development, a view that underwrites the UNESCO's commitment to the 'eradication of illiteracy' by the year 2000 as a means to modernization (Graff, 1986).

. . .

(5) Literacy as an instrument of cultural and scientific development. We take it as going without saying that writing and literacy are in large part responsible for the rise of distinctively modern modes of thought such as philosophy, science, justice and medicine and conversely, that literacy is the enemy of superstition, myth and magic. Frazer (1911–1915/1976) in his compendium of myths and beliefs, *The Golden Bough*, argued for the progressive stages of mankind from magic to religion to science, a view he shared with such philosophers as Comte (1830–42) and Hegel (1910/1967). In fact, it is usual to trace our modern forms of democratic social organization and our modern modes of thought to 'the glory that was Greece.' The Greek achievement has been credited, at least by some, to their alphabetic literacy:

> The civilization created by the Greeks and Romans was the first on the earth's surface which was founded upon the activity of the common reader; the first to

be equipped with the means of adequate expression in the inscribed word; the first to be able to place the inscribed word in general circulation; the first, in short, to become literate in the full meaning of that term, and to transmit its literacy to us.

(Havelock, 1982, p. 40)

The importance of writing to the advancement of philosophy and science has, in recent times been examined and defended in a series of major works by such writers as McLuhan (1962), Goody and Watt (1963), Goody (1986), Ong (1982), works which trace a new orientation to language, the world and the mind, to changes in the technology of communication. To an important extent, it was this series of books that turned literacy into a research topic.

(6) Literacy as an instrument of cognitive development. As with cultural development, so too with cognitive development. Genuine knowledge, we assume, is identifiable with that which is learned in school and from books. Literacy skills provide the route of access to that knowledge. The primary concern of schooling is the acquisition of 'basic skills,' which for reading consists of 'decoding,' that is, learning what is called the alphabetic principle, and which for writing, consists of learning to spell. Literacy imparts a degree of abstraction to thought which is absent from oral discourse and from oral cultures. Important human abilities may be thought of as 'literacies' and personal and social development may be reasonably represented by levels of literacy such as basic, functional or advanced levels.

Now the doubts:

(1) Writing as transcription. Writing systems capture only certain properties of what was said, namely, verbal form – phonemes, lexemes, and syntax – leaving how it was said or with what intention radically under-represented. The fact that visual signs can be routinely turned into verbal form obscures the fact that they can be verbalized in several, perhaps many, different ways by varying the intonation and emphasis and give rise to radically different interpretations. Far from writing being mere transcription of speech, writing is coming to be seen as providing a model for speech itself, we introspect language in terms laid down by our writing systems. Learning to read in part is a matter of coming to hear, and think about, speech in a new way . . .

(2) The power of writing. Rousseau raised the objection to claims about writing that has become the touchstone of modern linguistics. He wrote: 'Writing is nothing but the representation of speech: it is bizarre that one gives more care to the determining of the image than to the object' (cited by Derrida, 1976, p. 27). That writing was simply transcription of speech was, as we have seen, first advanced by Aristotle but it was being used by Rousseau to criticize the lack of attention to speech. Saussure (1916/1983) for similar reasons, attacked 'the tyranny of writing,' the fact that linguistic theory took as its object written language rather than spoken: 'The linguistic object is not defined by the combination of the written word and the spoken word: the spoken form alone constitutes the object' (pp. 23–24 or p. 45). So convinced are modern linguists of the derivative quality of writing that the study of writing has been largely neglected until very recently. Second, oral languages are not the 'loose and unruly' possession of the people that the early grammarians took them to be; all human languages have a rich lexical and grammatical structure capable, at least potentially, of expressing the full range of meanings. Even sign-language, the language of the deaf, which for years was thought to be little more than gesture and pantomime, has been shown to be adequate

in principle to the full expression of any meaning (Klima and Bellugi, 1979). And finally, oral discourse precedes and surrounds the preparation, interpretation, and analysis of written discourse (Finnegan, 1988; Heath, 1983). Writing is dependent in a fundamental way on speech. One's oral language, it is now recognized, is the fundamental possession and tool of mind; writing, though important, is always secondary.

(3) The superiority of alphabet. Only in the past decade has a clear case been made against the universal optimality of the alphabet as a representation of language (Gaur, 1984/1987; Harris, 1986; Sampson, 1985). First, counter to the received view, the alphabet was not a product of genius, that is, it was not the miracle of discovery of the phonology of language, but merely the adaptation of a syllabary designed for a Semitic language to the particularly complex syllable structure of the Greek language. Furthermore, an alphabet is of limited use in the representation of a monosyllabic language with many homophones as is the case in Chinese; a logographic system has many advantages for such a language. Nor is the simplicity of the alphabet the major cause of high levels of literacy; many other factors affect the degrees of literacy in a country or in an individual. Finally, our tardy recognition of the literacy levels of non-alphabetic cultures, especially the Japanese who routinely out-perform Western children in their literacy levels (Stevenson et al., 1982) has forced us to acknowledge that our view of the superiority of the alphabet is, at least in part, an aspect of our mythology.

(4) Literacy and social development. Some modern scholars have argued that literacy not only is not the royal route to liberation, but is as often a means of enslavement. Lévi-Strauss (1961) wrote:

> Writing is a strange thing. It would seem as if its appearance could not have failed to wreak profound changes in the living conditions of our race, and that these transformations must have been above all intellectual in character . . . Yet nothing of what we know of writing, or of its role in evolution, can be said to justify this conception.
>
> If we want to correlate the appearance of writing with certain other characteristics of civilization, we must look elsewhere. The one phenomenon which has invariably accompanied it is the formation of cities and empires: the integration into a political system, that is to say, of a considerable number of individuals, and the distribution of those individuals into a hierarchy of castes and classes . . . It seems to favour rather the exploitation than the enlightenment of mankind. This exploitation made it possible to assemble workpeople by the thousand and set them tasks that taxed them to the limits of their strength. If my hypothesis is correct, the primary function of writing, as a means of communication, is to facilitate the enslavement of other human beings. The use of writing for disinterested ends, and with a view to satisfactions of the mind in the fields either of science or the arts, is a secondary result of its invention – and may even be no more than a way of reinforcing, justifying, or dissimulating its primary function.
>
> (pp. 291–292)

While the contrast between enlightenment and enslavement may be overdrawn by Lévi-Strauss, enlightenment is an effective means of ensuring the adoption of orderly conventional procedures. A number of historical studies have suggested that literacy is a means for establishing social control, for turning people into good citizens, productive workers, and if necessary, obedient soldiers (Ariès, 1962).

. . .

Similar complexities occur when we look more closely at industrial development. Simple claims regarding the relation between general levels of literacy of a population and economic development have not stood up to scrutiny. Cipolla (1969) and Graff (1979, 1986) have reviewed the disorderly relationship between popular literacy and economic development from the Middle Ages through the nineteenth century. They both noted that advances in trade, commerce, and industry sometimes occurred in contexts of low levels of literacy. Moreover, higher levels of literacy do not reliably presage economic development.

. . .

Consequently, it is easy to overstate or misstate the functionality of literacy. Literacy is functional, indeed advantageous, in certain managerial, administrative and an increasing number of social roles. But the number of such positions which call for that level or kind of literacy is limited. Literacy is functional if one is fortunate enough to obtain such a position and not if not. Other, more general, functions served by literacy depend on the interests and goals of the individuals involved. The notion of 'functional' literacy, unless one addresses the question 'functional for what' or 'functional for whom' is meaningless.

(5) Cultural development. Over the past two or three decades cultural historians and anthropologists have made us aware of the sophistication of 'oral' cultures. Havelock (1963, 1982) provided evidence that much of the 'glory that was Greece' had evolved in an oral culture; writing had less to do with its invention than with its preservation. W. Harris (1989) showed that the degree of literacy in classical Greece, far from being universal, was quite limited. Probably no more than ten per cent of the Greeks in the era of Plato were literate. Thomas (1989) and Andersen (1989) have shown that classical Greek culture was primarily an 'oral' culture, favoring the dialectic, that is discussion and argument, as instruments of knowledge and that writing played a small and relatively insignificant part. Consequently, it is unlikely that we can simply attribute the intellectual achievements of the Greeks to their literacy. Indeed, Lloyd (1990, p. 37) found that the discourse that gave rise to the distinctively Greek modes of thought 'was mediated mainly in the *spoken* register.' And anthropological studies of oral cultures, far from sustaining the earlier claims of Lévy-Bruhl (1910/1926, 1923), have revealed both complex forms of discourse (Bloch, 1989; Feldman, 1991) and complex modes of thought which, for example, allowed Polynesian navigators to sail thousand-mile voyages without the aid of compass or chart (Gladwin, 1970; Hutchins, 1983; Oatley, 1977). Consequently, no direct causal links have been established between literacy and cultural development and current opinions run from the ecstatic 'Literacy is of the highest importance to thought' (Baker, Barzun, and Richards, 1971, p. 7) to the dismissive 'Writing something down cannot change in any significant way our mental representation of it' (Carruthers, 1990, p. 31).

(6) Literacy and cognitive development. It is simply a mistake, critics say, to identify the means of communication with the knowledge that is communicated. Knowledge can be communicated in a number of ways by speech, writing, graphs, diagrams, audio tapes, video. The role of the school is not to displace children's pre-school perceptions and beliefs but to explicate and elaborate them, activities that depend as much or more on speech as on writing. Emphasis on the means may detract from the importance of the content being communicated. Furthermore it overlooks the significance of content in reading and learning to read. Reading ability depends upon not only letter and word recognition but in addition on the general knowledge of events that the text is *about*; consequently, a strict distinction between basic skills and specialized knowledge is indefensible.

Secondly, the use of literacy skills as a metric against which personal and social competence can be assessed is vastly oversimplified. Functional literacy, the form of competence required for one's daily life, far from being a universalizable commodity turns out on analysis to depend critically on the particular activities of the individual for whom literacy is to be functional. What is functional for an automated-factory worker may not be for a parent who wants to read to a child. The focus on literacy skills seriously underestimates the significance of both the implicit understandings that children bring to school and the importance of oral discourse in bringing those understandings into consciousness in turning them into objects of knowledge. The vast amounts of time some children spend on remedial reading exercises may be more appropriately spent acquiring scientific and philosophical information. Indeed, some scholars find the concern with and emphasis on literacy puzzling. Bloch (1993) pointed out that even in the tiny remote village of rural Madagascar which he studied, in which literacy has essentially *no* functional or social significance, everyone, educated or not, is 'absolutely convinced of the value of schooling and literacy' (p. 8). For the first time, many scholars are thinking the unthinkable: is it possible that literacy is over-rated?

Thus we see that all six of the major assumptions regarding the significance of literacy are currently under dispute. Yet despite the fact that virtually every claim regarding literacy has been shown to be problematic, literacy and its implications cannot be ignored. Derrida (1976, pp. 30–31) pointed out 'this factum of phonetic writing is massive: it commands our entire culture and our entire science, and it is certainly not just one fact among others.' Addressing this complexity by the enumeration of pros and cons, advantages and disadvantages of literacy – the so called balanced perspective is, as we have just seen, of limited use. What is required is a theory or set of theories of just how literacy relates to language, mind and culture. No such theory currently exists perhaps because the concepts of both literacy and thinking are too general and too vague to bear such theoretical burdens.

[Olson goes on to explicate two traditions that have formed the basis for theories of literacy: social theory emanating from Durkheim and Weber which 'set out to relate cognitive change to social change but allowed no significant role to literacy in the transformations they described'; and the Toronto School (McLuhan, Havelock and Innis of communication theory), which argued that 'the cultural differences described by Lévy-Bruhl and others could be accounted for in terms of specific technologies of communication (a view popularly encapsulated in McLuhan's saying, "the medium is the message")'. If you are interested in the theoretical underpinnings of our everyday accounts of literacy, then this section is well worth pursuing. Olson's own view, propounded more fully in *The world on paper*, is that not only has literacy 'permitted the accumulation of treasures which are stored in texts but also . . . that it involves a diverse set of procedures for acting on and thinking about language, the world and ourselves'. These procedures have enabled us to model not only what is said and heard but what is intended and interpreted – the 'reading between the lines' that is the deeper basis for meaning and communication than the surface features of orthography, phoneme/grapheme relationships etc. which educators have overemphasised. The argument is complex and nuanced, and we encourage you to read the book in its entirety. In what follows we have excerpted Olson's eight principles which explain the implications of literacy for Western culture.]

Principle one: writing was responsible for bringing aspects of spoken language into consciousness, that is, for turning aspects of language into objects of reflection, analysis and design . . .

Principle two: no writing system, including the alphabet, brings all aspects of what is said into awareness . . .

Principle three: that which the script-as-model does not represent is difficult, perhaps impossible, to bring into consciousness . . .

Principle four: once a script-as-model has been assimilated it is extremely difficult to unthink that model and see how someone not familiar with that model would perceive language . . .

Principle five: the expressive and reflective powers of speech and writing are complementary rather than similar . . .

Principle six: an important implication of literacy derives from the attempt to compensate for what was lost in the act of transcription . . .

Principle seven: once texts are read in a certain new way, nature is 'read' in an analogous new way . . .

Principle eight: once the illocutionary force of a text is recognized as the expression of a personal, private intentionality, the concepts for representing how a text is to be taken provide just the concepts necessary for the representation of mind . . .

[Olson then goes on to draw out the implications of these principles for a revised understanding of reading, literacy and thinking. He concludes the book thus:]

Mind, in part, is a cultural artefact, a set of concepts, formed and shaped in dealing with the products of literate activities. These artefacts are as much a part of the world as the stars and stones with which they were once confused. Inventing these artefacts put an indelible stamp on the history of culture; learning to cope with them puts an indelible stamp on human cognition.

It would be a mistake to insist that intellectual uses of literacy all took the same form in all cultures. But there seems little doubt that writing and reading played a critical role in producing the shift from thinking about things to thinking about representations of those things, that is, thinking about thought. Our modern conception of the world and our modern conception of ourselves are, we may say, by-products of the invention of a world on paper.

Task B3.4.1: Olson and the literacy debates

Throughout these sections we have encountered writers who are engaged in on-going debates with one another. In some cases, for example that of Street, authors discuss their opponents directly and critically. In other cases, for example, that of Adams, references to her detractors are for the most part subtle and indirect. Olson provides us with a different approach: he appears to take on board his opponents' criticisms and revises his claims in light of their arguments. You might want to consider how effectively he has incorporated their ideas, and how persuasive you find his rhetorical strategy.

➤ How do Olson's six myths line up against Street's account of the autonomous model of literacy?

➤ Do you feel that he has accurately represented and responded to Scribner and Cole's and to Street's positions?

➤ Does his idea of 'The world on paper' indeed manage to overcome the limitations and prejudices of autonomous models of literacy?

★ **Task B3.4.2: Transcending the literacy thesis?**

You might want to discuss the above question – and other questions that this passage raises for you – with a friend or colleague. We would suggest, as a first step, trying to summarise for yourselves the main points of Olson's argument. From there, you might want to consider the various strengths and weaknesses of the argument, especially in light of the examples of literacy practices discussed by other authors – and by yourselves – in previous texts. Once you have your head around what Olson is saying, you might then return to the issue raised above and address the following questions:

➤ To what extent has he managed to transcend the debates over the literacy thesis and the great divide in order to offer a fresh approach?

➤ What problem is Olson wrestling with? Why is it important to have a grand theory of the relationship between literacy, society and mind?

➤ Olson emphasises that his new theory is made possible by shifting the focus from writing to a focus on reading. What is the significance of such a shift?

➤ According to Olson's theory, does one need to be literate to experience the 'world on paper'? In other words, does oral participation in literate culture accrue the same advantages as actually being literate?

➤ What other conditions, if any, need to be present in order for literacy to have the effects that Olson claims for it?

Commentary

Throughout this book we have invited you to reflect upon and/or discuss different texts, all the while hinting that we have done the same already. With regard to this text (and another in the next section) we decided to give you opportunity to eavesdrop upon our conversation. In what follows we bring largely unedited excerpts from our tape-recorded and transcribed discussion of Olson's chapter (and book).

What's the main point?

A: Maybe we should stop for a minute and say, 'what's the main point?' not just of the section on the myths and doubts, but of the whole book. So, he's rejected the idea that writing is completely different from – literacy's completely different from speaking, he's rejected the idea of this, no?

B: Has he? Let's just dive into one piece, where I think it's a grey area. I suppose you can't consider this without taking into account the bigger point he's making. The bigger point he's making, I think, is that writing systems enable us to model language. Whereas, in oral cultures, without literacy, you can do a lot of the other things that literacy has been credited with, and that's what the myths are, but you can't do that – you can't model language. So, let me just try a quote and see whether that holds up, actually. So, the argument is, not only has literacy permitted the accumulation of treasures, which are stored in text, 'but also' – this is the big one – 'that involves a diverse set of procedures for acting on and thinking about the language, the world and ourselves'. So, those are all quite big ones, 'language', that was the metalinguistic point, 'the world', which, sounds to me like 'great divide', and 'ourselves.' 'These procedures have enabled us to model not only what is said and heard but what is intended and interpreted.' Now, here, in that sentence the bit about 'reading between the lines'. Now, that seems to me a very strange claim from a linguistic point of view, as though – it looks as though he's saying, 'reading between the lines is not facilitated by oral language'. But, the whole of bloody pragmatics is about reading between the lines.

A: Well, let me tell you what I think his argument is here, and then let's see how that holds up. Back to what the main point is – this is my understanding: that, in speaking, we use all sorts of other non-linguistic cues to communicate what we're thinking, what we're intending.

B: Paralinguistic.

A: Yeah, raising our voices, gesturing, intonation, and repair, also, if we've been misunderstood. Whereas, in writing, we don't have that, which is, of course, one of the disadvantages of writing as opposed to speaking. So, what ends up happening when you read, if you have been inculcated into this type of literate culture, as he describes it, and I don't think he says it's necessary that that's going to happen. But if you have been inculcated into such a culture, then you are accustomed to trying to figure out what the author's intention is. It puts much more of a burden on you as a reader and you have to start trying to read between the lines, something you're not as actively engaging in in oral intercourse.

On the difference between spoken and written texts

B: Yeah, I still don't buy that. Why is there such a difference? So, there's a theoretical and empirical problem there, it seems to me. The empirical problem is, he's missed the extent to which texts do, in fact, have paralinguistic features, he's missed, in some ways, the whole multimodal dimension of texts. So, the notion of intonation not being replicated in writing, misses the point that what is done by intonation in sound systems, might be done by other modalities, if you like, visual and such-like, in texts. And certainly, there's framing, there's inverted commas, there's layout, there's all Gunther Kress's multimodality, that I think does a great deal of the work that the paralinguistic stuff does in speech.

A: It's true, I wouldn't want to say that you don't have any of that. And, of course, also, genre plays a big role. We know to expect certain types of intentions for certain types of texts. But, still, without setting up a 'great divide' where you have intentions readily apparent in all cases of speech, and they're never apparent in cases of writing, there still seems to be a difference in the affordances. It seems easier to express – or to clarify one's intentions in speech. It's not just expressing one's intentions, it's also being able to monitor whether you're being understood.

B: And to mark the fact there are such things in the first place, I think that's what he's saying.

A: Yeah. He makes a big deal out of illocutionary force. So you walk into a room and you say, 'Wow, it's hot in here.' Now, that's a speech act, he wants someone to open the window, but, if no one gets up to open the window, then you might say, 'Gee, it's so hot in here, I'd really appreciate it if someone would open the window.' And, if that doesn't work, then you make a direct request. But, in writing, you can't do that, you say, 'It's hot in here,' and then either the reader's picked up on it or they haven't.

B: But equivalence might be, for instance, signing marriage registers, where you are now married. Or, signing a cheque, that money is now yours. Now, you could say, we can't know about that without having the rest of the context, and, in a way, that would be the sort of point the other side might raise: that is, you can't isolate the written from spoken features. But even in the written part itself, there are procedures, affordances and features, which are like those oral ones, which could include a whole range of things: colour, light, etc. You only have to think of the way forms are designed to see how authority is invoked in writing. Here is authority being done, here is illocutionary force, it's being done by the set-up, and those boxes and those colours and the highlights, and the big letters. It's saying, 'this is a legal requirement, if you miss this, you will not be allowed to get a passport,' or something similar. That is as powerful as an intonation pattern, isn't it?

A: There's still a difference. There still seems to be –

B: Of what kind is the difference? Is it just a difference of – you see, that's what I meant, at the beginning, by saying I think there's an empirical question and then there's a theoretical question. The empirical question seems to me to cover a range of things, and, empirically, you could find all kinds of similarities and differences between writing and speaking. I'm not sure if you would find something that was very divide-like.

A: I think part of the issue is, it's not just about – it's tempting to set up these kind of hypothetical situations – I have a friend that I talk to on a day-to-day basis in person, and I have friends who I correspond with on email, and it's tempting to set-up and say, 'let's take a look empirically and see if there's a difference', but I don't think that's his point. The point is that given that I've been brought up in a literate society, with what he calls at one point, 'bookish parents', and I've been inducted into this way of relating to the world on paper, then I also relate to my interpersonal interactions in the same way, but that my mind somehow has been affected by this way of relating to text.

Literate culture or a narrow subculture

B: So, let me try one counter-example there, and he sort of hedges this one, which is 'phonological awareness'. And, at one point, he seems to be implying, exactly along those lines, that acquaintance with written language pushes you towards an awareness of phonological – phonemes, that you don't have in speech, because you don't need to worry about it. And, yet, empirically, we know, and all this debate about phonics, is precisely the fact that people engage a written text without realising that phonological level. And the whole Margaret Meek and Ken Goodman stuff was that people can be literate, or engage in a literate society, without even knowing the word 'phoneme', and what all that phonological awareness is about. So, that's a counter.

A: That's probably the shift from writing to reading. I think he's saying the phoneme, the phonological issue, the whole alphabet system, is not as important, what's important is the meaning element. That's how I understood it, that what's important is that we have this concern with meaning that we might not have in a non-literate culture. I've put it in a different way than he does, but I think that's what he's getting at, that we get obsessed with interpreting.

B: Now, you see, you've located it. And that example of the kind of home background, brings that out, you've located it in a very particular subset of literate society. All the ethnography of literacy work says, there are lots of things that people are doing with literacy, and this particular, slightly middle-class, reflexive attention to interpretative text, is a feature of a very specific subculture of literacy.

A: I think that's what he's talking about. Maybe we should look at his definition of literacy a minute, because I think this ties in –

B: But he's generalising to the whole of literacy here.

A: No, I don't think he is.

B: Oh, that's interesting!

A: But I might have misread it. Look on page 273. 'Literacy is a social condition, in reading and writing texts one participates in a "textual community" a group of readers . . . who share a way of reading and interpreting a body of texts. To become literate in a domain is to learn to share a "paradigm". To become literate, it is not enough to know the words; one must learn how to participate in a discourse of some textual community.'

B: Which is the pragmatic –

A: He's talking about something very specific. He's talking about being able to participate in what you've described as that middle-class group of people who engaged in interpretative reflexivity.

B: I read this to cover all kinds of communities, not only the middle-class one. So, this would include David Barton's pigeon fanciers, they're engaged in a community of practice to do with pigeons, so they share – here you are, 'textual community'. So, he is saying, all literate communities have these features and, yet, I'm saying, actually, only some of them would have a feature that would lead towards this special meta-awareness. So, the pigeon fanciers, there's no reason why their engagement with writing should lead them to model text, and particularly phonology, but all the other grammatical features of language, and the meta-features, none of that is necessary if you're engaging in 'pigeon literacy', if we call it that.

A: I think that's a good point, but he wouldn't argue with that.

B: 'Knowing which texts are important, how they're to be read and interpreted, how they're to be applied in talk and action' – that's all the pragmatics of literacy, I would say. Yeah, that's fine. That's a good point. But that doesn't, itself, lead to the meta-point that he's thrown in.

Privileged domains

A: No, I think you're right. Go on to the next page. He talks about 'privileged domains': law, religion, politics, science, and literature. He writes that literacy is 'the competence required for participation in these privileged domains'.

B: 'Privileged domains, which are bureaucratic' – yes, I remember this bit. That's right, he says, 'certain kinds of literacy', he says it in other places, as well. So, he's picking out those sectors of the literacy community as being the ones that generate this meta-awareness.

A: And do you accept that? Do you accept that participation in scientific, literate culture, for instance, will lead to –

B: Ah, but it's not literacy that's doing that, it's the whole engagement, it's the social practice. If we take it that it's only the subset, then it's not the technology of writing, it's the social context.

A: The question is, would it be possible to have that social context without reading, whereas reading and writing is so completely a part of that social context that you can't do without it?

B: It's a funny question in a way, because there are so many different – I mean, there isn't just one legal, scientific, religious whatever, over time and over space. So, each of these subsets will have their own practices, and many may not generate the same levels of meta-awareness. Because you have legal, scientific and religious communities without literacy.

A: I think you're right, when you begin to narrow it down and narrow it down and narrow it down, you end up with something – there's not much left.

A definition of literacy

A: Let's go back to the definition a minute, because I don't think we talked about it directly. 'Literacy is both a cognitive and a social condition, the ability to participate actively in a community of readers, who have agreed on some principles of reading, of hermeneutics, a set of texts in a working agreement of the appropriate and valid interpretations of those texts.'

B: So, at the moment, he's being very general, that is, all reading involves communities, hermeneutics, interpretation, and that seems to me –

A: And a set of principles for the interpretation, which would seem to me to be very significant in terms of thinking, because one could treat the text as being completely literal and with no room for manoeuvre, in which case I don't think it would lead to any sort of cognitive consequences.

B: So, there's nothing about the text, as such, yet, that is any different from other modalities, in this account, because other modalities will also have signs, visuality, gesture, which you also know you have to interpret, and which I could run the same thing through. The definition wouldn't change at all: 'Participate actively in a community of *gesturers*, a set of texts, in the broader sense of text, to be treated as significant. A working agreement and the appropriate or valid interpretation of those texts.' That all applies to all modes, it seems to me. But, I think that the heart of it is the next sentence. 'That definition helps to understand how the kind of literacy developed and shared by a community of readers, a particular community of readers, towards the end of the medieval period and the beginning of the early modern, could provide both a new way of reading and a new way of looking at and thinking about the world.' So, now, in the whole of the world and its modalities, and the whole of literacy and its ways, we've come down to this early European, again, history, which has a very particular thing which does this new way of looking and thinking about the world. Now, if we want to claim that that's true of Europe – and it sounds dreadfully ethnocentric, but if we did, there's nothing in here that says it's literacy that does that. He's made a leap, hasn't he?

A: No, I don't think he's saying that it's literacy, I think he's saying it's this particular interpretative convention, this particular way of thinking about texts, which affects the way of thinking about the world. I think he's talking about a particular intellectual movement which has become very consequential.

B: It isn't the late European world of bourgeois thought on paper, it's the world.

A: No, it's what happens to the world when the late European bourgeois community subjects it to paper.

B: No, to this kind of paperwork. Because everyone else is doing paperwork, busily, around the world, and those who aren't doing paperwork are still doing the things in the definition.

A: Before we go on and see whether that's ethnocentric, if you narrow it down to late European particular way of interpreting a particular set of texts, by a particular group of bourgeois, mostly men, Europeans, do you still find that problematic?

B: Yes, I think –

A: That there are cognitive consequences to that interpretative move, that's what I'm asking.

B: I'd be quite happy to talk about cognitive consequences to the interpretative move of late European society, up to a point, although it's ethnographically hard to establish. There may be something worth considering, but I can't see the point of attaching that to paper and to literacy, rather than to a social movement.

A: Could it have happened without literacy, that social movement?

B: Well, that's one of those questions, can we do that?

A: It comes back to what you were saying about this community of gestures, which I thought was very clever, but I'm wondering whether it's also true, could a community of gestures develop the same sort of –

B: Well, how about a community of logographs? Because, at the moment, this is a very particular world, on paper, which is phonological, alphabetic, and all those things, in this period.

A: Yeah, well, it seemed like you could have – art criticism could have the same sort of issues around interpretation that you have in textual criticism.

Getting carried away

B: Okay, but what I'm thinking is, how about Persia, Achaemenid Empire, fifth century BC, there's certainly some literacy there, there's huge amounts of iconography, and there's lots of other stuff going on, they're ruling the world. Now, that was two and a half millennia before this European stuff. And they seem to be doing all the things that are in here, cognitive and social activities, participating actively in community, hermeneutics, text treated as significant, working agreement on appropriate or valid interpretation. That's how that community operated, literacy is in there. But, would he say, 'Oh, it's the literacy that's done all that, rather than the politics or whatever, or the theology, the Zoroastrian kind of character of it all.' You know, they freed the Jews from Babylon, you know, they were early democrats, perhaps more so than current world powers. I get quite carried away with that.

A: You certainly are getting carried away.

B: Thank you, yeah, okay. So, is he going to include them in his account of the world on paper, of their world. For one, it's not paper, it tends to be stone that they tend to do it on, now, does that make a difference? Why is it paper?

A: I would think it does, by the way.

B: We're now getting into printing press.

A: Yeah, I would think that the fact that you can create, easily, lots of a certain text, would make people more – I mean, there's even a saying in Hebrew, you say, 'it's not written in stone', because if it's written in stone, you can't change it, whereas, with paper, you can play around with it, there's a flexibility to the world on paper that you don't have with the world engraved in stone.

B: That's odd, because one of the Goody's arguments is the complete opposite, which is there's a flexibility in the world of speech, which means you lose it the moment you've said it, whereas paper fixes and holds. And there it is, you can guarantee, it's now written down, therefore –

A: That's true, but it's not – I mean, I guess I would talk about speech being fluid, paper holding things, but stone not only holding but setting them in a way that you can't move them.

B: Okay. So, both paper and stone are not ephemeral, whereas speech is ephemeral, which is the big distinction they're making. But I wonder, I mean, we've got into that debate now, in terms of his world on paper, would not the world of either the Achaemenians, or the ancient Egyptians, with their papyrus, would they count in his –

Are pictures worth a thousand words?

A: I think not, for the following reason. I'm not sure I agree with this but I'll try and represent his idea, is that you cannot express a proposition with a picture. You can represent an image, you can represent a thing, you can have a picture of a tree, but you can't have a picture which says, 'trees are important to the ecology of the Earth'.

B: Well, I'm not convinced of that. He uses the example that you can't have a negative in a picture. We're surrounded by negative imagery, ranging from 'no smoking', to 'do not put your feet on the seats'.

A: Those are conventions –

B: Yeah, that's the point. Exactly that.

A: – which are sort of down the boundary between the picture and, I guess, language.

B: I think that would be my point. So, you can do those things. You can do them because you mix the conventions, or you mix the modalities, I suppose you're saying. So, he can't say figures alone can't do some of this kind of semantic work, including giving orders and denials. You can just by playing with them, cleverly. But, mostly, always locating them in other modes and genres. So, he is trying to hold on to this particular subsection of it. Now, to be fair, look at the next paragraph, he adds two caveats. Everything we've just been talking about. One is that 'culturally significant uses of writing have traditionally been defined too narrowly by defining literacy in terms of dominant public culture, science, literature.' What he appears to have just said, only now he recognises them as part of a range. In which case, where does that range fit in his argument? Is the whole of that range the world on paper? Which would sound like some kind of not less ethnocentric argument, but then it becomes a slightly determinist one, because it is the literacy that's doing it. Or, is it only picking out the early modern European period again?

A: He says, at the end of the paragraph, 'criticism of text is the important part of thinking and an important link between literacy and thought'. So, in a community in which people are engaged in criticising text, then you have that development of high-order thinking, and in a community in which you don't, then you don't get it.

B: So, I think what I would probably want to do is, rather than judging which are higher and which lower, take an ethnographic approach and say, there are different interpretations of text, different kinds of interpretations, and the differences stem from social and political conditions. So, there will be people who read the Torah or the Bible or whatever as literal accounts, almost as if they were in stone, and there will be people who have Olson's meta-awareness and treat the text more flexibly.

A: I want to take this discussion to another level. Let's grant that he's narrowed literacy down to a particular moment in European history, a particular bourgeois way of treating text, and it's ethnocentric. But now I'm trying to develop kids' thinking in schools, shouldn't I be trying to get them to be engaging with texts in the way that he describes?

B: Definitely. But that then is a particular relationship of one world to one kind of paper. I would be happy to then discuss and analyse and compare with other ways of reading texts and other forms of texts, if you want to use paper as a form of text.

A: So, your issue is *the* world on paper, with the definitive –

B: *The* world, and *on paper*, as opposed to a world, in particular –

A: Texts.

Task B3.4.3: Insert your own voice

Now that you have read this debate between us, you might like to join in – that is, insert yourself into the dialogue. One way of doing this might be to read the text aloud and to say your own comments at appropriate points; or you might make use of the literacy event involved in reading this spoken text by actually writing your own words in between the passages from the two of us.

➤ Do you find yourself siding with one of us more than the other?

➤ Or do you disagree with both of us and want to present a third voice?

Perhaps you could also engage in this discussion with some friends and interpellate a number of voices. And more boldly, you could try to say or write what you think Olson or one of the other authors in this section would have to say. We hope that such dialogic interaction with the text, whatever approach you adopt, will help clarify for you both the textual meanings and your own views.

Unit B4
Literacy as social practice

The studies cited in Sections B2 and B3 were concerned with cognition and with 'problems' of acquisition, whilst the studies in this Section B4 emphasise understanding of literacy practices in their social and cultural contexts. This approach has been particularly influenced by those who have advocated an 'ethnographic' perspective, in contrast with the experimental and often individualistic character of cognitive studies.

Developments in literacy studies have been usefully summarised in articles by Barton and Hamilton (1998, see Section B4.1), Collins (1995) and Street (2000; see also Annotated Bibliography). Heath's classic study of community literacy practices, *Ways with words* (1983), was a seminal text in this tradition closely associated with the ethnography of communication perspective, and you might find it helpful to consult that as you engage with the texts presented here. The material included here focuses on the everyday meanings and uses of literacy in specific cultural contexts. Bartlett and Holland, for instance, apply new ideas about literacy and identity to work in Latin America, whilst Barton and Hamilton focus on literacy practices in on a town in northern England. Recent books and articles have also located these approaches to literacy within the broader context of multilingual literacies (cf. Section B4.3), of multimodality and of what Gee et al. (1996) term 'the new work order' (see Section C3.1). There has also, recently, been a debate within social approaches to literacy regarding what Brandt and Clinton (2002) refer to as 'the limits of the local' – they and others (cf. Collins and Blot, 2003) question the 'situated' approach to literacy practices as not giving sufficient recognition to the ways in which literacy usually comes from outside of a particular community's 'local' experience. Street (2003; also available at http://www.tc.columbia.edu/cICE/Archives/5.2/52street.pdf) summarises a number of these texts and the arguments they put forward and offers some counter-arguments from an ethnographic perspective.

B4.1 LITERACY PRACTICES

David Barton and Mary Hamilton, along with other colleagues at Lancaster University such as Roz Ivanic, have been responsible for a considerable number of publications in the field of literacy as a social practice (see Annotated Bibliography) and their work has been hugely influential both in the UK and internationally. Their ethnographic study of everyday literacy practices in Lancaster, England, which they refer to here as 'local literacies' following the title of their 1998 book, ranks with Shirley Brice Heath's *Ways with words* as one of the classic texts in this approach. The selection here is chosen to highlight the conceptual apparatus developed by those working in social approaches to literacy. Drawing upon Heath (1983), Scribner and Cole (Section B3.2), and Street (Section B3.3), they develop further the concepts of literacy events and literacy practices.

Barton, D., Hamilton, M. and Ivanic, R. (2000) *Situated literacies: reading and writing in context* (London: Routledge), 'Literacy practices', Barton and Hamilton, pp. 7–15.

Text B4.1
D. Barton,
M. Hamilton
and R. Ivanic

Literacy practices

A *social theory of literacy: practices and events*

In this chapter we provide a framework in terms of a theory of literacy. It is a brief overview of a social theory of literacy. This can be seen as the starting-point or orienting theory, which the detailed studies in this book then expand upon, react to and develop. We define what is meant by literacy practices and literacy events and explain some of the tenets of a social theory of literacy. This is pursued in Barton and Hamilton (1998), where a further example of situated literacies not covered in this book can be found.

We present here the theory of literacy as social practice in the form of a set of six propositions about the nature of literacy, as in Figure 1.1. The starting-point of this approach is the assertion that *literacy is a social practice*, and the propositions are an elaboration of this. The discussion is a development on that in Barton (1994, pp. 34–52), where contemporary approaches to literacy are discussed within the framework of the metaphor of ecology. The notion of *literacy practices* offers a powerful way of conceptualising the link between the activities of reading and writing and the social structures in which they are embedded and which they help shape. When we talk about practices then, this is not just the superficial choice of a word but the possibilities that this perspective offers for new theoretical understandings about literacy.

Our interest is in social practices in which literacy has a role, hence the basic unit of a social theory of literacy is that of *literacy practices*. Literacy practices are the general cultural ways of utilising written language which people draw upon in their lives. In the simplest sense literacy practices are what people do with literacy. However practices are not observable units of behaviour since they also involve values, attitudes, feelings and social relationships (see Street 1993, p. 12, and Street, 1984 for an early account of literacy events and practices). This includes people's awareness of literacy, constructions of literacy and discourses of literacy, how people talk about and make sense of literacy. These are processes internal to the individual: at the same time, practices are the social processes which connect people with one another, and they include shared cognitions represented in ideologies and social identities. Practices are shaped by social rules which regulate the use and distribution of texts, prescribing who may produce and have access to them. They straddle the distinction between individual and social worlds, and literacy practices are more usefully understood as existing in the relations between people, within groups and communities, rather than a set of properties residing in individuals.

D. Barton,
M. Hamilton
and R. Ivanic

Literacy is best understood as a set of social practices; these can be inferred from events which are mediated by written texts.

There are different literacies associated with different domains of life.

Literacy practices are patterned by social Institutions and power relationships, and some literacies are more dominant visible and Influential than others.

Literacy practices are purposeful and embedded in broader social goals and cultural practices.

Literacy is historically situated.

Literacy practices change and new ones are frequently acquired through processes of informal learning and sense making.

To avoid confusion, it is worth emphasising that this usage is different from situations where the word *practice* is used to mean learning to do something by repetition. It is also different from the way the term is used in recent international surveys of literacy to refer to 'common or typical activities or tasks' (OECD/Statistics Canada, 1995). The notion of practices as we have defined it above – cultural ways of utilising literacy – is a more abstract one that cannot wholly be contained in observable activities and tasks.

Turning to another basic concept, *literacy events* are activities where literacy has a role. Usually there is a written text, or texts, central to the activity and there may be talk around the text. Events are observable episodes which arise from practices and are shaped by them. The notion of events stresses the situated nature of literacy, that it always exists in a social context. It is parallel to ideas developed in sociolinguistics and also, as Jay Lemke has pointed out, to Bahktin's assertion that the starting point for the analysis of spoken language should be 'the social event of verbal interaction', rather than the formal linguistic properties of texts in isolation (Lemke, 1995).

Many literacy events in life are regular, repeated activities, and these can often be a useful starting-point for research into literacy. Some events are linked into routine sequences and these may be part of the formal procedures and expectations of social institutions like work places, schools and welfare agencies. Some events are structured by the more informal expectations and pressures of the home or peer group. Texts are a crucial part of literacy events and the study of literacy is partly a study of texts and how they are produced and used. These three components, practices, events and texts, provide the first proposition of a social theory of literacy, that *literacy is best understood as a set of social practices; these are observable in events which are mediated by written texts.* The local literacies study (Barton and Hamilton, 1998) was concerned with identifying the events and texts of everyday life and describing people's associated practices. Our prime interest there was to analyse events in order to learn about practices. As with the definition of practices, we take a straightforward view of events at this point, as being activities which involve written texts; discussion throughout this book returns to the definitions of these terms. An example of an everyday literacy event, taken from the local literacies study, is that of cooking a pudding; it is described below.

This work complements other studies, primarily in Linguistics, which focus on the analysis of texts. The study of everyday literacy practices points attention to the texts of everyday life, the texts of personal life; these are distinct from other texts which are more usually studied such as educational texts, mass media texts and other published texts. Work in the field of literacy studies adds the perspective of practices to studies of texts, encompassing what people do with texts and what these activities mean to them. In our own work, practices remain central and we are led to examine how texts

D. Barton,
M. Hamilton
and R. Ivanic

fit into the practices of people's lives, rather than the other way round. Nevertheless, we see the full study of written language as exemplified in the chapters in this book, as being the analysis of both texts and practices.

Once one begins to think in terms or literacy events there are certain things about the nature of reading and writing which become apparent. For instance, in many literacy events there is a mixture of written and spoken language. Many studies of literacy practices have print literacy and written texts as their starting point but it is clear that in literacy events people use written language in an integrated way as part of a range of semiotic systems; these semiotic systems include mathematical systems, musical notation, maps and other non-text based images. The cookery text has numeracy mixed with print literacy and the recipes come from books, magazines, television and orally from friends and relatives. By identifying literacy as one of a range of communicative resources available to members of a community, we can examine some of the ways in which it is located in relation to other mass media and new technologies. This is especially pertinent at a time of rapidly changing technologies.

When baking a lemon pie in her kitchen, Rita follows a recipe. She uses it to check the amounts of the ingredients. She estimates the approximate amounts, using teacups and spoons chosen specially for this purpose. The recipe is hand written on a piece of note-paper. It was written out from a book by a friend more than ten years ago. The first time she read the recipe carefully at each stage, but now she only looks at it once or twice. The piece of paper is marked and greasy by having been near the cooking surface on many occasions. It is kept in an envelope with other hand written recipes and ones cut out of magazines and newspapers. The envelope and some cookery books are on a shelf in the kitchen. The books range in age and condition and include some by Robert Carrier. Sometimes she sits and reads them for pleasure.

. . .

Rita does not always follow recipes exactly, but will add herbs and spices to taste; sometimes she makes up recipes; at one point she describes making a vegetable and pasta dish similar to one she had had as a take-away meal. She exchanges recipes with other people, although she does not lend her books.

Looking at different literacy events it is clear that literacy is not the same in all contexts; rather, there are different *literacies* (cf. Street, 1984). The notion of different literacies has several senses: for example, practices which involve different media or symbolic systems, such as a film or computer, can be regarded as different literacies, as in *film literary* and *computer literacy*. Another sense is that practices in different cultures and languages can be regarded as different literacies. While accepting these senses of the term, the main way in which we use the notion here is to say that literacies are coherent configurations of literacy practices; often these sets of practices are identifiable and named, as in *academic literacy* or *work-place literacy* and they are associated with particular aspects of cultural life.

This means that, within a given culture, *there are different literacies associated with different domains of life*. Contemporary life can be analysed in a simple way into domains of activity, such as home, school, work-place. It is a useful starting-point to examine the distinct practices in these domains, and then to compare, for example, home and school, or school and work-place. We begin with the home domain and everyday life. The home is often identified as a primary domain in people's literacy lives, for example by James Gee (1990), and central to people's developing sense of social identity. Work is another identifiable domain, where relationships and resources are often structured quite differently from in the home. We might expect the practices associated with cooking, for example, to be quite different in the home and in the work-place

D. Barton,
M. Hamilton
and R. Ivanic

– supported, learned and carried out in different ways. The division of labour is different in institutional kitchens, the scale of the operations, the clothing people wear when cooking, the health and safety precautions they are required to take, and so on. Such practices contribute to the idea that people participate in distinct *discourse communities*, in different domains of life. These communities are groups of people held together by their characteristic ways of talking, acting, valuing, interpreting and using written language. (See discussion in Swales, 1990, pp. 23–7.)

Domains, and the discourse communities associated with them, are not clear-cut, however: there are questions of the permeability of boundaries, of leakages and movement between boundaries, and of overlap between domains. Home and community, for instance, are often treated as being the same domain; nevertheless they are distinct in many ways, including the dimension of public and private behaviour. An important part of the local literacies study was to clarify the domain being studied and to tease apart notions of home, household, neighbourhood and community. Another aspect is the extent to which this domain is a distinct one with its own practices, and the extent to which the practices that exist in the home originate there, or home practices are exported to other domains. In particular, the private home context appears to be infiltrated by practices from many different public domains.

Domains are structured, patterned contexts within which literacy is used and learned. Activities within these domains are not accidental or randomly varying: there are particular configurations of literacy practices and there are regular ways in which people act in many literacy events in particular contexts. Various institutions support and structure activities in particular domains of life. These include family, religion and education, which are all social institutions. Some of these institutions are more formally structured than others, with explicit rules for procedures, documentation and legal penalties for infringement, whilst others are regulated by the pressure of social conventions and attitudes. Particular literacies have been created by and are structured and sustained by these institutions. Part of this study aims to highlight the ways in which institutions support particular literacy practices.

Socially powerful institutions, such as education, tend to support dominant literacy practices (cf. Street and Street, 1991). These dominant practices can be seen as part of whole discourse formations, institutionalised configurations of power and knowledge which are embodied in social relationships. Other vernacular literacies which exist in people's everyday lives are less visible and less supported. This means that *literacy practices are patterned by social institutions and power relationships, and some literacies are more dominant, visible and influential than others*. One can contrast dominant literacies and vernacular literacies; many of the studies in this book are concerned more with documenting the vernacular literacies which exist, and with exploring their relationship to more dominant literacies.

People are active in what they do and *literacy practices are purposeful and embedded in broader social goals and cultural practices*. Whilst some reading and writing is carried out as an end in itself, typically literacy is a means to some other end. Any study of literacy practices must therefore situate reading and writing activities in these broader contexts and motivations for use. In the cooking example, for instance, the aim is to bake a lemon pie, and the reading of a recipe is incidental to this aim. The recipe is incorporated into a broader set of domestic social practices associated with providing food and caring for children, and it reflects broader social relationships and gendered divisions of labour.

Classic studies of literacies in the home, such as those by Heath (1983) and Taylor and Dorsey-Gaines (1988), have offered classifications of the functions and uses of

D. Barton,
M. Hamilton
and R. Ivanic

literacy for individuals . . . It is [however] very clear from our local literacies work that a particular type of text, such as diary or letter, cannot be used as a basis for assigning functions, as reading or writing any vernacular text can serve many functions; people appropriate texts for their own ends. Just as a text does not have autonomous meanings (cf. Street, 1984) which are independent of its social context of use, a text also does not have a set of functions independent of the social meanings with which it is imbued.

A first step in reconceptualising literacy is to accept the multiple functions literacy may serve in a given activity, where it can replace spoken language, enable communication, solve a practical problem or act as a memory aid – in some cases, all at the same time. It is also possible to explore the further work which literacy can do in an activity, and the social meanings it takes on. For instance, there are ways in which literacy acts as *evidence*, as *display*, as *threat*, and as *ritual*. Texts can have multiple roles in an activity and literacy can act in different ways for the different participants in a literacy event; people can be incorporated into the literacy practices of others without reading or writing a single word. The acts of reading and writing are not the only ways in which texts are assigned meaning (as in Barton and Hamilton, 1998, Ch. 14).

It is important to shift from a conception of literacy located in individuals to examine ways in which people in groups utilise literacy. In this way literacy becomes a community resource, realised in social relationships rather than a property of individuals. This is true at various levels; at the detailed micro level it can refer to the fact that in particular literacy events there are often several participants taking on different roles and creating something more than their individual practices. At a broader macro level it can mean the ways in which whole communities use literacy. There are social rules about who can produce and use particular literacies and we wish to examine this social regulation of texts. Shifting away from literacy as an individual attribute is one of the most important implications of a practice account of literacy, and one of the ways in which it differs most from more traditional accounts. The ways in which literacy acts as a resource for different sorts of groups are a central theme of Barton and Hamilton (1998), which describes some of the ways in which families, local communities and organisation regulate and are regulated by literacy practices.

Literacy practices are culturally constructed, and, like all cultural phenomena, they have their roots in the past. To understand contemporary literacy it is necessary to document the ways in which *literacy is historically situated*: literacy practices are as fluid, dynamic and changing as the lives and societies of which they are a part. We need a historical approach for an understanding of the ideology, culture and traditions on which current practices are based. The influences of one hundred years of compulsory schooling in Britain, or several centuries of organised religion, can be identified in the same way as influences from the past decade can be identified. These influences are located partly in the literacy practices themselves, complemented by family memories which go back to the beginning of the century and earlier. There is also a broader context of a cultural history of three thousand years of literacy in the world, and the ways in which this shapes contemporary practices.

A person's practices can also be located in their own history of literacy. In order to understand this we need to take a life history approach, observing the history within a person's life (cf. Sheridan, Street and Bloome, 2000). There are several dimensions to this: people use literacy to make changes in their lives; literacy changes people and people find themselves in the contemporary world of changing literacy practices. The literacy practices an individual engages with change across their lifetime, as a result of changing demands, available resources, as well as the possibilities and their interests.

Extension

Related to the constructed nature of literacy, any theory of literacy implies a theory of learning. *Literacy practices change and new ones are frequently acquired through processes of informal learning and sense making* as well as formal education and training. This learning takes place in particular social contexts and part of this learning is the internalisation of social processes. It is therefore important to understand the nature of informal and vernacular learning strategies and the nature of situated cognition, linking with the work of researchers influenced by Lev Vygotsky, such as Sylvia Scribner, Jean Lave and colleagues (Scribner, 1984; Lave and Wenger, 1991). For this it is necessary to draw upon people's insights into how they learn, their theories about literacy and education, the vernacular strategies they use to learn new literacies. We start out from the position that people's understanding of literacy is an important aspect of their learning, and that people's theories guide their actions. It is here that a study of literacy practices has its most immediate links with education.

Task B4.1.1: Literacy events and practices

We would now like to suggest some ways you can take hold of Barton and Hamilton's seminal analysis of literacy events and practices and begin to apply the ideas in contexts you are familiar with. On the one hand this should help clarify the ideas and on the other it can help test out their value and indeed their robustness – do they work when applied in contexts you know about and, if not, how might they need to be modified? How do they compare with the other ideas about literacy that were outlined in earlier sections, regarding 'acquisition' and 'cognitive consequences'?

We envisage readers pausing for a moment after reading the text, to reflect individually upon some questions for a few minutes before moving on to the next passage. You might start with questions designed to prompt and facilitate your thinking about the texts. In this case we suggest you take an example, comparable to the 'cooking literacy' cited by Barton and Hamilton, such as cinema literacy, and ask similar questions.

➤ What kinds of literacy events and practices are associated with going to the cinema?

You might monitor your own behaviour as you first read a review in a newspaper or journal; then look up the local cinemas to see when that film is on; you will perhaps check your diary to see when you are free to go and then phone some friends to go with you, accessing their numbers via your mobile or home telephone. Numeracy events link in here with literacy events, as Street, Baker and Tomlin (2005) have recently demonstrated. The film itself involves considerable use of written text, with credits at the beginning and end, but you might also look out for uses of text in the film set itself: for example, in the film *Capote*, the suspect's diaries were shown to the viewer and played a key part in Capote's writing up of the crime. Barton and Hamilton ask questions about 'domain' – where is the literacy event situated? They point out that domains sometimes overlap, as between home and community, but sometimes when we look closer they are differentiated by the participants and those differences are important to the kind of literacy engaged with. In the case of cooking literacy, the stance and attitude taken by participants to both the activity and the text will be different whether it takes place in the home domain or in the workplace. Similarly, cinema literacy straddles a number of domains – it may begin in the home, indeed if you broaden the definition to take in film watching more generally, then it may remain in the home as you bring back a DVD from a hire shop to show in your own sitting room. There will still be literacy events and practices associated with this, including reading about the film and also identifying films and their genres as you look along the video shop shelves.

Having provided a description of some such everyday literacy events and practice you are familiar with, in order to put Barton and Hamilton's scheme into practice, you might now begin to use your own experiences to ask more penetrating questions of these ideas and concepts.

Task B4.1.2: Structures and institutions

One way of doing this might be to engage in discussion with another reader. The questions we envisage at this point might arise from 10–15-minute small group discussions as part of a seminar or workshop. Here you might pursue Barton and Hamilton's ideas further by asking about the 'structuring' of the domains in which particular literacies are involved. They say:

> Domains are structured, patterned contexts within which literacy is used and learned. Activities within these domains are not accidental or randomly varying: there are particular configurations of literacy practices and there are regular ways in which people act in many literacy events in particular contexts. Various institutions support and structure activities in particular domains of life.

In discussion you might ask:

➤ Which institutions support and structure the literacy practices you are focusing on?

Cinema practices are embedded in much larger commercial activities, ranging from Hollywood production companies to small Independents. Different cinemas may show films from different sources. You may find different kinds of reading associated with these structures: the local art cinema may provide lengthy, academic-like accounts of films with contrary and complex reviews; the UGC and Odeon may provide brief snapshots of the films on show with the aim of persuading you to go. You may even choose a film in connection not only with the review and commentary but with the kind of text written about it – if you want an escape then the lighter advertising text may do, if you want 'serious' reflection and insight you might look for a kind of text that provides this, irrespective of whether the commentary itself is positive or negative.

You may be familiar with the concept of 'genre' from literature and indeed film studies and it may be helpful here in developing the idea raised earlier by Barton and Hamilton that 'literacy is not the same in all contexts; rather, there are different *literacies*' or, you might add, different 'genres' of literacy. But they also link this variation to social institutions not just individuals, as we have seen, and these in turn implicate 'power relationships – some literacies are more dominant, visible and influential than others':

➤ What kinds of power relationships are involved in the literacy practices you have chosen to focus on?

For example, in the cooking example you might discuss the gender implications of locating cooking in the home or in a restaurant and check out whether the texts associated with these different domains reinforce their potential to create social hierarchy. With respect to the cinema there may be rankings associated with art cinema and Hollywood, again associated as we noted above with different genres of writing. One finding such a discussion may generate is that literacy is only part of the picture being described, that we can't just isolate literacy from its social context. This would fit with the arguments about literacy being explored in this section that focuses on social practice approaches.

B4.2 LITERACY AND IDENTITY

In a paper that develops nicely the notions of literacy events and practices previously discussed by Barton and Hamilton, Bartlett and Holland argue that we should 'reconsider and broaden these conceptions of practice'. Drawing on innovations in the cultural historical school of psychology, sociocultural theory, and social practice theory, they propose an expanded conception of the space of literacy practice. They link work in literacy to broader social theory, such as Bourdieu's concept of *habitus*, although they indicate limits here in 'his tendency to underplay the importance of culturally produced narratives, images and other artifacts in modifying habitus'. They propose three concepts that might help move both social theory and literacy studies forward: figured worlds, artefacts, and identities in practice. You might consider how such concepts could be applied in your own context and what they would add.

Bartlett, L., and Holland, D. (2002) 'Theorizing the space of literacy practices', *Ways of Knowing Journal*, 2(1), 10–22.

Text B4.2
L. Bartlett
and D. Holland

Introduction[1]

'Practice' indexes a meta-theory in anthropology, sociology, linguistics, education and other fields of study. It signals a shift away from fetishizing culture, language, literacy and other social phenomena. No longer do we distill these processes from social life and conceive them as self-perpetuating essences capable of animating human actors. Instead we use the phrase 'in practice' to invoke pragmatics and a core of actors using cultural resources (which themselves undergo transformation) toward some culturally given end, all the while immersed in the flow of social life. In this article, we invoke cultural historical concepts of 'practice' developed from Bakhtin, Leont'ev, Vygotsky, and others to enhance practice theory and the notion of literacy practices, which is central to the field of literacy studies. Our main task is to elucidate a theory of the *space of practice*, including key concepts such as *figured worlds*, *artifacts*, *hybrid actors*, and *identities in practice*. Literacy, numeracy and other such activities can be productively analyzed using this approach, as we demonstrate in the second half of the paper when we apply the proposd concepts to an analysis of literacy practices in a Brazilian classroom.

Literacy studies

The field of literacy studies, while incorporating cognitive and psychological approaches, maintains a strong social tradition emanating from sociocultural anthropology (Heath 1983, Street 1984), cultural psychology (Scribner and Cole 1981), socio- and applied linguistics (Gee 1990, Barton and Hamilton 1998, Barton 1994, Baynham 1995), among other approaches. In the 1960s and 1970s, literacy studies remained mired in the claims that literacy had universal cognitive, social, or economic 'consequences' for individuals and/or societies (see, e.g., Goody 1968 and 1977, Ong 1982). In 1984, by integrating contemporary literacy research and adding his own ethnographic research on literacy practices in Iran, Brian Street initiated a paradigmatic revolution. He demonstrated that literacy had to be reconceived as embedded in and working through particular cultural, historical, political, and social contexts. In developing his 'ideological model,' so named in order to capture the negotiations of power involved in reading and writing (as well as in studies about reading and writing), Street relied on two concepts: literacy events and literacy practices.

Street adopted the notion of events from Shirley Brice Heath, who in her ethnography of three communities in the Southern United States defined literacy events as 'occasion[s] in which a piece of writing is integral to the nature of participants' interactions and their interpretive processes' (Heath 1982: 50). With the concept of literacy practices, Street wished to embed these moments within a larger

1 Acknowledgements: We would like to thank Dave Baker; Mike Baynham, and Betty Johnston, the organizers of the Literacy and Numeracy Conference in Leeds in July 2001, as well as the other conference participants, for their intellectual camaraderie. We are also indebted to two anonymous reviewers for the *Ways of Knowing Journal* for their insightful comments.

Extension

social, cultural, and ideological frame that would include participants' 'folk models of those events and the ideological preconceptions that underpin them' (Street 1993: 12–I 3).[2] A focus on literacy practices incorporates not only the social, political, and historical contexts of literacy events, but also the relations of social power that envelop them.

More recently, literacy theorists have endeavored to link literacy practices to the discourses that situate them. Discourses, according to Gunther Kress, are 'systematically organized sets of statements which give expression to the meanings and values of an institution. Beyond that, they define, describe and delimit what it is possible to say and not possible to say (and by extension – what it is possible to do or not to do) with respect to an area of concern of that institution, whether marginally or centrally' (Kress 1989: 7). In other words, discourses are institutionally defined, socially acceptable ways of thinking, doing, or saying. Baynham offers the example of the Back to Basics movement, a powerful discourse elaborated by groups with particular political interests that redirected schooling and school literacy practices for a decade (Baynham 1995: 10).

Linguist James Gee defined discourses much more widely. He characterized 'Discourse' (with a capital 'D') as:

> saying (writing)-doing-being-valuing-believing combinations . . . ways of being in the world; they are forms of life which integrate words, acts, values, beliefs, attitudes, and social identities as well as gestures, glances, body positions, and clothes. A Discourse is a sort of 'identity kit' which comes complete with the appropriate costume and instructions on how to act talk, and often write, so as to take on a particular role that others will recognize.

> (1996: 127)

For Gee, Discourses display social identities. Gee argued that second Discourse mastery is achieved through acquisition, or apprenticeship through immersion. However; he argued, the acquisition of a liberating literacy, defined as a way of using a Discourse to 'critique other literacies and the way they constitute us as persons and situate us in society' requires learning through overt instruction and the explicit juxtaposition and comparison of Discourses (138–141) . . . literacy researchers often incorporate a notion of discourse, though the term's connotations vary widely in contemporary work.

In sum, social studies of literacy or what has been dubbed New Literacy Studies, centers around the concept of literacy practices, which includes participants' cultural models of literacy events, social interactional aspects of literacy events, text production and interpretation, ideologies, discourses, and institutions (Baynham 1995: 1–5).

We propose to augment this theoretical frame by focusing on the production of literacy identities in relation to social structures and cultural worlds. To do this, we expand Bourdieu's concept of linguistic habitus by joining it with more recent developments in studies of identities-in-practice.

2 For Street, this shift entails a methodological change as well, from a sociointeractional analysis of the moment to broader, long-term participant observation in multiple domains of literacy (Street 2001: 11).

Proposed extension of theoretical frame

L. Bartlett
and D. Holland

Bourdieu's social practice theory explores the ways in which social structures influence actors and practice (1977). While people cannot escape the influence of social structures, structures cannot persist without at least a modicum of people's unforced compliance and the continual reconstruction of structures to fit changing conditions. The concept of *habitus* captures this dynamic. *Habitus* is composed of socially and historically constituted, durable, embodied dispositions to act in certain ways. It results from a person's history of interactions with structures, and strongly influences future actions. The key moment in Bourdieu's theory occurs in practice, in the encounter between structures (history brought to the present in institutions) and *habitus* (history brought to the present in person) (Holland and Lave 2001). Bourdieu's theory suggests that we analyze literacy events with an eye to the ways in which historical and social forces have shaped a person's linguistic *habitus* and thus impinge upon that person's actions in the moment.

However; Bourdieu's theory remains limited by his tendency to underplay the importance of culturally produced narratives, images and other artifacts in modifying *habitus*. We propose to strengthen a practice theoretical approach to literacy studies by specifying the space of literacy practice, examining in particular the locally operant figured world of literacy identities in practice, and artifacts.

The concept of the *figured world*[3] helps us rethink practice approaches. A figured world is a socially produced and culturally constructed 'realm of interpretation in which a particular set of characters and actors are recognized, significance is assigned to certain acts, and particular outcomes are valued over others' (Holland et al. 1998: 52). Figured worlds are populated by a set of actors and agents who engage in a limited range of meaningful acts or state changes in a particular situation. For example, a figured world of literacy might include 'functional illiterates,' 'good readers,' and 'illiterates' who struggle to become literate or demonstrate their literacy in a variety of settings, including the classroom, the marketplace, and home, Figured worlds are invoked, animated, contested, and enacted through artifacts, activities, and identities in practice.

Cultural worlds are continuously figured in practice through the use of cultural artifacts, or objects inscribed by the collective attribution of meaning (see Holland et al. 1998, Chapters 2 and 3). An artifact can assume a material aspect (which may be as transient as a spoken word or as durable as a book) and/or an ideal or conceptual aspect. These objects are constructed as a part of and in relation to recognized activities – e.g., the tokens of sobriety and life stories significant in Alcoholics Anonymous, 'sexy' clothes and gender-marked labels such as 'babes' or 'male chauvinist pigs' in college student romance, or patients' charts and medications in psychiatric hospitals. Artifacts meaningful to the figured world of literacy might include blackboards or textbooks (in the classroom), reading assessment scales, road-signs or signing ceremonies (in public space). Such artifacts 'open up' figured worlds; they are the means by which figured worlds are evoked, grown into individually and collectively developed. Artifacts are social constructions or products of human activity,

3 Boaler and Greeno (2000) have used the concept of 'figured worlds' to describe the figuring of mathematics classrooms in the United States and the kinds of learner identities that the different figurings afford. (See also Luttrell and Parker 2001.)

L. Bartlett
and D. Holland

and they in turn may become tools engaged in processes of cultural production. Significantly, a particular person may even, in practice, be collectively constructed as a social artifact. Individuals regularly get construed as symbols of something – say of beauty, or intelligence, or geekiness. They can then be used to signify in the figured world. Their invocation, presence or absence can serve, by evoking a world of social action peopled by valued and devalued types, to discipline others. People constantly produce artifacts that may become important in refiguring cultural worlds, giving flesh to new identities, and so eventually transforming habitus.

Cultural artifacts are essential to the making and remaking of human actors. In the theoretical strands interwoven by Holland et al. (1998), humans plus artifacts compose hybrid actors. Writing in the 1920s and early 1930s, Vygotsky and other members of the cultural historical school envisioned a fusion of humans and cultural artifacts. Through Vygotskian semiotic mediation, such artifacts are central to human's abilities to modulate their own behavior, cognition and emotion. In such practices, the reliance on artifacts as tools of self-management can become routine to the point that one resorts to them out of awareness, automatically. In other words, frequent practices become 'fossilized.' From a Vygotskian perspective, through this process of 'heuristic development' – a sort of opportunistic, symbolic bootstrapping – humans achieve a modicum of control over their own behavior and thus some degree of agency.[4]

Holland et al. extend Vygotsky's idea of semiotic mediation to the development of *identities in practice*. People use objectifications of social identities, e.g., images, narratives, labels, or memories of past events, to manage their own feelings, thoughts, behavior and actions on a broad scale. Over time and in practice, then, people organize mental and emotional labor through hybrid action with cultural and social artifacts. Thus, in addition to positional aspects of identities, which 'have to do with one's position relative to socially identified others, one's sense of social place, and entitlement,' Holland et al. emphasize figurative aspects of senses of self that develop in relation to 'figured worlds – storylines, narrativity, generic characters, and desire' (125). In this way they unite a cultural and a social approach to the question of identity formation. Holland et al. emphasize figured worlds as spaces of practice wherein actors form as well as perform. Particular persons are figured collectively in practice as fitting certain social identities and thereby positioned in power relations. Over time actors grow into such worlds, figuring themselves as actors in those worlds and gaining a sense of their position, their standing, in the relations of power that characterize the particular community of practice. Identities, conceptualized in this fashion, have a double-sided quality. They are simultaneously social phenomena and phenomena of the person. They are social in that they participate in relations of power and are imagined in social narratives. Moreover, particular persons are socially figured (constructed) according to these identities. At the same time, identities are personal phenomena in that they are important on intimate terrain as well. A person may construct herself for herself in the figured world. Personal identities with their figurative or narrativized aspects and their relational or positional aspects are important components of 'history in person' (see also Holland and Lave 2001).

4 Actor Network theorists such as Latour, Callon, Law and others also describe hybrid actors – actors composed of humans plus artifacts. While discussing analogous and interrelated processes to those described in Holland et al. 1998 actor network theorists focus on the institutionalization of artifacts as agents.

By adopting cultural artifacts of particular figured worlds and rehearsing them in communities of practice, social actors develop the ability to challenge the incapacitating effects of negative social positioning. Holland et al. argue that, while social positioning becomes embodied as habitus and generally remains out of awareness, semiotic mediation through cultural artifacts offers one means of acquiring some voluntary control over one's thoughts, feelings, and actions. In other words, the social construction of appealing, culturally plausible artifacts in a figured world offers an opportunity for social change, one person at a time.

[In the last section of the paper, based on Bartlett's fieldwork (Bartlett, 2001), they apply the concepts of figured world, artefacts, and positional and figured identity formation to literacy in contemporary Brazil.[5]]

Conclusions

In this article, we offered an enhanced theoretical approach to literacy practices. Previous studies situated literacy events within an ideological framework that included participants' cultural models of literacy. The concept of figured worlds both expands the notion of cultural models and augments our understanding of social practices. We argue that selves form in relation to, and practices are embedded within, socially organized and historically situated spheres of activity called figured worlds (Holland et al. 1998: 40–41). Social actors learn to refigure the meanings of certain practices and reposition themselves socially through the use of cultural artifacts, which evoke figured worlds. By 'space of practice,' we mean to go beyond reduced ideas of practice to conceive of these practices as embedded in historically contingent, collectively produced, motive oriented, artifact-mediated, relational activities and the figured worlds they manifest. We view individual practices as components of cultural activities that are informed by relevant figured worlds and the cultural artifacts that evoke and sometimes re-imagine these worlds. From the Brazilian case, we described the figured world of the educated person, an ever changing, but somewhat durable, complex of ways to figure literacy activities and personages. People such as Eunisa and Maria (adult learners in the Brazil case study) and their shamers [i.e. people who have made them feel shame] have developed their practices and senses of themselves in relation to that figured world. To counter the habitual traces of symbolic violence and foster students' social identities as educated people, literacy programs must engage cultural notions of 'the educated person' and elaborate alternative figured worlds of education, with compelling artifacts of its own.

Task B4.2.1: Beyond events and practices?

We would now like to suggest some ways you can extend your understanding of the article by Bartlett and Holland. For starters, you might pick up our claim

5 This research was funded by the IIE-Fulbright Commission and the Inter-American Foundation.

in introducing this text that it 'develops nicely the notions of literacy events and practices discussed previously by Barton and Hamilton'. Bartlett and Holland say that they want to go farther than Barton and Hamilton, arguing that we should 'reconsider and broaden their conceptions of practice'. You might start by considering: how do you use the term 'practice'? In many professional contexts, including educational ones, the term 'practice' refers to what people actually do, often seen as differentiating 'practitioners' from theorists. The term is also used to refer to repeated activities from which we learn new ways of thinking and doing – we learn by 'practice'. Street sees 'practice' as including not only activities and behaviours but the participants' ideas, concepts, models about this activity (Street, 1988, 2000). Are these the meanings you attribute to the term or do you have yet other ways of using it? Having thought about this for a while, you might go back to the paper and check out how Bartlett and Holland are using the term 'practice'. For instance, they 'propose an expanded conception of the space of literacy practice', expanding the notion of literacy events and practices in Barton and Hamilton. As we saw above, practices in that context had a precise meaning – indeed Barton and Hamilton state: 'When we talk about practices then, this is not just the superficial choice of a word but the possibilities that this perspective offers for new theoretical understandings about literacy.' You have already given some thought to what these 'new theoretical understandings' might be. Now Bartlett and Holland are asking you to move further:

> In this article, we invoke cultural historical concepts of 'practice' developed from Bakhtin, Leont'ev, Vygotsky, and others to enhance practice theory and the notion of literacy practices, which is central to the field of literacy studies.

Without going back ourselves to these early writers, we find ourselves asking:

➤ What sense do Bartlett and Holland provide for 'enhancing' the notion of practice in the context of literacy studies?

Their main contribution, they claim, is to invoke 'the *space of practice*, including key concepts such as *figured worlds*, *artifacts*, *hybrid actors*, and *identities in practice*'. You might ask:

➤ How, then, are these different from what we saw in Barton and Hamilton?

➤ What meanings did these terms have for you before you encountered them here?

Reflecting on your own uses can provide a good starting point for then seeing how differently terms are being used by authors who are trying to help us understand things differently.

Task B4.2.2: Entering 'figured worlds'

Having clarified your own meanings of the terms being addressed here, you might now like to check out how they compare with others' uses. You might consider in turn the terms *figured worlds, artefacts, hybrid actors* and *identities in practice* and discuss whether you have met them before and if so in what contexts. As with 'practices' you may be familiar with a particular meaning of some of the terms but are being asked to suspend these as your authors delve into other meanings. Eventually we will all want to come round to the questions:

➤ What has this got to do with literacy?

➤ In what ways do these concepts add leverage in making sense of literacy as a social practice?

B4.2.3: Applying Bartlett and Holland's analytic frame

At this point it might be appropriate to move on to try to apply Bartlett and Holland's concepts to your own list and reflect on what they add. Indeed, Bartlett and Holland themselves conducted such an exercise in order to develop and test out their ideas. You might take a similar situation to that described in the Brazilian context – where Bartlett and Holland describe classrooms that are more than just places for imparting dominant knowledge. They use the Brazilian case to 'describe the figured world of the educated person, an ever changing, but somewhat durable, complex of ways to figure literacy activities and personages'. More concretely, they try to show how 'People such as Eunisa and Maria (adult learners in the Brazil case study) and their shamers have developed their practices and senses of themselves in relation to that figured world'. You might then try to find a situation in which you can similarly try out the concept of 'figured world' or of 'the space of literacy practices', such as a classroom, or a work situation or some everyday scene in which literacy plays a significant part – travel centres, bookshops etc. In looking at those familiar scenes through these new lenses, you might then ask:

➤ Does your conception of 'literacy' alter?

➤ How does this view of literacy compare with those you encountered in the articles in Section B1–3 or in the newspaper reports cited in Section A1?

By describing and then reflecting on concrete situations from your own experience, you will be in a strong position to 'take on' the complex concepts being provided by the authors you are encountering in this resource book. This, we hope, helps put you at the centre of the intellectual activity – in Bartlett and Holland's terms, you will be 'figuring' your world, or the world of your authors and coming to your own conclusions about what they mean and whether they are relevant to the figured world you already occupy.

B4.3 MULTILINGUAL LITERACIES

Marilyn Martin-Jones and Kathryn Jones's edited volume of papers *Multilingual literacies* (2000) provided an essential addition to the literature on social literacies by engaging with the issue of multilingualism and its relationship to speakers' knowledge and use of different literacies. In their Introduction to the volume they ask 'Why multilingual literacies?' and their answers provide a basis for both the research described there by different authors and for future research and practice in the field. They summarise what will by now be familiar to the reader, the approach to literacy from New Literacy Studies, but in this case they show how multilingual contexts, different languages, language varieties and scripts add other dimensions to the diversity and complexity of literacies. In this sense they provide an up-to-date commentary on and extension of the work already included in this section of the handbook.

Text B4.3 M.
Martin-Jones
and K. Jones

Martin-Jones, M., and Jones, K. (2000) *Multilingual literacies: reading and writing different worlds* **(Amsterdam and Philadelphia: J. Benjamins), 'Introduction: multilingual literacies', pp. 1–15.**

'Why multilingual literacies?'

Both of the terms in the title of this volume derive from debates that have taken place in adjacent fields of research: in the sociolinguistic study of Bilingualism and in the New Literacy Studies. The terms may have different connotations for different readers, so our aim here is to unpack this inter-textuality and to give brief insights into the debates that led to the increasing use of both terms. We will take each in turn, starting with the term 'literacies'.

Like other academics and practitioners who locate themselves within the New Literacy Studies tradition, we talk about literacies in the plural to signal a critique of the a-social, a-historical skill/ability understanding of reading and writing associated with what Brian Street has called the 'autonomous' view of literacy (Street 1984, 1993, 2001). Literacies are social practices: ways of reading and writing and using written texts that are bound up in social processes which locate individual action within social and cultural processes. These practices are partly observable in specific events, but also operate on a socio-cognitive level. They include the values, understandings, and intentions people have, both individually and collectively about what they and others do (Jones 1999: 39). Focusing on the plurality of literacies means recognising the diversity of reading and writing practices and the different genres, styles and types of texts associated with various activities, domains or social identities (see Street 1984; Barton 1994; Baynham 1995; Gee 1990; Ivanic 1998 for a fuller discussion of these arguments).

In multilingual contexts, different languages, language varieties and scripts add other dimensions to the diversity and complexity of literacies (see Hornberger 1989, 1990 for a detailed illustration of this). We use the term 'multilingual' rather than 'bilingual' in order to capture the multiplicity and complexity of individual and group repertoires. We do this for four main reasons. Firstly, the term multilingual provides the most accurate description of the communicative repertoires of many of the individuals and linguistic groups referred to in this volume: many have more than two spoken or written languages and language varieties within their communicative repertoire. These include the languages and literacies associated with their cultural inheritance, the regional varieties of English spoken in their local neighbourhoods and some form of standard English. Thus, for example, the Welsh speakers in the rural community described in the chapter by Kathryn Jones (Chapter 11) speak a regional variety of Welsh associated with Dyffryn Clwyd (the Vale of Clwyd in north east Wales). They also speak a regional Welsh variety of English. In addition, they read and write standard English. Another, slightly different example comes from the chapters by Eve Gregory and Anne Williams (Chapter 2) and by Adrian Blackledge (Chapter 3). The people whose literacy experiences are presented in these chapters speak Sylheti, a regional language spoken in the Sylhet region of Bangladesh but they read and write Bengali, the standard national language of the country. In the London context, described in Chapter 2, many Sylheti speakers are fluent in the English vernacular of East London, whilst in the Birmingham context, described in Chapter 3, many speak the local West Midlands variety of English. The shaping of the communicative repertoires of local linguistic minority groups of migrant origin depends, in this way, on the patterns of settlement in Britain.

Secondly, we have adopted the term 'multilingual' because it signals the multiplicity and complexity of the communicative purposes that have come to be associated with different spoken and written languages within a group's repertoire. As with the local vernacular varieties of English mentioned above and standard British English, the languages and literacies in the communicative repertoires of groups of migrant or refugee origin carry traces of the social structures and language ideologies of the country of origin. As Schieffelin, Woolard and Kroskrity (1998) and Blommaert (1999) have recently emphasised, language ideologies are intimately bound up with people's day-to-day choices with regard to the languages used for reading and writing in different public domains and for spoken communication in the more private spaces of their lives. Thus, for example, Sylheti speakers see Bengali as having more prestige and as being the 'appropriate' language of literacy, whilst Sylheti continues to be used as an important emblem of identity. Similarly, the Panjabi speakers of Pakistani origin introduced in the chapters by Yasmin Alam (Chapter 13) and Rachel Hodge and Kathryn Jones (Chapter 15) speak Panjabi and write in Urdu, the national language of Pakistan. Spoken and written Urdu is seen as carrying greater prestige than Panjabi, a language which is primarily used in its spoken form but one which still commands considerable language loyalty in Britain and in the Panjab area of Pakistan.

Some spoken or written languages in a group repertoire are acquired and used for highly specialised purposes. Take, for instance, the languages used for reading religious texts, during different forms of religious observance. Several of the Muslim groups mentioned in the chapters of this volume (Chapters 2, 3, 5, 7, 8, 12, 13, 14 and 15) use Qur'anic Arabic for reading aloud from the Qur'an. Urdu and English are also used by some groups of South Asian origin for silent reading of books on the principles of religious practice. People from local Hindu groups, such as the Gujarati and Panjabi speakers introduced in Chapters 8 and 14 respectively, use Hindi and Sanskrit for doing the readings from Hindu epics such as the *Gita*, *Mahabharat* and *Ramayan* which are associated with religious observance. These readings are usually accompanied by religious songs and chants in the same languages.

The third reason why we use the term 'multilingual' is to take account of the fact that in any linguistic minority household or local group, among speakers of Welsh, Gujarati or Cantonese, there are multiple paths to the acquisition of the spoken and written languages within the group repertoire and people have varying degrees of expertise in these languages and literacies. As the chapters in this volume show, the degree of expertise that individuals attain depends on how they are positioned with regard to access to different spoken and written varieties. For example, among some groups of migrant origin such as those from Bangladesh (see Chapters 2 and 3) or Pakistan (see Chapters 13 and 15), women have had fewer opportunities than men to acquire literacy in English, and even the literacies of their local community. Many young people from these linguistic minority groups have not had the opportunity to acquire the literacies of their cultural inheritance because of the lack of provision in Britain for the teaching of languages other than English or the prestigious languages of the European Community. This is an issue which is brought out in the chapters by Raymonde Sneddon (Chapter 7) and Ahmed Gurnah (Chapter 12). Where opportunities are available for young people to learn to read and write in their family's preferred language(s), they often have insufficient time to develop the expertise required to use the written languages for purposes which are meaningful to them and to other members of their family. Some languages and writing systems demand considerable investment of time and effort in the early stages of learning. An Ran stresses this point in Chapter 4 as she presents her study of Chinese children learning to read and write Chinese with their mothers at home, in an urban British context.

The fourth reason why the term 'multilingual' is more useful than the term 'bilingual' is because it focuses attention on the multiple ways in which people draw on and combine the codes in their communicative repertoire when they speak and write. The term 'bilingual' only evokes a two-way distinction between codes whereas, as we have noted above, in multilingual settings, people typically have access to several codes which they move in and out of with considerable fluency and subtlety as they speak and write. Whilst a monolingual norm may operate for the production of texts in an institutional context, the talk around those texts may be 'multilingual', incorporating elements of the text and stretches of talk in different language varieties. This phenomenon is captured particularly well in the long extracts of spoken data presented by Mike Baynham and Helen Lobanga Masing in Chapter 10.

The contrasts between codes in a multilingual repertoire are often employed by speakers and writers as a meaning making resource. This is what has come to be widely known as the metaphorical function of codeswitching (Blom and Gumperz 1972; Gumperz 1982; Heller 1988). In recent writing on codeswitching, it is acknowledged that the meaning making potential of codeswitching is infinite (Auer 1990). Moreover, as we have seen in recent empirical research in Britain (Li Wei 1994; Rampton 1995) the codeswitching practices of individuals and groups are continually shifting, with young people's practices being the most fluid and changeable.

Lastly, we should add that by combining the terms 'multilingual' and 'literacies' we intend to signal that the configurations of languages and literacies considered here are not viewed in a deterministic light. We also want to stress that specific practices which involve the use of different spoken and written languages are always undergoing a process of reaffirmation and redefinition, both within individual repertoires over individual life spans and at a broader cultural level.

Task B4.3.1: Why multilingual literacies?

We find here a new direction for discussions of literacy as social practice in the emphasis on *Multilingual literacies*, and we now propose some tasks. The editors introduce their volume with the question 'Why multilingual literacies?' and you might similarly want to start there:

> What difference does it make to think of literacies across different languages (and scripts?) rather than to work with a monolingual conception of literacy? Martin-Jones and Jones claim that 'attention to multilingual contexts, different languages, language varieties and scripts adds other dimensions to the diversity and complexity of literacies'.

Kathryn Jones provides an example, from her own background and research, of Welsh speakers in the rural community who speak a regional variety of Welsh associated with Dyffryn Clwyd (the Vale of Clwyd in north east Wales). They also speak a regional Welsh variety of English. In addition, they read and write standard English. The choices as to not only which language but which regional variety to use and as to how to write it are conditioned by context, by social relations and by hierarchies of power – it might be harder to use a regional variety when dealing with bureaucracy and under these pressures writers may switch to either the standard in the local language or, as in many cases in Wales, into English. That issue has been a cause of strong political debate in Wales (as similarly in multilingual countries such as Belgium and South Africa) – the President of France recently walked out of a European Union meeting when one of his members of parliament spoke in English rather than French; even the powerful feel threatened by other people's choices.

When we add a variety of scripts to the variety of languages the situation becomes more complex. In their Introduction to *Multilingual literacies*, Martin-Jones and Jones cite a number of articles in the book that deal with people who speak Sylheti, a regional language spoken in the Sylhet region of Bangladesh. These people also read and write Bengali, the standard national language of the country. In the London context many Sylheti speakers are fluent in the English vernacular of East London, whilst in the Birmingham context many speak the local West Midlands variety of English. Sylheti and Bengali are both written in Bengali script – with perhaps some variations such as those between written English and German – whilst certainly most children of Bengali migrants in London will now also be familiar with English (or 'roman') script. Switching between these languages and scripts depends on local factors, such as whom you are talking or writing to, and broader issues, such as the relations between Sylheti and Bengali immigrants in different parts of England. Again these examples might stimulate your own reflections on your language and script usage.

Martin-Jones and Jones add two further aspects of such choices: the use of scripts in association with religious observance, as with Hindi and Sanskrit for doing the readings from Hindu epics such as the *Gita, Mahabharat and Ramayan*; and Qur'anic Arabic for reading aloud from the Qur'an. They also raise the issue of access to different spoken and written varieties, some of which may seem harder to acquire as a second language or script.

In the light of these fresh insights and the rich data associated with them, you might like to reflect on your own experience and respond to the following questions:

➤ How would you describe your own engagement with literacy in these terms?

➤ Are you monolingual, or do you have a number of languages and/or scripts?

➤ If the former is the case, do you always use 'standard' when you are writing or do also have a repertoire of local varieties or dialects and if so do you try to represent these when you write certain genres, such as letters?

➤ If the latter is the case, what are the conditions in which you choose to use different languages or scripts?

Task B4.3.2: Multilingual literacies in your own experience

As you explore your own experience with these different dimensions of language and script variety, you might like to discuss with others how your experiences vary. Having established a preliminary account of your own trajectory and current use in response to the questions above and using some of the concepts and headings offered by Martin-Jones and Jones, you will be in a good position to make comparisons. This might lead to further questions:

➤ How different are your learning trajectories?

➤ Are you equally constrained by family pressures or institutional constraints?

➤ Did you move country or region at some point in your life and did this affect your language and script choice differently from those who have always lived in the same place?

You might want to obtain the book *Multilingual literacies: reading and writing different worlds* and read some of the chapters there about different languages and cultures, especially noting those that speak directly to your own experience.

Task B4.3.3: Mapping multilingual literacies in your community

As with the other activities you have engaged with through these sections of this resource book, you might now find it helpful to undertake an exercise that calls upon the specific concepts and findings of this text. Again you might write down some of the findings that have emerged from the preceding reflection and discussion – such as examples of different scripts and your experience of them; or an autobiographical account of your language learning history; or a map or spider diagram of the varieties of language and script you currently encounter in daily life. The larger questions about culture, identity and power that have arisen in the other readings in Sections B3 and B4 could then be brought to bear on these descriptions. You might find the questions below helpful for focusing this activity, although they will not cover all experiences and you might want to provide further examples of your own.

➤ What is the significance of Martin-Jones and Jones's statement: 'In multilingual contexts, different languages, language varieties and scripts add other dimensions to the diversity and complexity of literacies'?

➤ What is the importance of code switching (between languages and/or between scripts) in your own experience or that of someone you know? How does the work of Martin-Jones and Jones and their colleagues help you to describe and explain these processes?

B4.4 LITERACIES AT WORK

In this Section B4 on literacy as social practice, we have built upon the conclusion of Section B3 'Consequences of Literacy', by including texts that illustrate the way literacies change in different contexts (multilingualism, work) and other social aspects of literacy (e.g. identity). The following text by Gowen can be seen as bringing to bear on the workplace, many of the debates signalled earlier, with again a preference being indicated for social perspectives on literacy. She challenges dominant assumptions in workplace education and amongst many employers regarding the 'low literacy' skills of the workforce (assumptions which you might like to link with the texts in Section B2 on literacy acquisition and Section B3 on the consequences of literacy) and instead describes the everyday literacy practises evident in their lives (which you might link with other texts in Section B4 on 'literacy as social practice'). She suggests that if this knowledge were brought to bear in the workplace – the literacy knowledge of workers themselves and knowledge about these skills by employers – then the account of 'falling standards' and 'low skills' might be revised in a more positive direction.

Gowen, S. (1994) '"I'm no fool": reconsidering American workers and their literacies', in P. O'Connor (ed.) *Thinking work: theoretical perspectives on workers' literacies* (Sydney: Adult Literacy and Basic Skills Action Coalition), Vol. 1, pp. 123–135.

Text B4.4
S. Gowan

Mr. Stone: She [the supervisor] have picks, certain people she do certain things for. She don't think I'm smart enough to know that, but I told her just because I didn't go all the way through school don't mean I'm no fool. I know what be going on. She told me I notice too much. It's not the idea that I notice too much. If my eyes see it, I can't help but notice it.

Edward Stone works as a housekeeping aide in a large urban, public hospital in the Southeastern United States. In 1989, he attended classes in a workplace literacy program designed to improve his basic skills. Mr. Stone's goals in attending the program included passing the General Education Diploma (GED) and earning a promotion to the hospital's Security Department. But although Mr. Stone attended classes faithfully for the duration of the nine-month program and made considerable improvement in his reading and writing skills, he is still, as of this writing (1994), scrubbing floors and cleaning bathrooms in the hospital.

Mr. Stone's story, moreover, is not an isolated anomaly in an otherwise efficient process of ongoing worker education and advancement. Unfortunately, it is all too typical of current conditions in the American workplace. Mr. Stone's story tells us many things. It is at its core a tale of the tragic waste of human capability. When we ask why Mr. Stone has not advanced at work, the most common answer is that his skills are deficient and he lacks the credentials (a high school diploma or a GED) to successfully advance beyond entry-level work (for examples of this position see *The Bottom Line*, United States Departments of Labor and Education, 1988 and *America's Choice*, National Center on Education and the Economy, 1990). While this analysis has informed much of the nation's current educational policy, it explains only a portion of what needs to be fixed in the American work-place to ensure entry-level workers of adequate wages and decent work. It offers at best a distorted and inaccurate picture of the Mr. and Ms Stones in the American labour force because it fails to acknowledge what they do know, how they use (or do not use) this knowledge at work, and how the environments in which they work are neither constructed nor chosen as sites to display the many skills and abilities they possess.

In this chapter, therefore, I suggest another interpretation of Mr. Stone's story, and in the telling invite readers to reconsider American workers and their literacies by exploring two questions that are rarely addressed: In what ways do American educational policies and workplace structures contribute to men and women like Edward Stone remaining in entry-level jobs for a lifetime? And why is it that in a time of staggering economic and social change, workers' literacy levels are blamed for the economic distress of the nation?

Industry and schooling

The background for this story is familiar to many who have studied work in late-twentieth century America, but it is important to revisit this background to link it to national educational policy. At the turn of the century, American workplaces were reordered according to principles of scientific management. Frederick W. Taylor devised this system as a way to organise large numbers of the population into efficient assembly line workers (Whyte, 1984). As we know, the assumption behind Taylor's method was that tasks should be broken down into their simplest, least intellectually demanding forms. Workers then were trained to perform these tasks with mechanical efficiency. In the Newtonian sense, workers literally became extensions of machines, fine-tuning their individual skills to perfection. But Taylor's methods were more than merely prescriptions for performance. They were also part of a sweeping social reorganisation of the workplace that took both the application of personal knowledge and the control of work away from workers and placed both in the hands of professional, highly educated managers (Clawson, 1980; Whyte, 1984). Thus Taylorism not only produced an efficient workplace but also a hierarchy with high-wage, well-educated managers overseeing pools of low-wage, high-turnover workers who needed only basic educational skills to perform their work.

. . .

American schools, in their roles as educators of the future workforce, adapted many of Taylor's methods. Thus, for the masses, education has consisted of the skills needed to perform well in a highly industrialised economy. These skills included basic content matter with a heavy emphasis on obedience, punctuality, good manners (Erickson, 1984; de Castell and Luke, 1983). Problem-solving, critical thinking skills, and other forms of more creative reasoning were generally left to the elite classes who would fill managerial positions. Rather than being a failure at education, then, it could be argued that our schools have, through scientific, discrete, isolated instruments of precision in curriculum, pedagogy, and assessment reproduced the industrialised model that has driven the economy. Standardised tests, tracking, basal readers, and pull-out programs all echo Taylor's model of separation, segmentation, hierarchy, and control. The application of scientific management in the classroom has also disenfranchised teachers and parents, extending the effects of the general disenfranchisement to much of the working class . . .

The consequences of change

Since the end of the 1970s, however, global economic linkages, technological advances in production and communication, demographic shifts, and a decline in the birthrate have come together to create national alarm over the economy. Yet, even though there is growing awareness of the need to reorganise the workplace in the schools, much of the 'public discourse' (Hull, 1991) has chosen to focus on the literacy levels of the current workforce and the 'failure' of the schools as the problems that must be solved in order to make America great again. What this discourse accomplishes is a casting of blame for the ultimate flaws in Taylorism and industrialisation and the nation's resultant inability to compete in a more competitive and sophisticated global economy directly on American workers and the schools that have educated them. But, if we accept the argument that schools have successfully produced workers for an industrial economy – minimally educated workers who perform well in assembly line work – then blaming those same schools for not producing workers who have adequate literacy skills for more complex (post-industrial) jobs distracts the public from the simple fact that American businesses are in trouble for a wide variety of reasons that have nothing to do with worker illiteracy. These reasons include, but are not limited to, outdated and ineffective managerial practices, enormous economic disparities between workers and managers, institutionalised racism and sexism, shrinking benefits, loss of decent, full-time work, increases in work-related stress and injuries, and deeply rooted hostilities between labour and management.

Restructuring work

When the national conversation is not sniping at worker illiteracy, it is touting the need for massive workplace change, often referred to as restructuring, re-engineering or re-inventing. These transformations are derived from new theories of management and work procedures and have created a vast emerging market for publishers and consultants . . . Theoretically, in this new model, workers are valued as members of a democratic community committed to long-term achievement based on continuous learning, shared problem-solving, and participatory management. Some of the

S. Gowan

strategies generally recommended to accomplish this transformation include programmatic changes to achieve 'high performance', such as cross-training, chain-of-customers, and Just-in-Time (JIT) inventories as well as more organisational changes, such as becoming a 'learning organisation', with flattened hierarchies and worker 'empowerment' . . .

[Gowen argues that employers may invoke this more flattened hierarchy (cf. Gee et al., 1996, on the 'New Work Order') but the way they address educational and training issues in the workplace stems from a more hierarchical vision that misses the skills workers already have.]

. . .

S. Gowan

I would like to suggest that many entry-level workers already possess important skills and knowledge that are needed in more participatory work organisations, and that management is unable, because of its privileged and isolated position in the hierarchy, to recognise this.

High performance in the House of God

With this general background in place, let us return to the story of Edward Stone. But rather than begin with an examination of his workplace, we will start with a visit to Mr. Stone's church – the House of God, Rib Shack, and Used Car Lot. The House of God is located on the corner of a busy street in the heart of the working class African American community in Bayside, on the gulf coast. On sunny days, the well-dressed congregation will gather under the trees to eat ribs, visit, tell tales, talk junk, watch children play and maybe think about buying a car. The House of God, to my mind, exhibits many of the principles of the 'new' workplace . . . There are several aspects of the organisation of the House of God that lead to this interpretation. First, the hierarchy is very flat. There is a minister, of course, and he leads the services. But he has a lot of help. His nine children are all a part of the service as well, as is everyone over the age of about 16. And while he stands in the front and preaches, other members of the congregation join in – singing, testifying, speaking in tongues, dancing – 'getting happy'. The service is rarely about one man at a podium speaking to his congregation. Instead, there is action at all levels, participation, autonomy and creativity.

Moreover, each member plays a variety of parts (in the discourse of high performance they are 'cross-trained'). They play in the band, sing in the choir, collect the tithe and help with the Bible reading. They watch the children and clean the bathrooms. While there are deacons and members of the Prayer Board, even these roles are not rigidly defined. For example, the chairwoman of the Prayer Board also serves refreshments like red velvet cake, coffee, coca-cola, and sausage and biscuits in the basement between Sunday School and church. The pastor's oldest daughter assists him with the scripture reading. Sometimes he reads and she repeats or answers. Other times she reads and he interprets. Sometimes they read together. Sometimes the whole congregation chimes in, sometimes not.

Within the House of God, Edward Stone is a valued and important member. His skill with video and audio equipment enables him to tape each church service for members who wish to hear or see the performance again at home. Mr. Stone sets up the equipment carefully before each service, and puts it all away each Sunday afternoon. Other members make copies of the tapes and sell them for a small fee to members and guests. Mr. Stone's skills are an important resource in the small church community.

Many times, Mr. Stone also helps with the cars that the church buys and sells. He is one of a number of men in the congregation who helps repair and market these cars. There is never a very large inventory of cars – usually one is located and repaired for a specific customer (an example of just-in-time or JIT method of inventory control). When someone from the community needs a car and is short on money, it is possible to barter goods and services with the church in exchange for the car.

Mr. Stone's wife Sheila and her sisters work in the Rib Shack. They spend a great deal of time arguing and tasting and re-adjusting – making sure the sauce is just right and the meat is tender. Because many of their customers are also members of their congregation, they are especially invested in the quality of the goods they produce. Because they each take such pride in their work, they become critics and customers themselves, producing fine food for one another as well as for the community. In the language of high performance, these women have organised themselves as a 'chain of customers' to ensure a superior product.

The House of God sanctuary is located on a corner lot, but it also shares its space with the Rib Shack and the car lot. The space taken up by all three enterprises is much smaller than that taken up by most of the other small churches in Bayside. This efficient use of space is similar to Whyte's (1991) analysis of the Japanese use of space in the manufacturing process. He argues that it is their efficient use of both human and material resources that make Japanese industries more economical than American counterparts.

The House of God also has avoided a great deal of administrative procedure, bypassed the need for secretarial staff and technology, and thus kept costs low by not relying on print materials to relay information. In this setting, print materials would be an added layer of bureaucracy rather than a useful tool for communicating. For example, in the church service, there is no written text to direct the people in the production of the service. There are no hymnals, no bulletins, no print materials to mark the steps or to organise information. Rather, the service flows from one event to another, with events often overlapping one another. This obvious lack of text serves to emphasise the presence of the one true text, the Bible. In the House of God, the Bible is the one single focal point for reading and discussion. Nearly all members carry one with them to each service. Mr. Stone, for example, carries a full-size King James version in a rich brown leather case. Inside the case are yellow highlighters, blue ink pens and number 2 pencils to mark and comment on the pieces of text that form the basis of each Sunday School lesson and church service. The efficiency of only one text in the service emphasises its importance and draws the congregation closer together as they read, respond and mark the words of God.

Members of the House of God cannot, however, explain exactly how they know when to do something or exactly what to do – when to start singing, for example, or which part of the scripture to read aloud. They say they just know it. They don't need or want a set of instructions written out for them because this would only detract from their activity. There is no rehearsal, no list of procedures, only performance which shifts in subtle ways to match the mood of the group (see Heath, 1983, for a description of similar 'church knowledge' in Trackton). In other words, there is no written agenda that prescribes the behaviours of the congregation. Rather, the rules of performance are negotiated and re-negotiated by the members of the church community at each church service.

While these behaviours are different from 'mainstream' church services, they are clearly *not* examples of 'pre-literate' knowing. Many members of the congregation are quite literate and read a variety of texts for a variety of purposes. Rather than a compensation for low literacy, it is an efficient way of getting the work of the church done – the work of creating a meaningful, artistic product crafted with love and caring – a peak spiritual experience within a community of believers. It is a way of knowing characterised by intuition and creativity rather than by a set of steps. It is also a way of knowing that bears little resemblance to the hierarchical, linear, controlled, segmented, non-participatory, industrial Protestant church services I am more accustomed to.

Some of the members of the House of God hold decent jobs as teachers or as supervisors in state and local government or public service organisations. A few own small businesses. But most are stuck in entry-level jobs or have only temporary work generally in settings that offer little opportunity to apply the skills and knowledge they display consistently within their church community.

The crisis in the American workplace is not simply about literacy, I would argue, but also about the organisation of work that does not allow workers to use the skills they already possess. In order to consider this point, let us move to Mr. Stone's workplace, the hospital where he is a housekeeping aide. Here Mr. Stone performs a job that is considered entry-level for wages that place him below the poverty line. While he does have benefits, without a GED, he has no opportunity for promotion or for an increase in pay. His supervisor, a white woman, believes that he is 'slow' and cannot make decisions or think critically. She expects him to work for her in silence, never questioning what she says or does. Those workers who do question the supervisor find themselves 'written up' or transferred to the night shift. This silencing is handled differently by different workers. Most have resigned themselves to the fact and have developed other activities to keep themselves alive. Some find extra work in the informal economy – catering, repair shops, running the numbers assisting in running an unofficial lottery. Others develop hobbies like gardening, painting or photography. Still others drink or smoke reefer on the job, and live from pay day to day off to pay day. Most of them see no opportunity for better work, and remain in the same positions for years. As I have described in detail elsewhere (Gowen, 1992), for many entry-level employees, work in the hospital has many of the life-sapping qualities described by Terkel (above).

In 1989, King Memorial Hospital offered literacy classes for these workers. In conceptualising workplace problems in terms of literacy, hospital management did what Senge (1990) terms 'burden shifting'. That is, it mistook deep-seated organ-isational problems with the distribution of power, privilege and wages for literacy problems, and assumed that some education would improve workers' productivity and performance.

After the workplace literacy classes ended and very few employees had been promoted to higher jobs or had earned any new credentials, many workers expressed bitterness and disappointment. Most learners in the program resisted the paternalistic forms of management and the glass ceilings inherent in the hospital. The job-based curricula did little to address those issues, but rather encouraged workers to more fully adapt to the organisational structure of the hospital. As a result, workers often acted incompetent or illiterate as their single means of maintaining any control over their work.

The problem at the hospital was not addressed by literacy classes. In fact, in some ways the classes made the problem worse because in defining the problem as literacy, the underlying causes of worker alienation were never addressed. Thus, workers like Mr. Stone did not change their behaviour significantly, and management believed that these workers were even more 'hopeless' than before. In looking at Mr. Stone at church and at work, we have a sketch of one worker as he lives his life in two very different contexts. At church, Mr. Stone is a busy, well-dressed man with a job to do, but at the hospital, Mr. Stone is a slumping, tired man with a torn uniform and a deep, quiet gaze. This sketch helps answer the questions posed at the beginning of this chapter.

In what ways do American educational policies and workplace structures contribute to men and women like Edward Stone remaining in entry-level jobs for a lifetime? In any serious attempt to restructure education and work, we must look beyond the skill levels of individual workers and consider how both the ways workers are taught and the environments in which workers perform their work have a great deal to do with how skilled and knowledgeable they appear to be. Industrialised, hierarchical organisations of work, by definition, require little in terms of knowledge and ability on the parts of workers. And when worker education is reduced to industrial perfor-mance – sequences of tasks broken down into small parts, mastered to efficient perfection, and repeated in the same manner over and over again – competence becomes the ability to perform like a machine. Models of education and work that focus on these rote tasks do little to recognise and celebrate the skills and abilities men like Edward Stone possess. They do nothing to tap into his rich store of knowledge about performance, about community and ironically about technical expertise. Mr. Stone cleans the floors because he doesn't have a high school diploma or a GED, and so the skills he does possess are rendered invisible because the hospital will not promote him, or anyone else, without the proper credential (docility certificate?).

One way to raise the skill levels of workers, then, would be to create environments that allowed for, indeed encouraged, workers to use the skills they have and to constantly develop new skills and knowledge. This means organisations that are fluid, open to change, collaborative, that actively support ongoing education for all workers, and that distribute profits fairly.

Why is it that in a time of staggering economic and social change, the idle worker is blamed for the problems of a nation?

The perception of a literacy crisis is one sign that a culture is undergoing rapid and large-scale social change (Graff, 1987), which is what appears to be happening at the moment in the American workplace . . .

. . . in blaming workers for being deficient, the reality that there are no longer good jobs available for much of the workforce is not addressed . . . While recent research (Kirsch, Jungeblut, Jenkins and Kolstad, 1993) suggests a strong correlation between worker literacy as measured by the NALS (National Adult Literacy Survey) and economic productivity, there is no data that supports the conclusion that increasing worker literacy would increase their real earned income.

Educating the workforce to be more literate in general, for not only economic purposes but for purposes of family and community life are important goals for education. But blaming workers' literacy deficiencies for the economic troubles of the nation is to mistake consequences for solutions. The troubles in the workplace go much deeper than whether or not a worker can perform SPC, understand how to file an insurance claim by reading the benefits package materials, or draw high-level inferences from job-related print materials. There is much that must be changed about work and wage before even highly literate employees will remain productive, healthy and committed to their work over the long term.

Extension

. . . And we can reject notions of general worker deficiency when we develop workplace literacy programs. Deficit approaches to workplace literacy may improve individual performance for the short term, but they will do little to help workplace organisations restructure themselves into more humane and democratic workplaces. And it also appears to do little to improve the quality of life for workers like Edward Stone. What it does accomplish is a maintenance of the status quo, especially in terms of power and privilege. Literacy educators who uncritically support workplace literacy programs will probably ensure themselves profitable consulting work, but may do little for those they are trying to help.

★ Task B4.4.1: Workplace literacies: theory and policy

Now that we are nearly at the end of Section B, we might use the Gowen text to reflect on where the account of workplace literacies fits into the discussions of the nature of literacy, its consequences and acquisition (Sections B1–3). For example, we have placed her text to the ideological side of our diagram (Figure A2.1) of autonomous and ideological models, although she does not explicitly draw upon these terms. This leads us to pose some further questions that help you make these broader links:

➤ Do you think we are justified in locating Gowen at the more 'ideological' end, or are there passages in the text that would locate her in another theoretical position?

➤ What other texts might be associated with her work?

➤ How do arguments about literacy skills and practices in the workplace in Gowen's text link with the earlier texts in Section B?

David Barton, whose account of social approaches to literacy we saw in Section B4.1, offers some help in addressing these questions as he directly addresses workplace literacies from a theoretical stand. In a chapter in the revised edition of his book *Literacy: an introduction to the ecology of written language* (2006) he links new ideas about workplace literacies with the notion of 'Domains' of literacy, suggesting that what counts as literacy, the accompanying events and practices, vary from one domain to another. Like Gowen, then, he argues that 'ethnographies of workplace literacy practices show a more complex picture' than that evident in much of the policy debate. You might go back to Barton's work and consider how far it complements that of Gowen:

➤ Does it help your understanding of workplace literacies to bring the two authors together?

Task B4.4.2: 'Seeing' workplace skills

Gowen raises challenging questions as to how we might 'see' what is going on at the workplace, especially with respect to the skills that workers need to accomplish their work. In particular, of course, literacy skills are increasingly seen as a key component of the workplace, because of their assumed contribution to enhancing 'effectiveness' and 'competitiveness'. Gowen shows that as Mr Stone engages in different domains of work he demonstrates skills which appear not to be recognised by his employers. Indeed she is scathing about the way 'the skills he does possess are rendered invisible'. There are methodological and theoretical issues at stake here with regard to how we can 'see' what is going on. At the broadest theoretical and ideological level, she argues that employers cannot 'see' their workers' skills because they are trying to blame the workers for their own deficiencies as economic managers. If workers like Mr Stone are only cleaning the floors, despite possessing far more sophisticated skills than this, this may be because they have not acquired the requisite formal educational qualifications, such as the GED, and consequently have not been promoted at work. Moreover, they have not acquired the educational credentials because they were not given the time off or the resources to do so, or the courses on offer were not adequate for their promotional and participatory needs. She writes (p. 128):

> While I clearly recognise the need for and strongly support increased investment in on-going and comprehensive worker education, I would like to suggest that many entry-level workers already possess important skills and knowledge that are needed in more participatory work organisations, and that management is unable, because of its privileged and isolated position in the hierarchy, to recognise this.

Gowen worries that the kinds of courses that were provided, and which Mr Stone for instance attended, were more geared to creating docile workers than to providing the skills that would enable them to move upwards in the job hierarchy. She argues (p. 132):

> In any serious attempt to restructure education and work, we must look beyond the skill levels of individual workers and consider how both the ways workers are taught and the environments in which workers perform their work have a great deal to do with how skilled and knowledgeable they appear to be.

This is strong critical stuff and you might want to challenge some of Gowen's claims. You might consider:

➤ What kinds of skills and knowledge do you think, from your reading, Mr Stone and other workers possess that employers might build upon?

➤ What would be appropriate methods for 'seeing' workplace skills? (You might review the various quantitative and qualitative methods signalled in earlier texts, such as formal tests or ethnographic approaches.)

➤ What other literature on workplace literacies do you know and how does it compare with Gowen's approach?

One further example here that might help with this methodological and comparative task is Mike Rose's *The mind at work* (2004). Rose describes how complex are the skills employed by a waitress as she calculates how many customers to serve at once, what mix of goods to bring with her to the serving room and distribute, how to divide the work in terms of time and space. There are interesting points of comparison here with Gowen's Mr Stone as he engages in different domains of work, and demonstrates skills which appear not to be recognised by his employers. There are, then, methodological and theoretical issues at stake here in explaining why Gowen and Rose are able to 'see' these skills whilst others are not, and you might also draw upon Barton's notion of 'domains' and the concept of 'social practices' that runs through Section B4 to address such questions. From your reading or from your own experience, such as in restaurants or travelling, or staying in hotels, you might answer the following questions:

➤ What skills can be identified amongst the workers in each site?

➤ How did you identify these skills, for example from direct observation, by asking people, by measuring them with tests?

➤ How did the skills you have described compare to those evident in the accounts by Gowen, Rose and Barton or others you have read?

In Section C we will provide some further more concrete tasks in relation to workplace literacies and you might want to look ahead to Section C3.1 'Workplace Literacies' to pursue this topic.

The final text in Section B, in which Reder and Davila review the debates about the 'Literacy Thesis', offers a useful summary of the theoretical positions in the section as a whole, and reading it now, after the Gowen text, might enable you to begin to relate the theoretical aspects of this work to more empirical studies of this kind.

B4.5 THE LITERACY THESIS REVISITED

Reder and Davila provide a helpful overview of the debates we have been considering in this section, summarising many of the key texts we have addressed. In particular they 'review recent progress in resolving tensions between conceptions of literacy as a system of locally situated cultural practices and conceptions of literacy as a broader system of written language that transcends specific individuals and local contexts'. Such theoretical tensions, they argue, have arisen out of earlier, long-standing literacy debates of the kind we have become acquainted with through the earlier seminal articles in the Extension – the Great Divide, the Literacy Thesis, and Social Practices approaches. They survey recent reviews and critiques of the 'New Literacy Studies' – Brandt and Clinton (2002), Collins and Blot (2003), Street (2003) – and try to draw out the new theoretical ground emerging here. They then address emerging concerns, in particular those raised by Brandt and Clinton concerning the adequacy of current literacy theories framed in terms of locally situated social practices. This new work brings together both the theoretical debates reviewed earlier and also their practical application both to applied linguistics in general and to education in particular. This provides a good bridge into Section C where there will be opportunities to develop such applications in your own contexts.

Reder, S., and Davila, E. (2005) 'Context and literacy practices', *Annual Review of Applied Linguistics*, 25, 170–187.

Text B4.5
S. Reder and
E. Davila

The current debate regarding the nature of literacy has intellectual roots that can be traced back to earlier contrasts Street (1984) drew between 'autonomous' and 'ideological' models of literacy. This important contrast was itself a reaction to influential debates at the time about the consequences of literacy for individuals and societies. We focus here on a related but quite distinct contrast evident in the more recent work, that between the *local* and *remote* (sometimes termed 'global' or 'distant') contexts for literacy events and practices. There is not space here to review in detail the well-known and important controversies about the 'consequences of literacy.'

As ethnographic studies of literacy practices in a variety of contexts accumulated during the 1980s, theorists began to systematize new ways of understanding the development, acquisition, and use of literacy. The approach termed the 'New Literacy Studies' (Gee, 1990; Street, 1995) was based on two key principles: seeing *context* as fundamental to understanding literacy, and eradicating any clear distinction between orality and literacy.[1] Operating with these core principles, ethnographic studies explored how text and speech are intertwined in daily use and how local contexts inevitably determine the shapes and uses of literacy. As a counterpoint to the many problems of the Literacy Thesis, the New Literacy Studies (NLS) research turned away from a general examination of broad sociopolitical and economic forces and began a careful consideration of concrete, local uses of literacy (e.g., Barton, 2001; Barton and Hamilton, 1998; Barton, Hamilton, and Ivanic, 2000; Heath, 1983; Street, 1993).

Brandt and Clinton: limits of the local

In their 2002 article, *Limits of the Local: Expanding Perspectives on Literacy as a Social Practice*, Deborah Brandt and Katie Clinton consider how the NLS framework has shaped literacy research, especially the growing collection of ethnographies of literacy. As the

---

1 Later scholars extended the leveling of differences between orality and literacy to the leveling of such categorical differences among other modalities as well, within frameworks of both *multimodal* literacy (Kress and van Leeuwen, 2001) and *metamedia* literacy (Lemke, 1998).

S. Reder and
E. Davila

title of their article suggests, Brandt and Clinton are not satisfied that literacy can be fully understood by looking only through the lens of the local context in which a literacy event takes place. They ask: 'Can we not see the ways that literacy arises out of local, particular, situated human interactions while also seeing how it also regularly arrives from other places – infiltrating, disjointing, and displacing local life?' (2002, p. 343). They contend that by privileging the local context as the *only* relevant context, NLS creates a 'great divide' between local and global contexts that is not only unnecessary, but also hinders our understanding of the forces at play in everyday literacy events.

Brandt and Clinton describe the reach and depth of the NLS theoretical perspective as they discuss Besnier's (1995) ethnography of literacy in a Polynesian community:

> So absorbed into local context does literacy appear in this study, in fact, that Besnier suggests that we can treat literacy practices as windows into a group's social and political structure – that is, not only can one look to local contexts to understand local literacy, but one can also look to local literacy practices to understand the key forces that organize local life. This is the radical analytical accomplishment of the social-practice perspective.
>
> (Brandt and Clinton, 2002, p. 343)

Though they acknowledge the fundamental importance of local context, Brandt and Clinton disagree with Besnier's formulation of literacy practices as simply a reflection of the local context. They argue that local context alone is insufficient to explain the uses and forms of literacy. They find an example of the limits of the local context in Besnier's own work: Local residents commonly ignore the content of English slogans on the t-shirts they wear. Besnier uses this example to point to the power of the local context – these slogans have no meaning for local t-shirt wearers and so they are ignored and do not enter into local literacy practices in any way. Brandt and Clinton argue on the contrary that the presence of these slogans demonstrates the connections between the local context of this Polynesian island and more remote contexts.

Brandt and Clinton readily admit that literacy research must be rooted in people's intimate everyday experiences with text. However, their critique of NLS rests on the idea that the local and global contexts are not two discrete realms. Rather than restrict their analytical framework to consider only how literacy is shaped by *local* social and cultural phenomena, the authors suggest that literacy practices can include transcontextualizing components. To this end, they propose the constructs of *localizing moves* and *globalizing connects*. The concept of *localizing moves* describes the work people do when they shape literacy practices to meet personal needs and to match local social structures. *Localizing moves* have been abundantly described in NLS ethnographies of literacy.

A *globalizing connect* describes a local literacy practice that has far-reaching implications and uses outside of the local context. Brandt and Clinton provide an example in the shape of a local representative of a national agricultural company. This representative reads the local weather forecast and talks to local farmers in order to gauge crop outputs. In other words, he is a participant in the same types of literacy practices as the local farmers themselves. However, he uses this local literacy event in a different context when he relays local information to headquarters and thus plays a role in a literacy event that unfolds on a much larger scale. This example shows how local literacy events can serve multiple interests and play a part in remote literacy events and large-scale processes of knowledge creation.

Brandt and Clinton also use the concept of literacy sponsors to highlight the ways that multiple forces can be at play in local literacy practices. The idea of literacy sponsors (Brandt, 2001) refers to the institutions, policies, and people that make the acquisition and practice of literacy possible: the government, corporate scholarship foundations, religious groups, and so on. Literacy sponsors often wield power over uses of literacy and they can provide and control access to literacy materials (textbooks, the Internet, etc.). Using literacy sponsors as an analytical tool highlights the tension among different immediate and remote forces at play in a given literacy practice. Brandt and Clinton explain this concept:

> When we use literacy, we also get used. Things typically mediate this relationship. Attention to sponsors can yield a fuller insight into how literate practices can be shaped out of the struggle of competing interests and agents, how multiple interests can be satisfied during a single performance of reading or writing, how literate practices can relate to immediate social relationships while still answering to distant demands.
>
> (2002, pp. 350–351)

Thus, when looking at literacy events, the local context is only part of the picture. The written materials at the center of a literacy event are often not locally produced. Their presence allows for remote actors to play a role (more or less consequential) in local practice. Brandt and Clinton highlight the material aspects of literacy as the key factor that allows multiple remote actors to influence a given literacy event and to shape local literacy practices.

It is important to note that Brandt and Clinton do not advocate a wholesale disavowal of the importance of the local context, nor do they contend 'that the technology of literacy carries its own imperatives no matter where it goes' (2002, p. 344). Rather, their formulation of context allows for distant influences on local practices to be clearly identified not as disinterested 'autonomous' forces, but as ideological players in their own right. They deny the existence of some remote, 'autonomous' literacy and they view distant influences on local practices as integral, subjective participants in local literacy events. They contend that 'local literacy events cannot exhaust the meanings or actions of literacy' (2002, p. 344). Brandt and Clinton continue:

> Social practices are not necessarily the shapers of literacy's meaning; indeed, they may be the weary shock absorbers of its impositions. That people manage to absorb or mollify these demands in different ways may be evidence of local ingenuity, diversity, agency, as much recent research emphasizes, but it is just as much evidence of how powerfully literacy as a technology can insinuate itself into social relations anywhere.
>
> (2002, p. 354)

Brandt and Clinton repeatedly note that literacy as a technology has the ability to travel, integrate, and endure. It is these unique properties that contribute to literacy's transcontextualizing capabilities. Brandt and Clinton contend that there is no divide between local and global contexts: People's everyday intimate experiences of literacy are in conversation with remote forces at play in the larger sociocultural context.

Extension

S. Reder and
E. Davila

Street: yes, but not autonomous remote influences

. . .

In specifically discussing the *Limits of the Local*, Street agrees with Brandt and Clinton's focus on the *relationship* between the local and the 'distant' as a more fruitful focus for research than either realm in isolation. However, he cautions that Brandt and Clinton not confuse 'distant' forces at play in literacy events with 'autonomous' literacy. Street emphasizes that 'distant' influences are indeed ideological. Brandt and Clinton seem to answer this concern in their discussion of literacy sponsors and the subjective control they can wield over the shape of local literacy practices.

Street acknowledges that 'we need a framework and conceptual tools that can characterize the relation between local and "distant"' (2003b, p. 4). However, he contends that NLS provides ample theoretical space for this type of analysis in its conceptualization of literacy events and literacy practices. . . . practices function as a framework that accommodates 'distant' influences on local literacy events.

The paired concepts of literacy events and literacy practices effectively highlight the difference between a local event and the larger forces that shape the participants in that event. However, it seems that these concepts provide an analytical *space* for understanding the relationship between the local and the distant, but without further development these concepts do not yet constitute a coherent framework for understanding this relationship. What exactly are these 'distant' forces? If we concede that literacy is not an autonomous entity, then what is the nature of literacy within the broader sociocultural context? Likewise, how do these 'distant' forces impact individual literacy events? The concepts of literacy events and literacy practices provide an answer as to *where* the local and the distant collide (in many everyday literacy events), but they fail to provide an answer as to *how* this interaction occurs.

. . .

If we acknowledge that local literacies do not exist autonomously, but commonly draw on perspectives that participants have developed through participation in other literacy practices – school literacies, work literacies, religious literacies, bureaucratic literacies – then we see that a 'single essentialized version' of local literacy practices ignores much of the context that participants use to create the practice in the first place. Likewise, 'global' literacy does not exist in an essentialized, pure form, but only emerges as one piece of hybrid literacy practices that are always, necessarily locally constituted. We come to see that 'local' and 'global' (or distant, remote) contexts do not exist in contrast to one another, but as constituents of a larger whole. Street's conceptualization of all literacy practices as hybrid constructions echoes Brandt and Clinton's analysis of local literacy practices as 'weary shock absorbers' of the impositions of distant participants.

Collins and Blot: a proposed resolution with power and identity

. . .

Collins and Blot note the need for an explanation that adequately addresses the quotidian reality of literacy as a locally-determined social practice while at the same time accounting for the unique place that literacy inhabits in modern Western society and thought. Such an analysis would shed light on the continuing patterns of access to, and use of, literacy among various groups in society. To achieve this end, Collins and Blot draw on post-structural theorists – primarily Bourdieu, de Certeau, Derrida, and Foucault – as they bring language, education, texts, and identity into the core of an argument about literacy and power in modern Western society. In their work, Collins and Blot agree with many NLS researchers, and they find much that is useful in their work. However, what Collins and Blot find missing in ethnographic accounts of literacy is an 'account of why literacy matters in the way that it does in the modern West' (2003, p. 65). This question arises from the many long-standing and recurring connections between literacy practices and the exercise of power in society. Because an investigation of this issue would necessarily involve a scope of study larger than the immediate ethnographic context, this sort of analysis has not been a primary concern in many NLS accounts of literacy.

Collins and Blot contend that considerations of *power* have largely been absent from most ethnographies of literacy. They cite Heath's (1983) seminal work as an example. Though this work provides an extraordinarily detailed view of how the different literacy practices of various groups in society impact (help or hinder) children as they encounter school literacy and discourse practices, Heath does not include an overt discussion of the ways that power in society has shaped what we know as 'school literacy.' She does not address the ways in which forces outside of the immediate context have contributed to the significance of 'school literacy' and guaranteed its preeminent place in education and in society.

This argument about the partisan nature of 'school literacy' is strongly reminiscent of Street's (1984) core contention that all literacy events carry ideological meanings. Literacy education in schools does not simply teach a set of decontextualized, discrete cognitive skills. Rather, the types of literacies that are taught – for example, sustained silent reading, comprehension questions, fill-in-the-blank forms – contribute to an organization of society according to the vision of those who have captured the power to create, endorse, promote, and institute particular brands of literacy in society.

As they discuss Heath's (1983) work in terms of ideological literacy and power, Collins and Blot praise the work for its eloquent and detailed description of the differences in literacy practices among communities, and for its implicit acknowledgment that 'school literacy' is only one type of literacy among equals. But Collins and Blot claim that the book comes with a surprise ending. Throughout the book, Heath discusses locally-developed projects and strategies designed to incorporate the skills students acquire at home and in the community into their developing 'school literacy' practices. The surprise comes in an epilogue which details changes in federal education policies that blocked and reversed many of these local efforts and replaced them with programs based on a more autonomous view of literacy that emphasized decontextualized, skill-based training and standardized testing. Collins and Blot contend that the body of Heath's analysis is missing a key point that ties her micro-analysis of language and literacy in local contexts to decidedly nonlocal federal policy decisions that nevertheless impact local life.

For Collins and Blot, the key point is that 'writing is usually associated with power, and particularly with specifically modern forms of power' (2003, p. 5). This leads them into a detailed consideration of the nature and consequences of power in society. Drawing on the work of the French post-structuralists, they see power not only as a macro-level force imposed in the form of institutions, bureaucracies and overt violence, but also as an intimate presence in all facets of everyday life. Power relations on a societal level create the shape of everyday life that in turn determines how individuals are educated, how each of us fits into society, and how we are able to define our identities. Thus, macro-level power translates into intimate and personal decisions about micro-level identity and conceptions of self. This analysis includes 'school' or dominant literacy as a mode of delivery of macro-level power, whereas identity includes conceptions of a literate self built through years of education, bureaucratic involvement, and employment. Thus Collins and Blot see literacy and power going hand in hand. Collins and Blot attempt to bridge the local/global divide with careful consideration of power and identity at the micro- and macro-levels.

Discussion: connecting local and remote contexts

These authors present different conceptions of *context* in their understandings of literacy. Although they agree that theories of literacy as social practices need to represent nonlocal contextual influences more explicitly, they differ in how they suggest we understand such distant influences. A key difference among their theories is in how they propose to connect the local and global contexts of literacy.

Street argues that the NLS already has the requisite theoretical framework in place, in which local contextual features interact in as yet unspecified ways with more global *literacy practices* to generate locally constructed *literacy events*. Brandt and Clinton propose a framework in which literacy events are understood in terms of both *localizing moves* and *globalizing connects*. Collins and Blot attempt to integrate local and distant influences through the dynamic interplay between micro- and macro-levels of *identity* and *power* in discourse and interaction.

In accepting Brandt and Clinton's argument that 'remote' influences need to be accounted for, Street cautions against formulating these as 'autonomous' influences. But without further development, it is not clear how the NLS framework of literacy practices offers a less 'autonomous' formulation of remote influences than that proposed in the Brandt and Clinton framework. Why should the social and cultural forces included in NLS conceptions of literacy practices be considered less 'autonomous' and somehow integrally linked to the local context, whereas the concept of global connects proposed by Brandt and Clinton is labeled 'autonomous'? Street seems more comfortable with Collins and Blot's power-based formulation, although again it is not theoretically clear why 'power' should wield a less 'autonomous' type of global influence than 'sponsorship' or other remote influences considered by Brandt and Clinton. Although power as formulated by Collins and Blot is certainly 'ideological' in NLS terms, it is not clear why *remote* sources of power that influence *local* interactions are operating in a more 'ideological' framework than other types of remote influence. How are we to tell? How do we avoid replacing an autonomous theory of literacy with an autonomous theory of power? Further theoretical elaboration and clarification are needed here.

Part of the difficulty may be that Street's (1984) contrast between 'autonomous' and 'ideological' models of literacy does not serve well as a dichotomous classification of contextual influences on social interactions. The original distinction, rooted in the debate about the Literacy Thesis, was intended to contrast ways of understanding the apparent 'consequences' of literacy. When conceptualizing the manner in which distant influences are involved in the construction of local literacy events, 'autonomous' and 'ideological' may not be suitable contraries. *From the perspective of local interactants*, might some distant influences be perceived as having relatively more 'autonomous' influence than others? How are we to tell? At the very least, we need here a better formulation of the ways in which remote influences on locally constructed literacy practices may or may not be 'autonomous.'

Although many theorists adhere to the distinction between 'ideological' and 'autonomous' models of literacy, others focus more on a related distinction between conceptions of literacy as 'situated' versus 'decontextualized.' From our perspective, it is less productive to ask *whether* (or which aspects of) literacy practices are *situated* than to ask about what contexts those literacy practices are situated *in*. In building theories based on close examination and analysis of local practices, NLS has not dealt systematically with identifying what makes a context 'local.' The context in which literacy practices are said to be situated is usually taken as a given for both the participants and the observer. But how do we locate the boundaries of the contexts in which literacy practices are situated? Where are the spatial and temporal margins? Although such questions about context boundaries have long been asked in microethnographic investigations (e.g., Shultz, Florio and Erickson, 1982), they also come to the fore again in discussing 'local' versus 'remote' influences on literacy.

There are several promising theoretical directions that can build on and extend the ideas developed in the three pieces reviewed here toward connecting local and global contexts of literacy practices. We will sketch two possibilities here.

[They go on to describe work on 'dual-context framework', citing Engeström and others and on actor-network theory citing in particular Latour. They then link this back to the work of Barton and Hamilton (see Section B3.1) which builds on this via the notion of textually mediated social worlds, and suggest this may be a way forward in resolving the dilemmas raised earlier.]

The insights of Barton and Hamilton may offer an important theoretical path forward. Future research may be able to extend these ideas by borrowing yet another construct from ANT, that of irreversibility. As noted previously, irreversibility in ANT is the extent to which an actant-network, at a given point in its development, is able to return to an earlier state in which alternative possibilities for future network development exist. An important feature of irreversibility to consider is its variable and continuous quality. This may provide some important new theoretical machinery for representing the remote influences of literacy (i.e., of inscriptions) within social networks. We suggest that the contexts inscribed by written materials in relatively irreversible states of actant networks will endow literacy with the appearance of having a relatively fixed ('autonomous') influence on social practices, whereas in more reversible network states, the inscriptions will endow literacy with influence that appears less 'autonomous.' In other words, when social groupings are in a state of flux (i.e., power players still forming alliances and meanings still have loose definitions) there is more focus on the players and their not-disinterested involvement is more readily apparent. When stable states of networks become institutionalized, the static (irreversible) relations of power seem 'natural' and the influence of the tools of the powerful (e.g., literacy) *seem* to be inherent in the tools themselves. In this way, the powerful influence of the people who control literacy is misassigned to literacy itself, thereby endowing literacy with an *apparently* 'autonomous influence.' This may provide a step towards resolving the issues noted earlier about characterizing the nature of distant literacy influences on local interactions.

S. Reder and
E. Davila

[Reder and Davila go on to suggest that these theoretical debates pose a major challenge for literacy educators and how they can take account of 'how contexts shape literacy practices'.]

Task B4.5.1: Summarising the literacy debate

Reder and Davila provide a helpful overview of the debates we have been considering in this section, summarising many of the key texts we have mentioned. So, first it might be useful to use this text in order to review and reflect upon your own take on these issues. Does the summary provided by Reder and Davila match your own? They go over the issues raised in Section B3 and B4 especially, regarding what they refer to as 'The Great Divide, the Literacy Thesis, and Other Binaries'. They summarise the 'social practices' perspective, citing familiar authors such as Barton and Hamilton (see Section B4.1) and Street (B3.3) and cite a recent critique of one aspect of this approach, namely what Brandt and Clinton (2002) refer to as 'The limits of the local'. They give space to the response by Street (2003; accessible at http://www.tc.columbia. edu/cice/) and by Collins and Blot (2003). The key issue is whether 'ethnographic' approaches to literacy as social practice have over-privileged 'the local' at the expense of addressing aspects of literacy that can be understood only in terms of 'remote contexts' – the 'global'.

In particular Reder and Davila claim to be offering a way out of the apparent impasse amongst these authors by calling on more recent work by Barton and Hamilton that employs actor-network theory and Wenger's 'communities of practice'. Barton and Hamilton, they suggest, provide a useful bridge between these fields and literacy studies by calling upon Wenger's concept of 'reification'. Building on this they develop the notion of 'textually mediated social worlds'. This concept, suggest Reder and Davila, can provide the forward 'path' that the previous debates were lacking. Using this notion, we can reconcile the remote aspects of literacy that may come to local users from afar, as in many global examples of new literacies, with the immediate and local meanings embedded in people's own communities of practice. These ideas may also complement the work of Bartlett and Holland (Section B4.2) that talks of 'figured worlds' in which the 'space of literacy practices' is construed and enacted. Furthermore, they also evoke Olson's idea of a 'world on paper' (Section B3.4) – you might want to consider how, if at all, these different conceptions differ, and whether these are differences that make a difference.

At least, that is a brief summary of what we 'take' from our reading of Reder and Davila and the other texts cited here. You might want to write a similar paragraph from your own perspective and address the following questions:

➤ Is the 'problem' as we have laid it out – the relationship between local and global?

➤ Is the solution, as we have interpreted Reder and Davila's use of Barton and Hamilton, one that links communities of practice with textually mediated social worlds?

➤ Or would you want to pose both 'problem' and 'solution' differently?

Task B4.5.2: Continuing the literacy debate ⭐

Having clarified your own position, you might like to enter into discussion with others and check out how their position relates to yours. In some cases you may be able to work towards an agreed synthesis of the ideas posed here; in other situations the contrast with different people's positions might help you clarify your own and maintain a basically different view. Some of the questions that the text raised for us include:

➤ Have New Literacy Studies ethnographies over-privileged the local dimensions of literacy practices, thereby missing out on the influence of more remote forces?

➤ How do the global and local interact? What is the mechanism whereby they influence one another? At one point Reder and Davila quote Brandt and Clinton referring to the local as 'weary shock absorbers'. Is that a useful metaphor? If not, what would work better?

➤ What are the implications of New Literacy Studies for educational practice?

After discussing these questions among yourselves, you may be interested in reading the following excerpts from our discussion of the article, and perhaps responding to issues raised and/or positions advanced by us.

Commentary: Does 'global' equal 'autonomous'?

B: The question about local–global relations from Brandt and Clinton was this: If we recognise that there are distant non-local influences on local practices, does that bring the notion of autonomous back in? I think using the word 'autonomous' in there, given the history of the word in literacy studies, is regrettable. It would have been better to have talked about 'distant' and 'non-local' in other ways, rather than muddy the waters by implying that autonomy appears there. And I think Reder and Davila slightly muddle that one up too.

A: Their criticism seems valid: by focusing too much on the local idiosyncrasies of literacy practices, you miss sight of the fact that these practices are embedded in global discourses, and there are other actors that don't appear on the ground but that are affecting that. But I guess you're right that there's no reason to ascribe to them an autonomous model of literacy just because –

B: You want to take account of the distance.

A: Yeah. The pairs global–local and autonomous–ideological are not the same. One is a way we think about literacy and the other is the different factors that we're thinking about when we're looking at the world.

B: And I think, to be fair, I think now, Brandt and Clinton would probably agree with that, what they were trying to get at was the distance bit. But there's another issue here, which Reder and Davila didn't really pick up on, and that's that methodologically, certainly anthropological use of ethnography, by definition, looks at the global all the time. There's never been an isolated and separate 'local'. Now, some people have characterised us doing that, and some representations occasionally might look like that, but, really, that's not how ethnography is done.

A: She brings up Besnier as an example of someone who misses the point.

B: Yes, I'd like to see how he would reply to that, actually. I think he was fully aware of the global. For instance, one of his themes was about missionaries coming with printing presses. And another was that people then use that to learn writing literacy, which they use to write letters to other people from Nukulaelae who've gone off to Australia. So, he's fully aware that there is this backwards and forwards movement. And he's also aware that the T-shirts signify, semiotically, as it were, an outside world, while at the same time, it doesn't matter what the letters on it are, because that signifying is only semiotic, it doesn't really do a *semantic* job, if you like.

A: So, you think they misunderstood him – because, when they quote him there, they're quoting him as saying exactly the opposite.

B: Yeah, as though he missed the signifying practices piece of the T-shirts.

A: Yeah, I'm not sure where it was, but it's exactly about the T-shirts, where they say that – it's on p. 173 – 'Local residents commonly ignore the content of English slogans on the t-shirts they wear. Besnier uses this example to point to the power of the local context – these slogans have no meaning for local t-shirt wearers, and so they are ignored and do not enter into local literacy practices.'

B: I don't think he would deny that the wearing of the T-shirt is a signifier of some kind, it's just that the actual content of the slogan is irrelevant. And I've seen that idea extended. In fact, we had a discussion about this the other day. People in California wearing T-shirts with Chinese writing on it. They couldn't read the content, but the fact that it was Chinese writing signified a certain position and set of ideas.

A: I can guess how they may bestow it with meaning. I haven't been to Polynesia, but, for instance, in Israel, you have a very similar thing where people wear T-shirts with nonsense words on them. It's always very funny to me, because they're not even slogans, they just have these various nonsense words: 'Texas – Lightning – Fantasy'. But the meaning is that English is a high-status language, so even if it doesn't, content-wise, mean anything, it does mean something wearing English and not Hebrew, because Hebrew has provincial connotations while English seems cosmopolitan.

B: And then what's Chinese on these T-shirts I was thinking of? I remember one of the Chinese girls saying, 'well, again, these aren't real characters'. But they're character-like, and that's all that matters, you just need to signify. You know, we can't read that calendar sitting over there from Tibet, but it's still sitting there signifying – foreign lands and all kinds of other things, without having to worry about how it works as a writing system. So, I would claim that Besnier fully understands that and that's what he's saying in the passage they're using there. But, maybe what matters more than whether they've got Besnier right, is whether there's a bigger point here. The bigger point has to be that literacy practices do come from outside, and that they then operate indexically, signify a range of things, from local interactions to how do we connect with the missionaries, capitalism, Australia, or wherever else? My answer to them is, methodologically, that's exactly what anthropology thinks it's doing. Do you imagine that ethnographers only, as it were, look at that immediate local context? That's an odd representation, really.

Does literacy have a common core?

A: But is there something common in all these many local instances of literacy? I guess this is the other part of what they're saying. Literacy is coming from other places, it's not locally grown. It's locally adapted, but is there some kind of common core that is being adapted in all these instances which then, we don't need to call it autonomous, but since it's common to all these places, it's worth looking at – abstracting from the local?

B: Still, I'm not so sure it's as uni-directional as your question suggests. People readjust it, mediate it, adapt it. The global–local relationship is more dialogical. What that slightly does, it moves us away from – well, it answers your core question by saying, maybe there isn't really a core, it's always moving. And that was Street's hybridity point, actually, which I think they misrepresented. Reder and Davila, on page 176, link the notion of hybrid with what Brandt and Clinton call 'weary shock absorbers'. Now, I think hybridity is a much more elaborate idea than 'weary shock absorbers'.

A: Yeah, 'weary shock absorber' – the shock absorber doesn't do anything but absorb.

B: Yeah, it's almost passive.

A: And it's 'weary' because it's being beaten down, all the time, by these things coming in. It has no agency.

B: And yet they say, this 'conceptualisation of all literacy practices as hybrid constructions echoes Brandt and Clinton's analysis of local literacy . . . as "weary shock absorbers."'

A: Now, why do they say that? I'm trying to remember the whole paragraph.

B: 'They're constituents of a larger whole,' is part of their point, but that whole isn't only the shock absorber metaphor, that whole might be, taking hold, bouncing back, mediating, absorbing, adjusting and all kinds of other processes. So, that was odd, actually.

A: I think you're right, 'hybrid' gives you a much more – it's much more respectful of the local than the 'shock absorber'. Though, in fairness, they say: 'That people manage to absorb or mollify these demands', according to Brandt and Clinton, 'in different ways may be evidence of local ingenuity, diversity, agency', and so forth 'is just as much evidence of how powerfully literacy as a technology can insinuate itself into social relations.' So, they're trying to make the point that it's both ways, whereas you're anxious to show that the local is important, they're anxious to show that the global's important, and it's just two different emphases.

B: I think that's right, if you look at it as emphases. Although I think the inclination in their writing is to keep privileging the global.

A: Because they feel that everybody else is privileging the local. And what Reder and Davila point out is that a lot of the early New Literacy Studies were answering the people who were emphasising the global, or the autonomous.

B: That's why they got 'autonomous' and 'global' muddled then, because it was answering a different debate.

A: But I think that their criticism of 'hybrid', and also which ties in to the criticism of practices, is that it doesn't give you the mechanism. It gives you an analytical space for understanding the relationship.

B: That's the heart of it, probably.

A: Yes, this, in my mind, was the key paragraph of the whole thing: 'It seems that these concepts provide an analytical *space* for understanding the relationship between the local and the distant, but without further development these concepts do not yet constitute a coherent framework for understanding this relationship . . . The concepts of literacy events and literacy practices provide an answer as to *where* the local and the distant collide (in many everyday literacy events), but they fail to provide an answer as to *how* this interaction occurs.'

B: 'A framework for understanding' – that's what Collins and Blot claimed they were doing. Now, is this criticism valid?

A: Well, my understanding, when they say a 'coherent framework', what they're basically saying is, 'we want to know the mechanism'. That's how I interpret it. You have these forces that join together in a hybrid, and we know how to look at the relationship, but how do they join together? What happens in that space?

B: Street's answer, in the reply to Brandt and Clinton, was, 'the relationship between events and practices provides an account of that' –

A: A description, maybe, but you still don't have –

B: A way of problematising?

A: It's a way of asking the question, but it's still not an answer. I'll give you an example of what an answer would look like. Say we take the idea of irreversibility, as I understood it, and I don't know actor-network theory very well, but the idea is that you have this system of relations which begins to incorporate technology, and it begins to assign technology a role in that system. And, at a certain point, the system – it gets so embedded, that it's irreversible, that you can't go back. So that the only way of communicating between clerks in the Home Office and asylum seekers is in writing, that becomes irreversible. And so there we have a mechanism.

B: And the mechanism is irreversibility. It's an odd mechanism, because it's a sort of negative.

A: Well, the mechanism is the incorporation of the technology into social relations which eventually become so deeply embedded that it becomes naturalised as irreversible. I don't know if I'm giving actor-network theory a very good hearing here.

Events and practices

B: So, one mechanism that we might both be more familiar with would be 'sedimentation', in the way that Kate Pahl [2001] uses the term.

A: Explain that for the record.

B: Well, to take Pahl's example, there is a child doing some drawing, and it might just be a singular event, but we see him drawing some of the same kind of images, particularly of sheep, a farmhouse, a woman, who turns out to be their grandmother who lives in Wales, and then that's reinforced by letters and telephone calls, and visits to this person's house. So, gradually, over time, there's a pattern of relations that evoke some of the same images, and it could be the sheep, the grandmother, the house. So, that the next time that child, you know, sitting in a school classroom, does a drawing that has all of those components in it – that's not an isolated incident. I would say it's part of a practice, that would be my way of describing it. Kate Pahl, bringing in Bourdieu, would say, 'What's happened there is that these various components have sedimented', that is, by recurring sufficiently often, have taken on a certain consistent shape and pattern, which then has indexical meaning. Every time the little picture appears, it actually signifies a family relationship, a history, personal feelings, and a whole set of things, which are more than you would identify just by seeing any one event on its own. And that sedimentation is what becomes *habitus*, in the Bourdieu pantheon. Now, that doesn't seem to be far away from events and practices, because my question would be, 'how does an event – how do we claim that an event is part of practices?' Here's an event, it could come and go, they do a drawing of a sheep and they don't do one again and off we go to other things. Or, it keeps recurring. Ah, what are the practices this is a part of? And it could be family literacy practices or it could be something else, family kinship practices, where practice captures both the events and the models of the events, the ideas about them, including the affect that goes with it. So, you get a pattern.

A: So, I guess the mechanism in the practice approach would be that it gets repeated over time, that people get exposed to these repetitive events – they get initiated into the community of practice, and it becomes sedimented in their *habitus*.

B: Let's add to that another mechanism, which is that they construct models of it, to represent it to themselves. So, they don't just do it, this isn't just behaviours.

A: Let's make this concrete; it's getting very abstract. Let's take the literacy practice – something that everyone's been exposed to: 'reading around the room'.

B: Reading circles.

A: Where everyone reads a few sentences, and the teacher stops from time to time and asks a question about what's happening. So, this is something which you find in thousands of primary schools all around the world, it's a practice, a recurring event, teachers were exposed to it when they were kids, and so it's become part of their *habitus*, everyone knows what it looks like, and it's become reified as an educational ideology, that this is how you teach reading.

B: It's a model, as well, of what we should be doing, we have ideas about it and why we do it, not just behaviour. That seems to me a key component to keep in there. It's not just behaviour, it is also patterned ideas about behaviour.

A: And just to play with this for a minute, what is the idea?

B: Well, that's what I'm projecting, that we'd need to know in order to see what this practice really was. If all we did was describe the behaviour, I wouldn't have thought we'd arrived at a description of the practice.

A: For the sake of argument, one of the ideas might be that –

B: Well, I would say 'shared', that sharing reading helps the collaborative under-standing, so it's a kind of collaborative model of the reading process, rather than a separate, individualised model, which certainly existed in schools in some contexts.

A: I'd add to that maybe it has something to do with examination, also. The teacher has to hear the child read out loud to make sure that she or he is doing it.

B: Yeah, that could be true. Now, these are two conjectures at the model level, but if you don't do that, all you've got is behaviour. And I would take ethnography, back to that discussion, to be quintessentially about searching for *emic* models. What do the participants think they're doing? Not just 'what are the participants doing?', that isn't enough, but 'what do they think they're doing?'

A: So, the reification, to close the book on the reification part, is that that this becomes considered to be reading, and it's a thing called reading.

B: A thing called reading, that's a good way of putting it, and that would be a good little title for a section, 'a thing called reading'.

A: Now, to get into the question they're asking about the mechanism, how has this practice view that we've talked about, how is that a mechanism for the meeting of the global and the local?

B: Well, I would say because you can't envisage either local or global, they're only reifications, too, except through practices. The global doesn't exist – a metaphor I like to use – it's not a satellite flying around out there. 'Local' and 'global' are only themselves heuristics, for describing sets of practices. Now, those practices will embed in them features that are local in the sense of familiar to people in an environment and features that come from somewhere else.

A: And it's those features that come from somewhere else that are the question. How do you, when you look at the school – let's say we're doing an ethnography of reading circles in school, how do you invoke those other contexts? Because you can't necessarily see them. In our discussion, we mentioned that it happens all over the world, not only in schools but also in religious circles and in families. You invoked all these other contexts but, actually, when you're just sitting there in the classroom doing an ethnography, you don't necessarily see those other contexts.

B: Ah, well, that might only be an empirical question. I think, at a theoretical level, there is no essential difference between invoking difference, if you like, in a very local situation, where someone from next door walks in, and invoking difference because the Americans have just started bombing you – I don't know why that came to mind, but, still, as an example of a global intrusion. At a theoretical level, there's no necessary difference between the degrees of distance. They may be worth characterising, and they will be different in some ways, but at the fundamental, theoretical construct of proximity-distant they're the same. I would say it's built into all – certainly to all ethnography, but also to all experience. Someone walks in the door from outside, they have shifted our 'local'.

A: So, to take Besnier as an example, if I'm an ethnographer out there and I see they're wearing shirts that have a foreign language on them, I could then begin to trace back where their shirts came from, how I got them.

B: Utterly, totally. Including the writing system piece of it, which would be quite interesting. Okay, they didn't write this themselves, and we're not interested in that. Yeah, but it's a writing system, where did that come from? Oh, someone else invented it. Does that matter? Well, maybe it does, at some level.

A: And then it's a question of what your interests are, ultimately, how you decide to focus the context, because everything could be a context for what's happening.

B: And that is true not only of the researcher, it's true of the people, the participants. And that seems to be one of the most exciting, as it were, anthropological insights. As Dell Hymes says, 'everyone's an ethnographer'. We're not just sitting outside describing laboratory rats moving about in cages. We've got models, and they have models, too.

A: So, one of the questions is, what context are they orienting themselves to?

B: Exactly.

A: And if they're orienting themselves to very, very local contexts, then perhaps the global's been less influential here.

B: So, what the mix of local and global is – that's what I would use hybridity for, really – will vary. It may even vary, it will vary, with context, with situation, if you like, if you want to call it that. Each situation someone's in will mix the local and the global slightly differently. You could argue that there's an institutionally built-in thing that academics – I'm on dangerous ground here – that academics might be more inclined to bring in the distant and the comparative, because that's part of the nature of their work. But, as I said that, I began to think that it may be true of certain academic traditions and not others. I'd like to assume it was built in to anthropology. So, the moment you say something, comparative method looms up, 'well, what might it look like somewhere else? And are they taking any account of that?' But it's very hard to think of a practice that doesn't invoke the distant as well as the local, actually, now we've got into this. There might not be any.

A: Perhaps one of the answers to this issue, or one of the ways of responding to this is to say that the minute literacy gets involved, you have an amplification of the global, because literacy is a way of carrying things in space and time.

B: That's a good way of putting it, yeah; although other semiotic systems might also have this effect.

Searching for a better metaphor

B: But, that – I think – I've just picked up something here that I think we might need to challenge, which is: 'What exactly are these "distant" forces?' If we concede that literacy is not an autonomous entity, then what is the nature of literacy within the broader sociocultural context? Likewise, how do these "distant" forces impact individual literacy events?' I wouldn't want to answer either of those questions. The 'are' and the 'is' are almost ontological kinds of descriptors, if you like. What I want to know is, how do we describe the relations, the incorporation of relative degrees of local and distant in any one event?

A: You could answer, though, this question of what are these distant forces? The answer, which I think that Reder and Davila give in the end, is that these distant forces are very powerful international organisations, global organisations, which have an ideological view of literacy which they're trying to impose upon the local.

B: Does that answer the 'are'? Certainly, it might answer the 'how do they work?' How do they impact on –

A: But why isn't it also an answer to the 'are'? It's also who they are. The UN is sponsoring a literacy programme, which comes into the village, and begins to promote a certain view of literacy, which, that's a distant force, it collides with the local, if you will.

B: But, then, if we want to understand what's happening, we then need to look at what are the relative degrees of incorporation and engagement between the local and these particular forces. So, I'm still slightly less interested in the 'are', although I can see the point, you know, if we're sitting here and someone walks in the door, I'm less interested in the 'are', as it were, the essentialised, reified notion of what this person is bringing, than how we – how the interaction shifts. You know, it's the stone that's fallen into the water, and the waves are now moving, the ripples. I suppose I'm more interested in the ripples than the stones, might be a way of putting it.

A: Well, just in the relationship, in the interaction –

B: So, of course, I have to know the quality of the stone, that's what they're saying, really. This stone has landed in this pond, and I'm interested in the ripples, exactly. And they say, 'yeah, but you need to take account of where it's come from and what it looked like before it landed'. And that's what your UN would be, then, so we have to study the UN.

A: Is there some way in which we can characterise that meeting, which repeats itself over and over again, that begins, sort of, what practices look like when they're global–local interactions as opposed to local–local interactions, and I know that's a problematic distinction.

B: But I wouldn't want to use, for instance, the word 'impact'. I still think that they're over-privileging the 'distant'. The word 'impact' is really problematic in the literacy field, especially at the educational level. So, here are these local people, and this thing called literacy is going to impact on them, and so they are shock absorbers. I think, you know, there is a model running through here.

A: And then your pond-and-stone metaphor looks the same way.

B: That's true, because the pond is just waiting there to be shocked by this stone arriving. But, I'm interested in the ripples. I suppose that's still 'impact', so you're right, in a way. I'm struggling with that same relationship, so I would also want to see what happens when the turtle or the fish leap out of the water and run around in the UN's headquarters, or whatever, and impact on the land creatures, so it isn't just one way. And I think they are interested in a direction of movement, and I'm more interested in the to-and-fro – that's what I meant by 'hybrid'. And they did pick that up, but then they lost it with their shock-absorber, really.

★ Task B4.5.3: Insert your own voice

As we suggested at the end of our discussion on Olson in Section B3.4.3 you might now like to join in the discussion, to insert yourself into the dialogue. One way of doing this might be to read the text aloud and to say your own comments at appropriate points; or you might make use of the literacy event involved in reading this spoken text by actually writing your own words in between the passages from the two of us.

➤ Do you find yourself siding with one of us more than the other?

➤ Or do you disagree with both of us and want to present a third voice?

Perhaps you could also engage in this discussion with some friends and interpellate a number of voices. And more boldly, you could try to say or write how you think Brandt and Clinton might have responded. We hope that such dialogic interaction with the text, whatever techniques you adopt, will help clarify for you both the textual meanings and your own views.

We now move on to Section C in which a number of the themes explored here are treated as the basis for concrete Explorations of your own. As you engage in these activities you might like to draw upon the conceptual and reflective insights developed in the commentaries on Section B and you might extend further particular activities you developed here.

SECTION C
Exploration

This section provides scope for you to explore and research aspects of literacy of particular interest to you. Most of the issues and examples explored build directly on topics addressed in Sections A and B, while some introduce relatively new topics and ideas.

C1   Exploring literacy as social practice
C1.1 Investigating literacy practices – an ethnographic perspective
C1.2 Literacy log

C2   Literacy and education
C2.1 Phonics, whole language and English orthography
C2.2 Children's literature – code, content and practice
C2.3 Academic literacies

C3   Literacy at large
C3.1 Workplace literacies
C3.2 Everyday writing in modern society
C3.3 International policy and practice in the literacy field
C3.4 'Literacy problems' and the mass media

The first Exploration, Section C1.1, introduces you to some tools and methods for investigating literacy events and practices, which you can apply to all the various domains of literacy examined in and beyond the other explorations in this section. The second exploration, Section C1.2, gives you an opportunity to take an inventory of your own experiences with literacy over the course of a single day.

The next three explorations focus on literacy and education: learning to read and write, children's literature, and what it means to be literate in the university. Section C2.1 involves further investigation of a topic central to the phonics versus whole language debate introduced in Section B2: that is, the complexities of using – or ignoring – the phonetic code of the English language. Section C2.2 also investigates issues related to children's acquisition of literacy, but goes beyond the issues of decoding in exploring the political implications of children's literature and related literacy practices. The fifth exploration (Section C2.3) moves us from children's literacy practices to the unique literacy demands of the University, or 'academic literacies'.

The remaining four explorations provide you with opportunities to examine 'literacy at large': for example, in the workplace (Section C3.1) and in everyday activities (Section C3.2). Section C3.3 looks at literacy outside of western society, applying, among other frames, controversies about the 'great divide' studied in Section B3 to United Nations literacy campaigns in the developing world. Finally, Section C3.4 takes us full circle to a topic with which we introduced the book: media representations of literacy 'crises' and how to cope with them (Section A1). In particular, we examine the recent synthetic phonics debate in England, which builds on many of the issues studied in Section B2 'Literacy Acquisition'.

In these units we raise a number of questions for exploration, point you to materials and sources that will assist you in addressing those questions, and – in some cases – demonstrate what such an exploration might look like. Throughout, we provide bibliographical and other suggestions for further resources.

Unit C1
Exploring literacy as social practice

C1.1 INVESTIGATING LITERACY PRACTICES – AN ETHNOGRAPHIC PERSPECTIVE

In Section C you are given opportunities to follow up the academic texts in Section B and the principles and ideas of Section A by engaging in investigations of your own. In this first segment, we map out some of the methods by which literacy practices can be investigated. These ideas may be applied across the board to the explorations below.

We describe a process for collecting and analysing data about a literacy practice, but do not necessarily suggest that you follow this model as is or in the order given. Rather, our intention is to model for you some of the key components of such an investigation. You will need to adopt and adapt these components selectively in accordance with your own questions and objects of inquiry.

Key questions

Recalling the concepts we have discussed above, such as the distinction between events and practices (see Section B4.1), we start by identifying a literacy event, that is an activity in which a written text plays a role. We use the description of a literacy event as a basis to analyse a literacy practice, that is both the social practices of reading and writing and the conceptions or 'models' of literacy that participants use to make sense of them (see Street, 2000). In studying events and practices we examine the following dimensions and questions:

Setting
- ◼ Where does the event take place?
- ◼ What is happening there?
- ◼ How is that site organised?

Participants
- ◼ Who is involved in the event?
- ◼ What social and semiotic resources do they bring to the situation?
- ◼ What are their roles?

Text(s) and other objects
- What texts are present as part of this activity?
- How are the texts identified by the different participants?
- What assumptions have each text's authors made about its prospective readers?

Actions and sequencing
- What are the participants doing?
- Is there any particular order to these actions?
- How do participants know the event has begun or terminated?

Rules
- What are the conventions – explicit and implicit – that govern participants' activity?
- How do we know how to read the implicit rules?
- Who is allowed to say and do what and when?

Interpretation
- How do the participants and observers make sense of the event and the texts involved in it?
- What are the meanings of literacy in this practice?

Contexts
- How might we situate this event in historical and geographical context?
- How is it informed by previous events and practices, and by forces operating elsewhere?
- What relevant histories are brought to bear upon it?
- How have practices evolved over time,
- How have they moved from place to place?
- How do these trajectories affect the way the practice is currently experienced?

Pulling it all together
- What does it mean to be literate in these practices?
- How does this meaning of literacy compare with official literacies promoted in policy and taught in school?
- To what extent are participants' models of literacy autonomous or ideological?
- What are the consequences of being (il)literate in this practice?
- What roles does literacy play, if any, in social differentiation and relations of power?

An Illustration

Let us take, for example, ordering a meal in a restaurant, which typically involves engagement with a written text – a menu – so may legitimately be seen as a 'literacy event'. In attempting to identify the social practice in which the event is located we may fairly confidently claim that the social practice is to do with the activity of ordering a meal. It is enacted daily by countless waiters and customers in innumerable literacy events (see Rose, 2004, for a detailed account of such practices). We might observe, record and take notes on a number of such events; collect texts and photograph sites and artefacts; and converse with participants. In order to extrapolate from the event to the practices that give it meaning, we might carefully and systematically describe their key components – setting, participants, text(s) and other objects, actions and sequencing, rules, interpretation, and contexts – and their implications vis-à-vis the issues raised in this book. We briefly outline how we might apply this framework to the literacy practice of ordering a meal.

Setting

- Where does the event take place?
- What is happening there?
- How is that site organised?

In the example of ordering a meal, the setting is a restaurant, in the case we have in mind, a small café with about 10 tables, 30 chairs and a long bar situated in the middle of London, England. Large windows cover two of the walls, such that the entire café is visible from the busy street outside. Empty burlap coffee sacks labelled 'Ethiopia', 'Guatemala' and 'Columbia' decorate the wall behind the bar, and newspapers are strewn over some of the tables. At the back of the bar is a door to the kitchen, from which clanging noises of metal pots can occasionally be heard. Most of the tables are populated by one or two diners, with the exception of one group of four girls by the entrance.

Participants

- Who is involved in the event?
- What social and semiotic resources do they bring to the situation?
- What are their roles?

The key participants in the event we have in mind include two diners and a waitress. The diners' role is to select their meal; the waitress's role is to consult the diners and transmit their selection to the kitchen. (Sometimes, there are other people involved in this event, for example, the manager may oversee the process, a diner from another table may eavesdrop or even intervene, etc.) We might describe the diners and wait staff in detail:

- What are the diners wearing?
- How old are they?
- How often do they come to this restaurant?
- What do they do for a living? What's the relationship between them? And so on.

Text(s) and other objects

- What texts are present as part of this activity?
- How are the texts identified by the different participants?
- What assumptions have each text's authors made about its prospective readers?

We've already mentioned a number of texts present in the restaurant – i.e. the newspapers, coffee sacks – and the participants may be orienting to them in different ways. The central text in the event of ordering a meal is the menu. We might first identify the range of knowledge and skills necessary to handle this text at different levels, for example looking at the script, choice of language, genre, organisation, layout, pictures, etc. For example, in the café we described above, while most of the menu is written in English, the list of hot drinks appears in Italian: espresso, macchiato, cappuccino, latte etc. What might this detail tell us about the café's intended clientele?

We should also note that the menu is not the only material artefact involved in the event (see Bartlett and Holland, Section B4.2 for use of the concept of artefact to signal how material objects are used by participants to help 'figure' their world). The diners are seated around a table, which is set with salt, pepper and sugar cubes, and the waitress is armed with a pen and pad. These and other objects also serve to define the event, constraining and enabling action, and signifying meanings. For example, we noticed that the diners are very attentive to the waitress's use of her pen and pad: after one orders the other pauses and waits for the waitress to finish writing before beginning to place his or her own order.

Actions and sequencing

- What are the participants doing?
- Is there any particular order to these actions?
- How do participants know the event has begun or terminated?

In our case, the event begins when the waitress approaches the table. Key actions include small talk ('How are you doing today?' 'Cold and wet, but otherwise well . . .'), clarifications about dishes ('Are there any nuts in that salad?'), recommendations ('Everyone loves the burger'), placing the orders ('I'll have the soup'), clarifications about the orders ('Would you like the chips or baked potato?') and a final 'Will that be all?' to signal that the interaction has come to a close. After recording the activities in a number of similar events, you may be in a position to describe a common sequence and implicit rules that govern the interaction.

Rules

- What are the conventions – explicit and implicit – that govern participants' activity?

- How do we know how to read the implicit rules?
- Who is allowed to say and do what and when?

Occasionally, these rules may be spelled out, for example a 'No Smoking' sign, or a notice on the menu requesting that diners refrain from consuming food not purchased in the restaurant on the premises. Most rules are not made so explicit, but none the less constrain participants' behaviour. For example, in the case of ordering a meal, if the diners respond, 'Yes' to the waiter's question, 'Are you ready to order?' there is an implicit expectation that they will not linger too long in deciding what they want. How long is too long? Another implicit rule is that the interaction may be more drawn-out if the restaurant is empty, but should be conducted economically if many other diners are waiting. One way we know how to read these implicit rules is by speaking with participants, who typically sense them, even if they had not thought about them before being questioned by you. Another way to detect the rules is by observing how participants respond when a novice – often the researcher – inadvertently transgresses them.

Interpretation

- How do the participants and observers make sense of the event and the texts involved in it?
- What are the meanings of literacy in this practice?

In this regard, we might listen to the diners' conversation before the waitress came over. One of the diners noticed that some 'errant apostrophes' have appeared in the headings for 'Drink's', 'Cake's', and 'Entrée's'. Given our grounding in literacy in this volume, we might ask further questions about these writing practices:

- What meanings do they attach to this over-exuberant punctuation?
- How does it affect their estimation of the restaurant, the quality of its food and/or clientele?
- Do they attempt to correct the menu, crossing out the superfluous apostrophes, or drawing the waitress's attention to the 'problem'?

Contexts

- How might we situate this event in historical and geographical context?
- How is it informed by previous events and practices, and by forces operating elsewhere?
- What relevant histories are brought to bear upon it?

The assumption built in to the account of events and practices is, as we noted above (see also Section B4), that events make sense because they are located in practices. The very idea of a social practice presupposes a history, that is the repetition of previous events that accumulate into a relatively consistent practice over time. In order, then, to make sense of the present events we might ask:

- How have these practices evolved over time?
- How have they moved from place to place?
- How do these trajectories affect the way the practice is currently experienced?

In the case of ordering a meal, we might look at the history of this particular restaurant, neighbourhood and cuisine. For example, until recently it was difficult to find Italian coffee in London cafés and we might consider whether and why that has changed:

- Has there been an influx of Italians into the neighbourhood?
- If not, what does this change say about the meaning of coffee for those who order it?
- And to what extent are these changes the product of global forces, for example those captured and/or disseminated by the Starbucks chain?

Given that this event is taking place in England, we might also consider:

- How, if at all, do these changes affect the primacy of tea in English identity?

And finally, we might pull back from the specific event and setting to consider broader social issues:

- How does the drinking of coffee index social status and relationships?
- Are there particular people one might or might not drink coffee with? Why?
- Are there particular restaurants, cafés, settings that we would or would not drink coffee in? Why?

Pulling it all together

After describing in detail some related literacy events, and analysing the literacy practices they reflect, you might want to reflect on these practices with regard to some of the key questions raised in this resource book:

- What does it mean to be literate in these practices?
- How does this meaning of literacy compare with official literacies promoted in policy and taught in school?
- To what extent are participants' models of literacy autonomous or ideological?
- What are the consequences of being (il)literate in this practice?
- What roles does literacy play, if any, in social differentiation and relations of power?

This account we have provided is intended to give you some initial ideas about how to go about investigating literacy events and practices. In the other explorations in this section we detail some specific practices and the types of questions that have been asked about them by other researchers. You may choose to further investigate some of these practices, or pursue a literacy event and the practices it is embedded in that have received less attention. Either way, we recommend that you seek the advice of researchers who have conducted such investigations before (see below).

For further information

Some helpful references on methodology include:

Agar (1996) This provides an overview of how anthropologists learn to 'make the familiar strange'.

Barton and Hamilton (1998) (especially Ch. 4 – 'Ethnography in practice') A detailed study of literacy events and practices in a northern town in England; the authors are acutely self-conscious about both the literacy theory they draw upon and the ethnographic methods they employ.

Bloome et al. (2005) The authors provide detailed micro-ethnographic accounts of classroom practices – a must for anyone studying literacy in school settings.

Freebody (2003) This introductory textbook on qualitative research in education contains detailed guidance on key elements of the research process. The sections on analysing interaction and texts are particularly helpful.

Green and Bloome (1997) The authors helpfully distinguish between 'doing an ethnography', which has belonged mainly to professional anthropologists, and 'adopting an ethnographic perspective' which is more widely available, though it still involves drawing upon social and cultural theories, of the kind outlined in this volume, to make sense of the data.

Heath and Street (forthcoming) The authors are anthropologists who have worked in the field of language and literacy for many years and apply their experience to considering 'how' to apply ethnographic perspectives to these areas.

Hymes (1974) Hymes was one of the original founders of the 'ethnography of communication' tradition and he takes the reader through how they might apply ethnographic perspectives to issues of communication, including spoken and written language.

Kamberelis and Dimitriadis (2005) Part of the growing series of support books for students in language and literacy wishing to do qualitative study in these areas (see also Heath and Street above).

Rampton UK Linguistic Ethnography Forum (2004) Rampton and his colleagues in the UK have attempted to bring together work in sociolinguistics with the insights and methods of ethnography.

Scollon and Scollon (2004) An introduction to 'nexus analysis', a research methodology that integrates study of discourse, social interaction, history, persons and technology.

C1.2 LITERACY LOG

Throughout this book we have discussed literacy practices in various domains and contexts – school, home, work, etc. – and have invited you to reflect on your own experiences with such practices. In the following exploration, we invite you to look more systematically at your own involvement in various literacy events and practices (see Section B4.1). We are also building on the 'Encounters with Literacy' (Section A4), in which we introduced you to a variety of literate domains through texts that might be encountered in them. In this exploration we ask:

- What are the domains of literacy you encounter in your daily activities?
- In what literacy practices do you participate?
- What texts do you consume and produce?

In order to address these questions, we recommend that you keep a detailed diary of all the literacy events in which you participate over the course of a typical day (or two), attending to the relevant texts, participants, roles, contexts, rules etc. (see Section C1.1 for a list of relevant dimensions, though we don't recommend doing an in-depth analysis of *every* literacy event in which you participate). A camera is a helpful and expedient tool for engaging in this activity. (See Jones et al. (2000) and Satchwell (2005) for examples of how literacy diaries and clocks have been used in literacy research.)

You may find it helpful to compare your literacy log with that of a classmate, friend or colleague, explaining the contours of the different events and your participation in them. Some questions to consider include:

- How does your participation change over the course of the day?
- What social and cognitive demands do the different literacy events make upon you and others?
- How did you learn to effectively participate in them?
- What conclusions can be drawn from this activity vis-à-vis the core issues discussed in this book?
- How relevant the scope of the book is to your literacy encounters, comparing, for example, the texts in Section A4 to the texts in your own log.

Unit C2
Literacy and education

C2.1 PHONICS, WHOLE LANGUAGE AND ENGLISH ORTHOGRAPHY

In Section B2 we included texts, commentary and tasks that addressed the issues of 'learning to read'. In particular, in Section B2.1 and B2.2 we discussed the debate between phonics and whole language approaches. The following explorations allow you to pursue one aspect of that debate more closely: the complexities of English orthography (i.e. the way print represents sounds), and the way they enable and constrain phonetic decoding. Two questions are addressed:

- What problems and challenges does English orthography pose for phonetic decoding?
- What are the problems and challenges of reading without highly developed knowledge of phonics?

Playing with the phonetic code

The English orthographic system (i.e. the way print represents sounds) is complicated, and contains many 'irregularities'. One of the challenges in teaching phonics, as advised by Adams and others (e.g. Section B2.1), is how to present this system to children. In order to understand and appreciate this problem better, in this exercise you will construct a (very) partial phonetic code and then test its use. First, analyse the code used in sentence 1 provided in Table C2.1 (overleaf) and draw up a chart of symbol–sound (or 'grapheme–phoneme', to use the linguistic terms) relationships (for example 'she' might be represented as /sh//ee/).[1]

Now, 'decode' sentence 2 using only the symbol–sound relationships in the chart you have just created (and not the more complete phonetic knowledge you bring to this exercise). Using only this partial phonetic code, some of the words may be undecipherable, or become distorted.

1 Following linguistic conventions, we use < > to signify letters and / / for sounds. For example <g> (the letter) can be used to spell /g/ and /j/ (the sounds).

Table C2.1 Encoding and decoding with phonics

1. She read the book at night

Symbol	Sound
<sh>	/sh/ as in **sh**arp
<e>	/ee/ as in s**ee**d
<r>	
<ea>	
<d>	
<th>	
<e>	
<b>	
<oo>	
<k>	
<a>	
<t>	
<n>	
<igh>	
<t>	

2. It was a cool read, and I raced through it.

- What were the difficulties? Why do they arise, and how do we deal with them in our everyday reading?
- How might phonics teaching systems deal with these problems?

Commentary

Some orthographic systems, such as Finnish or Spanish, are largely transparent, which means that each grapheme corresponds to only one phoneme. In contrast, English is far more complicated: 26 letters are used to represent 44 different sounds. And many sounds can be represented with more than one grapheme, for example great, they, late, wait, tray, straight and weigh all share the same vowel sound /ay/. Moreover, speakers with different accents pronounce their sounds differently. Phonics programmes deal with this problem in various ways. Most of them carefully control the vocabulary used in the texts children read, minimizing the 'irregular' words, and gradually increasing phonic complexity as pupils learn more graphemes. These controlled texts were traditionally compiled in 'basal readers', which have been severely criticised by the whole language movement as boring and turning children off of reading – hence the emphasis on 'real books'.

For more information on the English orthographic system and its historical development see the interview with Richard Venezky at http://www.childrenof thecode.org/interviews/venezky.htm. For criticism of basal readers see Goodman and National Council of Teachers of English (1988), Goodman (1989) and Shannon (1987).

Playing the psycholinguistic guessing game

Just as the preceding exercise demonstrated some of the problems involved in using a 'pure phonics' approach to reading, the following exercise is designed to demonstrate the problems of trying to read with only limited phonic knowledge.

Try to read the passage in Figure C2.1.

The cat ¥atc℘§d the ¥itc∈.

The ¥itc∈ dr∈⅁℘⌋ a sli∏Ψ n℘℘t into a big ca∈ldr∠ψ.

He c℘℘ld s℘℘ a sm℘lψ on the faΨΨ of the ¥itc∈.

C2.1 Reading without decoding (courtesy Ruth Miskin)

- How was the experience of reading?
- Were you able to decipher the text?
- What allowed you to make sense of it?
- What was difficult?
- What cues did you use?
- What skills and knowledge facilitated the process?
- If the picture was removed, could you work out the words?

Commentary

We encountered this exercise when participating in a teacher training workshop conducted by Ruth Miskin, developer of a synthetic phonics programme called *Read, Write, Inc.* (see http://www.ruthmiskinliteracy.com/index.html). Miskin summarises the exercise: 'Once a child can work out the words (decode) he can then begin to sort out the message (comprehend). If he can't decode the words easily, he can't begin to understand (even the simple passage above).' In reflecting on this exercise you might want to consider:

- How accurate a simulation of early reading is this?
- We have provocatively titled this exercise 'playing the psycholinguistic guessing game', but is it a fair illustration of the whole language approach to reading? What are the problems with it?

C2.2 CHILDREN'S LITERATURE – CODE, CONTENT AND PRACTICE

The articles on early literacy development that we looked at in Section B2, along with the examples of early literacy encounters in Section A4, were primarily about how children learn to make sense of text – without attending to the contents of what they read. However, reading is always reading *something*, and children learn from what they read even as they learn to read it. In this Exploration we invite you to examine critically the contents of children's literature.

Key questions

These include:

- What are the topics and issues typically addressed in children's literature?
- What implicit and explicit messages are embedded in the stories?
- What identities are made available to children readers? What social roles are valued, censured and/or absent in the stories?
- How has children's literature changed over time?
- What 'curriculum' is enacted in the way adults and children interact around children's literature (for example in the ritual of the bedtime story)?

These questions may seem somewhat abstract at this point; we flesh them out in the illustration opposite, which is followed by more detailed questions and ideas for concrete explorations.

Possible sources of data

Your local community library is a natural place to start looking for books and/or conducting ethnographic observation of how parents and children engage with children's literature. Likewise, most large bookstores devote a section of their store to children's literature, and prominently feature the most popular books (or the ones that they hope to sell the most – the way the store is organised, and the commercial logic guiding that organisation, are the topic for another exploration).

We recommend that you consider both classic children's literature (e.g. Dr Seuss, Beatrix Potter, Maurice Sendak, A. A. Milne, Jean de Brunhoff, E. B. White), and more recent attempts to twist traditional children's stories (e.g. Jon Scieszka and Lane Smith's *The true story of the three little pigs*, or Ahlberg and Ahlberg's *The jolly postman*). On-line you'll find numerous web logs ('blogs') devoted to reviewing and discussing children's literature, including librarian-authored Kid's Lit (http://kidslit. menashalibrary.org/), ten-year-old Destiny's Book Reviews (http://odd-ducks.com/ destinys-book-reviews/) and Cybils, the 2006 Children's and YA Bloggers' Literary Awards (http://dadtalk.typepad.com/cybils/).

An illustration

We exemplify the type of analysis we have in mind through consideration of Jean de Brunhoff's (1933) classic *The story of Babar, the little elephant*. We have chosen *Babar* because it is very well known, and has also been critically examined by a number of analysts (our favourite critical discussion, to which this section is indebted, is Kohl, 1995; see also: Dorfman, 1983; Hourihan, 1997; and Lurie, 2004). You may have encountered one or more of the books in the *Babar* series when you were younger, or may read it to children now. If so, you may want to try to recollect your own impressions of the story before we begin critically examining it:

- Did you enjoy it?
- What were your favourite parts?
- What was the point of the story?
- Did it provide any moral lessons?

One of us remembers enjoying the story very much as a little boy (though he could recall no details), and was thus very surprised to encounter Herbert Kohl's (1995) provocatively entitled essay, 'Should we burn Babar?' Below we have provided a rereading of the story in the light of Kohl's fascinating essay (which we heartily recommend).

But first, before reading the content of the story, it might be helpful to pause and examine the story in terms of decoding, of the kind discussed in Section B2.1. Take, for example, the first paragraph of the story:

> In the Great Forest a little elephant was born. His name was Babar. His mother loved him dearly, and used to rock him to sleep with her trunk, singing to him softly the while.

One way to approach this text is to inquire into its 'decodability' (see Mesmer, 2001), or how easily it may be decoded by beginning readers. Decodability is commonly thought of as a function of how phonetically regular the contained words spellings are, and the extent to which the phonemes used have already been learned by the children readers. So, for example, 'Babar' would be expected to have a high degree of decodability, while 'Gr*eat*' and '*whi*le' would be more difficult (see Section C2.1 for elaboration on the phonetic decoding issues involved here). Another issue one might look at is the length of words: a multisyllabic word such as 'elephant' is expected to be harder to read than monosyllabic words such as 'In' and 'born'. Finally, looking at the text beyond the individual words, you might notice that the first two sentences are relatively simple, containing limited information, while the third sentence is complex, containing three verb phrases, and therefore is expected to be harder to follow. Given this analysis, someone with a phonics emphasis might recommend a different book for early readers, for example, a book that uses repetition and rhyming in order to help children appreciate phonetic patterns, for example 'the cat sat on the mat'.

However, as we mentioned at the outset, we're going to go beyond analysis of the text's code, instead focusing on its content. You have already encountered the first page, which tells of Babar the elephant's birth and life with his loving mother in the natural paradise called the Great Forest. His idyllic childhood is disrupted one day when a 'cruel hunter' shoots his Mother. Babar flees the hunter and ends up in a town, where he is befriended by 'a very rich old lady', who takes him under her wing, providing him with human artefacts such as clothes, food, a bed, car and education. After two years of life in the town, during which time Babar has become a bourgeois gentleman, his cousins Arthur and Celeste come to visit him. He decides to go back to the Great Forest with them, where he is crowned King on account of the fact that 'he has lived among men and learned much'.

On one level this story is a typical *Bildungsroman* (coming of age story), in which the hero is separated from the protection of his or her home at a young age, undergoes adventures and overcomes adversity in order to mature eventually from child to adult. This is brought home in amusing fashion through the visual incongruities of an elephant dressed in a suit, doing aerobic exercises, driving a car and having a tea party. However, a deeper analysis of the story reveals what Kohl sees as troubling messages regarding materialism and colonialism.

The story's materialism is evident in the centrality of shopping throughout. Babar's first thought upon arriving in the town is amazement at the houses and people. His

Then he bought:

a shirt,
collar and tie,

a suit of a delightful
green colour,

C2.2 Jean de Brunhoff, *The story of Babar, the little elephant*

second thought was 'What lovely clothes they have got! I wish I could have some too!' The very rich old lady 'loved making others happy, so she gave him her purse'. Next there is a long and detailed sequence of pictures of all that Babar bought: 'a shirt, collar and tie, a suit of a delightful green colour, a lovely bowler hat, and shoes and spats'. Likewise, when Arthur and Celeste come to visit him in the city, Babar immediately takes them clothes shopping and then to a teashop. 'Every day he [Babar] drove out in the car that the old lady had bought him. She gave him everything that he wanted.' The message is clear: buying things makes you happy, and good, kind people give you everything you want.

Kohl notes that Babar didn't dress up as a taxicab driver, salesman or factory worker. He donned a suit and tie, bowler hat and even spats, symbols of the upper class. And, in keeping with his appearance, he lives a life of leisure, cruising around the countryside in his convertible, strolling through the park with the old lady, and socialising with her friends at dinner parties. Where did the old lady's money come from? How must others live in order to afford the old lady and Babar such a comfortable lifestyle? These questions are not addressed in the story, though Kohl suggests that perhaps the old lady is in the elephant hunting business, reminding us that the cruel hunter is also a member of her class. Kohl sees the story's materialist ethos and main characters as teaching children to equate money with goodness (p. 25):

> The people in Paris don't all live like the Rich Lady, her friends, and the people who serve them. Providing young children with a steady diet of the untroubled lives of the rich is one way to equate wealth with well-being . . . However, it is possible to live a full and decent life without great wealth, and it may be that the acquisition of great wealth always comes at the cost of other people's impoverishment.

The elephants at the outset have no consumer items, and in the opening scenes of the book their lives seem happy and complete. However, when Babar, Celeste and Arthur arrive back in the Great Forest, the elephants cry, 'What lovely clothes! What a beautiful car!' and immediately embrace Babar as their King. So the story is not just about Babar's journey from wild youthfulness to civilised maturity, it is also about the taming or colonisation of the primitive elephant society. As such, the books can be read as an apology for European colonialism: the Great Forest is Africa and the elephants are the 'primitive' natives made better and happier by adopting European culture as symbolised by bourgeois clothing (cf. MacKenzie, 1986; Said, 1978; Street, 1975). Rather than resisting the civilisation that killed his mother, Babar flees *towards* the town, and adopts its culture and ways. He brings this culture with him upon his return to the Great Forest and, in a later book in the series, *Babar the king*, he constructs a western-style city in the middle of his elephant kingdom.

Babar and beyond – possibilities for further reflection and exploration

How relevant is this adult reading for how children experience the book?

Kohl remarks, 'It's easy to take children's literature more seriously than children take it, and it's sensible, in the midst of critical musings, to remember that sometimes an elephant in a green suit is just an elephant in a green suit' (p. 24). You might want to pursue this question by reading and discussing the story with some children.

- What do they make of the story?
- What are their favourite characters and scenes, and why?
- What lessons do they draw from the story?
- What do they think of the interpretation we have offered here?

How has the Babar series evolved since The story of Babar?

The first story was written in 1931 in France. Since then, the author's son, Laurent de Brunhoff, has brought the series up to date, in part in response to the criticisms levelled against the early books (see Lurie, 2004). You might find it interesting to compare recent stories in the series to the early ones:

- How have they changed?
- What messages are embedded in the current Babar corpus?

What are the messages implicit in other popular children's books?

You might like to select some other children's books and subject them to a critical reading similar to the reading of Babar provided above. Guiding questions might include:

- Who are the main characters?
- What do they represent?
- What are the key categories (e.g. boys/girls, wild/civilised) and what characteristics are attributed to each?
- Who has power in the story, and how is it exercised?
- What lessons are offered vis-à-vis how to deal with 'difference' and conflict, succeed in life, be happy, etc.?

How are these implicit messages received? How do children and adult readers interact with them in practice?

The above analysis focused primarily on the text itself, while largely ignoring the social and cultural practices of its consumption. Underlying this analysis were certain assumptions about its readers, how they approach children's literature (e.g. unproblematically) and what they make of the text. But to truly appreciate the effect of this and other texts, and to test those assumptions, you would need to go one step further and investigate adults and children's interactions around the text. Very often adults will provide a running commentary on a story they read to their children, asking questions, clarifying elements, speculating about motives and even arguing with various elements. Likewise, children may puzzle over different aspects of the story and ask for explanations. You might observe (and, ideally, record) and analyse readers' joint engagement with the text, and also interview the children about what they've read and how they make sense of it.

■ How does such a practice-based view of the text influence the analysis of its content?

For further information

Freebody and Baker (1985) and *Baker and Freebody (1987)* Systematic study of the way beginning school books attempt to constitute children's identities, thereby initiating them into the culture of schooling.

Kohl (1995) In addition to the essay on the *Babar* books, which served as the primary source for our above discussion, Kohl discusses a wide range of other stories and issues, including a critique of biographies of US civil rights leader Rosa Parks and a discussion of children's interpretations of *Pinocchio*.

Luke (1988) This historical account of the development of literacy policy in the postwar period in British Columbia integrates textual interpretation, political and economic history, and analysis of teaching and learning practices (as prescribed in teachers' manuals).

Street (1975) This book looks at the use of 'anthropological' themes in fictional work during the late nineteenth and early twentieth centuries. Street identified borrowings from the academic literature that fed into the work of popular authors of Empire, such as Rider Haggard, John Buchan, Edgar Rice Burroughs, Rudyard Kipling etc. In these apparently innocent fictional accounts lay key 'scientific' and ideological themes of the time, such as evolution, race, heredity, environment and the notion of the 'primitive'.

C2.3 ACADEMIC LITERACIES

In this exploration we leap from the literacy requirements and texts associated with early childhood to those of the university. Since, as a reader of this book, you are likely a participant in such literacy practices, this exploration has a secondary aim: to enable you to reflect on the styles and expectations for 'academic literacy' you have encountered – and are likely to encounter in the future – and to consider in the light of these what strategies and genres are best suited to your own individual needs. We will help you to do this by setting out five explorations. In Section C2.3.1

we ask you to reflect upon some of your own experience with writing in various contexts. In Section C2.3.2 we invite you to write a book summary and we provide some models based on summaries we have done on recent books in the field of academic literacies. Section C2.3.3 involves comparison between academic and other texts: we ask you to undertake a text analysis of two pieces, one written for an academic journal and one for a lay audience; we then ask you to undertake a 'textual translation' in which you take a lay text and rewrite it as an academic text or vice versa, and we illustrate this with examples from our own writing of a text written for a philosophy conference that was then rewritten for an audience of school teachers. Section C2.3.4 involves an application of what has been learned from all of these texts and explorations to your own writing. The activities conclude with Section C2.3.5: analysing our writing in this book (in the spirit of reflexivity and critique that we have tried to maintain throughout).

The overall approach adopted here is based on work in the field of 'academic literacies' that is explicated below and that applies a 'social practice approach to literacy' (Section B4; see also Hyland, 2006) to the requirements for writing held by institutions, faculty and students. There are many different 'writing styles' envisaged by these various participants, and one of the major problems is that these different expectations are not always made explicit – rather it is assumed that 'writing is writing – just do it'. Students for instance may be asked to 'write up' a discussion as though that writing were simply a transparent representation of what had been said, a 'dump' of the oral language, whereas in fact there are very particular genre and style requirements for such writing depending upon the context, the field of study, the personal preferences of tutors etc. We will try to explore these issues here, providing some background reading, some tasks and some suggestions for making explicit and enhancing your own writing proficiency according to the context and demands you encounter.

C2.3.1 Reflecting on your own writing

Before engaging closely with the literature we cite and beginning the other explorations we propose, just reflect upon your own experiences with writing in various contexts:

- Do you find some contexts, topics and audiences easier to write about than others?
- Has academic writing (and reading) posed any particular problems for you?
- What ideas and activities were helpful for you in finding your way in the world of academic literacy?

It should be interesting to contrast your own experiences with those of others; such a discussion may even provide a good basis to make generalisations about the nature of academic literacy, and to generate ideas for how best to induct students into it. In what follows we suggest some additional activities for exploring academic literacy.

C2.3.2 Summarising an academic book or article

A common first task in academic work is to review the literature on a topic: summarising – and, ideally, critiquing – what has been written about a certain topic or issue and providing an overview of the state of the art in the field. In the Further Information section we have provided examples of brief summaries of recent books in the area of academic literacy, and offer an overview of the field in the next paragraph.

Recent and forthcoming publications on *academic literacies* have explored the issues involved in student writing and faculty perceptions, expectations and feedback, using combinations of ethnographic-style study of *practices* and critical analysis of *texts*. These approaches, building on the social practice perspective indicated by the papers in Section B4, assume that reading and writing are socially and culturally embedded practices. Becoming academically literate, then, involves learning to read, write and think in an academic way, which includes language and interaction amongst members of the institution. Again it is practices as well as texts that are foregrounded and institutions as well as individuals. Researchers explore such issues as appropriateness and varieties of language; discourse communities within the academy; the gap in expectations between students and faculty; and learning as 'social events'. The findings revolve around evidence-based research and conceptualisation of literacies in keeping with contemporary pluralistic models. The very coincidence of so many works appearing at the same time across different countries and research traditions suggests:

- the emergence of a powerful field of enquiry that is attempting to shift the ways in which we understand and research student writing in academic contexts
- that long-term research programmes, rooted in revised theoretical framing of underlying assumptions about literacy in general and academic literacy in particular, represent a positive way forward in this field
- that applications grounded in such theory and research provide a new way for both academics and new learners to combine theory and practice in understanding writing in the academy in both new and more traditional contexts.

Before you start to write your own summary you might reflect upon our summaries in the Further Information section below and ask:

- Do our summaries meet your requirements at this stage?
- Do they offer a helpful model as to how such writing might be done?
- If you have criticisms then take these into account in writing your summary.

Writing your own review

Now use these brief summaries to model one of your own. Select a book or article in the field that you feel you would like to explain to others, because it is helpful and/or because you want to challenge the position taken by the author(s). To get you started, you might call upon the terms and the style used in the genre we present below. We have noted a number of the key words that appear in our summaries:

> *accessible; refers to; tended to be hidden; providing a research basis; influential; shifts the focus; evidence; offers insights; go well beyond; particularly interested in; focus; implications; move beyond; attempt to; pitched at a more theoretical level; aiming; locate; more subject than; major point; argue; drawing on models.*

1 You might go back over our summaries and see whether there are other terms that you think are key.
2 Then organise them into themes that help give a piece structure, for example:
   ■ Description of the piece: *refers to; particularly interested in*
   ■ Author's focus or argument: *argue; major point; aiming*
   ■ Relationship to other arguments: *(which) tended to be hidden; pitched at a more theoretical level; more subject than; move beyond; shifts the focus; drawing on models*
   ■ Evidence base: *providing a research basis; evidence*
   ■ Implications: *influential; implications*
3 Go back to the chosen article or book and skim read to check whether these terms and headings capture what you want to say about it.
4 Now use these terms and any you have added, and this structure, including any further headings, to begin to write your own critical review of the article or book you have chosen.
5 Did your opinions of the article or book change as a result?

C2.3.3 Academic and lay literacies

Textual analysis

Choose two texts, one for an academic journal and the other for a lay audience, written by the same author, and analyse the differences between them. (One way to locate appropriate texts would be to check the c.v. or web page of a favourite academic author for articles in the popular press.)

■ What makes an academic text 'academic'?
■ What are the advantages of the two different types of writing?
■ Create a list of comparative characteristics of the academic and lay genres you are analysing – attending for example to discourse structure, syntax, word choice, authorial stance, etc.

Textual translation

Take a lay text and rewrite it as an academic one (or vice versa). This 'translation' process is something that we've found ourselves engaged in many times. In what follows we provide you with a recent example, which may help you further develop your understanding of academic and other genres of writing. One of the authors wrote an academic paper about dialogue in schools, initially for a conference in philosophy in education, and later as a working paper in the King's College London 'Working Papers in Urban Language and Literacies' series (http://www.kcl.ac.uk/depsta/education/wpull.html). The first three paragraphs of the working paper draft are reproduced below (as text 1). Later, he was invited to give a presentation on the same topic for an audience of school teachers, and asked to prepare a brief abstract, reproduced overleaf (as text 2). He had thought that this text did a good job of presenting the ideas in a non-academic fashion, but the organiser of the event thought he could do better. She responded to the proposed abstract as follows:

> My only question might be around how well the [practitioner conference] audience would identify with the language . . . Of all people, [the early childhood educators] would most certainly identify with the notion of educational dialogue but I guess we need to be sure that it doesn't all sound too academic?

The third attempt appears as text 3 (p. 215). Review these three texts, and judge for yourself their relative advantages.

- What makes one more 'academic' than the others?
- What is gained and/or lost in translation?
- How might you improve upon them?

Text 1 – Extract from article for academic working paper and conference

Dialogue in schools – toward a pragmatic approach
Dialogue, as an ideal, has become rather fashionable. It is proposed as remedy to a broad variety of issues, including irrationality, false consciousness, multicultural strife, ineffective learning, textual understanding, the creation of civil society, postmodern ethics and what it means to be human. It is enthusiastically embraced by educators working in philosophical enquiry, sociolinguistic research, teacher preparation and policy. Having crossed every other threshold, one is tempted to conclude, its entrance into our classrooms is merely a matter of time.

Yet, ethnographic and linguistic studies repeatedly show that the overwhelming majority of classroom interactions adhere to the infamous Initiation-Response-Evaluation (IRE) framework (Cazden, 2001).[1] In this

1 Recent UK studies include: Burns and Myhill (2004), Galton (1999), Moyles (2003), and Smith et al. (2004).

deeply ingrained pattern, teachers *initiate* discourse by lecturing or asking predominately predictable, closed questions, usually designed to test pupils' recall of previously transmitted knowledge and/or to discipline inattention. Pupils *respond* with one- or two-word answers. Teachers *evaluate* student responses, praising correct answers ('well done!') and censuring error ('you haven't been paying attention!'). Teachers dominate talk by controlling the topic and allocation of turns, by speaking more often than pupils and for longer periods of time and, indirectly, by privileging pupil contributions that are essentially a revoicing of previous teacher utterances.

The persistence of non-dialogical teaching in the face of so much enthusiasm should give us pause: Why hasn't dialogue become a common form of classroom discourse? True believers round up the usual suspects: 'inept' teachers, an over-crowded curriculum, managerialism, the audit society, 'youth today'. While each of these explanations may account for part of the failure to make schools more dialogical, I am troubled by this general line of reasoning, in which theories of dialogue themselves remain largely unquestioned. In this essay, I seek to shift the focus: rather than positing a dialogical ideal and decrying schools for not living up to that standard, I question prevailing common sense about educational dialogue against the background of current structures and cultures of schooling. I argue that *idealistic* models of dialogue are ultimately inimical to formal educational practice, and propose in their stead a *pragmatic*[2] approach better suited to the school context.

Text 2 – Abstract for presentation to audience of school teachers

Getting over Socrates: toward a practical approach to dialogue in schools
Educational dialogue is an old idea that has come back into fashion. Yet, notwithstanding all the recent excitement, our classrooms remain over-whelmingly monological. The persistence of non-dialogical teaching in the face of so much enthusiasm should give us pause: Why hasn't dialogue become a common form of classroom discourse? True believers round up the usual suspects: 'traditional' teachers, an over-crowded curriculum, managerialism, the audit society, 'youth today'. While each of these factors may contribute to the failure to make schools more dialogical, I am troubled by this general line of reasoning, in which theories of dialogue themselves remain largely unquestioned. In this presentation I seek to shift the focus: rather than positing a dialogical ideal and decrying schools for not living up to that standard, I question prevailing common sense about educational dialogue against the background of current structures and

---

2 'Pragmatic' here is intended to invoke James's philosophical Pragmatism, not 'pragmatics' in the linguistic sense.

cultures of schooling. I argue that idealistic models of dialogue are ultimately inimical to formal educational practice, and propose in their stead a practical approach better suited to the school context.

Text 3 – Abstract for practitioner audience, revised in light of criticism that Text 2 might sound 'too academic'

Getting over Socrates: toward a practical approach to classroom dialogue
Teaching through dialogue is an old idea that has come back into fashion. Educators around the world are encouraging teachers to promote discussion and debate, to give pupils more opportunities to express themselves, to probe pupil understanding, and to generally talk less. Yet, despite all the excitement for such 'dialogic teaching', teacher monologues dominate talk in most classrooms. Why has traditional classroom talk persisted despite all the calls to change it? In this presentation I question the common sense about educational dialogue against the background of the way schools are currently organised and run. I argue that currently popular models of dialogue are overly idealistic. In their stead I propose a practical approach better suited to the realities of schooling.

C2.3.4 Application to your own writing

Having laid the ground by looking at the background literature and some analyses of other people's writing, you are now in a good position to apply these ideas to your own writing.

- Take a draft, two or three pages in length (not a piece you consider to be finished), and work with friends or colleagues on analysing and improving it.
- Then reflect on your own piece of writing in the light of Crème and Lea's account of the writing process (see p. 217). For instance, they argue that each writing task is different: it has different 'elements' and requirements and can be characterised in terms of 'type', 'genre', 'structure', 'style'. Look in particular at the question of genre and consider what text type your writing belongs to.

C2.3.5 Analysing the writing in this book

Finally, go back over some of the texts you read earlier in this resource book and consider how well they have matched up to the demands laid out above:

- What textual genres were included in this volume?
- Did the authors take sufficient account of audience and context?
- How did they cope with the interdisciplinary nature of the field (and its readership)?

- Did the authors just go off on their own tack without worrying about whether you were following?
- Apply these parameters to our own writing throughout the volume.

Since the resource book is designed to help you develop your understanding and knowledge of the field of literacy, it is particularly important that the literacy we as authors use to do this meets these requirements; we cannot simply hide behind the 'authority of the book'! You should be in a stronger position to make your own judgement in this after working through the above activities. We hope we have met the standards you will by now have set for yourselves and that you have enjoyed the readings and the activities as well as learned something from them. Some brief summaries of recent publications on academic literacies follow.

For further information

Chris Candlin and Ken Hyland (1999) edited a collection of essays under the title *Writing: texts, processes and practices*. Calling on authors from a range of international contexts, they argue for an 'integrated and multidisciplinary perspective' on 'the study of academic and professional writing'. They see three dimensions underlying writing research; 'the description and analysis of texts, the interpretation of processes and the exploration of the connections between writing and the institutional practices which in large measure are constituted and sustained through writing'. The major point that comes from this complex compilation of articles is the importance of evidence-based research in an area that may be more subject than most to anecdote and generalisation, given that academics themselves are the participants and therefore liable to have strong interests and ideas about their own practice.

Carys Jones, Joan Turner and Brian Street (1999) likewise locate their edited volume *Students writing in the university: cultural and epistemological issues* in these new approaches, aiming to 'raise awareness of the underlying complexities concerning student writing in the university'. Pitched at a more theoretical level than many of the manuals for study skills that pervade the field, the authors attempt to clarify what it means to represent and to do research about student writing at the university, taking account not only of researcher models but of those of students and tutors themselves. The research on which the articles are based aims to move beyond the narrow confines of current policy debates in this area – concerned with competencies, measurement, accreditation, certification and surveillance – to 'explore the epistemological, cultural, historical and theoretical bases of such writing'. The implications of such reconceptualisation for practice are considerable and, like the other work emerging in this field, the authors have an eye on practical outcomes as well as wanting to give serious credibility to research in the area.

Mary Lea and Barry Stierer's (2000) *Student writing in higher education: new contexts* likewise locates the research dimension of the field within the major changes taking place in higher education, in both the UK and other settings including South Africa and Australia. The focus of this book is upon 'new contexts' within which the writing and assessment practices of university courses are currently located, and the authors are particularly interested in innovative approaches identified in both traditional academic and more professional subject areas. The implications of this research for university teachers are considerable and go well beyond what is being prescribed by new agencies devoted to 'raising standards' in university teaching, such as the Institute of Learning and Teaching in England.

Roz Ivanic's (1998) *Writing and identity* offers insights into students' own perceptions of the writing process, particularly as it relates to issues of identity formation and their relation to institutional pressures. Using detailed longitudinal evidence from a cohort of mature students, the author shifts the focus from the pathologised student with writing 'problems' to the complex institutional procedures and to the ideas and images of those involved. This includes both students themselves and faculty as they make writing requirements central to their interpretation of the learning process. This seminal work is influential to many of the other texts summarised here, again providing a research basis for understanding complex processes that have tended to be hidden beneath policy considerations, traditional assumptions or new study skills work units focused upon 'quick fix' solutions to apparent student problems.

Theresa Lillis's (2001) *Student writing: access, regulation, desire,* like Roz Ivanic's, derives from collaborative research with mature students in higher education. The 'access' in the title will be familiar to those working in HE in the UK at present – it refers to, on the one hand, government policy for 'access' for 'non-traditional' students and, on the other, in the author's terms, to issues of discourse, language and meaning as representational resources to which access may be 'regulated' by the processes and mechanisms of academic institutions. Likewise, 'regulation' refers to issues of meaning making in academic writing and the varieties, across fields, disciplines and institutions, of ways in which meaning is construed and defined. Finally 'desire' refers to the varying and often contested aims of different parties regarding access and choice and the making of meaning. Drawing on Lea and Street's and Ivanic's models, Lillis unpacks the ways in which becoming an 'insider' is defined and controlled and opens up the field of academic literacies to questions of power and value.

Mary Lea and Phyllis Crème's (2003) *Writing at university: a guide for students* is a 'how to' book that is rooted in the principles of academic literacies approaches and so is less 'technical' and 'fix it' than many others in the field. The book is targeted at university students and their academic tutors and aims to make the reader more aware of the complexity of the writing process, taking account for instance of the many different 'writing styles' required by different courses and tutors. They offer practical guides intended to build upon the student's prior experience but extending it in the light of the kinds of writing assignments they are likely to be required to produce. They engage, for instance, with the relationship between reading and writing and the use of personal and textual cohesion, taking the reader through such issues as 'You and your writing', 'First thoughts on writing assignments' to 'Writing your knowledge in an academic way' and finally 'Completing the assignment'.

Unit C3
Literacy at large

C3.1 WORKPLACE LITERACIES

The activities we suggest below with regard to workplace literacies build upon the text by Gowen in Section B4.4. In this Exploration we suggest that you attempt to address Gowen's arguments for yourself by looking at specific examples and then reflect back on her text in the light of the data you collect. We also suggest you use this specific case to link back to the theories and methods outlined in this resource book: for instance, we propose you use a method of working that is derived from some of the concepts and ideas you encountered in Section B4, in particular the distinction between literacy events and practices (ideas we also developed in Exploration C1.1). By the end you will be in a good position to reflect and comment upon the usefulness of this as opposed to other approaches.

We suggest you do the Exploration in your own workplace, or members of your family or friends might be able to facilitate access to their workplaces. Obviously you need to be sensitive but often workers are happy to engage in discussion with researchers if their aims are well laid out beforehand and there is no hidden agenda.

Having identified a workplace you could then map out a research plan for gaining access, asking specific questions of the kind detailed below and then analysing your data.

Gowen provides detailed ethnographic-style accounts of the everyday literacies her subjects brought to bear on such tasks as taping church services, repairing and marketing cars, managing a restaurant etc. You might try to observe some similar examples of people at work, in particular examining the literacy dimension. For instance, in Section C1.1 we sketched an account of a waitress or waiter that encompassed reading menus, writing orders, passing slips of paper to chefs, preparing bills etc. and you might also refer to the book by Rose (2004) that we mentioned there for further categories of this kind. You might find similar categories and use a similar procedure in the workplace you have chosen. One way of doing this might be to mark out a period of time during which you will observe workplace practices and begin to ask questions of some participants. Ideally, for a major research project this might be a year or more; for a minor study, one week might be sufficient. Keep a detailed day diary in which you describe the events and practices you observe and keep notes on questions and issues that arise – you will want to consult these later as you try to make sense of what you have found out.

We recommend moving into the research site gradually, taking account of the sort of dimensions, issues, and questions raised in Section C1.1 'Investigating Literacy as a Social Practice'. You might want to read that Exploration again now. If for instance you have five days to undertake the research, you might focus your attention as follows:

Day 1 – Physical environment
- Describe where the workplace is situated.
- Describe the room in which the activity you intend to focus on is situated and its physical character (including, of course, signs and other literacy artefacts).

Day 2 – Social environment
- Begin to take notice of who is meeting with whom.
- Are there hierarchies, role, gender, age differences?

Day 3 – Skills or tasks
- Drawing upon Gowen, you might begin to consider what are the workplace skills that each participant brings to bear. For instance, you might observe the balance between speaking and writing, and within writing the balance between use of computers and handwriting.

At this point you are just noting questions and considering which ones it might be possible to raise and which should be shelved. Again, you are taking it slowly and not rushing to ask questions directly yet.

Days 4–5 – Interviews
Having sifted the questions you began to develop for yourself above, you might now try to address some of them to the workforce. Depending on how well you feel you are getting on with those in the workplace, you might develop more questions that locate the events described up to now within larger historical and social practices:
- What training have different participants had in the different literacy and oral skills required?
- What did they bring from their last workplace that has been relevant here?
- Do they see their work life as a continuity of developing skills or are the different practises so different they require separate skills?

Post-field work analysis – Revisiting Gowen

You will now have a number of pages of notes and comments and can review them with some of the earlier questions in mind but also with an eye to whether they raise new questions and how well they help you to address the kinds of issues raised by Gowen. We recommend that you now go back to the Gowen piece and consider whether your data are commensurate with her questions, claims and conclusions:

- Are there some questions you can answer – for example what skills do the workforce bring from their home environment?
- And some that are harder and would require more and perhaps different research – for example whether the workforce are being denied the kind of educational and literacy support that would facilitate their promotion?
- What would be required to get the kind of data Gowen accumulated and what are the limits both of her and your data regarding the kinds of claims and arguments that can be made?
- Did the people you spoke with or listened to express any views on the nature of literacy and the kinds of literacy skills required?
- Does your research raise new and different questions not addressed by Gowen?

Links to the theories and methods outlined in this resource book

In the light of texts you have been reading in this resource book, you might analyse whether your respondents' views can be characterised in the terms employed by different academic sources, for instance autonomous or ideological; skills or practices.

Gowen talks about the ways in which 'post-industrial' models challenge earlier perspectives on the workplace. Does your data speak to these larger issues? Did the employers and friends you are discussing this with raise these issues? For example, did they indicate a difference between industrial and post-industrial, or did they use other terms to describe such a shift, such as 'new work order' or 'post-Fordist'?

We proposed that you use the distinction between literacy events and practices to facilitate your workplace observation. You should now be in a good position to reflect and comment upon the usefulness of this as opposed to other approaches.

Implications for your own ideas and assumptions

You could then move back out from the particular domain of workplace literacy to consider what the implications are for theory more generally of the particular findings in your data.

One aim of your activity is to enable you to question your own assumptions as well as those of the authors we have been considering in this section. You might review this whole experience from this perspective and take stock of where you have got as you enter the last stages of the book.

C3.2 EVERYDAY WRITING IN MODERN SOCIETY

Despite claims that literacy is not what it used to be (see for instance Section C3.4), there is increasing evidence that in everyday life people are using writing for a wide variety of purposes and in a range of ways, including diaries, letters, notes and memos and making observations on social life around them (see in particular Barton and Hamilton's accounts of 'everyday literacy practices' in Section B4.1 and Gowen's concern for the detail of workers' home as well as workplace literacies in Section B4.4). We provide here an opportunity to explore these issues further, with reference to the Mass Observation Project (MO), a famous UK example of 'ordinary' people using writing to 'speak for themselves'. In this exploration, you will first respond to a MO 'directive' to reflect on your own everyday writing experience. Next, you will contrast your response to those of one of the 'official' MO respondents. Finally, we offer some possible directions for further inquiry into everyday writing processes, through the MO archive and other means of inquiry.

Begun in 1937 as a way of giving voice to ordinary people's views of the abdication crisis and continued through the war as a way of countering the dominant propaganda about how people were supposed to be feeling, MO has continued into the twenty-first century with a Panel of 'Observers' who write regularly in response to 'directives' that ask their views on such everyday matters as family changes, health, everyday interpretations of science, issues of 'race', gender, nationhood, the role of the royal family, the death of Princess Diana, Britain's involvement in wars (Falkland, Iraq) etc. (see p. 224 for details of how to access the material).

We here propose that you act as one of the MO 'Observers' and answer an actual 'directive', which was sent out in the spring of 1991. In doing so you can both reflect on the content issues raised there by the observers and commentators – the nature of writing in everyday life – and also engage in the writing that actual participants do, thereby using your own experience to address the concerns about literacy raised here, and indeed throughout the resource book.

The spring 1991 MO directive asked the correspondents to write about the writing process itself – what did it mean for them to write in this way and what other forms of writing did they engage in, for example letters to newspapers, minutes for local committee meetings, keeping a diary etc. Detailed answers to this directive were published in Sheridan et al. (2000), especially Section II, 'Dialogues and writing practices', which mainly consists of extracts from correspondents' own writing.

Responding to an MO directive

Provide a response to the following directive on 'The uses of writing and reading'. (While many of the questions deal with the task of writing for MO, treat these as more general questions about your own everyday experiences with writing.)

MASS-OBSERVATION: DIRECTIVE SPRING 1991
PART II – THE USES OF WRITING AND READING
(Please remember to start this part on a new sheet of paper)

This section is about your everyday uses of reading and writing and your ideas about them. The yellow form enclosed with this directive is for use as a sort of diary. The form asks about all kinds of reading and writing. Instructions on how to fill it in are on the reverse side of the form.

The following twelve questions are mainly about your writing for Mass-Observation, whether it's a diary, a directive reply or a special report. People who have been writing for us for a long time will probably find it easier to answer than newcomers, but I'd be grateful if everyone would have a go.

You will probably find it easier to answer if you read the questions all through first and there will be some overlap.

1. Before you start writing for M-O do you discuss your ideas with anyone else? If you do, who are they? Do people know that you are a 'Mass-Observer'?
2. One you've written your contribution, do you read it out to anyone, or show them what you've written? Has any ever asked you not to write about them?
3. Do you need to be in a particular sort of mood to write for M-O? If you do, please describe it?
4. When you write, do you need to be in a particular place? Do you have a special chair, table or desk? Do you write at home or at work? Do you ever write while travelling or away from home?
5. Do you need to have a particular pen or pencil or type of paper? Do you prefer to type or word-process?
6. Do you need privacy and silence to write or can you write with people and noise around you?
7. Do you get started as soon as a directive arrives or do you like to mull it over? Do you answer all in one go or in different sessions? Do you make notes or do a draft first?
8. Have you kept copies of what you send us? Do you ever have after-thoughts'?
9. What do you think you get personally out of writing for Mass-Observation? Do you think writing for M-O has changed you? In what way?
10. In your opinion what is the value of this kind of writing and of the whole project?
11. Do you do other kinds of writing apart from your M-O work? Please describe. How are they different from your M-O writing? (style, pace, mood etc).
12. Lastly, we have had the honour of receiving your photographs but most of you have never seen us. Can you put into words what you imagine we are like at the Mass-Observation Archive? What do you think the Archive is like? When you write do you have a reader in mind? If so, who is it?

Contrasting your responses to those of MO correspondents

The MO correspondents' answers to these questions are described and analysed by Sheridan and colleagues in their (2000) book *Writing ourselves: Mass Observation and literacy practices*, which you might like to consult and compare these answers with your own. We reproduce here some examples of these answers taken from the book.

One of the researchers interviewed a Mrs Wright in her home about how she responded to directives and she answered:

> When it arrives I read through it and I think about it – odd moments you know – like waiting for the train or on the train going up to work and sort of scribble bits down on bits of paper here there and everywhere. I scribble notes to myself – if I had this piece of paper in my bag I'd probably scribble all notes all over it and think, 'That's along the lines of what they were talking about then'. I remember that and scribble a note down to myself and then I sort of – it's only on a day where I've got the time, then I sit down and sort of say, 'Oh well there's that note there and there's this one here, and oh, there's another bit of paper there' and put them all together then. When I've got the time, which might not be for – nearly 'til the next directive is due – I sit down and write it all out.
>
> I'm usually sitting in the chair [in the living room] and there's probably football or something on the telly that I don't want to watch so I write it then. My husband and son are quite used to it now. I usually do my books in the chair, the finances and a crossword or something, you know – I'm not usually sitting watching television, I'm usually doing something else as well, knitting, or – anything.
>
> I like to think about the directive especially exceptional points like [question] 12 in this directive [the Uses of Writing and Reading] struck me as unanswerable and I have given it a lot of attention. I answer as much as I have time for in each session but break off to talk, get refreshments or watch a TV programme. A session is flexible according to what else is going on, but I would wait until I felt I could give it at least an hour's attention. For diaries or the Gulf Crisis I would make notes first and then write up trying not to change things with hindsight. If I write on the train I would consider that a draft copy, as the writing would be illegible. Sometimes I make notes on the directive itself when reading through as ideas spring to mind.
>
> I avoid questions that I don't want to answer and – it's the same with talking to you – I'd change the subject.
>
> (Sheridan et al., 2000, p. 141)

How does this compare with your own response to the directive above? Mrs Wright, for instance, says question '12 in this directive [the Uses of Writing and Reading] struck me as unanswerable'.

- Did you respond in this way to any of the questions?
- Do you 'scribble' on the train as she does?
- Or like Mrs Wright, do you mix writing with everyday home activities, like making tea or watching television?
- She has quite strong views on the writing process, from resisting the questions that MO asked her to mapping out time and space for writing – does this correspond at all to your own everyday writing practices?
- What does all this tell you about yourself as a writer?

Further lines of inquiry

The preceding activities were designed to stimulate your interest in everyday literacy practices and in the Mass Observation Project. You may wish to follow these topics up with original investigations. The MO archives provide a wealth of data for analysis (see below for access information), allowing, for example, investigation of how literacy practices, writing styles, etc. have changed over time and/or in response to various events. Alternatively, you might want to engage in ethnographic observation of others' everyday literacy events and practices, using the methods and tools outlined in Section C1, or to gather friends and colleagues together for a discussion of your different answers to the above directive and reflections on the associated questions.

For further information

Information on MO, including a list of publications and details of how to visit and use the Archive are available through the Archive website: http://www.massobs. org.uk/. If you cannot actually get to the Archive in Brighton, examples of the material in the Archive, the observers' responses to directives, early diaries etc. are now available in microfiche format and in digital form.

Sheridan et al. (2000) An account of a research project in which MO correspondents were interviewed in their homes about their writing practices, both for MO and more generally. Provides both analysis by the authors based on social literacy theory and lengthy passages from the correspondents' own accounts.

C3.3   INTERNATIONAL POLICY AND PRACTICE IN THE LITERACY FIELD

Readers might be interested in moving beyond their immediate country of work or home location and the literacy issues raised there, some of which we have signalled specifically for the UK and USA, and to explore broader policy issues and practice in the international context. Here there has been a long history of countries in the 'North' developing ways of bringing literacy to the 'South'. In the immediate post-Second World War era, this tended to be framed in a rather postcolonial way, and metaphors of 'bringing light into darkness' or of 'curing ills' were frequent. UNESCO has been deeply involved from this time in developing policy and in urging member states to bring resources to bear on literacy 'problems'. The organisation publishes annual statistics on literacy levels, and the comparison of these is often crucial for economic decision making, investment etc. More recently, the organisation's reports have paid more attention to qualitative approaches to the complex relationships between 'literacy and development', and the recent *Global monitoring report on literacy* offers a rich up-to-date resource for exploring these issues further. We here focus on this as the most up-to-date and generally available report on literacy in international contexts. We suggest you access the report on the website (http://portal.unesco.org/education/en/ev.php-URL_ID=43283andURL_DO=DO_TOPICandURL_SECTION=201.html) and then address some of the questions we pose overleaf.

As the website indicates, 'Global Monitoring focuses on how the world is doing in implementing the policies and actions for achieving the Millenium [*sic*] Development Goals (MDGs) and related development outcomes'. It is a framework for 'accountability in global development policy'. The GMR on literacy 'aims to stimulate renewed national and international awareness of the crucial importance of literacy for achieving all the Education For All (EFA) goals'. To get to grips with this topic, then, you will need to become familiar with at least some of the frequently used acronyms and their policy histories, notably Millennium Development Goals (MDGs) and the Education For All (EFA) goals. Across ten chapters, the document summarises these international policy positions and projects as they apply to literacy, unpacks different definitions of literacy, introduces new qualitative concepts (such as 'literate environments') to the dominant quantitative discourse and eventually sets 'priorities for action'. The GMR drew upon a large number of commissioned papers (over 120) which are all also available on the website. If you are not familiar with the scale of such enterprises in international policy making, then the GMR on Literacy provides a helpful way in. Since you begin with considerable knowledge of the field, following the materials you have read and the activities you have engaged in through the earlier parts of this resource book, you are well placed to act as an 'expert' in relation to the enterprise. Indeed, you might reflect on what it means to be an 'expert' in such a field.

In the following exploration you will move from (1) reflection on what you already know (and have learned from this volume) to (2) checking assumptions against data, (3) applying all to this to the GMR, (4) engaging in discussion and feedback (including with policy teams via email sites etc.) and (5) writing up your findings, and finally (6) doing research of your own on policy and practice regarding literacy in your region.

Reflection

First, reflect on what you already know about literacy and its place in the policy context.

- Write down a page of key issues and concepts you have encountered in government and other policy documents.
- What phrases and metaphors stand out from these documents – for example 'light into darkness', 'challenge', 'rights', 'cure' etc?
- How are approaches to literacy in policy documents similar to and/or different from those encountered in this volume?
- What is included under the heading of 'literacy'? For instance, in many cases 'numeracy' is seen as included within literacy – is this how you have approached it? (If you are interested in numeracy and its relationship to literacy see Street et al. 2006).

Checking assumptions against data

Second, make use of your reading in this volume to check on the assumptions about literacy that are prevalent in policy statements, whether in the media or in official documents and reports (see p. 229 for url links to major documents in this field). For example, you might consider:

- Do the public statements assume the kind of 'crisis' we saw in the very first newspaper reports we examined in Section A1?
- Where do the policy makers stand on the kinds of issues we unpacked in Section B, as different academics contested the space of literacy theory and its application?
- Do they, for instance, go along with Adams and Snow (Section B2.1 and B2.3) in emphasising cognitive aspects of literacy acquisition or with Goodman (Section B2.2) and Scribner and Cole (Section B3.2) in taking a more holistic view that includes social dimensions?
- Given how new the 'social practice' approaches cited in Section B4 are, we might expect to find less attention to this in the policy statements. Is this the case? Or are there documents, reports, newspaper accounts that seem more attuned to the Barton and Hamilton (Section B4.1) view of 'situated literacies', the Bartlett and Holland (Section B4.2) conception of 'the space of literacy practices' or the Martin-Jones and Jones (Section B4.3) concern for 'multilingual literacies'?
- If not, then you might reflect on what you or they think is the role of academics in relation to policy. Are the authors in Section B4 indulging academic debates that have little significance for policy or practice? Should they be more attuned to the applications of their work?

We raise this final issue in part because the authors in Section B2 have had a great deal of influence over policy. Adams, for instance, was lead author of a major report in the USA that was also frequently cited by the UK government as it developed a more centralised policy and curriculum on literacy in the late 1990s.

■ What might be the reasons for the differences in degrees of influence the various approaches to literacy have had in influencing policy?
■ Are some authors just whistling in the dark because dominant discourses are too powerful for their new ideas to take hold? Or perhaps their ideas are unrealistic or unworkable?

Apply to GMR

Third, having explored these issues with respect to the material you have encountered in this resource book, and public policy statements, you will now be in a good position to extend your insights to the GMR document cited on p. 225 which we use here as a particularly full and up-to-date account of these issues. The aims of this exploration are to reflect upon the influence on policy of the different academic approaches discussed in the resource book, and to explore the differences between literacy policy in 'western' developed countries and in the 'developing' world. In particular consider:

■ Where does the GMR stand, do you think, on the learning or cognition or social practices approaches?
■ Is the position mapped out there similar to that with which you are familiar from UK or USA policy statements and documents?
■ Is the international dimension of literacy simply subsumed to a 'westernised' framework of thought and policy or does it take on some of its own features?

For instance, it had been assumed until recently that literacy levels in westernised countries were not a 'problem' – at least until the 'crisis' discourse began to take hold (see Sections A1, C2.1). In relation to so-called 'developing' countries, the assumption has perhaps been held for longer that 'low' literacy rates are an impediment to 'development', a 'disease' to be 'cured', a 'problem' to be solved. Economic, social, individual 'progress' are often associated with the acquisition of literacy, as we have seen (cf. Section B4). So you are now well placed to assess:

■ Does this view hold even more strongly with respect to countries seen as 'underdeveloped', 'behind'?
■ Where does the GMR Report stand on these issues?
■ What impression does it give of countries in the 'South' and which of the various arguments does it use – implicitly or explicitly – to underpin its account?

You might find it helpful to keep notes, a record of your reflections at this stage, and to link them with the page references for the articles and sources in the resource book or those you have found for yourself as part of the activities.

Discussion and feedback

Fourth, having used such reflections in order to establish your own starting position, you might now move outwards and enter into discussion with others on these issues. These days, such discussion can take place electronically, through web links etc. as well as through face-to-face encounters. The web page cited previously for the Global Monitoring Report on literacy has a link for 'feedback' and you might use this to raise some of the issues signalled earlier as you engage in your own activity. Members of the GMR team in Paris are able to respond to such feedback and you might take their comments into account as you build up a fuller picture of the international policy arena for literacy. (A similar facility is available in the UK for accessing discussion forums on adult literacy (and numeracy) via the National Research Development Centre (NRDC) website – http://www.nrdc.org.uk/. And in the USA you might consult the National Center for the Study of Adult Learning and Literacy (NCSALL) – http://www.ncsall.net/)

Mark out some themes, issues and/or questions that arise in these various forums, both national and international, as you engage in discussion with those already working in these fields. If you are reading this resource book as part of a course, then feed these themes into workshop or seminar discussions. Or you might know of local specialist groups interested in international development issues (for example the National Center for the Study of Adult Learning and Literacy (USA); UNESCO Institute for Lifelong Learning (Hamburg); UK Commission for UNESCO; World Development Forum; British Association for Literacy and Development; etc.) and you could join these, attend meetings and raise some of the questions about literacy you have been exploring and reflecting on.

Write up findings

Fifth, one outcome of such discussions can be for you then to write up your findings so far. In a more formal context, this could take the form of a traditional research paper or essay in which you address a key question that has arisen or explore some concepts/ideas that are ambiguous or contested. Possible questions to guide your writing:

- What does work on literacies and development in international contexts have to say to the learning and teaching of literacy in your own country?
- What changes when you bring to bear on current policy debates about literacy the theoretical literature you have been reviewing in this resource book?

Like the Mass Observation 'observers' discussed above (Section C3.2), you may have found yourself collecting some written record of your activities as you work through this resource book, or you might have stored on the computer some of the materials we have come across here, such as selections from the GMR, NRDC etc. and your own notes and reflections. If you have engaged in 'feedback' or 'discussion groups' on the websites, you might save some of these exchanges and perhaps come back to them later as you compare international and national policies and practices in this field. Or you might simply keep a notebook where you write your reflections and note the references you have used. Whatever form your records take, you are now in a position to reflect like the MO respondents on what this means for your view of 'writing' in your life and indeed in contemporary society more generally. Since this resource book is about literacy, you can use your own literacy as a resource for exploring the questions it raises.

Research of your own on policy and practice regarding literacy in your own region

Sixth, using the examples cited in chapter 3 of the GMR on Literacy, 'Country efforts: increasing momentum', you might follow up the local situation in your own country and region. That chapter

> examines selected elements from a sampling of national Education for All (EFA) plans, considers public financing and household costs and continues the 2005 Report's attention to teachers, focusing particularly on projected needs. It stresses the necessity of maintaining momentum towards gender parity, despite the disappointment of the missed goal, and the growing urgency of other crucial issues: social inclusion; redressing the balance between primary education and the inclusion of youths and adults in literacy programmes; education in difficult country circumstances (e.g. in situations of conflict).

- Which of these issues can you identify in your own context?
- What are the government and local agencies in your region doing about it?

You could also go back over the issues raised above, as you engaged in reflection, discussion and exercises and select key ones to focus on as you investigate local practice. You might then consider producing your findings as a 'Report' of the kind evident in the GMR document.

For further information

International Agency Documents: the UNESCO GMR Report on Literacy 2005 together with the 'background papers' produced in association with it, has a comprehensive bibliography and url list for both academic research and agency reports in this field: http://portal.unesco.org/education/en/ev.php-URL_ID=43180 andURL_DO=DO_TOPICandURL_SECTION=201.html. For details on the UK see the National Research Development Centre (NRDC) website – http://www. nrdc.org.uk/. An equivalent organisation in the USA is National Center for the Study of Adult Learning and Literacy (NCSALL) http://www.ncsall.net/. For details of a project on numeracy as well as literacy you might consult the following which also provides a useful bibliography on work in this area: Street, B., Baker, D. and Rogers, A. (2006) 'Adult teachers as researchers: ethnographic approaches to numeracy and literacy as social practices in South Asia', *Convergence*, XXXIX (1), 31–44.

C3.4 'LITERACY PROBLEMS' AND THE MASS MEDIA

For the past two decades the media have been full of accounts of 'falling standards' in literacy, of 'crises' in the capacity of people to read and write, and of the dire consequences for national prosperity of this growing 'illiteracy epidemic'. Indeed, we opened this book in Section A with excerpts from three newspaper articles discussing precisely such an alleged literacy crisis and what should be done about it. In this final exploration you will investigate these and other media representations of literacy and related problems in light of your reading of and reflection on the texts in Sections A and B.

Key questions

You might consider:

■ How do the mass media present 'literacy' and why it is or is not a problem? What aspects of the issue are included in or excluded from the media's discussions?
■ What solutions are recommended?
■ What benefits are promised if the problem is resolved?

These questions are of course central to the discussions in Section B: the texts in B1 discuss what is included in the term 'literacy', the texts in B2 suggest explanations for problems in literacy acquisition and possible solutions, and the texts in B3 analyse the consequences of literacy. Comparing these texts and your reflections on them to the mass media accounts, consider:

■ What issues are highlighted and/or marginalised in the media representations?
■ Are there any inaccuracies or misleading passages?

In Section B you encountered a number of different traditions with competing interpretations of 'literacy', literacy problems, solutions and their consequences: for example psychological (Adams, Snow, Olson), psycholinguistic (Goodman), cultural psychological (Scribner and Cole), anthropological (Goody and Street) and New Literacy Studies (the authors in Section B4). One overarching issue in analysing the mass media representations is to consider:

■ Which academic views are given the most weight – implicitly or explicitly – in these popular accounts?
■ How has academic research been positioned in the public debates?

Possible sources of data

There are plenty of resources for finding data on this topic:

■ The articles in the Introduction (Section A1). Revisit our synopses and brief extracts, and of course also the complete texts of the original articles (available in your local library).

■ Just check your daily newspaper; we predict that there will be a relevant story or opinion-editorial piece quite soon!

■ Search newspapers. One helpful source, which may be available to you if you're affiliated with a university, is Lexis-Nexis (http://www.lexisnexis.com/academic/), which allows for searching by keyword (e.g. 'literacy', 'illiteracy', 'phonics', 'crisis') and also downloading the text of the full articles. See list of suggestions of specific articles in For Further Information section (see p. 233).

■ Special interest groups and organisations working in the area often provide summaries and/or the full text of articles of interest to them. See, for example, the UK National Literacy Trust (http://www.literacytrust.org.uk/literacynews/index.html), or the National Research and Development Centre (NRDC) for adult literacy and numeracy (http://www.nrdc.org.uk).

■ Video news programmes. Check your library for video-recordings. Also, many news programmes now have on-line archives of reports (see for example the BBC programmes in the illustration below).

An illustration

For an example of an analysis of a media representation see the article 'Literacy makeover: educational research and the public interest on prime time' (Lefstein, in press), which is also available on-line at http://www.tcrecord.org/Content.asp?ContentId=13450 (requires subscription). This article is an analysis of BBC *Newsnight* reports on the synthetic phonics debate broadcast on 26 May, 20 June and 20 July 2005 (currently available on-line at the BBC website: http://news.bbc.co.uk/1/hi/programmes/newsnight/4584491.stm, and http://news.bbc.co.uk/1/hi/programmes/newsnight/4700537.stm). The article explores the questions outlined above, with a particular emphasis on how educational research is represented in the news reports and in the subsequent studio debates.

One interesting issue that emerges in this article is the extent to which *Newsnight* reporters attempt to force the issue into the classic phonics versus whole language 'reading wars' frame discussed in Section B2. Consider for example the following exchange between *Newsnight* Moderator Kirsty Wark and Dominic Wyse, a Lecturer in Primary Education at Cambridge University.

> WYSE: I think the – the research picture – there's a very good American
> Reading Panel report which surveyed hundreds of studies on phonics

and concluded that statistically there was no great advantage of synthetic phonics, which is what we're talking about, over analytic phonics. And –

WARK: Wait – in laymen's terms analytic phonics is?

WYSE: Well, that's a good question actually [chuckles]. Analytic phonics is basically about taking larger chunks of words, analysing them –

WARK [interrupting]: Look and see.

WYSE: Uh, well, yes.

WARK: But is it – do you think that the way that children learn is about the mix of the way they're taught, what is on the page, and about how to approach the page rather than the pure sounds?

WYSE: I think the big point about learning to read is there is no simple answer, and anybody who says . . .

Wark's summary of Wyse's explanation of analytic phonics as 'look and see [*sic*]' is baffling. Wyse hadn't said anything to suggest such a characterisation, which indeed is erroneous. Where did Wark's idea come from? 'Look and *say*' is a term critics use to (perhaps unfairly) characterise whole language. Wyse chooses not to contest Wark's misrepresentation, in part because that would further complicate the definition, and perhaps also on account of being bullied. Wark next presents what she assumes to be Wyse's position on how children learn to read: 'the mix of the way they're taught, what is on the page, and about how to approach the page rather than the pure sounds'. Note that Wark's interventions here reflect an attempt to place the debate into the customary reading wars frame (for example, invoking the so-called look-and-say method), including positioning Wyse as an advocate of whole language. Wyse's position, however, does not fit into either the whole language or phonics camps, though the viewer of the programme might have a hard time understanding that.

Reconsidering Section B2

Following your viewing of these programmes and/or reading of this article – and of course your own explorations of other mass media representations – reconsider the way we have presented the issues in Section B2. In other words, whereas before we asked you to judge the media accounts in light of Section B2, we now suggest that you assess Section B2 in light of the media representations:

- Should the 'reading wars' divide between phonics and whole language still be the dominant frame of reference?
- If so, how accurately have the different positions been presented in the Section B2 texts?
- And to what extent has the discussion proceeded beyond that dichotomy?
- What other frames of reference have you identified?
- Do these also fall into the kind of black/white, on/off dichotomies that have characterised the 'reading wars'?

For further information

Specific newspaper articles that provide a rich basis for analysis

Adey, P. (2003) 'Benefits of the strategies debatable?', *Times Educational Supplement*, 11 April, p. 21.

Bradbury, M. (1994) 'We gave the world a universal language. Why can't we teach it to our own children any more?', *Daily Mail*, 23 March, p. 8.

Cassidy, S. (2005) 'Government exaggerated literacy and numeracy crisis', *The Independent*, 25 January, p. 18.

Judd, J. (1993) 'Literacy depends on how you read the figures: is it a real decline in standards or just a wobble?', *The Independent*, 9 December, p. 31.

Kelly, M. (1998) 'Spelling out the crisis in literacy', *The Scotsman*, 19 January, p. 17.

Phillips, M. (1998) 'Spare the teachers and spoil the child', *Sunday Times*, 18 October, p. 19.

Times Higher Education Supplement (1998) 'Superb timing as academy leads way on standards', 16 October, p. 14.

Times Higher Education Supplement (2007) 'We must tackle the literacy crisis', 30 March, p. 12.

Academic analyses of media coverage of literacy crises

Berliner and Biddle (1995) Written by two psychologists, this book seeks to assess the accuracy of the myths of US educational crisis: that standards are falling, that schools are a failure and that educational expenditures are of no avail.

Welch and Freebody (1993) A discussion of the reasons for an alleged 'literacy crisis' in Australia and elsewhere in the western world.

Maeroff (1998) An edited collection of articles about media representations of schooling in the USA, written by historians, scholars of media studies, educationalists and journalists. See especially chapter 7, 'Reading and the media' by Dorothy Strickland.

Smith et al. (2003) This book looks at the media treatment of educational issues (including chapter 5 on literacy research) in terms of the political and economic interests at play.

Larson (2001; second edition 2007) A number of authors review the claims made for literacy and for standards with particular reference to the No Child Left Behind legislation in the USA.

Research studies of literacy standards (to compare mass media reports to more academic sources)

Brooks (1997), Hilton (1998), Levine (1998), OECD (1995), Robinson (1997), Street (1996; see also other comments in same issue of *Literacy across the Curriculum*) and Tymms (2004).

Conclusion
Coming to terms with new literacies

Throughout this volume we have mainly addressed literacy as reading and writing of print. However, in looking forward, we feel it is important to point beyond this dimension of literacy. We conclude, therefore, by signalling two areas ripe for further enquiry, which we label here *new literacies* and *multimodality*. Whilst recognising that this is not the place to delve into this area as deeply as we would like and as the work warrants – that, indeed, is for another volume – we provide a brief overview that we hope offer a helpful way into this area.

Understanding literacy in its social context these days involves, according to some researchers (see for example references in the 'New Literacies' section of the Annotated Bibliography), even more attention than before to locating the language and literacy dimensions within broader semiotic systems. Kress and van Leeuwen (1996), for instance, describe these different communicative resources as 'modes' – visual signs, notation systems, colour, layout, kinaesthetic and other ways of signifying meaning that do not necessarily draw upon a language system directly. Hence the growing field of 'multimodality'. With respect to visual mode they have suggested ways in which theoretical perspectives developed within the language area could be applied to other modes, what they term a 'grammar of visual design'. Science educators such as Carey Jewitt (2006) have focused on the semiotic dimension of learning about science in schools. There is much work to be done on relating the literacy dimension to which this volume is devoted to the broader themes associated with such 'multimodality'. Some of the literature on this theme has referred to these varieties of communicative practices as 'new literacies' (Street, 2006), although the term is often used to focus particularly on new technologies such as those associated with the internet and digital forms. Street, however, has warned of the dangers of a new 'technological determinism' if literacy is taken to refer just to a particular technology.

Growing attention is being paid to the educational dimension of multimodality and new literacies, in ways that link closely to many of the texts and activities we have engaged with above (cf. Abbott, 2000). If there is more 'mixing' of modes these days and if the new digital technologies such as the internet are leading to new communicative practices, then how should we be facilitating learners to take up and use them (Cope and Kalantzis, 2000; Hawisher and Selfe, 2000)? Some argue that for many children this is now second nature and it is their parents who need most help. But not all children have been exposed to the varieties of modes and communicative practices. And there are many examples (cf. Leander and Sheehy, 2004) where schools incorporate new technologies into old ways of thinking that fail to take full account of their 'affordances'. In any case, the whole point of 'education' is that it helps us reflect critically on our 'skills' and naturalised practices, so there is always need for educational approaches to such new communicative practices.

In the light of the detailed accounts of print literacy evident throughout this volume, you might like to ask whether these practices and skills are really so 'new'. Hasn't here always been a 'mix' of 'modes' of communication – visual, linguistic, sound? Old Bible manuscripts, for instance, created their meaning not only through the words on the page but through use of illuminated highlighting, such as at the beginning of a text, and similarly Islamic calligraphy has long used decorative representations of letters to do more than just impart the content meaning of passages of the Qur'an – the very appearance of the lettering at the entrance to a mosque, for instance, attests to the glory of Allah. And in non-religious contexts, too, the use of 'visuals', whether to illustrate children's books or to advertise consumer goods, is a well known feature of our communication systems (see Section A for some vivid illustrations).

We hope that by reading this resource book you will feel you are in a good position to take such a critical and reflexive view of new literacies and of multimodality. We hope that, as a result of engaging with the texts and activities we have outlined above, you will feel confident to take on this new dimension of 'literacy' and to keep moving on even as you close this particular volume.

Annotated bibliography

LITERACY ACQUISITION

GOODMAN, K. S. (1982) *Language and literacy: the selected writings of Kenneth S. Goodman* (ed. Gollasch, F. V). Boston: Routledge and Kegan Paul. This volume gathers a selection of papers written by Kenneth Goodman (see Section B2.2) between 1964 and 1977. Included are some of the classic statements of Goodman's positions, divided into three sections: 'The reading process', 'Miscue analysis' and 'Approaches to research'. Goodman explains in the book's foreword his motivation for publishing this collection: 'many references and treatments of my ideas are now being based on secondary sources rather than my own statements. It is hoped that greater accessibility will make it possible for readers to check out representations and characterizations of my beliefs and convictions themselves' (p. viii).

ADAMS, M. J. (1990) *Beginning to read: thinking and learning about print.* Cambridge, MA: MIT Press. Another classic volume in the history of research into reading acquisition, this book summarises and integrates a vast body of (primarily psychological) research on literacy acquisition. Adams's review was commissioned by the US Office of Educational Research and Improvement 'to provide guidance as to how schools might maximize the quality of phonic instruction in beginning reading programs'. The book is divided into six sections: a historical survey of the field, including the public debate over phonics; the importance of phonics; what skilled readers know and are able to do; what needs to be taught; learning how to read; and conclusions. She summarises the gist of her position thus: 'In brief, reading depends integrally on deep and thorough knowledge of spellings and spelling-sound relations. At the same time, both the use and acquisition of such knowledge depend on the child's fuller understanding of and interest in the reading process' (p. 11). Appended to the volume is a (dissenting) Afterword by Dorothy Strickland and Bernice Cullinam. The book is almost 500 pages long; Steven Stahl and colleagues prepared a 150-page summary: *Beginning to read: the new phonics in context (a précis of the classic text)*, published by Heinemann (1990).

NUNES, T. and BRYANT, P. (eds) (2004) *Improving literacy by teaching morphemes.* London: Routledge. This edited volume sidesteps the phonics/whole language debate that has been the focus of many of the readings and tasks in this volume (Section B2, C2.1), instead drawing attention to a relatively neglected dimension of literacy: morphological knowledge. Morphemes are the smallest unit of meaning in the language, such as the suffixes '-s', '-est' and '-ing' in the words 'morphemes', 'smallest' and 'meaning' in this sentence. Knowledge of such morphemes can help readers make sense of (and write) spellings that might be seen as 'irregular' in a pure phonics approach. The book presents findings from a number of studies demonstrating the benefits of the teaching and learning of morphemes for literacy acquisition.

CONSEQUENCES OF LITERACY

FINNEGAN, R. (1988) *Literacy and orality*. Oxford: Blackwell. Ruth Finnegan is a social anthropologist who has worked especially in West Africa, attuned to linguistic and cultural meanings and in particular to the role of orality in 'traditional' societies. She brings this experience and perspective to bear on the debates regarding literacy, challenging the hypothesis made famous by her anthropologists colleague Jack Goody regarding the 'great divide' between literacy and orality. She rejects the technological determinism of this approach and challenges the view that the presence or absence of literacy is a fundamental differentiating factor – between either societies or individuals. She instead focuses on cultural and contextual factors, drawing upon a wide range of recent work in history and anthropology as well as first-hand field work in Africa, Europe and the South Pacific. A key overview of the controversies from one of the major players in the field.

GOODY, J. (ed.) (1968) *Literacy in traditional societies*. Cambridge: Cambridge University Press. Goody is the central figure in debates about the 'effects' or 'consequences' of literacy. This collection of essays, published in 1968, include a famous piece co-written with Watt on 'The consequences of literacy' that set the tone for debate for subsequent decades. The volume as a whole remains a major point of reference for more recent critical perspectives, of the kind evident in the work of Finnegan, Street, Barton and other authors summarised here. In fact, the essays in this volume do represent more of a mix than is often recognised, that by Kathleen Gough on literacy in Kerala already laying the ground for critiques of the over-determinism for which Goody and others have been berated. A range of anthropologists, working in Africa, China, India, Thailand and Melanesia plus some historical work on pre-industrial England makes this a rich scholarly volume that certainly demands scrutiny in the new literacy environments that engage scholars today.

SOCIAL PRACTICE APPROACHES TO LITERACY

STREET, B. (1995) *Social literacies*. London: Longman. This is a collection of Street's essays that particularly helped to introduce the idea of a 'social practice' view of literacy to a US audience. It reproduces essays that developed the distinction between 'autonomous' and 'ideological' models of literacy, distinguished between literacy events and literacy practices and provided a definitive critique of traditional approaches, such as that of Walter Ong. The book also includes essays on literacy and education and literacy and schooling.

BARTON, D. and HAMILTON, M. (1998) *Local literacies: reading and writing in one community*. London: Routledge. One of the seminal books in the field of literacy studies, this volume provides a report and analysis on many years of ethnographic-style field work by a team of researchers in the town of Lancaster, in the north of England. The researchers walked the streets, knocked on people's doors, hung around newsagents and book stores to capture the everyday uses of literacy amongst a variety of people. The authors reflect carefully on their field methods and offer advice to readers plus providing feedback to their own respondents who in turn comment on the methodology. In some ways this has become the UK equivalent of Shirley Heath's classic *Ways with words*.

COLLINS, J. and BLOT, R. (2002) *Literacy and literacies: texts, power, and identity*. Cambridge and New York: Cambridge University Press. The authors attempt to move literacy studies a stage beyond the mere adding on of more and more ethnographies of literacy, asking how literacy is implicated in domains of power and of subjectivity. The book provides a useful summary of previous research, critiquing both the 'consequences' debate and the situated approach and draws upon historical accounts to develop a new synthesis. In particular the focus is on power, cultural form and historical processes, with detailed reference to case studies.

GEE, J. P. (1990) *Social linguistics and literacy: ideology in discourses*. London: Falmer. One of the early moves in the direction of what Gee here terms 'New Literacy Studies'. Originally published in 1990, this collection of Gee's articles has since been updated and republished in 1996 and that volume especially is frequently referred to. The chapters entitled 'Literacy: from Plato to Freire' and 'Background to the "New Literacy Studies"' are especially relevant to the present volume, covering changing approaches to the study of literacy that eventually emerged as a social practice view. Gee has been credited for taking literacy out of school (although Heath, Cole, Graff, Street and others were making similar moves) although his position is rather that school 'mediates' community-based social institutions and public institutions and their literacies. In this volume too he makes the distinction between Discourse with a big 'D' and discourse in its more traditional sense, more focused on language and text analysis.

GRAFF, H. (1979) *The literacy myth*. New York: Academic Press. Another seminal text in the field of literacy studies, in this case rooted in historical accounts that challenge the dominant assumptions about literacy, assumptions that Graff refers to as the 'literacy myth'. Using data drawn from nineteenth-century Canadian cities, he shows how the myth that literacy leads of itself to social development and progress in fact disguises forces of inequality and discrimination. Drawing on historical data, both qualitative and quantitative, regarding the lives and livelihoods of men and women in three cities, he examines their work, migration, mobility and family partnerships. He then links these specific social data to general themes regarding the uses and meanings of literacy.

HEATH, S. B. (1983) *Ways with words.* Cambridge: Cambridge University Press. Probably the earliest of the social studies of literacy, and certainly one of the most influential, this book uses detailed ethnographic and linguistic study over a long period to show how literacy varies between different communities and between everyday life and the school. Dealing with the Piedmont Carolinas during the 1960s, Heath details the ways with words that characterise everyday life, whether on the veranda discussing letters, through bedtime stories or in children's narratives, and she contrasts these with the specific formal practices of schooling. There are two sections: 'Ethnographer learning' tells of her own ethnographic experience in tracking literacy in the three communities; and 'Ethnographer doing' shows how this more culturally sensitive approach was introduced into the teaching and learning process. An Epilogue, which has attracted considerable further attention, notes the difficulties that this attempt to build bridges actually encountered.

SCRIBNER, S. and COLE, M. (1981) *The psychology of literacy.* Cambridge, Mass.: Harvard University Press. Scribner and Cole were amongst the first to attempt to retheorise what counts as literacy and to look outside of school for empirical data on which to base sound generalisations. Their account of literacy amongst the Vai people of Liberia, West Africa, involved both ethnographic description of context and psychological testing and measurement of the consequences of different uses and forms of literacy. They used these approaches in order to test out claims in a 'real life' setting From this more empirical perspective, they challenged many of the claims about the cognitive consequences of literacy that derived mainly from abstract hypotheses not based in evidence. From this they argue that many of the assumptions about literacy in general are 'tied up with school-based writing'. This book became the basic reference point for the subsequent empirical and theoretical debates about the limits of the 'great divide' hypothesis.

GREGORY, E. and WILLIAMS, A. (2000) *City literacies: learning to read across generations and cultures.* London: Routledge. A more recent example of the application of social theories of literacy to new sites, in this case the city of London. Using a combination of ethnographic field work and linguistic analysis, the authors explore the lives and literacies of different generations living in two contrasting areas of the city, Spitalfields and the City at the end of the twentieth century. Differences between poverty and wealth and ways of learning and using literacy are identified across different contexts – classrooms, clubs, places of worship. Respondents are also given space to recount their own family histories and memories of literacy. Complementing Graff's account of nineteenth-century cities in Canada, the study links everyday literacies with those in classrooms, drawing attention also to issues of ethnicity and language variation.

RECENT BOOKS EXPLORING LITERACY IN EDUCATIONAL CONTEXTS

LARSON, J. and MARSH, J. (2006) *Making literacy real: theories and practice for learning and teaching.* Sage: London. In 'Framing literacies' Larson and Marsh attempt to reconnect what we know about literacy learning to what we do. The book takes three prominent theoretical frameworks – New Literacy Studies, critical literacy, and sociocultural theory – and illustrates what these frameworks look like in real case examples, articulating how the frameworks discussed work together to construct rich and complex contexts for literacy learning and progressive frameworks for research.

PAHL, K. and ROWSELL, J. (eds) (2006) *Travel notes from the New Literacy Studies: instances of practice.* Clevedon and Buffalo: Multilingual Matters Ltd. Another volume in this genre, edited by Rowsell and Pahl (forthcoming), also attempts to make links explicitly between theory and educational practice. At a theoretical level they attempt to combine the multiliteracies and the multiple literacies positions: 'To meet the demands of our changing communicational landscape, we need to adjust our notion of literacy and its implications on how we produce texts in multiple settings, at different times, by different sets of actors'. At the same time they want to follow through the implications of this for pedagogy and curriculum, and the authors in their volume provide examples of actual classroom practice where such shifts can be identified.

BLOOME, D., S. P. CARTER, B. M. CHRISTIAN, S. OTTO and N. SHUART-FARIS (2005) *Discourse analysis and the study of classroom language and literacy events – a microethnographic perspective.* Mahwah, NJ: Lawrence Erlbaum. The authors present a social linguistic interactional approach to the discourse analysis of classroom language and literacy events. Building on recent theories in interactional socio-linguistics, literary theory, social anthropology, critical discourse analysis and the New Literacy Studies, they describe a microethnographic approach to discourse analysis that provides a reflexive and recursive research process that continually questions what counts as knowledge in and of the interactions among teachers and students. They link close analysis of linguistic features of social interaction with what Gee (1990/1996) terms the 'social' turn in language study: they devote chapters to the social construction of identity; to power relations in classroom events and beyond; to the role of multiple literacies, not just spoken language or a narrow 'autonomous' model of literacy; and to the broader understanding of 'people's everyday lives' of the kind acknowledged in the oral history movement and the UK's Mass Observation Project (which receives some original treatment in chapter 5).

STREET, B. (ed.) (2005) *Literacies across educational contexts: mediating learning and teaching.* Philadelphia: Caslon Publishing. Grounded in the New Literacy Studies (NLS), this collection of essays challenges international colleagues to apply to diverse educational contexts some of the principles entailed in viewing literacy as a social practice. The volume includes sixteen case studies of innovative educational projects by researchers and practitioners working across the boundaries of traditional educational institutions and the everyday lives of their students. Their work also seriously tests and challenges NLS theory. The accounts include processes of literacy learning in school and out of school; in elementary, secondary, higher education, adult education; through field trips, school councils, service learning;

amongst lesbian, gay, bisexual, transgender and queer youth; in the Project Freire Literacy Academies in New York City and the Hispanic Academic Program in Northern California; via multi-grade schooling in the Peruvian Amazon and in heritage language and literacy programs in Hawai'i. The authors explore what it means for students to learn and teachers to teach literacies across local and global contexts as people move between cultures and communities in the twenty-first century.

MAHIRI, J. (2004) *What kids don't learn in school: literacies for urban youth.* New York: P. Lang. Following a graduate research class run by Jabari Mahiri at Berkeley that drew upon work in New Literacy Studies, the students went out into local neighbourhoods to engage in their own research and provide a series of detailed accounts of the uses and meanings of literacy amongst urban youths in different contexts. The edited book includes also responses from fellow academics.

LEWIS, C., ENCISCO, P. and MOJE, E. B. (forthcoming) *New directions in sociocultural research on literacy.* Mahwah, NJ: Lawrence Erlbaum Associates. [From the Foreword by B. Street] Amongst the outpouring of books that address what it means to think of reading and writing in terms of social theory, rather than more narrowly in terms of cognitive skills and educational measures, the present collection is both timely and distinctive. The authors bring together critical accounts of sociocultural theory with equally critical and incisive accounts of literacy. This task is timely because many of us are struggling with the limits of both fields at this moment. Sociocultural theory can offer us a way of recognising the learning processes and practices associated with reading and writing, a perspective that is especially important in educational contexts where literacy acquisition continues to be represented as decontextualised and atomised skills; but sociocultural theory has tended to shy away from the broader political and ideological issues that have led to such misconceptions in the first place. The authors in the present volume attempt to redress this balance by invoking the concepts of power, identity and agency in interpreting literacy learning and practice.

HULL, G. and SCHULTZ, K. (eds) (2002) *School's out!: bridging out-of-school literacies with classroom practice.* New York and London: Teachers College Press. The authors sketch (pp. 11–31) the major theoretical traditions that have shaped research on the relationships and borders of literacy in and out of school – the ethnography of communication, cultural historical activity theory, and the New Literacy Studies – and use research in the field of literacy in the United States to offer broader theoretical and practical frameworks for comparative work. This volume, complemented by numerous articles in key sites, has established a key benchmark for such debates about literacy in and out of school.

LARSON, J. (ed.) (2001) *Literacy as snake oil: beyond the quick fix.* New York: Peter Lang. The chapters of this edited book paint a gloomy picture of contemporary literacy policy in the United States, with implications for other countries moving towards more regulatory and mandated curriculum for teaching literacy in schools.

The authors argue that current literacy policy and programmes reduce literacy and its teaching to a limited and limiting set of technical tools, which are bundled into commercial packages. These packages are sold to schools and parents as a modern form of magical 'snake oil' that is guaranteed to cure all educational ills. The research community and government have colluded with commercial publishers in pushing this quick-fix approach, which has damaging effects on children and schools. The authors discuss these ideas in relation to specific contexts, ranging from reading theory and the work of the National Academy of Sciences Report on Reading in the USA to broader accounts of policy and reform and specific analysis of programmes. A second edition of the book, which includes discussion of literacy policy in the UK, is in press in 2007.

LITERACY AND DEVELOPMENT

FREIRE, P. (1972) *Pedagogy of the oppressed.* London: Sheed and Ward. Freire's work has been the most influential in world development circles in applying alternative theory and politics to the learning of literacy. Starting with field experience in Brazil, where he developed local literacy programmes intended to help poor people learn to 'read the world' as well as 'the word', his ideas spread to many Third World countries and eventually also to the USA and Europe. He evolved a theory of education for literacy based on the conviction that every human being is capable of looking at the world critically in a dialogue with others. The intended effect of this process is for the learner to transform their world, to bring radical self-awareness to the forces of oppression. This involves both general philosophical principles and precise technical details of the learning process – such as using key words to build up a literate vocabulary. This book was the first public presentation of Freire's philosophy and remains the seminal text in the field of literacy and development, whatever subsequent critiques and refinements might be now identified.

NEW LITERACIES

COPE, B. and KALANTZIS, M. (2000) *Multiliteracies.* London: Routledge. The authors in this edited volume look forward to the future of literacy teaching and learning in the context of rapidly changing communicative media and practices. Originally defined as the New London Group, the influential group of contributors, including a number not part of the original NLG, bring together different national and international experiences to the redefinition of what counts as literacy – or 'multiliteracies'. In particular, the role of new technologies in altering the ways in which literacy is produced and disseminated is seen as seminal to understanding and teaching. The authors are concerned, then, not only with theoretical and definitional perspectives but also with applications, notably in the field of education. Current debates about future directions in literacy cannot but take account of this major contribution to the field.

KRESS, G. and VAN LEEUWEN, T. (1996) *Reading images: the grammar of visual design*. London: Routledge (especially Introduction, pp. 1–14, and chapter 1, pp. 15–42). Kress and van Leeuwen offer a scholarly and precisely analysed account of the semiotics of visual images. Drawing upon Hallidayan linguistic theory, including a broader conception of 'grammar' than usual in schooled language studies, they systematically analyse the features of visual design as though they were a 'language', although now with the refinement that they see meanings as not just made once, as in traditional linguistics, but rather as resources that are continually being made and remade. They argue that western, post-industrial societies are in a period of profound transition in which formerly stable semiotic arrangements and framings are coming undone. How we can understand the new assemblages and recognise patterns in the new multimodal world – where, for instance, the screen may replace the page – requires new analytic frameworks of the kind they offer here. Different from traditional art history, which was also of course concerned with analysis of the 'visual', the authors here locate visual design within the broader range of communicative practices and their contexts. A ground-breaking text that has spawned many further accounts of specific features of the new landscape – including their own 'theoretical browser' *MultiModal Discourse*, this book remains a crucial point of reference.

HAWISHER, G. E. and SELFE, C. (ed.) (2000) *Global literacies and the World-Wide Web*. London: Routledge. Interested in examining how on-line literacy practices might force us to rethink what counts as literacy, the authors link new theoretical approaches with specific national cultural and educational contexts. Whereas some of the generalisation about the futures of literacy seems abstract and perhaps implicitly culturally biased, the authors of this book were given the remit of representing their own local cultural meanings and practices, before generalising about 'new literacies'. The authors, then, offer a more dynamic and socially grounded account of 'global literacies', indicating for instance that what may appear to be uniform practices in fact may have different meanings in different contexts. Certainly any whisper of technological determinism is eschewed in favour of more socially sensitive accounts. As the editors argue in the introduction, 'until culturally specific investigations of culturally determined literacy practices on the Web are undertaken, we are no closer to understanding the real complexity of the internationalness of the literacy environment offered by the Web, or to identifying the many small inaccuracies so effectively masked by the global-village narrative'.

ABBOTT, C. (2000) *ICT: changing education*. London: Routledge. Abbott addresses the implications for teachers of the new technologies that are entering classrooms. Schooling and teaching, he argues, will have to change in a variety of ways and this book offers support to teachers in helping children engage with ever more sophisticated new technologies. In doing so he attempts to combine technical skills with humanistic values.

JEWITT, C. (2006) *Technology, literacy and learning: a multimodal approach*. London: Routledge. An application to educational contexts of theories of multimodality and new technologies. Jewitt draws upon detailed qualitative classroom research in UK schools in the subject areas of science and English.

KRESS, G. (2002) *Literacy in the new media age.* London: Routledge. Definitions of 'literacy' have now to take account of new modes of communication, what Kress refers to as 'multimodality' where a mode might be linguistic, visual, kinaesthetic etc. This book offers a synthesis of approaches to this subject, including the seminal work of Kress himself.

LEANDER, K. and SHEEHY, M. (2004) *Spatializing literacy research and practice.* Bern: Peter Lang. Using research on classroom practices and school responses in the USA to new digital technologies, the authors use concepts of time and space and draw upon New Literacy Studies to make sense of the new literacies in educational contexts.

TUTLE, E. (1997) *Visual explanations: images and quantities, evidence and narrative.* Cheshire, CT: Graphic Press. A mathematician's attempt to link the fields of visual production and interpretation with that of mathematics: an original perspective on visual images that complements the approaches from multimodality.

WAGNER, D. and KOZMA, B. (2005) *New technologies for literacy and adult education.* Paris: Unesco Publishing. The book analyses two interconnected approaches to using ICT to support adult literacy and adult or basic education – ICT as institutional tools for attaining traditional literacy; and literacy as a broader set of text and technological skills, involving more socially defined approaches to communication and new knowledge.

References

Abadzi, H. (2003). *Improving adult literacy outcomes: lessons from cognitive research for developing countries.* Washington, DC: World Bank.

Abbott, C. (2000). *ICT: changing education.* London: RoutledgeFalmer.

Adams, M. J. (1990). *Beginning to read: thinking and learning about print.* Cambridge, MA: MIT Press.

Adams, M. J. (1991). Why not phonics *and* whole language? In W. Ellis (ed.) *All Language and the Creation of Literacy.* Baltimore, MD: The Orton Dyslexia Society.

Adams, M. J. (1993). Beginning to read: an overview. In R. Beard (ed.), *Teaching literacy balancing perspectives* (pp. 204–215). London: Hodder and Stoughton.

Adey, P. (2003, 11 April). Benefits of strategies debatable. *Times Educational Supplement,* 21.

Agar, M. H. (1996). *The professional stranger: an informal introduction to ethnography* (2nd ed.). San Diego and London: Academic Press.

Alexander, K., and Entwistle, D. (1996). Schools and children at risk. In A. Booth and J. Dunn (eds), *Family-school links: how do they affect educational outcomes?* (pp. 67–88), Hillsdale, NJ: Erlbaum.

Anbar, A. (1986). Reading acquisition of preschool children without systematic instruction. *Early Childhood Research Quarterly,* 1, 69–83.

Andersen, O. (1989). The significance of writing in early Greece – a critical appraisal. In M. T. Larsen and K. Schousboe (eds), *Literacy and society* (pp. 73–87). Copenhagen: Centre for Research in Humanities.

Anderson, C. A. (1966). Literacy and schooling on the Development Threshold: some historical cases. In C. A. Anderson and M. Bowman (eds), *Education and Economic Development.* London: Frank Cass.

Ariès, P. (1962). *Centuries of childhood: a social history of family life.* New York: Vintage Books.

Astle, T. (1784). *The origin and progress of writing as well hieroglyphic as elementary: also, Some account of the origin and progress of printing.* London.

Auer, P. (1990). A discussion paper on code alternation. In ESF Network on Codeswitching and Language Contact. Papers for Workshop on 'Concepts, Methodology and Data', Basel, 12–13 January. Strasbourg: The European Science Foundation.

August, D., and Hakuta, K. (1997). *Improving schooling for language-minority children: a research agenda.* Washington, DC: National Academy Press.

Bacha, N. N. (2002). Developing learners' academic writing skills in higher education: a study for educational reform. *Language and Education,* 16(3), 161–177.

Backman, J. (1983). The role of psycholinguistic skills in reading acquisition: a look at early readers. *Reading Research Quarterly,* 18(4), 466–479.

Baeder, J. (1996). *Sign language: street signs as folk art.* New York: H. N. Abrams.

Baker, C. D., and Freebody, P. (1987). 'Constituting the child' in beginning school reading books. *British Journal of Sociology of Education,* 8 (1), 55–76.

Baker, L., Serpell, R., and Sonnenschein, S. (1995). Opportunities for literacy learning in the homes of urban preschoolers. In L. M. Morrow (ed.), *Family literacy: connections in schools and communities* (pp. 236–252). Newark, NJ: International Reading Association.

Baker, S. W., Barzun, J., and Richards, I. A. (1971). *The written word.* Rowley, MA: Newbury House Publishers.

Bartholomae, D. (1985). Inventing the university. In M. Rose (ed.), *When a writer can't write: studies in writer's block and other composing-process problems* (pp. 134–165). New York: Guilford Press.

Bartlett, L. (2001). *Literacy and shame and comparative education projects in contemporary Brazil.* Dissertation. Chapel Hill, NC: Department of Anthropology at the University of North Carolina Chapel Hill.

Bartlett, L., and Holland, D. (2002). Theorizing the space of literacy practices. *Ways of Knowing Journal,* 2 (1), 10–22.

Barton, D. (1994). *Literacy: an introduction to the ecology of written language.* Oxford: Blackwell.

Barton, D. (2001). Directions for literacy research: analysing language and social practices in a textually mediated world. *Language and Education,* 15 (2–3), 92–104.

Barton, D. (2006). *Literacy: an introduction to the ecology of written language* (2nd ed.). Oxford: Blackwell.

Barton, D., and Hamilton, M. (1998). *Local literacies: reading and writing in one community.* London: Routledge.

Barton, D., and Hamilton, M. (2000). Literacy practices. In D. Barton, M. Hamilton and R. Ivanic, *Situated literacies: reading and writing in context* (pp. 7–15). London: Routledge.

Barton, D., Hamilton, M., and Ivanic, R. (2000). *Situated literacies: reading and writing in context.* London: Routledge.

Barton, D., and Ivanic, R. (1991). *Writing in the community.* Newbury Park and London: Sage.

Barton, D., and Padmore, S. (1991). Roles, networks and values in everyday writing. In D. Barton and R. Ivanic (eds), *Writing in the community* (pp. 58–77). Newbury Park and London: Sage.

Baynham, M. (1995). *Literacy practices: investigating literacy in social contexts.* New York: Longman.

Beard, R. (ed.) (1993). *Teaching literacy balancing perspectives.* London: Hodder and Stoughton.

Beard, R. (1999). *National Literacy Strategy: Review of research and other related evidence.* London: DfES.

Bell, S. G., and Yalom, M. (1990). *Revealing lives: autobiography, biography, and gender.* Albany: State University of New York Press.

Bereiter, C. (1977). Integration of skill systems in the development of textual writing competence. Unpublished manuscript, Ontario Institute for Studies in Education.

Berkenkotter, C., and Huckin, T. N. (1995). *Genre knowledge in disciplinary communication: cognition, culture, power.* Hillsdale, NJ and Hove: L. Erlbaum Associates.

Berliner, D. C., and Biddle, B. J. (1995). *The manufactured crisis: myths, fraud, and the attack on America's public schools.* Reading, MA: Addison-Wesley.

Besnier, N. (1989). Literacy and feelings: the encoding of affect in Nukulaelae letters. *Text,* 9, 69–92.

Besnier, N. (1995). *Literacy, emotion, and authority: reading and writing on a Polynesian atoll.* Cambridge and New York: Cambridge University Press.

Besnier, N. (2001). Literacy. In A. Duranti (ed.), *Key terms in language and culture* (pp. 136–138). Malden, MA: Blackwell.

Biber, D. (1986). Spoken and written textual dimensions in English: resolving the contradictory findings. *Language*, 62 (2), 384–414.

Bissex, G. L. (1980). *Gnys at wrk: a child learns to write and read*. Cambridge, MA: Harvard University Press.

Bitzer, L. (1968). The rhetorical situation. *Philosophy and Rhetoric*, 1, 1–15.

Bledsoe, C. H., and Robey, K. M. (1986). Arabic literacy and secrecy among the Mende of Sierra Leone. *Man*, 21 (2), 202–226.

Bloch, M. (1989). Literacy and enlightenment. In M. T. Larsen and K. Schousboe (eds), *Literacy and Society*. Copenhagen: Centre for Research in Humanities.

Bloch, M. (1993). The uses of schooling and literacy in a Zafimaniry village. In B. V. Street (ed.), *Cross-cultural approaches to literacy*. Cambridge: Cambridge University Press.

Blom, J. P., and Gumperz, J. J. (1972). Social meaning in linguistic structure: codeswitching in Norway. In J. J. Gumperz and D. H. Hymes (eds), *Directions in sociolinguistics: the ethnography of communication* (pp. 407–434). New York: Holt Rinehart and Winston.

Blommaert, J. (1999). *Language ideological debates*. Berlin: Mouton de Gruyter.

Bloome, D. (1993). Necessary indeterminacy and the microethnographic study of reading as a social process. *Journal of Research in Reading*, 16 (2), 98–111.

Bloome, D., Carter, S. P., Christian, B. M., Otto, S., and Shuart-Faris, N. (2005). *Discourse analysis and the study of classroom language and literacy events: a microethnographic perspective*. Mahwah, NJ: L. Erlbaum Associates.

Bloome, D., Puro, P., and Theodorou, E. (1989). Procedural display and classroom lessons. *Curriculum Inquiry*, 19 (3), 265–291.

Bloomfield, L. (1933). *Language*. New York: H. Holt and Company.

Boaler, J., and Greeno, J. G. (2000). Identity, agency, and knowing in mathematics worlds. In J. Boaler (ed.), *Multiple perspectives on mathematics teaching and learning* (pp. 171–200). Westport, CT: Ablex.

Bourdieu, P. (1977). *Outline of a theory of practice*. Cambridge and New York: Cambridge University Press.

Brandt, D. (1998). Sponsors of literacy. *College Composition and Communication*, 49 (2), 165–185.

Brandt, D. (2001). *Literacy in American lives*. Cambridge: Cambridge University Press.

Brandt, D., and Clinton, K. (2002). Limits of the local: expanding perspectives on literacy as a social practice. *Journal of Literacy Research*, 34 (3), 337–356.

Britton, J. N., Burgess, T., Martin, N., McLeod, A., and Rosen, H. (1975). *The development of writing abilities*. London: Macmillan.

Bronfenbrenner, U. (1996). *The state of Americans: this generation and the next*. New York: Free Press.

Brooks, G. (1997). *Trends in standards of literacy in the United Kingdom, 1948–1996*. Paper presented at the British Educational Research Association conference, from http://www.leeds.ac.uk/educol/documents/000000650.htm.

Bruner, J. S., Olver, R. R., Greenfield, P. M., and Harvard University, Center for Cognitive Studies (1966). *Studies in cognitive growth: a collaboration at the Center for Cognitive Studies*. New York and London: Wiley.

Brunhoff, J. de (1933). *The story of Babar, the little elephant*. New York: H. Smith and R. Haas.

Candlin, C., and Hyland, K. (1999). *Writing: texts, processes, and practices*. London: Longman.

Canieso-Doronila, M. L. (1996). *Landscapes of literacy: an ethnographic study of functional literacy in marginal Philippine communities*. Hamburg: UNESCO Institute of Education.

Caplan, G., and Grunebaum, H. (1967). Perspectives on primary prevention: a review. *Archives of General Psychiatry*, 17 (3), 331–346.

Carruthers, M. J. (1990). *The book of memory: a study of memory in medieval culture.* Cambridge: Cambridge University Press.

Carter, R. (1995). *Keywords in language and literacy.* London and New York: Routledge.

Chall, J. S. (1983). *Learning to read: the great debate* (updated ed.). New York: McGraw-Hill.

Chall, J. S., Baldwin, L. E., and Jacobs, V. A. (1990). *The reading crisis: why poor children fall behind.* Cambridge, MA and London: Harvard University Press.

Cicourel, A. V. (1992). The interpenetration of communicative contexts: examples from medical encounters. In A. Duranti and C. Goodwin (eds), *Rethinking context: language as an interactive phenomenon* (pp. 291–310). Cambridge: Cambridge University Press.

Cipolla, C. M. (1969). *Literacy and development in the West.* Harmondsworth: Penguin.

Clammer, J. R. (1976). *Literacy and social change: a case study of Fiji.* Leiden: Brill.

Clanchy, J., and Ballard, B. (1988). Literacy in the university: an anthropological approach. In G. Taylor (ed.), *Literacy by degrees* (pp. 7–23). Milton Keynes: Society for Research into Higher Education and Open University Press.

Clanchy, M. T. (1979). *From memory to written record: England 1066–1307.* London: Edward Arnold.

Clawson, D. (1980). *Bureaucracy and the labor process: the transformation of US industry, 1860–1920.* Monthly Review Press.

Coffin, C. (2002). *Academic writing: a toolkit for higher education.* London: Routledge.

Cohen, M. S. R. (1958). *La grande invention de l'écriture et son évolution.* Paris: Imprimerie Nationale Librairie C. Klincksieck.

Cole, M., and Scribner, S. (1974). *Culture and thought: a psychological introduction.* New York: Wiley.

Coleman, J. S., United States Office of Education and National Center for Education Statistics (1966). *Equality of educational opportunity.* Washington, DC: US Dept. of Health, Education, and Welfare, Office of Education.

Collins, J. (1995). Literacy and literacies. *Annual Review of Anthropology*, 24, 75–93.

Collins, J. (1996). Socialisation to text: structure and contradiction in schooled literacy. In M. Silverstein and G. Urban (eds), *Natural histories of discourse* (pp. 203–228). Chicago and London: University of Chicago Press.

Collins, J., and Blot, R. K. (2003). *Literacy and literacies: texts, power, and identity.* Cambridge and New York: Cambridge University Press.

Committee on the Prevention of Reading Difficulties in Young Children, Snow, C. E., Burns, M. S., and Griffin, P. (1998). *Preventing reading difficulties in young children.* Washington, DC: National Academy Press.

Comte, A. (1830–42). *Cours de philosophie positive.* Paris: Bachelier.

Cook, T. (1991). Clarifying the warrant for generalized causal inferences in quasi-experiments. In M. W. McLaughlin and D. C. Phillips (eds), *Evaluation and education: at quarter century* (pp. 115–144). Chicago, IL: National Society for the Study of Education, distributed by the University of Chicago Press.

Cook-Gumperz, J. (1986). *The social construction of literacy.* Cambridge and New York: Cambridge University Press.

Cooley, C. H. (1909). *Social organization: a study of the larger mind.* New York: C. Scribner's Sons.

Cope, B., and Kalantzis, M. (1993). *The powers of literacy: a genre approach to teaching writing.* Pittsburgh: University of Pittsburgh Press.

Cope, B., and Kalantzis, M. (2000). *Multiliteracies: literacy learning and the design of social futures.* London: Routledge.

Covey, S. R. (1990). *The seven habits of highly effective people.* New York: Simon and Schuster.

Cowan, P. (2005). Putting it out there: revealing Latino visual discourse in the Hispanic academic program. In B. Street (ed.) *Literacies across educational contexts: mediating learning and teaching* (pp. 145–169). Philadelphia: Caslon Publishing.

Creme, P., and Lea, M. R. (2003). *Writing at university* (2nd ed.). Buckingham: Open University Press.

Crystal, D. (1976). *Child language, learning and linguistics: an overview for the teaching and therapeutic professions.* London: E. Arnold.

Curry, M. J., and Lillis, T. (2004). Multilingual scholars and the imperative to publish in English: negotiating interests, demands, and rewards. *TESOL Quarterly*, 38(4), 663–688.

Dalby, D. (1969). Further indigenous scripts of West Africa: Manding, Wolof and Fula alphabets and Yoruba 'holy' writing. *African Language Studies*, 10, 161–181.

Daniels, P. T., and Bright, W. (1996). *The world's writing systems.* New York: Oxford University Press.

de Castell, S., and Luke, A. (1983). Defining 'literacy' in North American schools: social and historical conditions and consequences. *Journal of Curriculum Studies*, 15(4), 373–389.

Delgado-Gaitan, C. (1990). *Literacy for empowerment: the role of parents in children's education.* New York: Falmer Press.

Derrida, J., trans. Spivak, G. C. (1976). *Of grammatology* (1st American ed.). Baltimore: Johns Hopkins University Press.

Diringer, D. (1968). *The alphabet: a key to the history of mankind* (3rd ed.). New York: Funk and Wagnalls.

Dorfman, A. (1983). *The empire's old clothes: what the Lone Ranger, Babar, and other innocent heroes do to our minds.* New York: Pantheon Books.

Duranti, A., and Goodwin, C. (1992). *Rethinking context: language as an interactive phenomenon.* Cambridge: Cambridge University Press.

Emmison, M., and Smith, P. (2000). *Researching the visual: images, objects, contexts and interactions in social and cultural inquiry.* London: SAGE.

Erickson, F. (1984). School literacy, reasoning, and civility: an anthropologist's perspective. *Review of Educational Research*, 54 (4), 525–546.

Escamilla, K. (1994). Descubriendo la lectura: an early intervention literacy program in Spanish. *Literacy, Teaching, and Learning*, 1 (1), 57–70.

Evans-Pritchard, E. E. (1937). *Witchcraft, oracles and magic among the Azande.* Oxford: Clarendon Press.

Fairclough, N. (1989). *Language and power.* London and New York: Longman.

Fairclough, N. (1991). Discourse and text: linguistics: an intertextual analysis within discourse analysis. In *Critical discourse analysis: the critical study of language* (pp. 187–213). London: Longman.

Farrell, T. J. (1977). Literacy, the basics, and all that jazz. *College English*, 38 (5), 443–459.

Feldman, C. F. (1991). Oral metalanguage. In D. R. Olson and N. Torrance (eds), *Literacy and orality* (pp. 47–65). Cambridge: Cambridge University Press.

Fingeret, A. (1983). Social network: a new perspective on independence and illiterate adults. *Adult Education Quarterly*, 33 (3), 133–134.

Finnegan, R. (1999). Sociological and anthropological issues in literacy. In D. A. Wagner, R. L. Venezky and B. V. Street (eds), *Literacy: an international handbook* (pp. 89–94). Boulder, CO: Westview Press.

Finnegan, R. H. (1988). *Literacy and orality: studies in the technology of communication.* Oxford: Blackwell.

Floch, J.-M. (2000). *Visual identities.* London: Continuum.

Frazer, J. G. (1976). *The golden bough: a study in magic and religion.* London: Tavistock.

Freebody, P. (2003). *Qualitative research in education: interaction and practice.* London and Thousand Oaks, CA: Sage Publications.

Freebody, P., and Baker, C. D. (1985). Children's first schoolbooks: introductions to the culture of literacy. *Harvard Educational Review,* 55 (4), 381–398.

Freire, P. (1985). *The politics of education: culture, power, and liberation.* Hadley, MA: Bergin and Garvey.

Freire, P., and Macedo, D. (1987). *Literacy: reading the word and the world.* Hadley, MA: Bergin and Garvey.

Gadsden, V. L. (1993). Literacy, education, and identity among African-Americans: the communal nature of learning. *Urban Education,* 27 (4), 352.

Garfield, S. (2004). *Our hidden lives: the everyday diaries of a forgotten Britain, 1945–1948.* London: Ebury.

Gaur, A. (1987). *A history of writing.* London: British Library.

Gee, J. P. (1990). *Social linguistics and literacies: ideology in discourses.* London: Falmer.

Gee, J. P. (1996). *Social linguistics and literacies: ideology in discourses* (2nd ed.). London and Bristol, PA: Taylor and Francis.

Gee, J. P. (1999a). *An introduction to discourse analysis: theory and method.* London: Routledge.

Gee, J. P. (1999b). Critical issues: reading and the new literacy studies: reframing the National Academy of Sciences report on reading. *Journal of Literacy Research,* 31 (3), 355–374.

Gee, J. P. (2000). The limits of reframing: a response to Professor Snow. *Journal of Literacy Research,* 32 (1), 121–128.

Gee, J. P., Hull, G. A., and Lankshear, C. (1996). *The new work order: behind the language of the new capitalism.* St. Leonards, NSW: Allen and Unwin.

Geisler, C. (1994). *Academic literacy and the nature of expertise: reading, writing, and knowing in academic philosophy.* Hillsdale, NJ: Lawrence Erlbaum.

Gelb, I. J. (1952, 1963). *A study of writing.* Chicago: University of Chicago Press.

Gersten, R., and Woodward, J. (1995). A longitudinal study of transitional and immersion bilingual education programs in one district. *The Elementary School Journal,* 95 (3), 223–239.

Gladwin, T. (1970). *East is a big bird: navigation and logic on Puluwat atoll.* Cambridge, MA and London: Harvard University Press.

Goldenberg, C., and Gallimore, R. (1991). Local knowledge, research knowledge, and educational change: a case study of early Spanish reading improvement. *Educational Researcher,* 20 (8), 2–14.

Goldenberg, C., and Gallimore, R. (1995). Immigrant Latino parents' values and beliefs about their children's education: continuities and discontinuities across cultures and generations. *Advances in Motivation and Achievement,* 9, 183–228.

Goldenberg, C., Reese, L., and Gallimore, R. (1992). Effects of literacy materials from school on Latino children's home experiences and early reading achievement. *American Journal of Education,* 100 (4), 497–536.

Goodman, K. S. (1967). Reading: a psycholinguistic guessing game. *Journal of the Reading Specialist,* 6 (1), 126–135.

Goodman, K. S. (1989). Access to literacy: basals and other barriers. *Theory into Practice,* 28 (4), 300–306.

Goodman, K. S. (1989). Whole-language research: foundations and development. *The Elementary School Journal,* 90 (2), 207–221.

Goodman, K. S. (1992). I didn't found whole language. *Reading Teacher,* 46 (3), 188–199.

Goodman, K. S. (1994). Deconstructing the rhetoric of Moorman, Blanton, and Mclaughlin – a response. *Reading Research Quarterly,* 29 (4), 340–346.

Goodman, K. S. (1996). *On reading.* Portsmouth, NH: Heinemann.

Goodman, K. S., and National Council of Teachers of English, Reading Commission (1988). *Report card on basal readers.* Katonah, NY: R. C. Owen.

Goodman, Y. M. (1989). Roots of the whole-language movement. *The Elementary School Journal,* 90 (2), 113–127.

Goody, J. (1968). *Literacy in traditional societies.* Cambridge: Cambridge University Press.

Goody, J. (1977). *The domestication of the savage mind.* Cambridge: Cambridge University Press.

Goody, J. (1986). *The logic of writing and the organization of society.* Cambridge: Cambridge University Press.

Goody, J. (1987). *The interface between the written and the oral.* Cambridge: Cambridge University Press.

Goody, J., Cole, M., and Scribner, S. (1977). Writing and formal operations: a case study among the Vai. *Africa: Journal of the International African Institute,* 47 (3), 289–304.

Goody, J., and Watt, I. (1963). The consequences of literacy. *Comparative Studies in Society and History,* 5 (3), 304–345.

Gough, P. B., Alford, J. A., and Holley-Wilcox, P. (1981). Words and context. In O. J. L. Tzeng and H. Singer (eds), *Perceptions of print: reading research in experimental psychology.* Hillsdale, NJ: Lawrence Erlbaum Associates.

Gowen, S. (1994). 'I'm no fool': reconsidering American workers and their literacies. In P. O'Connor (ed.), *Thinking work: theoretical perspectives on workers' literacies* (Vol. 1, pp. 123–135). Sydney: Adult Literacy and Basic Skills Action Coalition.

Gowen, S. G. (1992). *The politics of workplace literacy: a case study.* New York: Teachers College Press.

Graff, H. J. (1979). *The literacy myth: literacy and social structure in the nineteenth-century city.* New York: Academic Press.

Graff, H. J. (1986). *The legacies of literacy: continuities and contradictions in western culture and society.* Bloomington: Indiana University Press.

Graff, H. J. (1987). *The labyrinths of literacy: reflections on literacy past and present.* London: Falmer.

Green, J. L., and Bloome, D. (1997). A situated perspective on ethnography and ethnographers of and in education. In S. B. Heath, J. Flood and D. Lapp (eds), *Handbook for research in the communicative and visual arts.* New York: Macmillan.

Greenfield, P. M. (1972). Oral or written language: the consequences for cognitive development in Africa, the United States and England. *Language and Speech,* 15 (2), 169–178.

Gumperz, J. J. (1982). *Language and social identity.* Cambridge: Cambridge University Press.

Hall, N., and Robinson, A. (1995). *Exploring writing and play in the early years.* London: David Fulton.

Hallam, E., and Street, B. V. (2000). *Cultural encounters: representing otherness.* London: Routledge.

Halliday, M. A. K. (1975). *Learning how to mean: explorations in the development of language.* London: Edward Arnold.

Halverson, J. (1991). Olson on literacy. *Language in Society,* 20 (4), 619–640.

Halverson, J. (1992). Goody and the implosion of the literacy thesis. *Man,* 27 (2), 301–317.

Hamilton, M., Barton, D., and Ivanic, R. (1994). *Worlds of literacy.* Clevedon: Multilingual Matters.

Harbsmeier, M. (1988). Inventions of writing. In J. Gledhill, B. Bender and M. T. Larsen (eds), *State and society: the emergence and development of social hierarchy and political centralization* (pp. 253–259). London and Boston: Unwin Hyman.

Harris, R. (1986). *The origin of writing.* London: Duckworth.

Harris, W. V. (1989). *Ancient literacy*. Cambridge, MA and London: Harvard University Press.

Hart, B., and Risley, T. R. (1995). *Meaningful differences in the everyday experience of young American children*. Baltimore: P. H. Brookes.

Hatch, E. (1992). *Discourse and language education*. Cambridge: Cambridge University Press.

Havelock, E. A. (1963). *Preface to Plato*. Cambridge, MA: Belknap Press, Harvard University Press.

Havelock, E. A. (1982). *The literate revolution in Greece and its cultural consequences*. Princeton: Princeton University Press.

Hawisher, G. E., and Selfe, C. L. (2000). *Global literacies and the World-Wide Web*. London: Routledge.

Heath, S. B. (1982). Protean shapes in literacy events. In D. Tannen (ed.), *Spoken and written language: exploring orality and literacy* (pp. 91–117). Norwood, NJ: Ablex.

Heath, S. B. (1983). *Ways with words: language, life, and work in communities and classrooms*. Cambridge: Cambridge University Press.

Heath, S. B., and Street, B. V. (forthcoming). *Ethnography: approaches to language and literacy research*. New York: Teachers College Press.

Hegel, G. W. F. (1967). *The phenomenology of mind*. New York: Harper and Row.

Heller, M. (1988). *Codeswitching: anthropological and sociolinguistic perspectives*. Berlin: Mouton de Gruyter.

Heller, S. (2004). *Design literacy: understanding graphic design* (2nd ed.). New York: Allworth.

Hildyard, A., and Olson, D. R. (1978). Literacy and the specialisation of language. Unpublished manuscript. Ontario Institute for Studies in Education.

Hilton, M. (1998). Raising literacy standards: the true story. *English in Education*, 32 (3), 4–16.

Holland, C., Frank, F., and Cooke, T. (1998). *Literacy and the new work order: an international literature review*. Leicester: NIACE.

Holland, D. C., Lachicotte, W., Skinner, D., and Cain, C. (1998). *Identity and agency in cultural worlds*. Cambridge, MA: Harvard University Press.

Holland, D. C., and Lave, J. (2001). Introduction. In D. C. Holland and J. Lave (eds), *History in person: enduring struggles, contentious practice, intimate identities* (pp. 3–33). Santa Fe, NM: School of American Research Press.

Hornberger, N. H. (1989). Continua of biliteracy. *Review of Educational Research*, 59 (3), 271–296.

Hornberger, N. H. (1990). Creating successful leanring contexts for bilingual literacy. *Teachers College Record*, 92 (2), 212–229.

Hornberger, N. H. (2003). *Continua of biliteracy: an ecological framework for educational policy, research, and practice in multilingual settings*. Clevedon and Buffalo: Multilingual Matters.

Hounsell, D. (1988). Towards an anatomy of academic discourse: meaning and context in the undergraduate essay. In R. Saljo (ed.), *The written world: studies in literate thought and action* (pp. 161–177). Berlin: Springer-Verlag.

Hourihan, M. (1997). *Deconstructing the hero: literary theory and children's literature*. London and New York: Routledge.

Howard, U. (1991). Self, education and writing in nineteenth century English communities. In D. Barton and R. Ivanic (eds), *Writing in the community* (pp. 78–108). Newbury Park and London: Sage.

Hull, G. (1991). *Hearing other voices: a critical assessment of popular views on literacy and work*. Berkeley: University of California. National Center for Research in Vocational Education.

Hull, G. (2000). Critical literacy at work. *Journal of Adolescent and Adult Literacy*, 43 (7), 648–652.

Hull, G. (2001). Constructing working selves: Silicon Valley assemblers meet the new work order. *Anthropology of Work Review*, 22 (1), 17–22.

Hull, G. A. (1997). *Changing work, changing workers: critical perspectives on language, literacy, and skills*. Albany, NY: State University of New York Press.

Hull, G. A., and Schultz, K. (2002). Locating literacy theory in out-of-school contexts. In G. A. Hull and K. Schultz (eds), *School's out!: bridging out-of-school literacies with classroom practice* (pp. 11–31). New York and London: Teachers College Press.

Hull, G. A., and Schultz, K. (eds) (2002). *School's out!: bridging out-of-school literacies with classroom practice*. New York and London: Teachers College Press.

Hutchins, E. (1983). Understanding Micronesian navigation. In D. Gentner and A. Stevens (eds), *Mental Models* (pp. 191–225). Hillsdale, NJ: Erlbaum.

Hyland, K. (2002). *Teaching and researching writing*. Harlow: Longman.

Hyland, K. (2006). *English for academic purposes: an advanced resource book*. Abingdon and New York: Routledge.

Hymes, D. H. (1974). *Foundations in sociolinguistics: an ethnographic approach*. Philadelphia: University of Pennsylvania Press.

Illich, I., and Sanders, B. (1989). *ABC: the alphabetization of the popular mind*. Harmondsworth: Penguin.

Ivanic, R. (1998). *Writing and identity: the discoursal construction of identity in academic writing*. Amsterdam: John Benjamins.

Jackson, N. E. (1991). Precocious reading of English: origins, structure, and predictive significance. In A. J. Tannenbaum and P. Klein (eds), *To be young and gifted* (pp. 171–203). Norwood, NJ: Ablex.

Jackson, N. E., Donaldson, G. W., and Cleland, L. N. (1988). The structure of precocious reading ability. *Journal of Educational Psychology*, 80, 234–243.

Jacob, E., and Jordan, C. (1987). Explaining the school performance of minority students. *Anthropology and Education Quarterly*, 18 (4).

Jewitt, C. (2005). Multimodality, 'reading', and 'writing' for the 21st century. *Discourse*, 26 (3), 315–331.

Jewitt, C. (2006). *Technology, literacy and learning: a multimodal approach*. London: Routledge.

Johnston, R. S., and Watson, J. E. (2005). *A seven year study of the effects of synthetic phonics teaching on reading and spelling attainment*. Edinburgh: Scottish Executive, Education Department.

Jones, C., Turner, J., and Street, B. V. (1999). *Students writing in the university: cultural and epistemological issues*. Amsterdam: John Benjamins.

Jones, K. (1999). *Texts, talk and discourse practices: exploring local experiences of globalisation*. Unpublished PhD thesis, Lancaster University, Lancaster.

Jones, K., Martin-Jones, M., and Bhatt, M. (2000). Constructing a critical, dialogic approach to research on multilingual literacy: participant diaries and diary interviews. In M. Martin-Jones and K. Jones (eds), *Multilingual literacies: reading and writing different worlds* (pp. 319–351). Amsterdam: John Benjamins.

Juel, C. (1988). Learning to read and write: a longitudinal study of 54 children from first through fourth grades. *Journal of Educational Psychology*, 80 (4), 437–447.

Kaestle, C. F. (1991). *Literacy in the United States: readers and reading since 1880*. New Haven: Yale University Press.

Kalman, J. (1999). *Writing on the plaza: mediated literacy practice among scribes and clients in Mexico City*. Cresskill, NJ: Hampton Press.

Kamberelis, G., and Dimitriadis, G. (2005). *On qualitative inquiry: approaches to language and literacy research*. New York: Teachers College.

Kao, G. and Tienda, M. (1995). Optimism and achievement: the educational performance of immigrant youth. *Social Science Quarterly*, 76, 1–19.

Kim, J. (2003). Challenges to NLS: response to '"What's "new" in New Literacy Studies'. *Current Issues in Comparative Education*, 5 (2), 118–121.

Kirsch, I., Jungeblut, A., Jenkins, L., and Kolstad, A. (1993). Adult literacy in America: a first look at the results of the national literacy survey. Washington, DC: National Center for Educational Statistics, US Department of Education.

Klima, E. S., and Bellugi, U. (1979). *The signs of language*. Cambridge, MA and London: Harvard University Press.

Koelle, S. W. (1854). *Outlines of a grammar of the Vai language, together with a Vai-English vocabulary*. London: Church Missionary House.

Kohl, H. R. (1995). *Should we burn Babar?: essays on children's literature and the power of stories*. New York: New Press.

Krashen, S. (1982). *Principles and practice in second language acquisition*. Oxford: Pergamon.

Kress, G., and Leeuwen, T. van (2001). *Multimodal discourse: the modes and media of contemporary communication*. London: Arnold.

Kress, G. R. (1989). *Linguistic processes in sociocultural practice* (2nd ed.). Oxford: Oxford University Press.

Kress, G. R. (1997). *Before writing: rethinking the paths to literacy*. London: Routledge.

Kress, G. R. (2002). *Literacy in the new media age*. London: Routledge.

Kress, G. R. (2004). *English in urban classrooms: a multimodal perspective on teaching and learning*. London: RoutledgeFalmer.

Kress, G. R., Jewitt, C., Ogborn, J., and Tsatsarelis, C. (2001) *Multimodal teaching and learning: the rhetorics of the science classroom*. London: Continuum.

Kress, G. R., and Leeuwen, T. van (1996). *Reading images: the grammar of visual design*. London: Routledge.

Kress, G. R., and Street, B. V. (2006). Multi-modality and literacy practices (Foreword). In K. Pahl and J. Rowsell (eds), *Travel notes from the new literacy studies: instances of practice* (pp. vii–x). Clevedon: Multilingual Matters.

Kulick, D., and Stroud, C. (1993). Conceptions and uses of literacy in a Papua New Guinea village. In B. V. Street (ed.), *Cross-cultural approaches to literacy* (pp. 30–61). Cambridge: Cambridge University Press.

Labov, W. (1973). The logic of non-standard English. In N. Keddie (ed.), *Tinker, tailor: the myth of cultural deprivation* (pp. 21–56). Harmondsworth: Penguin Education.

Labov, W., Cohen, P., Robins, C., and Lewis, J. (1968). *A study of the non-standard English of Negro and Puerto Rican speakers in New York City. Volumes I and II* (Cooperative research report No. 3288). Philadelphia: Linguistics Laboratory, University of Pennsylvania.

Larson, J. (ed.). (2001, 2nd edition 2007). *Literacy as snake oil: beyond the quick fix*. New York: Peter Lang.

Last, N., Broad, R., and Fleming, S. (1981). *Nella Last's war: a mother's diary, 1939–45*. Bristol: Falling Wall Press.

Latour, B. (1987). *Science in action*. Cambridge, MA: Harvard University Press.

Lave, J. (1988). *Cognition in practice: mind, mathematics and culture in everyday life*. Cambridge: Cambridge University Press.

Lave, J., and Wenger, E. (1991). *Situated learning: legitimate peripheral participation*. Cambridge: Cambridge University Press.

Lea, M. R., and Stierer, B. (2000). *Student writing in higher education: new contexts*. Buckingham and Philadelphia: Society for Research into Higher Education and Open University Press.

Lea, M. R., and Street, B. V. (1998). Student writing in higher education: an academic literacies approach. *Studies in Higher Education*, 23 (2), 157–172.

Leander, K. (2005). *Home/schooling, everywhere: digital literacies as practices of space-time*. Paper presented at the American Educational Research Association.

Leander, K., and Sheehy, M. (2004). *Spatializing literacy research and practice*. Bern: Peter Lang.

Lefstein, A. (in press). Literacy makeover: educational research and the public interest on prime time. *Teachers College Record*, 110 (7).

Legarreta, D. (1979). The effects of program models on language acquisition by Spanishspeaking children. *TESOL Quarterly*, 13 (4), 521–534.

Lemke, J. L. (1995). *Textual politics: discourse and social dynamics*. London and Bristol, PA: Taylor and Francis.

Lemke, J. L. (1998). Metamedia literacy: transforming meanings and media. In D. Reinking, M. C. McKenna, L. D. Labbo and R. D. Kieffer (eds), *Handbook of literacy and technology: transformations in a post-typographic world* (pp. 283–302). Mahwah, NJ: Erlbaum.

Levine, K. (1998). Definitional and methodological problems in the cross-national measurement of adult literacy: the case of the IALS. *Written language and literacy*, 1 (1), 41–61.

Lévi-Strauss, C. (1961). *Tristes tropiques*. New York: Atheneum.

Lévi-Strauss, C. (1962). *The savage mind*. London: Trafalgar Square.

Lévy-Bruhl, L. (1923). *Primitive mentality*. London: George Allen and Unwin.

Lévy-Bruhl, L. (1926). *How natives think*. London: George Allen and Unwin.

Lewin, K. (1936). *A dynamic theory of personality*. New York and London: McGraw-Hill.

Li Wei (1994). *Three generations, two languages, one family*. Clevedon: Multilingual Matters.

Liberman, I. Y., and Liberman, A. M. (1990). Whole language vs. code emphasis: underlying assumptions and their implications for reading instruction. *Annals of Dyslexia*, 40, 51–76.

Lillis, T. (1997). New voices in academia? The regulative nature of academic writing conventions. *Language and Education*, 11 (3), 182–199.

Lillis, T. M. (2001). *Student writing: access, regulation, desire*. London: Routledge.

Lloyd, G. E. R. (1990). *Demystifying mentalities*. Cambridge: Cambridge University Press.

Luke, A. (1988). *Literacy, textbooks, and ideology: postwar literacy instruction and the mythology of Dick and Jane*. London: Falmer Press.

Luke, A. (2003). Literacy and the other: a sociological approach to literacy research and policy in multilingual societies. *Reading Research Quarterly*, 38 (1), 132–143.

Lurie, A. (2004). The royal family: the Babar books by Jean de Brunhoff and Laurent de Brunhoff. *New York Review of Books*, 51 (20), 57–61.

Luttrell, W., and Parker, C. (2001). High school students' literacy practices and identities, and the figured world of school. *Journal of Research in Reading*, 24 (3), 235–247.

Macdonald, J. B. (1973). Reading in an electronic media age. In J. B. Macdonald (ed.), *Social perspectives on reading: social influences and reading achievement* (pp. 23–29). Newark, DE: International Reading Association.

Mace, J. (1995). *Literacy language and community publishing: Essays in adult education*. Clevedon: Multilingual Matters.

MacKenzie, J. M. (1986). *Imperialism and popular culture*. Manchester: Manchester University Press.

McLuhan, M. (1962). *The Gutenberg galaxy: the making of typographic man*. [Toronto]: University of Toronto Press.

Maddox, B. (2005). Literacy and the market: the economic uses of literacy among the peasantry in north-west Bangladesh. In B. V. Street (ed.), *Literacies across educational contexts: mediating learning and teaching* (pp. 137–151). Philadelphia: Caslon Publishing.

Maeroff, G. I., and Hechinger Institute on Education and the Media (1998). *Imaging education: the media and schools in America.* New York: Teachers College Press.

Martin, N., D'Arcy, P., Newton, B., and Parker, R. (1976). *Writing and learning across the curriculum, 11–16.* London: Ward Lock Educational.

Martin-Jones, M., and Jones, K. (2000). *Multilingual literacies: reading and writing different worlds.* Amsterdam: John Benjamins.

Meek, M. (1991). *On being literate.* London: Bodley Head.

Mesmer, H. A. E. (2001). Decodable text: a review of what we know. *Reading Research and Instruction,* 40 (2), 121–142.

Miller, G. A. (1988). The challenge of universal literacy. *Science,* 241 (4871), 1293.

Moffett, J. (1968). *Teaching the universe of discourse.* Boston: Houghton Mifflin.

Moorman, G. B., Blanton, W. E., and McLaughlin, T. (1994). The rhetoric of whole language. *Reading Research Quarterly,* 29 (4), 308–329.

Moynihan, D. P. (1965). *The Negro family: the case for national action.* Washington, DC: US Department of Labor.

Murnane, R. J., and Levy, F. (1993). Why today's high-school-educated males earn less than their fathers did: the problem and an assessment of responses. *Harvard Educational Review,* 63 (1), 1–19.

National Academy of Education (1996). *Quality and utility: the 1994 trial state assessment in reading.* Stanford, CA: Stanford University School of Education.

National Academy of Education Commission on Reading, Anderson, R. C., and National Institute of Education (USA) (1985). *Becoming a nation of readers: the report of the Commission on Reading.* [Pittsburgh, PA]: National Academy of Education.

National Assessment of Educational Progress (1981). *Reading, thinking, writing: a report on the 1979–1980 assessment.* Denver: NAEP.

National Assessment of Educational Progress (1994). *The NAEP 1992 technical report.* Princeton, NJ: Educational Testing Service.

National Assessment of Educational Progress (1995). *NAEP 1994 reading: A first look – findings from the National Assessment of Educational Progress (revised edition).* Washington, DC: U.S. Government Printing Office.

National Center for Education Statistics (1995). *Approaching kindergarten: a look at preschoolers in the United States. National Household Education Survey.* Washington, DC: United States Department of Education, Office of Educational Research and Improvement.

National Center on Education and the Economy (USA), Commission on the Skills of the American Workforce (1990). *America's choice: high skills or low wages!: the report of the Commission on the Skills of the American Workforce, June 1990.* [Rochester, NY]: National Center on Education and the Economy.

National Reading Panel (USA) (2000). *Teaching children to read: an evidence-based assessment of the scientific research literature on reading and its implications for reading instruction.* Washington, DC: National Institute of Child Health and Human Development, National Institutes of Health.

Needlman, R. (1997). *Pediatric interventions to prevent reading problems in young children.* Paper written for the Committee on the Prevention of Reading Difficulties in Young Children, National Research Council.

Nettles, M. T. (1997). *The African American education data book.* Fairfax, VA: Frederick D. Patterson Research Institute of the College Fund/UNCF.

Oatley, K. G. (1977). Inference, navigation and cognitive maps. In P. Johnson-Laird and P. Wason (eds), *Thinking: readings in cognitive science* (pp. 537–547). Cambridge: Cambridge University Press.

O'Connor, P. (1994). *Thinking work: theoretical perspectives on workers' literacies.* Sydney: Adult Literacy and Basic Skills Action Coalition.

Ogbu, J. (1974). *The next generation: an ethnography of education in an urban neighbourhood.* New York: Academic Press.

Ogbu, J. (1982). Cultural discontinuities and schooling. *Anthropology and Education Quarterly*, 13, 290–307.

Ogbu, J. U. (1990). Cultural model, identity, and literacy. In J. W. Stigler, R. A. Shweder, G. H. Herdt and University of Chicago. Committee on Human Development (eds), *Cultural psychology: essays on comparative human development* (pp. 520–541). Cambridge: Cambridge University Press.

Ohta, A. S. (2004). *The ZPD and adult L2 development: beyond social interaction.* Paper presented at the Annual Meeting of the American Association of Applied Linguistics.

Olson, D. R. (1977). From utterance to text: the bias of language in speech and writing. *Harvard Educational Review*, 47 (3), 257–281.

Olson, D. R. (1988). Mind and media: the epistemic functions of literacy. *Journal of communication*, 38 (3), 27–36.

Olson, D. R. (1994). *The world on paper: the conceptual and cognitive implications of writing and reading.* Cambridge: Cambridge University Press.

Olson, D. R., and Torrance, N. (1991). *Literacy and orality.* Cambridge: Cambridge University Press.

Ong, W. J. (1982). *Orality and literacy: the technologizing of the word.* London: Methuen.

Organisation for Economic Co-operation and Development, and Statistics Canada (1995). *Literacy, economy, and society: results of the first international adult literacy survey.* Paris: Organisation for Economic Co-operation and Development.

Pahl, K. (2001). Texts as artefacts crossing sites: map making at home and at school. *Reading, Literacy and Language*, 35 (3), 120–125.

Pahl, K., and Rowsell, J. (2005). *Literacy and education: understanding the new literacy studies in the classroom.* London: Paul Chapman.

Pahl, K., and Rowsell, J. (2006). *Travel notes from the New Literacy Studies: instances of practice.* Clevedon and Buffalo: Multilingual Matters.

Pattanayak, D. P. (1991). Literacy: an instrument of oppression. In D. R. Olson and N. Torrance (eds), *Literacy and orality* (pp. 105–108). Cambridge: Cambridge University Press.

Pearson, P. D. (2004). The reading wars. *Educational Policy*, 18 (1), 216–252.

Pianta, R. C. (1990). Widening the debate on educational reform: prevention as a viable alternative. *Exceptional Children*, 56 (4), 306–313.

Plummer, K. (1983). *Documents of life: an introduction to the problems and literature of a humanistic method.* London: Allen and Unwin.

Prinsloo, M., and Breier, M. (1996). *The social uses of literacy: theory and practice in contemporary South Africa.* Amsterdam: Benjamins.

Purcell-Gates, V. (1991). Ability of well-read-to kindergartners to decontextualise/recontextualise experience into a written-narrative register. *Language and Education: An International Journal*, 5 (3), 177–188.

Purcell-Gates, V. (1996). Stories, coupons, and the 'TV Guide': relationships between home literacy experiences and emergent literacy knowledge. *Reading Research Quarterly*, 31 (4), 406–428.

Qualifications and Curriculum Agency (QCA), and United Kingdom Literacy Association (UKLA) (2005). *More than words 2: creating stories on page and screen*. London: QCA.

Ramirez, J. D., Yuen, S. D., and Ramey, D. R. (1991). *Final report, longitudinal study of structured English immersion strategy, early-exit and late-exit transitional bilingual education programs for language-minority children. Executive summary*. San Mateo, CA: Aguirre International.

Rampton, B. (1995). *Crossing: language and ethnicity among adolescents*. London: Longman.

Rampton, B., and UK Linguistic Ethnography Forum (2004). UK Linguistic Ethnography – a discussion paper. Retrieved 21 July 2005, from http://www.lancs.ac.uk/fss/organisations/lingethn/papers.htm.

Reder, S., and Davila, E. (2005). Context and literacy practices. *Annual Review of Applied Linguistics*, 25, 170–187.

Reid, A. (1988). *Southeast Asia in the age of commerce, 1450–1680*. New Haven: Yale University Press.

Robinson, C. (2003). *Literacies – the new meanings of literacy*. UNESCO Position Paper.

Robinson, P. (1997). Literacy, numeracy and economic performance, *Working Paper No. 888*. London: Centre for Economic Performance, London School of Economics.

Robinson-Pant, A. (1997). '*Why eat green cucumbers at the time of dying?': the link between women's literacy and development*. Hamburg: UNESCO.

Robinson-Pant, A. (2005). *Cross-cultural perspectives on educational research*. Maidenhead: Open University Press.

Rockhill, K. (1987). Gender, language and the politics of literacy. *British Journal of the Sociology of Language*, 8 (2), 153–167.

Rogers, A. (1992). *Adults learning for development*. London: Cassell.

Rogers, A. (1994). *Using literacy: a new approach to post-literacy materials*. London: Overseas Development Administration.

Rogers, A. (2003). *What is the difference?: a new critique of adult learning and teaching*. Leicester: NIACE.

Rogers, A. (2005a). *Urban Literacy: Communication, Identity and Learning in Development Contexts*. Hamburg: UNESCO Institute for Education.

Rogers, A. (2005b). Literacy and productive skills training: embedded literacies. *Adult Education and Development*, 65, 59.

Rogers, A. (2006). Adult teachers as researchers: ethnographic approaches to numeracy and literacy as social practices in South Asia. *Convergence*, 39 (1), 31–44.

Rogers, A. (2006). DFID experience of adult literacy. *International Journal of Educational Development*, 26 (3), 339–346.

Rogers, A., Maddox, B., Millican, J., Jones, K. N., Papen, U., and Robinson-Pant, A. (1999). *Re-defining post-literacy in a changing world*. London: Department for International Development (DfID).

Rogoff, B. (2003). *The cultural nature of human development*. Oxford and New York: Oxford University Press.

Rogoff, B., and Lave, J. (1984). *Everyday cognition: its development in social context*. Cambridge, MA: Harvard University Press.

Rogoff, B., Paradise, R., Arauz, M. R., Correa-Chavez, M., and Angelillo, C. (2003). Firsthand learning through intent participation. *Annual Review of Psychology*, 175–204.

Rose, J. (2006). *Independent review of the teaching of early reading: final report* (No. 1844786846). London: Department for Education and Skills.

Rose, M. (2004). *The mind at work: valuing the intelligence of the American worker*. New York: Viking.

Rosen, H. (1972). *Language and class: a critical look at the theories of Basil Bernstein* (2nd ed.). Bristol: Falling Wall Press.

Rosen, H. (1988). The autobiographical impulse. In D. Tannen (ed.), *Linguistics in context: connecting observation and understanding* (pp. 69–89). Norwood, NJ: Ablex Publishing Corporation.

Rossell, C. H., and Baker, K. (1996). The educational effectiveness of bilingual education. *Research in the Teaching of English*, 30 (1), 7–74.

Rousseau, J.-J. (1966). Essay on the origin of languages. In J. H. Moran and A. Gode (eds), *On the origin of language: two essays by Jean-Jacques Rousseau and Johann Gottfried Herder*. New York: F. Ungar Publishing. Co.

Said, E. W. (1978). *Orientalism*. New York: Pantheon Books.

Sampson, G. (1985). *Writing systems*. Stanford: Stanford University Press.

Satchwell, C. (2005). *Literacy around the clock: an examination of the 'clock activity' as a method for identifying everyday literacy practices with further education students*. Paper presented at the Proceedings of 3rd International Conference – What a Difference a Pedagogy Makes: Researching Lifelong Learning and Teaching Conference.

Saussure, F. de (1983). *Course in general linguistics*. London: Duckworth.

Schieffelin, B. B., Woolard, K. A., and Kroskrity, P. V. (1998). *Language ideologies: practice and theory*. New York and Oxford: Oxford University Press.

Scollon, R., and Scollon, S. B. K. (2004). *Nexus analysis: discourse and the emerging internet*. London and New York: Routledge.

Scribner, S. (1984). Studying working intelligence. In B. Rogoff and J. Lave (eds), *Everyday cognition: its development in social context* (pp. 9–40). Cambridge, MA: Harvard University Press.

Scribner, S., and Cole, M. (1973). Cognitive consequences of formal and informal education. *Science*, 182, 553–559.

Scribner, S., and Cole, M. (1978a). Literacy without schooling: testing for intellectual effects. *Harvard Educational Review*, 48 (4), 448–461.

Scribner, S., and Cole, M. (1978b). Unpackaging literacy. *Social Science Information*, 17 (1), 19–39.

Scribner, S., and Cole, M. (1981). *The psychology of literacy*. Cambridge, MA: Harvard University Press.

Senge, P. M. (1990). *The fifth discipline: the art and practice of the learning organization*. New York: Doubleday/Currency.

Shannon, P. (1987). Commercial reading materials, a technological ideology, and the deskilling of teachers. *Elementary School Journal*, 87 (3), 307–329.

Sheridan, D., Street, B. V., and Bloome, D. (2000). *Writing ourselves: Mass Observation and literacy practices*. Cresskill, NJ: Hampton Press.

Shultz, J. J., Florio, S., and Erickson, F. (1982). Where's the floor? Aspects of the cultural organization of social relationships in communication at home and in school. In P. Gilmore and A. A. Glatthorn (eds), *Children in and out of school* (pp. 91–123). Norwood, NJ: Ablex.

Simeonsson, R. J. (1994). Promoting children's health, education and well-being. In *Risk resilience and prevention: promoting the well-being of all children* (pp. 3–31). Baltimore: Paul H. Brookes.

Singer, H., and Ruddell, R. B. (1976). *Theoretical models and processes of reading* (2nd ed.). Newark, DE: International Reading Association.

Slavin, R. E., Karweit, N. L., Wasik, B. A., Madden, N. A., and Dolan, L. J. (1994). Success for all: a comprehensive approach to prevention and early intervention. In R. E. Slavin,

N. L. Karweit and B. A. Wasik (eds), *Preventing early school failure: research, policy, and practice* (pp. 175–205). Boston: Allyn and Bacon.

Slavin, R. E., and Madden, N. A. (1995). *Effects of Success for All on the achievement of English language learners.* Paper presented at the Annual meeting of the American Educational Research Association.

Smith, F. (1971). *Understanding reading: a psycholinguistic analysis of reading and learning to read.* New York: Holt Rinehart and Winston.

Smith, M. L., Fey, P., Heinecke, W., Miller-Kahn, L., and Noble, A. (2003). *Political spectacle and the fate of American schools.* New York: RoutledgeFalmer.

Snow, C. (2000). On the limits of reframing: rereading the National Academy of Sciences report on reading. *Journal of Literacy Research,* 32 (1), 113–120.

Snow, C., Burns, S. M., and Griffin, P. (eds) (1998). *Preventing reading difficulties in young children.* Washington, DC: National Academy of Sciences.

Snyder, I. (2002). *Silicon literacies: communication, innovation and education in the electronic age.* London: Routledge.

Soltow, L., and Stevens, E. (1981). *The rise of literacy and the common school in the United States: a socioeconomic analysis to 1870.* Chicago: University of Chicago Press.

Soter, A. O. (1992). Whose shared assumptions? Making the implicit explicit. In D. E. Murray (ed.), *Diversity as resource: redefining cultural literacy.* Alexandria, VA: Teachers of English to Speakers of Other Languages.

Stanley, L. (1988). Historical sources for studying work and leisure in women's lives. In E. Wimbush and M. Talbot (eds), *Relative freedoms: women and leisure* (pp. 18–32). Milton Keynes: Open University Press.

Stedman, L. C., and Kaestle, C. F. (1987). Literacy and reading performance in the United States, from 1880 to the present. *Reading Research Quarterly,* 22 (1), 8–46.

Stevenson, H. W., Stigler, J. W., Lucker, G. W., Lee, S., Hsu, C., and Kitamura, S. (1982). Reading disabilities: the case of Chinese, Japanese, and English. *Child Development,* 53 (5), 1164–1181.

Stierer, B. (2000). School teachers writing at university: what kind of knowledge is at stake? *Teacher Development,* 4 (2), 199–221.

Stierer, B., and Bloome, D. (1994). *Reading words: a commentary on key terms in the teaching of reading.* Sheffield: National Association for the Teaching of English.

Street, B. V. (1975). *The savage in literature: representations of 'primitive' society in English fiction, 1858–1920.* London and Boston: Routledge and Kegan Paul.

Street, B. V. (1984). *Literacy in theory and practice.* Cambridge: Cambridge University Press.

Street, B. (1988). Literacy practices and literacy myths. In R. Saljo (ed.), *The written word: studies in literate thought and action,* vol. 23 of Language and Communication Series (pp. 59–72). Heidelberg: Springer-Verlag.

Street, B. V. (1993). *Cross-cultural approaches to literacy.* Cambridge and New York: Cambridge University Press.

Street, B. V. (1995). *Social literacies: critical approaches to literacy in development, ethnography, and education.* London and New York: Longman.

Street, B. V. (1996). Academic literacies. In J. Clay, D. Baker and C. Fox (eds), *Challenging ways of knowing: in English, mathematics and science* (pp. 101–134). London: Falmer Press.

Street, B. V. (1996). Review of International Adult Literacy Survey. *Literacy across the Curriculum,* 12 (3), 8–15.

Street, B. (1998). New literacies in theory and practice: what are the implications for language in education? *Linguistics and Education,* 10 (1), 1–24.

Street, B. V. (2000). Literacy as social practice. *International Journal of Psychology,* 35 (3–4), 387–397.

Street, B. V. (2001). *Literacy and development: ethnographic perspectives.* London: Routledge.

Street, B. V. (2003). What's 'new' in New Literacy Studies? Critical approaches to literacy in theory and practice. *Current Issues in Comparative Education,* 5 (2), 77–91.

Street, B. V. (2005). *Literacies across educational contexts: mediating learning and teaching.* Philadelphia: Caslon Publishing.

Street, B. V. (2006). Fresh hope for literacy: a critical reflection on Literacy for Life, EFA Global Monitoring Report, *Report on a Colloquium held on 24 January 2006 at the British Council, Spring Gardens, London.* London: British Association for Literacy in Development (BALID) and United Kingdom Forum for International Education and Training (UKFIET).

Street, B., Baker, D., and Rogers, A. (2006) Adult teachers as researchers: ethnographic approaches to numeracy and literacy as social practices in South Asia. *Convergence,* XXXIX (1), 31–44.

Street, B. V., Baker, D., and Tomlin, A. (2005). *Navigating numeracies: home/school numeracy practices.* Dordrecht: Springer.

Street, B. V., and Street, J. (1991). The schooling of literacy. In D. Barton and R. Ivanic (eds), *Writing in the community* (pp. 143–166). London: Sage Publications.

Stromquist, N. P. (2004). *Women's rights to adult education as a means to citizenship.* Paper presented at the Gender, Education and Development: Beyond Access Conference.

Stubbs, M. (1980). *Language and literacy: the sociolinguistics of reading and writing.* London: Routledge and Kegan Paul.

Swales, J. (1990). *Genre analysis: English in academic and research settings.* Cambridge and New York: Cambridge University Press.

Swindells, J. (1995). *Uses of autobiography.* London: Taylor and Francis.

Tannen, D. (1982). The myth of orality and literacy. In W. Frawley (ed.), *Linguistics and literacy* (pp. 37–50). New York: Plenum Press.

Tannen, D. (1985). Relative focus on involvement in oral and written discourse. In D. R. Olson, N. Torrance and A. Hildyard (eds), *Literacy, language, and learning: the nature and consequences of reading and writing* (pp. 124–147). Cambridge: Cambridge University Press.

Taylor, D., and Dorsey-Gaines, C. (1988). *Growing up literate: learning from inner-city families.* Portsmouth, NH: Heinemann.

Taylor, D., and Strickland, D. S. (1986). *Family storybook reading.* Portsmouth, NH: Heinemann.

Teale, W. H. (1986). Home background and young children's literacy development. In W. H. Teale and E. Sulzby (eds), *Emergent literacy: writing and reading.* Norwood, NJ: Ablex.

Teale, W. H., and Sulzby, E. (1986). Emergent literacy as a perspective for examining how young children become readers and writers. In W. H. Teale and E. Sulzby (eds), *Emergent literacy: writing and reading* (pp. vii–xxv). Norwood, NJ: Ablex Publishing.

Terkel, S. (1974). *Working: people talk about what they do all day and how they feel about what they do.* New York: Pantheon Books.

Tharp, R. G. (1989). Psychocultural variables and constants: effects on teaching and learning in schools. *American Psychologist,* 44 (2), 349–359.

Thomas, R. (1989). *Oral tradition and written record in classical Athens.* Cambridge: Cambridge University Press.

Tymms, P. (2004). Are standards rising in English primary schools? *British Educational Research Journal,* 30 (4), 477–494.

United Nations Educational Scientific and Cultural Organization (UNESCO) (2004). *The plurality of literacy and its implications for policies and programmes.* Paris: UNESCO.

United Nations Educational Scientific and Cultural Organization (UNESCO) (2005). *Education for all: the quality imperative.* Paris: UNESCO.

United States Departments of Education and Labor (1988). *The bottom line: basic skills in the workplace.* Washington, DC: United States Departments of Education and Labor.

Varenne, H., and McDermott, R. (1983). Why Sheila can read: structure and indeterminacy in the structure of familial literacy. In B. B. Schieffelin and P. Gilmore (eds), *The acquisition of literacy: ethnographic perspectives.* Norwood, NJ: Ablex Publishing Corporation.

Vellutino, F. R. (1991). Introduction to three studies on reading acquisition: convergent findings on theoretical foundations of code-oriented versus whole-language approaches to reading instruction. *Journal of Educational Psychology,* 83 (4), 437–443.

Vygotsky, L. S. (1978). *Mind in society: the development of higher psychological processes.* Cambridge, MA and London: Harvard University Press.

Wagner, D. (2004). Literacy (ies), culture (s), and development (s): the ethnographic challenge. *Reading Research Quarterly,* 39 (2), 234–241.

Wagner, D. A. (1993). *Literacy, culture and development: becoming literate in Morocco.* Cambridge: Cambridge University Press.

Weber, R. M. (1993). Even in the midst of work: reading among turn-of-the-century farmers' wives. *Reading Research Quarterly,* 28 (4), 292–302.

Welch, A. R., and Freebody, P. (1993). Introduction: explanations of the current international 'literacy crises'. In P. Freebody and A. R. Welch (eds), *Knowledge, culture and power: international perspectives on literacy as policy and practice* (pp. 6–22). London: Falmer.

White, K. R. (1982). The relation between socioeconomic status and academic achievement. *Psychological Bulletin,* 91, 461–481.

Whyte, W. F. (1984). *Learning from the field: a guide from experience.* Beverly Hills: Sage Publications.

Whyte, W. F. (1991). *Social theory for action: how individuals and organizations learn to change.* Newbury Park: Sage Publications.

Williams, R. (1976). *Keywords: a vocabulary of culture and society.* London: Fontana.

Worpole, K., Maguire, P., and Morley, D. (1982). *The Republic of letters: working class writing and local publishing.* London: Comedia.

Yin-yee Ko, D. (1989). *Toward a social history of women in seventeenth century China.* Unpublished doctoral dissertation, Stanford University.

Index